*Also by*
DOROTHY HERRMANN

With Malice Toward All

# S.J. PERELMAN
# A LIFE

*Dorothy Herrmann*

A FIRESIDE BOOK · PUBLISHED BY
SIMON & SCHUSTER, INC. · NEW YORK

*In memory of my father and stepfather,*
*Bernard Herrmann and John Douglass Wallop*

Copyright © 1986 by Dorothy Herrmann
All rights reserved
including the right of reproduction
in whole or in part in any form
First Fireside Edition, 1987
Published by Simon & Schuster, Inc.
Simon & Schuster Building
Rockefeller Center
1230 Avenue of the Americas
New York, New York 10020
Published by arrangement with The Putnam Publishing Group
FIRESIDE and colophon are registered trademarks of Simon & Schuster, Inc.
Manufactured in the United States of America
1  3  5  7  9  10  8  6  4  2  Pbk.

Library of Congress Cataloging-in-Publication Data
Herrmann, Dorothy.
S.J. Perelman : a life.
Reprint. Originally published: New York : Putnam, c1986.
"A Fireside book."
Bibliography: p.
Includes index.
1. Perelman, S. J. (Sidney Joseph), 1904–    —
Biography.   2. Authors, American—20th century—
Biography.   3. Humorists, American—20th century—
Biography.   I. Title.
[PS3531.E6544Z69  1987]    818'.5209   [B]    87-7480
ISBN 0-671-64199-9 Pbk.

Unless otherwise indicated, all photographs are courtesy of an anonymous donor.

The author gratefully acknowledges permission from the following sources to print material in their control:
   The Brown University Archives, Brown University, Providence, Rhode Island, for "Death," a poem by Nathanael West, © 1924, and "Even Stephen," © 1929, a poem by Laura West.
   Leila Hadley for excerpts from *Give Me the World,* copyright © 1958 by Leila Hadley.
   Hilton Kramer, executor, estate of Josephine Herbst, for excerpts from *Hunter of Doves* by Josephine Herbst, copyright © 1954 by Josephine Herbst.
   Abby and Adam Perelman, heirs of S. J. Perelman, for comedy material written by S. J. Perelman for Larry Adler, © 1942 by S. J. Perelman; and for *Nathanael West: A Portrait,* © 1933 by S. J. Perelman.

*(Continued on page 338)*

# Acknowledgments

This first biography of S. J. Perelman makes use of the recollections of many of his friends, relatives and colleagues, as well as personal documents and memorabilia.

In his passion for privacy, Perelman compartmentalized his friends. He knew a great many people, but few knew about the existence of other people in his life and the nature of his relationships with them. This biography could not have been written without the help of those friends, and I am deeply grateful for their cooperation and keen insights into a complex and in many ways mysterious man.

For the time they have spent with me and generous loan of letters, manuscripts, photographs and other documents, I would like to thank the following persons, listed here in alphabetical order: Celia Ernspos Adler, Mary Ahern, Alice H. Amore, Walter Arps, Helen Barrow, Archie Bashlow, George Bashlow, Tom Torre Bevans, Mrs. Tallman Bissell, Harriet Blacker, Dave Bogart, Nina Bourne, Professor Fredson Bowers, Edward R. Brace, Marshall Brickman, Heywood Hale Broun, George Brounoff, Joseph Brugger, Mel Calman, Teet Carle, Marian R. Clarke, Mrs. Robert Coates, Alistair Cooke, Alan Coren, Malcolm Cowley, Cheryl Crawford, Prudence Crowther, Parke Cummings, Hope Hale Davis, Robert Gorham Davis, Agnes de Mille, Maurice Dolbier, Andrew Duggan, William A. Dyer, Jr., Herman Elkon, Mr. and Mrs. Michael Ellis, Patricia Englund, Mary Faulconer, Pamela Fiori, Karl E. Fortess, Philip French, William K. Gale, Tom Glazer, Mrs. William Godley, Ruth Goetz, Edward Goldberger, Robert Gottlieb, Mrs. Theodore Greening, Dr. Jesse Greenstein, Mr. and Mrs. John G. Gude, Dorothy Guth, Leila Hadley, Mr. and Mrs. Philip Hamburger, Shirley Hazzard, Professor Constance B. Hieatt, John Hollander, Eleanor F. Horvitz, John Houseman, E. Howard Hunt, Mrs. Nunnally Johnson, Betty White Johnston, E. J. Kahn, Jr., Mrs. Susan Kaplan, Dr. and Mrs. I. J. Kapstein, Mr. and Mrs. Samuel Kaufman, Elia Kazan, Irene Kemmer, Louise Kerz, Donald Klopfer, Joseph Lash, James Lee, Joseph Leon, Jack Levine, Phyllis Levy, Dr. and Mrs. Edward LeWinn, Denver Lindley, Jr., Sue Lloyd, Dick Lochte, Philip Lukin, Mr. and

Mrs. Vincent Mason, Mrs. Paul McGhee, Diane Daniels Megargel, Richard Merkin, Mr. and Mrs. Frank Metz, Mr. and Mrs. Joseph Meyer, Vincente Minnelli, Sam Mitnick, Jean Montague, Betty Blue Moodie, Priscilla Morgan, Mrs. Ogden Nash, Charles O'Neill, Gisella Orkin, Jenna Orkin, Gene Patterson, Neva Patterson, Nat Perrin, Dr. Robert Perry, Letty Cottin Pogrebin, Mr. and Mrs. John Pomfret, John M. Richmond, Arnold Roston, Allen Saalburg, John Sanford, Martha Saxton, Constance Sayre, Dorothy Oliveson Schiff, Joseph Schrank, Peter Schwed, Mrs. C. P. Scoboria, Charles Selber, Israel Shenker, Ralph Steiner, Leon Stem, Janet Sternburg, Caskie Stinnett, Susan Sullivan, H. N. Swanson, Dr. Harold Taylor, Paul Theroux, Mrs. James Thurber, Lester Trauck, Harry Tugend, Dr. and Mrs. Leonard Wallenstein, Marjorie Weaver, Frederick B. Wiener, Walter F. Wiener, Delta Willis, B. Ruby Winnerman, Maxine Winokur, Mildred Wohlforth, William Wolf, James Wolford and William Zinsser.

I am also indebted to other persons, who for reasons of their own did not wish to be identified.

No single archive spans Perelman's long life and varied career. Mrs. Martha Mitchell and her staff at the Brown University Archives were of tremendous help in providing material on his college career, as well as on his work as a cartoonist and editor of the *Brown Jug*. I am also particularly indebted to Laurence B. Chase, who generously made available to me his undergraduate thesis on Perelman and West's years at Brown.

My gratitude goes also to the staff of the Berg Collection of English and American Literature, The New York Public Library, for granting me access to the S. J. Perelman manuscript collection. For help in researching other aspects of his literary and theatrical career, I wish to thank: the staff of the Columbia University Libraries, Rare Book and Manuscript Division; Lucille Wehner, Department of Special Collections, The Newberry Library, University of Chicago; Dr. Howard B. Gotlieb, Director, Special Collections, Mugar Memorial Library, Boston University; James Hutson, Chief, Manuscript Division, Library of Congress; Casindania P. Eaton and Nancy Johnson at the American Academy and Institute of Arts and Letters; Robert A. Tibbetts, Curator of Special Collections, Ohio State University Libraries; the staff of the Spruance Library of the Bucks County Historical Society; Val Almendarez at the Academy of Motion Picture Arts and Sciences; Bridget P. Carr, Manuscript Department, The Houghton Library, Harvard University; Gene M. Gressley, The University of

Wyoming Division of Rare Books and Special Collections; Leo M. Dolenski, Manuscript Librarian, Bryn Mawr College Library; Mrs. Lloyd W. Brown, Colchester Historical Society; Jeannette Blanco, Curator, Curtis Theatre Collection, University of Pittsburgh Libraries; Dorothy L. Swerdlove, Curator of the Theatre Collection at the Library of the Performing Arts, Lincoln Center; Norman Corwin; Flora Gill Jacobs; Dr. Abe Jankowitz; Walter and Miriam Schneir; H. B. Stecy; Linda H. Davis; Peter Davison; Dee Coakley; Bob Kempner; Elinor Langer; Stephen Banker of *Tapes for Readers;* Mary Ellen Ward of *Travel & Leisure;* Robin Breed and Judy Englander of Daphne Productions; and Victor D. Schmalzer of W. W. Norton and Company.

Paul G. Wesolowski of New Hope, Pennsylvania, is regarded as the world's leading expert on the Marx Brothers. For his help in researching the stormy professional and personal relationship between S. J. Perelman and Groucho Marx, he has my gratitude. I also benefited from reading Joe Adamson's lively analysis of the Marx Brothers' films.

Perelman worked for a number of motion picture studios during the thirties, and I am grateful to Herbert S. Nusbaum of MGM/UA Entertainment Company for allowing me to examine S. J. and Laura Perelman's contract files when they were employed as screenwriters at MGM.

I am also indebted to Rick Epstein of the *Delaware Valley News* in Frenchtown, New Jersey, for suggesting people in the Bucks County area who knew S. J. Perelman and Nathanael West. My thanks go to Dr. Joanna E. Rapf of the University of Oklahoma for letting me read her paper on Nathanael West and Boris Ingster. Dr. Jay Martin's excellent biography, *Nathanael West: The Art of His Life*, was of invaluable help in providing me with knowledge of West's life and career. I also appreciate his having made available to me his extensive correspondence with Perelman about West's biography.

I would especially like to thank my mother, Lucille Fletcher Wallop, for her criticism of the manuscript in its various stages and her editorial suggestions.

Marion Meade, author of a forthcoming biography of Dorothy Parker, generously shared with me her expertise in the difficult art of recreating another person's life. Her knowledge and friendship made my task much easier.

My gratitude, too, to Owen Laster at William Morris and Phyllis Grann at G. P. Putnam's Sons for their enthusiasm and interest in this biography. And I would like to thank Stacy Creamer and Mary Kurtz at Putnam's for their meticulous preparation and copyediting of my manuscript.

Finally, I would like to thank my husband, Lance Silverman, for his love, support and unfailing good humor during the fascinating— and exhilarating—years in which we shared our lives with S. J. Perelman.

DOROTHY HERRMANN
New York City
1985

# CONTENTS

INTRODUCTION                                                    13

### PART ONE 1904–1940

1  Joseph and Sophie                                           17
2  "Ah, the College Boys, the College Boys"                   28
3  "A Sumptuous Living"                                       46
4  "I Told You I'd Wax Roth Some Day"                         62
5  Enter Groucho Marx                                         71
6  Laura                                                      86
7  "A Dreary Industrial Town"                                 97
8  "Strictly from Hunger"                                    106
9  Tragedy                                                   128

### PART TWO 1940–1970

10  Aftermath                                                137
11  *One Touch of Venus*                                     147
12  Persona                                                  157
13  "To Count the Cats in Zanzibar"                          176
14  "Behind a Façade"                                        190
15  *Around the World in 80 Days*                            206
16  "A Writer of Little Leaves"                              217

17  *The Beauty Part*                               228
18  "A Living National Treasure"                    240

### PART THREE 1970–1979

19  "Alone in This Day of Humorists"                261
20  "Adieu to Onslow Square"                        269
21  "One Last Chuck of the Dice"                    287

WORKS BY S. J. PERELMAN                             301
NOTES ON SOURCES                                    303
SELECTED BIBLIOGRAPHY                               326
I N D E X                                           330

# INTRODUCTION

Sidney Joseph Perelman was unique in American humor. A brilliant stylist and erudite satirist, he had the gift of unabashed zaniness. For forty years his impish wit and outrageous fantasies embellished the pages of the *New Yorker*. And what a delight it was to flip through the magazine and come upon one of his inimitable titles—"Beat Me, Post-Impressionist Daddy" or "Is There an Osteosynchrondroitrician in the House?" or "No Starch in the Dhoti, S'Il Vous Plaît" or "Boy Meets Girl Meets Foot"—any one of which guaranteed the reader a verbal roller-coaster ride through a world of puns, double entendres, flashes of slang and dashes of Yiddish, all put together in a matchless style that almost concealed the bitterness beneath.

Perelman's writing was original, bizarre. He was irreverent, scornful, but always with a whimsical touch. He made fun of things by setting them on stage in a dazzling light, and poking them gently and deftly where it hurt. A marvelous parodist, he could play any role and pierce through to the heart of pretense and conceit. His pieces were filled with satirical names for the phoneys he despised: Barnaby Chirp, Harry Hubris, Irving Stonehenge, Robin Moonshein. He could write like the giddiest woman alive—casting himself into the role of "Fern Replevin, an utterly lovely creature of twenty-four, whose mouth wanders at will over her features," or pretend that he had spent the day "reclining on my chaise lounge in a negligee trimmed with maribou reading trashy bonbons and eating French yellow-backed novels."

In reality Perelman was a small dapper man with a neatly trimmed mustache, a soft hesitant voice and sad quizzical eyes behind steel-rimmed spectacles.

He wrote very slowly, painstakingly, brooding over each word and

13

tooling every sentence. He lived for seventy-five years and worked at writing incessantly from the age of twenty on. Humor was his livelihood, his raison d'être, his only key to fame and fortune, and he never stopped working at it, driving his brain to wilder and wilder heights. Nor did he ever become "arty," but spent his rare genius on almost anything that came to hand, from a hilarious piece for the *New Yorker* to a movie script for Jack Oakie. As a poor young man helping to support his parents and later as a husband and father, he took his responsibilities seriously.

He wrote twenty-one books, innumerable pieces for the *New Yorker* and many other magazines, and coauthored several stage plays, including the hit musical, *One Touch of Venus*. In 1956 he won an Oscar for his screenplay for *Around the World in 80 Days*. It was said that he was responsible for creating Groucho Marx's comic image, and although he denied this, as did Groucho, there is an echo in *Monkey Business* and *Horse Feathers* of Perelman's very special literate frenzy.

His erudition and vocabulary were legendary. E. B. White of the *New Yorker* once said, "Perelman commanded a vocabulary that is the despair (and joy) of every writing man. Sid is like a Roxy organ that has three decks, fifty stops and a pride of pedals under the bench. When he wants a word, it's there."[1]

Although he wrote incessantly on many trivial matters, Perelman never wrote seriously about his personal life. Time and again his publishers asked him for a full-scale memoir, but he always put them off, saying he didn't have the time or he had no use for people who dwelt on their past achievements. In May of 1960 Simon and Schuster were finally able to persuade him to sign a contract for an autobiography. He wanted to call it *Smiling, the Boy Fell Dead*, but had to change the title to *The Hindsight Saga* when a play by the same name opened on Broadway.

He tinkered with this autobiography off and on for nineteen years. When he died, only four chapters could be found among his papers. They were published posthumously in 1981 in a collection, *The Last Laugh*, which included seventeen other pieces which had appeared in the *New Yorker*. None of the four is autobiographical in the true sense. All deal rather superficially with his brother-in-law, Nathanael West, Dorothy Parker, the Marx Brothers, and with his career as a screenwriter in Hollywood. They are lighthearted, entertaining, but in no way deep or personally revealing. To the day of his death in a lonely hotel room in New York City, S. J. Perelman remained an intensely private man.

# PART ONE

1904–1940

# I

# JOSEPH AND SOPHIE

## (1904–1921)

I loathe writing. On the other hand, I'm a great believer in money. Often, when it seemed I couldn't pay the grocery bill, Providence has mysteriously intervened, and I don't mean my natal city, Providence, which can be counted on for absolutely nothing.

S. J. PERELMAN, *Life* interview, 1962[1]

I had the feeling that he wasn't quite pleased with his parents. Either he didn't like them or perhaps they weren't his style.

ALLEN SAALBURG[2]

As an adult, S. J. Perelman seldom spoke about his parents. They were mysterious figures to even his closest friends. The only clues to their identity were found in his humor, but his memories of them, like so much else he wrote about his life, were not to be trusted. His mother and father were "fantastically wealthy," he once wrote, adding that his father sometimes came to dinner wearing a sack suit "checkered with dollar signs" and the garden paths around their vast Newport estate were filled with rubies instead of the usual gravel.[3]

In reality, Joseph Samuel Perelman and his wife, Sophie, were poor, hardworking Russian Jews who had come to the United States during the massive wave of immigration in the late 19th century.[4] Sophie Perelman's background in particular was typical of many Jews fleeing Russia at that time. She was born in Velizh, a small town in the province of Vitebsk, in 1881, the year Czar Alexander II was assassinated. Sophie's maiden name was Charren or Charen. Her father was a peddler who came home only a few times a year. Her

17

mother died when Sophie was a small child. The family was a large one. There were six children in all, and green-eyed, vivacious Sophie was the youngest, the baby upon whom everyone doted.

Religious persecution of the Jews began after Czar Alexander's death, and in the late 1880s, the Charren family decided to come to America. According to a cousin, the family did not emigrate en masse, but rather came separately or in small groups. In 1889, a year after the Great Blizzard, Sophie, her father and her older sister Lena arrived in New York. Both girls were sent to work as soon as possible, "finishing" housedresses at home for a garment subcontractor. As they knew no English, they began attending night classes that the Board of Education ran several times a week to teach immigrants and their children the language of their new homeland as well as acquaint them with American customs.

Joseph's relatives were more educated and well-to-do. They came from Rostov, a town in Russia near the Black Sea. Rostov was not within the Pale of Settlement, the area of 386,000 square miles from the Baltic Sea to the Black Sea where most Jews were forced to live. In Rostov, in the early 19th century, the Jewish population was treated with respect. They were important members of the community. Joseph's family, at least on his mother's side, was quite rich, making a prosperous living as hay and grain dealers.

The name Perelman is Ashkenazic, meaning either "dealer in pearls" or "husband of Pearl." About David Perelman, Joseph's father, nothing is known other than Sid's claim that he was a designer of whiskey distilleries.[5] It is believed that Joseph's mother, Sarah Isrelvitz, was related to Johann Gottlob Wagner, a well-known 18th-century German maker of harpsichords, clavichords and pianos who in 1783 invented a type of square piano. Sarah's father, Jacob, was in the real estate business, although it is not known whether he practiced his trade in the United States or in Russia.

In 1887, the Perelmans' pleasant life in Rostov came to an end when Rostov became part of the community of the Cossacks of the Don. It was decreed that only Jews who had lived in Rostov prior to 1887 could continue to reside in the city. This was probably a compelling factor in the decision made by some members of the Perelman family to leave Russia for America.

Joseph Perelman was sixteen years old when he arrived in the United States in 1891 with his brother Harry and his aunt Mary

Isrelvitz, his mother's sister. Mary was married to David Davidoff, a Russian Jew who was also in the real estate business. They had two children, Anna and Sophie Jennie.

Many of the Eastern European Jews emigrating to the United States in the 1880s and 1890s were poor peasants from small villages or the ghettos of large cities. But Joseph's family was comfortably off. They arrived in the United States with $15,000, a considerable sum in those days.

Almost immediately, the family settled in Colchester, Connecticut. According to Alexander and Lillian Feinsilver, "Although a few Jewish settlers began drifting into Colchester in the 1880s, the first real settlement was in the 1890s through the impetus of the Baron de Hirsch Fund. Colchester was one of several farm settlements in eastern Connecticut aided by the Fund, including Oakdale, Montville and Chesterfield.

". . . At the very time that the Jews were coming in, the town of Colchester was undergoing a general decline. The Hayward Rubber Company, one of the biggest in the country, which had been the chief industry for almost half a century, closed its doors in 1893."[6]

As a result of this closing, hundreds of people left town to find work elsewhere. Local merchants were in trouble, as were the farms and the local bank. Farms were being sold at low prices and in great numbers, and advertisements for such property, stressing good business opportunities and low-cost living, attracted many of the recent Russian immigrants, including Joseph's family. A 1911 Report of the Immigration Commission revealed that "few had ever been farmers before . . . nearly all came to Connecticut with some money, and since the majority bought old farms there were fewer privations in the early days of the settlement than in the New Jersey colonies. It took a long time for most of these city-bred people, 90% of whom purchased land immediately on arrival, to master the cultivation and marketing of produce. . . . Presently, however, a new industry was started that soon overshadowed legitimate agriculture. This was the summer boarder industry."[7]

During the 1920s, Colchester became a booming summer resort very popular with Jews. In fact, Colchester has been called "the Catskills of Connecticut." One visitor to Colchester in its heyday was Nathanael West, who spent the summer there as a young boy.

As soon as they arrived in Colchester, Mary Isrelvitz and her brother Leon bought a farm with substantial acreage and several buildings, including a beautiful colonial house and schoolhouse. The price was $4,900.[8] Two years later, in 1893, Mary purchased a house and two acres on Hall's Hill Road in the center of town for $1,600.[9]

But the Davidoffs did not have the necessary skills to be good farmers. In 1896, Mary sold the farm for $3,200,[10] but retained the Hall's Hill property, leasing it to her husband for ten years at a rental of four dollars a month. By then this property consisted of two houses: one with six rooms, the other with fourteen rooms and a store.[11]

A few years later the Davidoffs moved to Brooklyn. They sublet the Hall's Hill property and sold the entire contents of their store.[12] On June 26, 1901, Mary Davidoff gave power of attorney to her nephew, Joseph Perelman, to dispose of the Hall's Hill property.[13] The following month he sold it at a considerable loss to Harris Cohen for $1,075.[14] The prosperous days of the family were over.

Vanished, too, was Joseph's dream of becoming an engineer. The family could not afford to send him to college, so he went to sea. Sid claimed that his father was the third engineer on the first ship into Havana Harbor in 1898 after the battleship *Maine* was blown up, an event that triggered the Spanish-American War. Joseph was shaken by the experience. Later he often told Sid about seeing sharks feeding off the bodies of American sailors.[15]

After his return from Cuba, Joseph married Sophie Charren and settled in Brooklyn, in a tenement apartment at 168 Seventh Avenue. Times were hard, and the only job Joseph could get was as a machinist in a Jersey City factory. It took him hours to get there by public transportation, and the pay was poor. Like many young men of his generation, Joseph was a socialist who abhorred the capitalist system. He dreamed of the time when workers would be decently compensated for their labor.

While he was still employed in Jersey City, Joseph heard that working conditions were better in Rhode Island, and that there were more opportunities for immigrants in the industrial city of Providence. In 1904, he and Sophie moved from Brooklyn to Providence, where Joseph's brother-in-law, Louis Bashlow, was already established.

They had another incentive for moving: Sophie had recently given birth to a son, Sidney Joseph. He was born on February 1, 1904, delivered at home by Dr. J. Elizabeth Hatton, who duly noted on his birth certificate that he was a "male-white" and that Joseph and Sophie had had one previous child, now deceased.[16]

Years later, when people asked S. J. Perelman what the initials

S. J. stood for, he always replied that his full name was Sidney Joseph and that his friends called him Sid. This was not quite true, for Perelman's first name was really Simeon, the Hebrew name of the son of Jacob who was the traditional eponymous ancestor of one of the tribes of Israel. Shortly after Simeon's birth, however, Joseph and Sophie had a change of heart. Did not the name Simeon sound strange and obviously foreign? What native-born American would be able to pronounce it? Other Eastern European Jews, striving to become assimilated into American life, chose Anglo-Saxon first names for their offspring: Murray, George, Alan, Arthur, Albert, Jeffrey and Sidney, to name only a few examples. It is possible that having been given a distinguished English name caused Perelman to become infected with the Anglophilia that obsessed him his entire life.

The New England city to which Joseph Perelman moved his family was undergoing drastic changes. Founded in 1636 by Roger Williams, the Puritan nonconformist, Providence for many years was an important shipping and shipbuilding seaport. After 1820, maritime commerce began to decline. In the next hundred years, Providence was transformed from a bustling seaport to a highly industrialized East Coast city. In 1824, the population numbered 15,000 but by 1930, it had swelled to 253,000, mainly because of the enormous numbers of European immigrants like Joseph Perelman who had flocked to Rhode Island looking for work.

Soon after his arrival in Providence, Joseph opened a dry-goods store on Chalkstone Avenue. But he had no talent for business, and was barely able to support his family by selling Amoskeag cotton and ginghams, as well as laces, needles and thread. The family occupied a tiny three-room apartment above the store, but soon moved to the second floor of what Rhode Islanders call a "triple-decker" at 8 Bernon Street. Joseph's cousin, Sophie Mason, her husband Louis, a tinsmith, and their young son, Vincent, lived nearby.

Sid's mother doted on him and took him wherever she went. While she waited on customers in the store, he played behind the counters with a darning ball or a tape measure. He was a small, dark-haired child, whose expression was quick and intelligent, even though his left eye had a divergent squint.

When he wasn't working in the store, Joseph was pouring over some socialist tract or Haldeman-Julius's five-cent Little Blue Books,

21

with their diatribes by Brann the Iconoclast or Colonel Robert Ingersoll, the fiery atheist. As Sid grew older and was able to read, his
father would pass this inflammatory literature on to him. Joseph was
"a gentle, quiet man, a Utopian socialist, who conveyed to Sid some
idea of human folly and social inequity and so set him to the satire
that so often gives its bite to his writing," I. J. Kapstein, one of Sid's
childhood friends, later commented.[17] Many of Perelman's funniest
pieces were attacks on commercialism, advertising and silly luxury
items—aspects of American life that must have deeply troubled his
idealistic socialist father.

"On the other hand, it must have been his mother's lively spirit
that gave sparkle to his," Kapstein added. "She was small, alert as
a bird, with a quick independence all her own. . . ."[18]

Sophie was not an intellectual like her husband, although she did
share his socialist views. Neither she nor Joseph attended synagogue
or practiced the Jewish faith, and so Sid grew up without any religious
training.

Both Sophie and Joseph spoke English as well as Yiddish. Like
many second-generation Jews, Sid never learned to speak Yiddish
himself, but he picked up a huge vocabulary of Yiddish words and
expressions. The language undoubtedly appealed to him because it
was rich in irony and filled with vivid, down-to-earth expressions. In
many of his pieces, he used it for its shock value in contrast to very
erudite and recondite English.

Besides his Jewish ancestry, with its tradition of skepticism, learning, and restless searching for identity, there was another important
influence on Sid's character. The outspoken iconoclasm of the New
Englander was there as well. Sid, who was educated entirely in New
England schools, was heavily influenced by Yankee philosophy. He
believed in speaking one's mind, standing against the crowd and in
pinching one's pennies, seldom squandering his money on cabs, gifts
for friends or other luxuries.

Like many New Englanders, he loved the land and took solace from
nature. As a boy one of his idols was Thoreau, and one of his favorite
lines in *Walden* was: "It is not worth the while to go round the world
to count the cats in Zanzibar."

When Sid was thirteen, he wrote an essay that won first prize in
a contest sponsored by a magazine called *The American Boy*, which
featured stories stressing heroic traits of young men. "It was entitled

'Grit,' and it extolled the valor of those taxi drivers who had stemmed the Prussian horde at the Marne. Grit, I explained, was raw courage in the face of overwhelming odds, fortitude under well-nigh unbearable pressure—in a word, pluck," Sid later recalled.[19]

Sid did not, however, want to be a writer. He wanted to be a cartoonist, possibly because he had seen "the chalk talks" at the local vaudeville theaters, in which artists created stunning effects with a blackboard and some chalk in a matter of minutes. When he was eleven or twelve, his parents had given him a blackboard and chalk as a birthday present, and he set to work trying to reproduce the characters in the comic strips in the Providence newspapers: the Katzenjammer Kids, Maggie and Jiggs, Krazy Kat, Mutt and Jeff. When he was in high school, his favorite comic strip was "Silk Hat Harry's Divorce Suit" by "Tad" Dorgan, which ran in the *Boston American*. Originally conceived as a burlesque of the trial of Harry K. Thaw for the murder of architect Stanford White, the series actually dealt with marital infidelity. Tad's two main characters—Judge Rumhauser ("Call me 'Rummy' ") and Silk Hat Harry—were unregenerate ladies' men who would resort to any stratagem to steal each other's current amour. The cartoonist's cynical view of the world was underscored by the fact that all his characters were actually dogs in human clothing. Their dialogue—which consisted of such lines as "Nobody's home but the telephone and that's in the hand of the receiver"—so tickled Sid that he repeated it to anyone within earshot.[20]

Cartooning began to consume Sid's life. He drew not only on the blackboard his parents had given him, but on the long cardboard strips around which the bolts of fabric were folded in his father's store. When he visited relatives, he spent most of his time sprawled on the floor drawing caricatures. George Bashlow, his cousin, remembers spending many winter afternoons with Sid in which they pretended to be their favorite cartoon characters and acted out comic strips from the newspapers.

By the time Sid was in his teens, Joseph had abandoned the dry-goods business. He had never been very successful at it, although he managed to accumulate enough money to buy a summer cottage at Riverside, a resort near Providence on upper Narragansett Bay. The great American dream of that time was to be a poultry farmer, and Joseph also bought a farm in rural Norwood, south of Providence, along with 5,000 chickens which he planned to raise for their eggs.

23

One of these chickens became enamored of Sophie Perelman and followed her everywhere.

This business, too, proved a failure. Many of the white leghorns died after birth, and egg sales were poor.

Sid did his best to help his parents on the farm, but most of his time was spent in being a student at Classical High School, which he attended after graduating from Candace Street Grammar School. His classmates remember him as an intensely shy, withdrawn boy, a not very outstanding student, who sometimes brought eggs to class, on which he had drawn funny faces. During the lunch hour, he would pass these around for the amusement of his fellow students. Although they laughed at his caricatures, some of his classmates wondered whether he ate the eggs in the cloakroom afterward. He looked as if he could not afford to buy lunch.[21]

To earn extra money, he worked after school in two local department stores. One was Shepards, where he worked in the candy department and "almost died from stealing the nougats." The other was the Outlet Company, where he was a stockboy in the men's shoe department, then in the rug department and finally in the men's clothes division, where he folded boxes in the basement and sent them upstairs to "stern men in blue serge suits."

At Classical High School, Sid studied English, mathematics, history, chemistry, physics, German, Greek and Latin. In the English classes, to enliven the lesson, he and Kapstein, whom he variously called "Io" and "Kappy," passed notes back and forth, on which they scribbled fantastic names. One of their favorites was "Iphigenia Horowitz." Just the sight of this name on a piece of paper sent either one of them into a fit of giggles.

Their English teacher was a lady named Marjorie Day. She believed that the works of Shakespeare were best appreciated if they were read aloud. Once, her rendition of *Julius Caesar*, in which she played all the parts, sent Sid and Kapstein into gales of laughter. In retaliation, she sent them to the principal's office. Unchastened, they made up a parody about Miss Day and sang it under their breaths a few days later in assembly while all the other students were singing the school version of the Triumphal March from *Aïda*.

Sid never forgave Miss Day for punishing him. Many years later, when he was in his sixties, he came across a photograph of some teachers in a newspaper, clipped it out and, after penciling in mustaches and beards on the women's faces, sent it to Kapstein with the legend "A Jew never forgets."[22]

World War I ended in 1918, during Sid's sophomore year in high school. Both he and Kapstein were vastly relieved to see it over, since they both had been convinced that they would be drafted as soon as they graduated. All during their freshman and sophomore years, they drilled every week on the school grounds with Springfield rifles.

In 1921, his senior year, Sid was chairman of the debating society. He also entered the Anthony Medal essay-writing contest at Classical High School. One of the judges, Benjamin Crocker Clough, an instructor of English at Brown University in Providence, thought Sid's essay deserved the medal. But since its title was "Why I Am an Atheist," inspired by the views of Robert Ingersoll, Clough was emphatically voted down by the other two judges—a minister and a lady librarian. Sid did not receive the prize.

Perhaps to console himself, he convinced Kapstein to play truant for a day and exchange the discipline of Classical High School for the dizzying high life of Boston. Kapstein was to remember that day as being quite pedestrian and unmemorable: They went to several bookshops on Cornhill and attended an afternoon vaudeville show before taking the train home. When Sid wrote about the escapade thirty-one years later for *Holiday* magazine, it included very different recollections. He described a chance meeting at Durgin-Park's Market Dining Room with Fred Allen, then billed as the World's Worst Juggler, and told how by pretending to be reporters for the *Yale Daily News*, he and Kapstein managed to interview Allen backstage at the Majestic after his show. The other events of their commonplace outing became transformed into a wild, Perelmanesque account of youthful debauchery in which he and "Kapustin" (Kapstein) spent all their money on Harvard pennants, tobacco jars made of human skulls and first editions of works by Arthur Machen, Edgar Saltus and George Gissing. After consuming three pounds of saltwater taffy apiece on the train back to Providence, they took to their beds for several days with severe stomachaches, at which point their parents learned the origins of the Harvard pennants and first editions. "Eventually, by pawning everyone's possessions, the scandal was averted," but not before Kapstein's father had given him a terrible thrashing.[23]

For Sid, beset by his parents' numbing financial problems, the world of fantasy was becoming a more intriguing place than reality.

Like many gifted children with dreams and ambitions, he felt confused and in conflict. He loved his parents, but he was also humiliated and frustrated by them. Hard as they worked, they remained powerless, nobodies.

And so in his youth he began to disengage himself from his parents and the crushing burdens of their drab chicken farm. Instead of doing his homework, he would head off for the vaudeville acts at the B. F. Keith Theatre, or the silent films at the Victory and Fay's. There he would sit in the shadowy darkness, mesmerized by the glamor of such stars as Jetta Goudal, Corinne Griffith, Norma Talmadge, Aileen Pringle, Louise Brooks and Nita Naldi. The Empire Burlesque on Westminster Street was another favorite haunt. And so was the Keith-Albee, where once on a freezing, rainy night in 1916 he saw four comedians in a skit called "Home Again," which had something vaguely to do with the horrors of ocean travel. The comedians called themselves the Four Marx Brothers, and the skit included a performance by a wag called Harpo who kept pulling ship's cutlery from his ample coat sleeves and manhandling female passengers.

On Fridays, after attending a vaudeville show or seeing a film, Sid might go to the Providence Public Library, where he would check out seven or eight books for the weekend's reading. His tastes were eclectic. He devoured Horatio Alger and Oliver Optic and romantic novels such as *In the Sargasso Sea* by Thomas Janvier, about two young boys who wandered into the Bermuda Triangle. He also consumed a great deal of what he called "mulch," popular fiction of the period: *The Sheik* by E. M. Hull, *Graustark* by George Barr McCutcheon, *The Mystery of Fu Manchu* by Sax Rohmer and *Three Weeks* by Elinor Glyn.[24]

In the Providence Public Library he also discovered the works of Joseph Conrad and Somerset Maugham, whose descriptions of faraway places excited his imagination and made him long to travel. James Joyce was another thrilling discovery. Like Joyce, Sid possessed a great mimetic talent so that when he began to write, he could create not only a first-person narrative from a female viewpoint, but evoke the inner voices of dogs, cats, even vegetables in the refrigerator. Once he did an entire piece from a coconut's point of view.

Foreign languages and literature also fascinated him. Although he read vast quantities of material, he was a very slow, meticulous reader, analyzing each word and studying the construction of every sentence.

Secretly he tended to compare himself at all times with the heroes he read about and invariably found himself lacking. "Shrimp-like" was how he later described himself, even though he was of average height—five feet nine and a half—and trim and quite muscular, with powerful arms. Yet, he continued to see himself as small, puny and unathletic—an inferior physical specimen in a society that valued male tallness and strength.

"Under a forehead roughly comparable to that of the Javanese or the Piltdown Man are visible a pair of tiny pig eyes, lit up alternately by greed and concupiscence. His nose, broken in childhood by a self-inflicted blow with a hockey stick, has a prehensile tip, ever quick to smell out an insult; at the least suspicion of an affront, Perelman, who has the pride of a Spanish grandee, has been known to whip out his sword-cane and hide in the nearest closet. He has a good figure, if not a spectacular one; above the hips, a barrel chest and a barrel belly form a single plastic unit which bobbles uncertainly on a pair of skinny shanks," he later wrote in a famous self-description.[25]

Psychologically it is understandable that he found it difficult to trust the affection of others. No doubt feeling that nobody could really love him for himself, he protected himself by withdrawing into a shell of cool detachment.

Although Sid yearned for the company of women, his intense shyness and lack of money were barriers. Once, he got up courage to ask a girl at school to a dance. She consented to go with him, although without much enthusiasm, as he was not good-looking or popular. The dance was a dressy affair, and Sid's date wore her fanciest gown. But he could not afford a tuxedo and called for her at her home in ordinary street clothes. Nor could he afford a taxi; they went to the dance by trolley. His date was humiliated.

So was Sid. Many years later, as soon as he could afford it, he began buying only the most expensive custom-made English clothes. They were so beautifully tailored they gave the impression their wearer had never suffered poverty, hardship and the terrible smell of thousands of chickens dying.

# 2

## "AH, THE COLLEGE BOYS, THE COLLEGE BOYS"

### (1921–1925)

In the fall of 1921, Sid accomplished what his father had been unable to do: He went to college, enrolling as a freshman at Brown University. Although founded in 1764 as a parochial school for Baptist ministers, Brown eventually accepted students of all religious faiths. In the 1920s, there were few Jewish students and even fewer Jews on the faculty. Perhaps the only exception was Percy Marks, a young English professor who had written *The Plastic Age*, a bestselling exposé of flaming college life.

The Jazz Age was in full swing when Sid entered Brown. In many respects, he would remain emotionally and artistically wedded to this era for the rest of his life. His personal relationships would reflect its illusions about sexual excitement and glamor, and his humor would retain much of its madcap zaniness and irreverence.

During the twenties, Brown's reputation as a rich boys' country club was already established. In 1923, Upton Sinclair published *The Goose-Step*, in which he had the following unkind words to say about it:

> ...Here is an extremely wealthy institution, catering to the sons of the plutocracy, and almost as snobbish as Princeton ...
>
> Brown in its day had such outstanding men as Lester F. Ward and Meiklejohn, now president of Amherst; but those days have passed, and there has followed a regime of intellectual dry-rot. It is a League of the Old Men, maintaining a caste system, based on seniority; any young instructor who arises to suggest a new idea is quickly taught his place ...
>
> Under such a regime what becomes of the students? Exactly the same

28

thing as we found happening to the students at Harvard, Wisconsin and California; they get drunk.[1]

In Sid's day, many Brown students studied just enough to get by, sneaking a look at their books between football games and fraternity hops. Having a winning personality was more important than intellectual achievement. A popular person had "pep"; he possessed that "old college spirit."

"The word 'pep' after the war had become a much overused part of America's vocabulary. It meant more than enthusiasm; it meant only enthusiasm over the 'right' things, as defined by the majority of society," observed Laurence B. Chase in his fine analytic study of life at Brown in the twenties. "One was considered to have 'pep' if he was a 'booster,' if he praised what everyone else was praising. . . . Only certain adventures allowed the participant to give evidence of his 'pep.' The distinction between 'peppy' and ordinary adventures could be made by the amount of outward group action required by the participant. On the college campus, therefore, if the student took part in freshman hazing and fraternity functions, if he belonged to two or three extracurricular activities, if he participated in a sport (or at least followed sports closely), if he praised the college uncritically, danced the latest dance, wore the latest cut of clothes, he had 'pep' . . ."[2]

According to this definition, Sid Perelman lacked "pep," since commuting every night from the campus to his parents' chicken farm gave him very little time for extracurricular activities. " 'The carpetbaggers,' as the commuters were called, were scorned by the campus residents," says Laurence B. Chase. "They were not members of the Brown community; they appeared on campus only to attend classes; then hurried away to their homes—or so the popular portrait went. They were worthy of scorn, because they did not participate, as a rule, in extracurricular activities, they took from Brown without giving, the undergraduates claimed."[3]

Sid seems to have coped with this situation by isolating himself from his classmates and immersing himself in his studies. According to Chase, "students on campus at the time, when they recall Perelman at all, remember a shy freshman, with thick steel-rimmed glasses, a boy who seldom indicated whether or not he recognized his classmates, a boy who seemed always to be in a hurry."[4]

Sid's Jewishness did not help the situation. Brown had many fraternities, but in the twenties Jews were barred from becoming members. This meant that he was denied an opportunity to participate in any extracurricular campus activities since these were all controlled by the fraternities.

As time went on, however, he managed to attract attention by contributing an occasional cartoon to the *Brown Jug*, the college humor magazine which appeared eight times during the school year. In the 1920s the college humor magazine was a special phenomenon, attracting many readers outside the student body, and the *Brown Jug* enjoyed an excellent reputation among its contemporaries, largely because of the quality of its art and cartoon work. Much of its literary humor, which was far less competent, mirrored the changes in mores during the decade and dwelled on three themes: drinking, petting and funny campus incidents.

Sid had continued to draw cartoons all through high school. At Brown, he began to turn out work that was ever more skilled and professional. One of his fellow employees in a small tobacco store in downtown Providence, where he worked as night manager after school, was Harry Krasnow, a graduate of the Rhode Island School of Design and an excellent draftsman. When Sid wasn't busy selling cigars and cigarettes, he took sketching lessons from Harry.[5]

Sid's first cartoon for the *Jug* depicted two men engaged in conversation while one played the piano. The caption read:

"What does your expression 'in your odd minutes' mean, Bob?"
"Why, your odd minutes are those when you are not working."
"I should think your odd minutes would be those when you are working."

Benjamin Clough, the Brown English instructor who had earlier voted for Sid's essay on atheism in the high-school writing contest, was impressed by his cartoon. In a review of the *Jug* in the March 4, 1922, *Herald*, he noted, "[The class of] 1925 gives a good account of itself among 'Jug' artists. Wells and Perelman seem to me to be especially promising."

At this point in his life, Sid had no intention of becoming a professional artist. Like Joyce and Maugham, he wanted to be a doctor. At first he did well in his science courses, receiving an A in biology in his freshman year—mainly because his skillfully executed biological drawings impressed the instructor. Confidently he signed up for basic anatomy the following year, but switched his major to English when he was faced with the assignment of dissecting a cat.

In 1921, the English faculty at Brown was the largest on campus, boasting a total of fourteen members. Judging from the ages of its instructors, Upton Sinclair's condemnation of Brown as a university of doddering old men would seem to have validity. Of the fourteen, only two—Ben Clough and Percy Marks—were young; the rest had been entrenched for years. Clough and Marks's youth, combined with an informal, relaxed attitude, made them extremely popular with students. A graduate of Harvard, Clough was a warm, compassionate individual who was known for his whimsical sense of humor. It was Clough who created the mythical character of Josiah Carberry, head of the Department of Ceramics, who has been a long-standing tradition at Brown. Clough had a falsetto voice and delighted in reciting the verse, "Jenny Kissed Me," while watching his listeners' reactions.[6] Perelman took at least one course from him and maintained a close friendship with him throughout his life.

The other popular young member of the English department was Percy Marks, whose novel *The Plastic Age* created a sensation when it was published in 1924. Although Marks insisted that his depiction of "Sanford College" was entirely fictitious, it was in fact a thinly disguised portrait of Brown University as a hotbed of drinking, swearing and sex. As soon as they could get hold of a copy, students began scanning its pages for characters reminiscent of themselves and their friends. Among other lurid revelations, Marks wrote that girls attending Sanford dances checked their corsets in the cloak room. Recalled Quentin Reynolds, a friend of Sid's who also attended Brown in the early twenties: "Since none of us barbarians knew any girls who wore corsets, there was a good deal of speculation about where and how the bachelor author had gathered his data."[7]

Marks was an avid supporter of H. L. Mencken, who crusaded against the materialistic values of the middle class, and soon Sid too became a devotee. He was particularly influenced by Mencken's *American Mercury*, which Mencken coedited with drama critic George Jean Nathan. The *Mercury* made its debut in 1924, and its caustic messages and outspoken views had a galvanizing effect on the public, particularly on college students, who carried the small, green-covered magazine everywhere. To be known as a reader of the *Mercury* meant that one was not a self-complacent Babbitt but a campus intellectual.

In addition to his English courses, Sid studied a number of foreign languages, including Latin, French, Italian and German. Although he never learned to speak any of them fluently, he knew them well enough to use them in his later prose with telling effect.

In February of 1922, during Sid's second semester, he met a young transfer student from Tufts University in Medford, Massachusetts—Nathan Weinstein.

Languid and slow-spoken, Weinstein was an easygoing New Yorker who definitely might be said to have lacked "pep." His nickname *was* Pep, however—a sardonic label, since he seemed to possess no energy whatsoever. His friends started calling him Pep when he was a teenager at summer camp in New York and was so exhausted by a hike up Mount Marcy that he slept for a day afterward.

Weinstein was six feet tall and had brown hair and brown eyes. Although handsome and well-built, he was physically uncoordinated. His old friend John Sanford recalls that his walk "was a sort of shamble, awkward and out of sync," as was his way of putting on a coat, "which made you think he was trying to climb down the arm-hole and come out of the cuff, or his way of picking up change, which couldn't have been harder for him if the coins were made of water. He was always tripping, always fumbling, always ill-related to still objects, and he was like that in everything you'd ever seen him put his hand to—everything but writing, and there alone he seemed to be at home, moving language with such ease and grace as he could never master in so little a thing as lighting a cigarette."[8]

When Weinstein arrived at Brown, he told some of his classmates that he had been in the United States Navy—a pure fabrication, as was his claim that he had graduated from De Witt Clinton High School in New York. In fact, Weinstein had not graduated from any high school. A skilled artist, he had somehow managed to doctor his high-school transcript, and with the help of ink and ink eradicator had given himself passing grades in the courses he had actually failed. He was admitted to Tufts in September of 1921, but never went to any of his classes and was asked by the Promotions Committee to withdraw in late November. Strangely enough, he wanted to continue his college career and he decided to apply for admission to Brown. The problem was, of course, how to be admitted, since his academic record did not exist.

By a curious set of circumstances, it seemed there was another

Nathan Weinstein at Tufts. Born in 1899 in Dorchester, Massachusetts, he attended high school in Boston, and then Harvard Dental School during World War I, before transferring to Tufts Medical School in 1921. Unlike the New York Nathan Weinstein, the Boston Nathan Weinstein was a conscientious student with a straight C average.

When he applied to Brown, *Nathaniel* Weinstein of New York (the name he used to apply to Tufts) used his given name, *Nathan* Weinstein. According to James F. Light, "From this slight change in name apparently, there occurred a result that may have been planned, but possibly was accidental: the college credits earned by the Boston Nathan Weinstein were credited by Brown University to the record of the New York Nathan Weinstein. This credit windfall was not made official until March of 1922, at which time Brown University evaluated the credits earned by the Boston Nathan Weinstein at Harvard Dental School and Tufts University. The evaluation lowered the earned credits slightly but the New York Nathan Weinstein (or Nathanael West) still retained fifty-seven college credits earned by another man. Some of these credits—in Chemistry, Biology, Physics and Economics—were in areas required in most colleges, and the acquisition of credits in these subjects, all of them uncongenial to West's mentality, undoubtedly helped West to stay in college and made it possible for him to graduate in two and a half years."[9]

Perelman and Weinstein did not meet until 1922 when they were enrolled in the same class. At first, Sid was put off by Weinstein's expensive, well-tailored clothing, most of which came from Brooks Brothers. "But when I got to know him," Sid later recalled, "he had a warm and fanciful humor and great erudition that made the rest of us feel sort of juvenile."[10]

The two young men soon found that they had a great deal in common. Both were the sons of Russian immigrants, although Weinstein's father, Max, was a tough-minded businessman whose speculative ventures in the construction business were usually successful. Both viewed the world satirically as well as romantically, and both cultivated sophisticated poses as a way of dealing with their own insecurity. Both also scorned sentimental displays of emotion.

Both men were avid readers and shared a mutual admiration for James Joyce. Sid often borrowed books from Pep, who possessed the largest student library at Brown. Weinstein liked to boast about his prodigious literary knowledge. He maintained that he had read all the works of Tolstoy by the age of nine and could improve on Dostoevsky by tearing out every other page of his novels. But, as John Sanford later quipped, "the question was, which page?"[11]

Weinstein, a Jew like Perelman, was also excluded from fraternity life. According to Jay Martin, he "wanted not to belong to a fraternity so much as to be pledged."[12]

Like Sid, Weinstein was an accomplished artist and cartoonist. At summer camp, he had contributed many cartoons to the camp magazine, among them a strip satirizing baseball, a game he liked to play but was not very good at, as he had a tendency to daydream in the outfield about his favorite writers. He also liked to make sketches of suffering saints and Christlike figures, as well as drawings in the styles of Aubrey Beardsley and Max Beerbohm.

At Brown, Weinstein briefly called himself "Nathaniel von Wallenstein Weinstein." Although Wallenstein was his mother's maiden name, "Nathaniel" and "von" were pure romantic inventions, perhaps reflecting his desire to create a noble and dashing identity for himself.

In high school, Sid had often made bookplates for his friends, and in 1923 he made one for Weinstein. Satirizing their elitism, it depicted a man embracing an ass. At the top a scroll bore the reader's name—Nath. V. Wallenstein-Weinstein; at the bottom was a quotation from Goethe—*"Lieb' ich wass andere lieben?"* ("Do I love what others love?")

Handsomely dressed and sophisticated, Pep Weinstein must have struck Sid as an exotic and glamorous figure. Born in New York City on October 17, 1903, he was the child of well-to-do parents, indulged not only by his mother and father but by his younger sisters, Hinda and Lorraine. Meanwhile Sid rode home every night to a run-down chicken farm and the spectacle of a father depressed and out of work, for Joseph, after borrowing $600 from his cousin's husband, Louis Mason, to help defray the cost of his son's college tuition, had given up his dream of self-employment and gone back to work as a machinist. His employers were Brown & Sharpe, manufacturers of precision instruments and tools in Providence. Laid off from that job in 1923, he would never work again, for Rhode Island was already in the throes of the Depression.[13] What money Sid earned—at the cigar store and in a factory where he electroplated car radiators—went to help support his parents. He had little to spare for himself.

Sid did no writing until his junior year, when he published a short humor piece for the *Brown Daily Herald*'s "Genial Cynic" column in the form of an advertisement:

Why Flunk?

Professional Tutoring by Two Freshmen!
We Won the Hartshorn Prize and the President's
Premiums in Algebra and Vergil
Why not have us tutor you in
    Dante
    Masse [sic]
    Billiards
    Psychology
    Money and Banking
    Wrestling
    Biochemistry?

We also substitute chapel and take care of finances. Register for Phi Beta Kappa with us—one cow-hide bag with every diploma while they last.[14]

Perelman signed the piece "S.J.P." From then on, he would use the initials S. J. instead of his full name. This way of signing himself was not unusual among Jewish writers of the period, including Sid's close friend, I. J. Kapstein. In an era of discrimination, the practice might be regarded as a kind of survival tactic: The use of initials might make an author sound less Jewish.

Most of Sid's energies were directed toward drawing rather than writing. As a sophomore he became associate art editor of the *Liber Brunensis*, the college yearbook, and did many of the sketches heading the pages devoted to various college organizations and activities. In that same year, he was also made a full-fledged member of the *Jug* board, a "Juggler of the Brush and Pen."

As a junior he continued drawing cartoons for the *Jug*, completing a series of woodcuts in 1923 which bore such inscriptions as "Cut in wood by Perelman," "Cut in Chapel by Perelman," "Moulded in cocoa by Perelman," and "Cut and dried by Perelman." Sometimes he signed himself wistfully as "Perelman/London," "Perelman/Sussex Downs, England," "Perelman/Somaliland" and "Perelman/Vancouver."

One of his cartoons for the *Jug* was entitled "After the Victory," a satire of a Brown post-game celebration. In the first part of the cartoon, cheerleaders and Brown students exude "pep" as they exclaim "Goody!", "Peachy!", "Boomkins!" and "Pat. Pend'g!" In the second part, entitled "As We Are Inclined to See It," the students have passed out and are being trundled off the field in a wheelbarrow. The strip was signed "Battery Recharged by Perelman" and "Engraved on linoleum by Perelman."

Much of what passed as college humor in Sid's day was plagiarized from other sources. William A. Dyer, Jr., editor of the *Brown Jug* in 1924, recalls spending many afternoons in the college library, poring over old jokes from *Harper's* magazines of the nineties. These jokes, he says, usually consisted of four lines which he would painstakingly reduce to two and then give to Sid to draw the accompanying pictures. Sid must not have felt that the jokes were very good, for when he turned in his cartoons, they had absolutely nothing to do with the point.

In his junior year, Sid became a member of the rather exclusive Sphinx Club, a faculty-student organization that met once a month. Its purpose was "the promotion of intellectual fellowship among its members." He also joined the English Club, which met every month to discuss contemporary literature. Meanwhile, he and I. J. Kapstein founded the Rabelaisians, an informal literary group. According to Kapstein, it was "about as Rabelaisian as a convention of choir boys."

In May of 1924, a piece by Perelman appeared in *Casements*, the Brown literary magazine, for the first time. Entitled "The Exquisites: A Divagation," it was a satire on the pseudo-sophisticated college student and consisted of a dialogue between two aesthetes named Herakletes and Meander who, like the Rabelaisians, consider themselves far above the common herd:

"Meander, I have abandoned my faith in Epicureanism."

"Surely not, fickle one."

"I swear it."

"You hesitate in an alarming fashion. Last week, you were a diabolist, the week before an ascetic. Lamentable . . ."

There was a short silence, broken only by hissing steam and distant shouts from the swimming pool. Meander opened his eyes and sighed.

"What is the youth of the land coming to, Herakletes? Where can we find the Paters and Beardsleys of this day and generation?"

Herakletes considered. Learning had indeed declined of late.

"You are right, Meander."

They walked slowly toward the locker-rooms, where Nubians awaited them to aid in completing their toilet.[15]

Although juvenile, this effort nevertheless reveals a self-mocking attitude, a device that Perelman would often employ in his later humor. Sid might fancy himself and his friends as true aesthetes, men of exquisite taste, but he could still find humor in their lofty pretensions. Another significant aspect of the piece is that it is a conversation between two men. The theme of male friendship appears in almost all of Perelman's cartoons during this period. A typical cartoon depicts two men, usually nattily attired, who are either talking or engaged in some strange and fanciful activity such as riding on vacuum cleaners or flying through the clouds.

Because of Sid's well-known friendship with Weinstein, one is tempted to view the cartoons as a tribute to their friendship. Actually Perelman was friendly with many other men at Brown, including Kapstein, Quentin Reynolds, Edward Goldberger, William Dyer, Jr., and Duncan Norton-Taylor, and some of the cartoons may symbolize his relationship with them or, perhaps more importantly, his desire to have a close male friend, a brother and soul mate who would not only challenge him intellectually but alleviate the loneliness and isolation he had felt as an only child. It would not be until the early thirties, when he seriously began to consider marrying Weinstein's sister Laura, that this theme of male companionship gave way to one of male-female relationships. His cartoons began to include men and women who were often engaged in romantic, conventionally sentimental pursuits such as canoeing in the moonlight.

In the same May issue of *Casements* in which "The Exquisites" appeared, N. von Wallenstein-Weinstein, as he was now signing himself, contributed a poem called "Death":

> *Cherished inspirer of minor poets,*
> *How many adolescent wails*
> *Have reached your fleshless ears!*
> *Shall I join that inane chorus*
> *With my poor echo of an old cry?*
> *Scold you for a thief,*
> *Cherish you as a friend,*
> *Beg you for more days,*
> *Or vainly dare you take me?*
> *Why must you disturb*
> *The mediocre mind to thought*
> *And scare small souls to God?*

*Casements* was patterned after many small literary magazines of the twenties. Although not an official Brown publication, it had the distinction of being banned in Providence after publishing several erotic stories. When he wasn't involved with the *Jug*, Sid spent a lot of time hanging around the *Casements* offices. Philip H. Van Gelder, a freshman on the *Brown Daily Herald*, recalled dropping by the *Casements* office one day and being told by Sid that Amy Lowell, the poetess, was going to be a contributor to the next issue. Although Van Gelder had misgivings about the truth of this story, he reported it to his editor, who printed it in the *Herald*. Members of the *Jug* besides Perelman must have enjoyed this joke at the *Herald*'s expense, since the *Jug* and the *Herald* spent most of their time sniping at each other in print.

Practical jokes were the rage in the twenties. Even sophisticated people spent time playing them on one another. The Brown campus had its share of buckets of water set over doorways and frogs placed in rumble seats. Sid was suspected of many of the cleverer ones.

In Sid's senior year, when he was editor of the *Brown Jug*, Fredson Bowers was the editor of the *Brown Daily Herald*. Bowers had just published a series of literary burlesques of popular contemporary writers in the college literary magazine. Among them was one on D. H. Lawrence. "Suddenly," Bowers writes, "the Providence chief of police and various ministers started getting anonymous letters protesting the 'filth' that was being published on the Hill, and demanding action. So of course the Dean got involved, and the editor of the magazine—Gordon Keith Chalmers, who later became president of Kenyon—and I were hauled on the carpet for an explanation. . . . this is what I then thought to be a typical Perelman jape, writing letters to the clergy and the police in such a high moral tone and demanding action. That is, it was a jape that fitted the *Brown Jug*'s idea of humor. But he never admitted it . . ."[16]

Sid's first humor piece for the *Brown Jug* was published in 1924. Called "The Tale of Poor Mary," it was a surrealistic account of a waif who subsists on the roots and berries she gathers in Chatham Square and then one day, as she is walking down Madison Avenue, sees the "natty" clothes in "Rooks Brothers' " windows:

> Various signs proclaimed the products "Nobby"—"Keen"—"Snappy" and so on. Mary gazed pensively. Suddenly her gaze fell upon three pencil-striped sacs in one corner, and, at this very moment, fortune

tapped her gently on the snout. It all seemed too good to be true. For a tense moment she gapped [sic] at them, open-mouthed. Then, with a happy shout, she burst through the great swinging doors of Rooks Brothers.

The manager looked up in amazement as Mary rushed impetuously into his office.

"My dear young lady—"

"Sir, are you the manager?"

"Yes, but . . ."

"Sir, I have an idea!"

"Yes?"

"Sir, in your window you have three pencil-striped suits. Consider the labour it took to stripe those suits. Think of the men, the toil, the time, the pencils! Why not have the whole process done by machinery? *Why not have the stripes woven right into the cloth?*"[17]

After yet another dinner of oak roots, which she is again reduced to eating after this debacle, poor Mary drifts gently off to sleep at the end of the tale.

Far less peaceful was the 1924 *Brown Jug* banquet, which was held partly to celebrate Sid's election as *Jug* editor. Percy Marks was the guest of honor. Edward Goldberger, Class of '27, remembers driving Marks in his father's car to the banquet, which was held in a restaurant in Wickford, on the outskirts of Providence. When they arrived, the party was already under way. Perched atop each table was a half-empty bottle of scotch, which, as Goldberger recalls, was "probably made yesterday." Not surprisingly, the party was very raucous. Members of the *Jug* were throwing rolls at each other when Sid decided that some sophistication was in order. He proceeded to entertain the group with a trick in which he pulled a piece of paper out from under a quarter, leaving the coin undisturbed. After that he decided to substitute a tablecloth for the piece of paper. Neither the quarter nor the tablecloth remained on the table, and all the silverware and plates tumbled to the floor with a crash. The sight of them seemed to have had a stimulating effect on the guests, for they began to wreck the restaurant, at which point the owner threatened to call the police. Marks then shooed everyone out of the premises. The *Jug* later paid for the damages.[18]

The *Jug* banquet was one of Marks's last appearances at a campus gathering. Soon afterward he was dismissed from his teaching post at Brown, supposedly because his thinly veiled portrayal of life at the university had offended President William H. P. Faunce, a Baptist minister and staunch advocate of Prohibition. Marks's dismissal upset his students, particularly Perelman, Weinstein and Kapstein, for he had encouraged their writing—and, as a Jew himself, given them pointers on how to cope with campus discrimination. In the June issue of the *Brown Jug*, an unsigned editorial was probably written by Perelman:

> O tempora, O morons! Year after year we have seen instructors re-engaged whose mental laxity was a watchword, whose classroom discipline was a joke, and whose lectures were more remarkable for their buffoonery than for their information. For these reasons alone, the campus worshippers of the Great God Sham flocked to their classrooms. Beacons of inspiration? Bunkum! Dispensers of canned idealism. Their classes are well-filled because they offer the easiest route to a degree. Yet those men are retained year after year, while really brilliant men are ousted on the most cowardly pretext. Frankly, we have in mind Mr. Marks.[19]

Marks was extremely distressed by his dismissal. Although he married soon afterward and went on to write several bestselling novels, he never returned to academia until the end of his life, when he taught English for a few years at the University of Connecticut. He died in New Haven, Connecticut, in 1956. By then he had long since disclaimed the novel that had made him famous. When people asked him how they might obtain a copy of *The Plastic Age*, he would write them back, imploring them not to read it because it was too "dated."[20]

Sid's election to the editorship of the *Jug* in his senior year represented a real triumph. He had overcome the stigma of being a "carpetbagger" and non-fraternity man. Once he became editor of the *Jug*, his image on campus immediately changed, and he began to be cultivated by the people who for three years had ignored him. "There were nineteen fraternities," he later told writer Alan Brien. "As a Jew, I wasn't invited to join any of them. That is, until I started to write and became editor of the humor magazine. Then two of them asked me to belong. I refused them flat, and that gave me great pleasure. Great pleasure."[21]

As soon as he took control of the *Jug*, Perelman began a crusade against what he regarded as the provincialism of the university. Since over two-thirds of *Jug* subscriptions were sold off-campus, he tried to make the magazine appeal to a wider audience by including humor that was not specifically Brown-oriented.

After the *Jug*'s second issue under Sid's editorship, the *Herald* complained that "The *Jug* has now published two numbers, both of them below the standard of other years, and last year in particular."[22] It cited the new editor's policies as the reasons for the failure.

Several days later Sid wrote a defense of his attitude in a letter to the *Herald:*

> With a vigor that borders on the fanatical, the editors of the *Herald* Saturday last fell on the defenseless *Jug* and tore it into ribbons . . .
> Basing their contentions on the rather obvious platitude that the college flapper, liquor and necking are time-worn, the statement was made that there is always to be found in college life and customs a distinctive humor. To be devastatingly frank, I believe that the only real and spontaneous humor in the college is that which concerns itself with the erotic.[23]

In the January 1925 issue of the *Jug*, he wrote his most scathing editorial, which included blasts at almost everything he found shallow and adolescent at Brown. This included the editorial policies of the *Herald*; the students' lack of interest in drama—they "would rather invest in six-weeks-old synthetic gin or Herbert Tareytons"; the recent fund-raising drives for new sports facilities, which he summed up as "MILLIONS FOR ATHLETICS AND NOT A CENT FOR AESTHETICS"; and the immaturity of most of the student body:

> Ah, the college boys, the college boys! I daresay that if all the sub-freshmen who are intending to come to Brown could see it for what it is, a fraternity-ridden and lethargic academy of very middle-class "boosters," they would change their minds about starting for Providence next fall. From the dot of nine o'clock when we rush in to fear God for fifteen minutes every morning till Cap Cameron [the campus guard] puts the last blowsy drunk to bed, the spectacle is the same.[24]

The *Herald* was quick to retaliate. "The editorial in question was a personal feeling which may be accepted outside the campus as an authentic report. Whether it was true or not . . . it was in bad taste to print it, and showed a rather unbecoming disregard for many pertinent factors which less precipitancy and cocksuredness would have recognized. The *Jug* needs a sense of humor in its editorials and less adolescent aping of the well-known comedy team of Mencken and Nathan, no dishonor to them."[25]

Also appalled by Perelman's iconoclastic attitude was Otis Randall, Dean of the College, who called him into his office, an action that was usually tantamount to dismissal.[26] The Cammarian Club, the student governing body, also administered a reprimand. Undaunted, Perelman got his revenge in the next issue of the *Jug*. He himelf drew the cover, which depicted a morose student in knickers outside the "Office of the Dean." Instead of writing the editorial page himself, he substituted a Mencken essay on the virtues of destructive criticism.

Still in a Menckenesque vein, he fired off a letter to the *Herald* about a campus ruling that permitted men with good grades to cut chapel:

> Gentlemen:
>     Permit me to call to your attention a peculiarly humorous state of affairs. At the present time men on the Dean's List are allowed to cut chapel as often as they like. The natural inference is that excellence in scholarship makes religious education unnecessary. I can see no mention made of this inducement in "Student Life at Brown," the naive propaganda publication of the university. I have no doubt that prospective students would be interested in knowing that a grade of B or better excuses them from worshipping the Creator in Brown University. Does not this rather fantastic ruling represent a departure from the old fear-God days?
>
> Faithfully,
> S. J. Perelman[27]

Not all of Sid's writing for the *Jug* was of the serious, high-minded variety. The fantastic, imaginative side of his personality often broke through in editorials such as the following:

> Students of criminology will find an interesting parallel to the Leopold and Loeb case in the notorious Dugong Hafiz episode. Dugong Hafiz, a student of chemistry at Harvard, was suddenly arrested on an inclusive charge of parricide. It was alleged that he had disposed of his parents in some way to his own pecuniary advantage. On investigation it was found that, acting on the suggestion of a famous advertisement, Hafiz had fed his mother and father on raisins and rusty well-water until they were chemically about 95% iron. He had then sold them to a dealer in scrap iron who, in turn, sold them to a Philadelphia foundry, where they were melted into ten-penny nails and doorknobs. . . .[28]

Although he claimed to have coauthored a one-act play, *Broken Hearts and Jaws*, with a member of the faculty, he was better known as a set designer for two of the bawdiest productions ever to be staged at Brown. The first was a fantastic backdrop for the annual St. Patrick's Day Show in 1924: *The Plastered Duchess, or A Musical Fiasco in Three Acts*, was a parody of Oscar Wilde's *The Duchess of Padua* and Percy Marks's newly published *The Plastic Age*. Written in part by Quentin Reynolds, who also starred as the Plastered Duke, it featured Pep Weinstein as a well-dressed villain named Macaroni.

*The Plastered Duchess* contained such lines as "Brevity is the soul of one that's lit." Although Sid was not supposed to have been involved in the writing, the following dialogue sounds suspiciously Perelmanesque:

> HERALD: "Oyez! Oyez! Hear ye! Hear ye! The Plastered Duke is staggering in! Down, down, ye lowly proletariat! Order, order, I say!
>
> *Enter Duke*
> DUKE: "A bucket of beer and a cheese sandwich!" (Mounts throne) "Well, well, what's on for today? Let's show some life for I have sundry and divers things to do. To meet a fair young bimbo at Tilden & Thurber's, for instance. She thinks she's going to nick me for some poils! It is to laugh. Ha-ha! And once again, ha-ha! How sharper than a serpent's tooth is the Yiddisher bimbo! But we tarry. Away! Away! My kingdom for a horse's neck! What is so rare as a day in July and August?"

*The Plastered Duchess* featured the usual hairy chorus of football players in yellow wigs who were greeted by a barrage of coins, eggs and vegetables thrown by the predominantly male audience. Sid's painted curtain depicted the play's characters, as well as a toilet with the caption "Pay Your *Herald* Subscriptions Here." At the play's conclusion, members of the audience surged forward and promptly began tearing up the curtain for souvenirs. Actually, they staggered forward, for both cast and audience were by then as "plastered" as the Duchess of the title. It was reported that Pep Weinstein never witnessed the audience's stampede. He had passed out in the second act.

The second set Sid designed was for *Red Hot Martha*, which was presented on St. Patrick's Day in 1925. This show was a burlesque of Percy Marks's latest novel, *Martha*. The hit song of the evening was a raucous takeoff on "Red-Hot Mamma," and encores were repeatedly called for, perhaps because the song contained the line "Red-Hot

Martha, Red-Hot Martha, pull your bloomers down!" Almost immediately after the final curtain, the *Herald* started a rumor that Perelman and several other students had written the lyrics. All his life he disclaimed authorship, insisting that he had been responsible only for the sets. In any event, when President Faunce became aware of the show's licentiousness he responded by putting an end to the St. Patrick's Day productions.

By then Sid had met Elizabeth Jane Linz, a pretty blonde junior at Pembroke College, the women's division of Brown. "Sliz," as Elizabeth was called, came from Wheeling, West Virginia. A talented actress, she had appeared in many college plays and was a campus leader. The caption under her yearbook picture states that hers was "an unusual personality—with both eagerness and detachment, keen interest and complete indifference."[29] She called Sid "Sidsy," and they continued to see each other after he left Brown and moved to New York.

Sid never graduated from Brown. "The only thing that interested me at Brown was the *Brown Jug*," he later said. "I was a very indifferent student and did the minimum of work necessary to remain in college."[30]

He was never able to pass trigonometry in his freshman year. He flunked the course again and again. Only three credits stood between him and a degree.

His parents were terribly disappointed, and Sid was furious at Brown, and even more furious at his own lack of mathematical ability. Ironically, his friend Pep Weinstein had somehow managed to get a degree from Brown in 1924 without even having graduated from high school. The caption under his yearbook picture—with its mysterious inscription reading "Evil to him who evil thinks"—gives some hint of his enigmatic personality and its contradictions:

> From his seat in 28 U. H., "Pep" looks across at the Dean's office and smiles placidly, for he is an easygoing, genial fellow. Addicted to reading the latest and the best, he introduced "Jurgen" and "De Maupassant" to us—for which we are truly thankful. He passes his time in drawing exotic pictures, quoting strange and fanciful poetry, and endeavoring to uplift *Casements*. He seems a bit eccentric at times, a characteristic of all geniuses. To predict his future would indeed be a hard task, so we'll leave the answer to the crystal and the astrologer. May his slogan always be, "Honi soit qui mal y pense."[31]

44

In the spring of 1925, the year he would have graduated, Sid received a letter from Norman Anthony, editor of *Judge*, a national humor magazine that had often reprinted his cartoons for the *Jug*. Anthony offered him a job as a cartoonist. *Life* and *Judge* were the most widely read humor magazines in the country. Some members of the *Jug* staff thought that Sid should hold out for *Life*, but stung by Brown's failure to give him a diploma, he snapped up Anthony's offer.

As a final blast at Brown University and the entire college educational system, he published a long quotation by intellectual historian Albert Jay Nock in *The Freeman*, a weekly journal of politics and the arts, in the June editorial page of the *Jug:*

> A university run by the students, with only the loosest and most informal organization, with little property, no examinations, no arbitrary gradations, no ignorant and meddling trustees! A university that would not hold out the slightest inducement to any but those who really wanted to be put in the way of learning something, and who knew what they wanted to learn; a university that imposed no condition but absolute freedom—freedom of thought, of expression, and of discussion! As one surveys actual university life in the United States, such a notion seems fanciful, almost fantastic . . .[32]

Next to his "graduation" picture in the yearbook was the following paragraph:

> Mr. Perelman is our leading sophisticate, chief rooter for Huxley and greatest admirer of Ezra Pound. . . . He was a quiet and ingenious lower classman; but he has since fought the good fight against Babbettism [sic] Sham, Hypocricy [sic], and Mediocrity. All are supposed to quiver before the vicious slashes of his pen and pencil. If we can judge from his ability to extract cigarettes from one and all, he will be a success in the world along with Mencken and Nathan.[33]

The words scarcely describe the struggle he had undergone. Yet he would be a success in the world. He had to be. His father, still unemployed and deeply depressed, had just been diagnosed as having cancer. He desperately needed an operation. What little money Sid's parents had saved was rapidly dwindling and soon would be gone. It would be up to Sid to support them, to make good at last the American dream.

# 3

## "A SUMPTUOUS LIVING"

### (1925–1929)

> I tied a red bandanna to a peeled willow stick and emigrated
> to New York in 1924 to earn, as I believed, a sumptuous liv-
> ing . . . I saw myself ensconced in a studio, with lightly draped
> models, wearing a Windsor tie and a beret and expertly ne-
> gotiating a palette, a loaded brush and a maulstick . . .
>
> S. J. PERELMAN
> to William Zinsser, 1969[1]

Sid's life as a fledgling cartoonist was drab and discouraging. His
contract with *Judge* required him to provide two cartoons a week, as
well as a short humor piece, for which he was paid a salary of thirty-
five dollars.

Getting the money was a job in itself, for *Judge* was in no hurry to
pay its contributors. Although the editors maintained that they paid
promptly on publication, the writers and cartoonists on the staff soon
discovered that the only way to get their money was to go to the
treasurer's office in person and threaten a lawsuit unless they were
paid.

Sid began to spend a great deal of his time in *Judge*'s reception
room, waiting with other writers and cartoonists for Joseph Cooney,
the treasurer, to come out of his office. Cooney "had a gray suit, and
they painted the office gray to make him invisible," Sid recalled.
"Hirelings waiting to be paid would see a red spot moving along the
wall, but by the time they realized it was Cooney's ruddy face he was
out the door."[2]

According to Parke Cummings, another writer who worked for *Judge*,
collecting a check could also be dangerous. The magazine's offices

were located on West 43rd Street and Twelfth Avenue, and visitors would have to cross railroad tracks to reach the building. At all times they ran the risk of being hit by a freight train.[3]

*Judge*'s editorial policy was lackadaisical. Although it billed itself as "The World's Wittiest Weekly," the magazine's idea of humor was a hodge-podge of cartoons and "he-and-she" jokes. Much of the material was supplied by its readers. "Krazy Kracks," "Funnybones" and "Epilaughs" each paid five dollars apiece for contributions. A major source of humor was Prohibition and the following "Epilaugh" poem is typical: "John Brown's body/Lies pickled to the ears/With what he has imbibed/It should keep for many years." "Funnybones" printed puns and jokes contained within the silhouettes of dog bones. Its contributions included the following: "The cheapest operation was Adam's; it cost but one bone." Another regular feature was "The Cheer Leaders," which reprinted excerpts from college humor magazines such as the *Brown Jug* and the *Princeton Tiger*.

Despite the level of its humor, *Judge* attracted some exceptional talent. Regular contributors included Stephen Leacock, Corey Ford, Gardner Rea, Donald McKee, Milton Gross and R. B. Fuller. Donald Herold and Ruth Eastman did many of the covers. George Jean Nathan was drama critic, and Pare Lorentz did the movie reviews.

In 1925, when Perelman joined the staff, the editorial responsibilities of the magazine were divided between Norman Anthony, a merry, monkey-faced man, and Harold W. Ross, who had previously worked on the *American Legion Weekly*. According to Corey Ford, Ross, unlike Anthony, "seldom laughed aloud. If something amused him, his upper body heaved spasmodically a couple of times, and his heavy lips parted in a broad silent grin, showing large teeth with a gap in the center. He wore his coarse brown hair brushed upright to a height of three inches, and now and then, when he was embarrassed or frustrated, he would rub a hand across his face and comb his fingers back through the thatch of hair in one prolonged gesture of confusion, or explode with a heartfelt 'Jesus!' and then grin at his own ineptness."[4]

Ross had been hired to boost *Judge*'s circulation. He wanted to change the magazine from a national monthly to a sophisticated weekly concentrating on New York City. But *Judge*'s publishers scoffed at the idea, and he soon resigned and went on to find backers for his project elsewhere.

Sid knew Ross slightly when he was coeditor of *Judge*. They did not become friends until the mid-1930s when Sid became a steady and important contributor to the *New Yorker*.

Sid's cartoons for *Judge*, like those for the *Brown Jug*, were heavily influenced by the work of John Held, Jr., and Ralph Barton, two popular cartoonists of the twenties. Many years later Sid told artist Richard Merkin that Barton had a more profound influence on his work than Held.[5]

John Held, Jr., was celebrated for his satiric, exaggerated portraits of flappers with angular figures, cropped hair and an unconventional style of dressing, including long ropes of beads, rolled-down stockings and unbuckled galoshes that "flapped" as they walked. He also liked to draw pseudo-primitive woodcuts illustrating such old ballads as "Frankie and Johnny" and "Let Sixteen Gamblers Carry My Coffin," and it was this type of drawing that Sid tried to imitate.

Ralph Barton was famous for his sophisticated caricatures in the *New Yorker* and *Vanity Fair* and was quite the opposite of the reclusive Held. Slight and dapper, with Rudolph Valentino–type good looks, he was an inveterate partygoer. Barton committed suicide in 1931 after his wife, the actress Carlotta Monterey, divorced him and married Eugene O'Neill.

Sid's first cartoon for *Judge* as a regular contributor appeared in the August 15, 1925, issue. Buried at the back of the magazine, it was entitled "The Flighty Pair" and depicted two men being tossed in the air through clouds. The caption read:

> "Don't breathe a word, Casper—but I think Lord Percy is horribly fastidious."
> "You said it, Dalmatia. He even insists on being measured for his coat of arms."[6]

Soon, at least one of Sid's cartoons appeared in every issue. Like his work for the *Brown Jug*, the drawings were surrealistic and, according to Richard Merkin, revealed an awareness of avant-garde artists like Henri Matisse. The dominant theme once again was the relationship of two men, both of whom were fashionably attired and engaged in a fantastic activity like sitting in bathtubs resting on clouds or riding on sheep. Again, the captions bore no relationship to the pictures.

Sometimes Sid's captions revealed a preoccupation with disease and death. One read "I've Got Bright's Disease and He's Got Mine," while another, depicting two men roller-skating, read:

> "Yes, Danzig, it's interesting to think of the two skeletons hidden away around here."
> "What—why, Plushface—where are they?"
> "Inside of us, m'dear, inside of us."[7]

The September 26, 1925, issue contained a cartoon that seems curiously prophetic of West's fatal automobile accident some years later. (A notoriously poor driver, West often alarmed his family and friends by speeding on narrow country roads and daydreaming at the wheel.) It depicted two men jumping exuberantly into the air as they waved diplomas. The caption read:

> "Was your cousin driving fast before the crash?"
> "Fast? He was driving so fast that the Pekingese on the seat beside him looked like a dachshund."[8]

At first Sid lived in New York at 46 West 8th Street, where he shared a furnished room with John M. Richmond, another Brown student. Four other Brown alumni rented rooms in the same building. Among them were a woman who under the pen name of "Susan Chester" wrote an advice-to-the-lovelorn column for the *Brooklyn Daily Eagle*, and I. J. Kapstein, who moved in a year later after graduating from Brown and getting a job as an assistant editor at Alfred A. Knopf.

Across the street was a delicatessen where Sid could buy a corned beef or pastrami sandwich, his favorite food. In the same block was the Troubadour Tavern, where poets in long capes came to recite their poetry. According to Richmond, Sid renamed the place the "Boobadour Tavern."[9]

On some evenings Sid dined with Richmond or Kapstein at Siegel's Restaurant on Sixth Avenue, where for seventy-five cents they could order a three-course meal with fifteen cents extra for homemade bread pudding. Kapstein remembered that they frequented another cheap restaurant where the waitress never failed to ask, "What kind of bread you want—white or rye?" Occasionally Sid and Richmond frequented bars and nightclubs that featured comedians such as Jimmy Durante.

Sid was a Jimmy Durante fan and followed him to the Silver Slipper and the Ambassadeurs. According to Sid, "in time the great Schnozzola favored me with his friendship and my entrance would evoke the singing triolet: 'Here comes that extra special friend of mine! Sit him down at table nine! See that he don't buy no wine!' "[10]

John Richmond recalls that "one night Nathanael West went with us to see Jimmy Durante. At that time Durante was a member of a group called Clayton, Jackson and Durante, and he came over after he did his act, and I remember said to Sid, 'Poilman . . . Poilman, I want to tell you something.' "

Richmond is of the opinion that Sid never wrote any material for Durante, although Sid always hoped that the comedian would offer him a job. Another Brown classmate, Philip Lukin, says that Sid did write some comic routines for Durante, but was never paid for his material.[11]

Perelman and Richmond lived at the West 8th Street apartment until 1926. Then they moved to a one-room apartment on Staten Island, where Richmond had been offered a job. They lived there for approximately a year and a half.

Walter "Fats" Saunders, another friend from Brown, lived nearby with his family in an old Victorian house overlooking the harbor. Sid would often spend hours in the Saunders attic, reading old copies of *Simplicissimus*, a German humor magazine published in Munich.

Even though his life seemed to be going well, Sid was seized with occasional spells of melancholia. One night, as he and Kapstein boarded the Staten Island ferry, he announced, "I don't think I have long to live."

The remark may have been triggered by his father's illness. Several months before, Joseph had undergone an operation for retroperitoneal sarcoma. Other complications ensued, and he died nine months later on October 2, 1926. He was fifty-one years old.[12]

When Sid realized that his father was dying, he took the train to Providence. His cousins, Archie and George Bashlow, met him at the station and drove him to the hospital. His father died soon after his arrival. After Joseph's burial at Lincoln Park Cemetery in Warwick, Sid stayed in Providence for about a week, helping his mother sort out his father's effects. She had decided to stay on at the farm in Norwood. When Sid returned to New York, John Richmond recalled that he was "very quiet" and more subdued than usual. He never discussed with his roommate his feelings about his father's death.

Three years earlier, Mary Davidoff had died at the age of seventy-one. As was customary in those days, the funeral was held at home. Sid never forgot the emotions he experienced at the Masons' house on Bernon Street, nightmarishly transformed by the presence of his great-aunt in her open coffin. Many years later, when a friend's relative died, he implored her not to let her children view the remains. All his life he would have difficulty coping with the deaths of people close to him and would often affect a callow indifference.

Sid and John Richmond moved back to Manhattan in 1927, renting the top floor of an office building at 180 Madison Avenue that had been converted into an apartment. According to Richmond, Sid hadn't much cared for Staten Island, since it had very few good delicatessens.

Richmond recalls that Sid as a young man was very selective in his choice of friends. "His analysis of people would always be in terms of whether the person had any intellect, any sense of humor, never on how much money he or she made."

It was during the mid-twenties that Sid became more self-conscious about his clothes. In imitation of Percy Marks, who had made an impression at Brown by carrying a cane, he bought himself a walking stick and carried it everywhere.

In New York, he continued to see Elizabeth Linz, who still called him Sidsy. "It was a strange relationship," a friend said, "because she was nothing like him. She was fascinated by him and constantly paid attention to him." No one knows why or when the relationship broke off, but perhaps it coincided with Sid's growing interest in Lorraine Weinstein, one of Nathanael West's younger sisters.

When John Richmond got married, Sid and Quentin Reynolds decided to live together. They were joined later by I. J. Kapstein. Perelman and Reynolds sublet an apartment on West 11th Street from Florence Haxton, editor of *Snappy Stories*, and Hope Hale, a writer whom Perelman later dated.

"I think we charged them only five dollars more than the sixty-five dollars per month we paid," Hope Hale Davis recalls. "Reynolds, a flamboyant type with a cane hooked over his arm, did the bargaining, but the young man in the background caught my attention. He was what my aunt would call 'dish-faced,' with thick dark brows arching high over very round, bright eyes. I sensed lurking beneath his shyness an oblique charm, exotic, outside my experience, and was glad when he and Florence discovered a common interest. They were both living on checks painfully extracted from the same publisher, in whose humor magazine, *Judge*, Perelman's pseudo-woodcuts parodied the melodrama and sentiment of the 1890s. . . .

"Among our age group," Mrs. Davis recalls, "wisecracks were in demand, but with Sid they were simply a takeoff point ('Put an egg in your shoe and beat it') for his flights of strange, anarchic comedy. When the company numbered more than two—and sometimes only two—he put on a continuous performance. I remember once catching through a crack in the door a glimpse of his rolling eye, and in my sudden wild giggles I lost forever the words to which he had added this irresistible mummery. I felt privileged, but it never occurred to me that Sid's humor had any other source than natural high spirits.

"I should have been more perceptive—if not then, at least after Sid began bringing his friend Pep Weinstein to my basement on East 58th Street. I did wonder, seeing their mood sometimes, if this was what people meant by Jewish melancholy. Pep was often morose, lamenting his dishonest school career, his laziness, his sense of failure. Even the way the two of them joked about Pep's then unpublished book, *The Dream Life of Balso Snell*, with its St. Puce character, a flea who lived in the armpit of Jesus Christ, showed their troubled feelings about their inescapable Jewishness. For Sid these would give rise to marvelous inventions such as Max Toplitz, Barney Bienstock's landlord *(Chicken Inspector #23)*, the builder of an apartment house called Toplitz Towers in Ilium, New Jersey. . . ."[13]

In the twenties, it was considered sophisticated to imbibe vast quantities of alcohol, but Sid, according to Mrs. Davis and other friends, was not much of a drinker. Never one to tolerate fools—drunken or otherwise—he would rid himself of boisterous guests by suggesting that they all go out for coffee. Then, after he had taken a goodnight cup with his friends, he and his date would depart.[14]

In January of 1927, Sid renewed his friendship with Pep Weinstein, who had just returned from a trip to Paris. Before he left the United States in October of the previous year, Weinstein had legally changed his name to Nathanael West.

Coincidentally or otherwise, Weinstein chose for himself the name of one of New England's most famous mariners—Nathaniel West, who was born in Salem, Massachusetts, in 1756. Nathaniel West had commanded privateers and, after his seafaring days were over, had become a wealthy merchant. On the other hand, Weinstein's selection of the name West may have been influenced by the example of his cousin, Sam, who, as Dr. Jay Martin has pointed out, "had been using it on Wall Street for some time."

West went to Paris in the hope of working on a novel, *The Dream Life of Balso Snell*. After a brief period of work as a construction superintendent for his father, he had convinced the family that he was unsuited to a career in real estate and persuaded them to pay for his attempt at novel writing.

West sailed for Paris on October 13, 1926, four days before his twenty-fourth birthday. Once there, he seems to have done little work on his novel. Magnificently dressed, he would stroll along the streets, listening to the chatter of pimps and prostitutes and jotting down slang words in his notebook. He told friends he wanted to write a glossary of Parisian slang, as used by the common people.

Although he intended to stay in Paris for an unspecified length of time, he was forced to return home after three months abroad. His father and uncle were heavily in debt, early victims of the Depression that was beginning to set in. Suddenly, West's dream of becoming a writer was a fantasy, a form of self-indulgence his parents could no longer subsidize. He was needed at home to help support the family, which was rapidly losing everything it had.

Overnight his life changed. No longer was he the pampered young man who could buy all the clothes and books his expensive tastes demanded. Like Sid, he had to work for a living, and the only job he could get was one as assistant manager of the Kenmore Hall Hotel at 145 East 23rd Street—a job relatives got for him when he was unable to find work himself.

Perelman saw a lot of West during this period, and it was then that their real friendship began. "He often visited me in the Village," Sid said, "curious about, though hardly envious of, the precarious life I was leading."[15] According to Lester Cole, Perelman became "an awe-inspiring figure for West," and from then on, West wrote with Perelman in mind as his most sensitive reader—and severest critic.[16]

Sometime during this period Sid became better acquainted with West's sister Lorraine. She was then seventeen years old, a tall, thin, dark-haired girl with a languid manner and a dry sense of humor.

Lorraine Weinstein—or Laura West, as she later called herself—

was the youngest child in the Weinstein family, having been born in New York City on May 23, 1911. Her sister Hinda—"Sis"—was seven years older.

Physically and temperamentally Laura had much in common with her brother, whom she adored and whose dream of becoming a writer she had always encouraged. Both were tall and languorous people, with a lively intelligence and wit that masked a rather melancholy temperament. For Perelman, whose literary talent included an ability to view the world from both a male and female viewpoint, Laura might have seemed the female embodiment of the traits he found so attractive in West.

At seventeen, Laura had some of the movie-star good looks that would automatically have attracted Sid, who had spent a good part of his adolescence in movie houses watching beautiful, soulful silent-screen stars. She had lustrous hair, large sensual blue eyes and an aquiline nose. Full-figured and graceful, she dressed elegantly. "She was attractive and striking-looking in a rather cool way," says a member of her family who recalls her as a young woman.

George Brounoff, a friend of West's, met Laura at a party when she was sixteen or seventeen years old. "She was very much like her brother, sort of reserved, with a lazy way of walking, a lazy way of talking, a sweet girl, not a very pretty girl, but bright. She was like her brother, very much like him."[17]

In 1928, Laura enrolled as a freshman at Pembroke College. In the brief semester while she was there before dropping out in 1929 to marry Sid, she seems to have followed her brother's relaxed example by involving herself in no extracurricular activities, aside from designing costumes for a couple of college plays. In fact, she gave the impression of being unhappy and ill at ease at Pembroke, perhaps because she found that most of the students were too unsophisticated, not at all like the people she knew in New York.

In February of 1929, her poem "Even Stephen" was published in the *Sepiad*, the Pembroke literary magazine:

EVEN STEPHEN
A Sound Poem: (Sensitive Miss Goldstein of 6B P.S. 186
reads a poem by Alfred, Lord Tennyson)

*Full-bodied six,*
*Five fathom deep,*
*At even:*

*My father Stephen*
*sleeps.*

*Nestles the vessels*
*Subtle slumber,*
*On sweet resting*
*Stephen?*

*Eve calls the oar*
*Haven a creeping:*
*Heaven.*
*Full fathom sleeping*
*O! Stephen.*

*Six, five and even,*
*Seven Stephen,*
*Seven!*
*Slumber subtle number.*
*Stephen. Even seven?*
*Even seven.*[18]

This poem was published under the name of Laura West. According to Laura's cousin, Mrs. Samuel Kaufman, it was Sid who suggested that she change her name. He felt that Lorraine sounded too much like a trade name; Lorraine hairnets were popular at that time.[19]

The transformation of Lorraine and Nathaniel Weinstein into Laura and Nathanael West may have reflected the family's desire to assimilate quickly into American life, for the Weinsteins evidently wanted to be as Americanized as possible. According to a member of the family, they looked down on relatives who retained the accents and customs of the old country.

Laura's adulation of her brother may also have influenced her choice of a new name. Not only did she attend the same university, she also chose the last name of West. She was so enamored of the name that even after her marriage to Perelman, she would sometimes sign her name "Laura P. West."

Sid seems to have had some ambivalence about Nathan and Lorraine changing their names to West, for he continued to refer to them by their original names, at least on official documents. His passport, issued on June 25, 1929, stated that he was accompanied by his wife, Lorraine. In case of death or accident, he listed the person to notify as "Mr. N. V. Weinstein of 115 West 86th Street."

Many years later, when Hinda Weinstein's daughter, Maxine, told

Sid she wanted to change her name, he urged her not to and so strong were his arguments that she followed his advice.

Meanwhile, his own interest in and affection for Yiddish had intensified. In 1928, he wrote I. J. Kapstein a letter outlining the steps by which a "nameless clod becomes the actively disagreeable outlaw." Eighteen Yiddish epithets were listed, including *pischer, schlemiehl, schnorrer* and finally, the ultimate condemnation, *pötz.*

The year of the stock market crash, 1929, was a watershed year for Sid, a time of tremendous growth and change. In March, he introduced West to "Susan Chester," the Brown graduate who had lived in his building on West 8th Street in New York. "Susan" was still writing a lovelorn column for the *Brooklyn Daily Eagle.* Thinking that Sid might find her mail a good source of comic material, she had asked him to dinner at Siegel's Restaurant. Perelman asked if he could bring West along.

Having at last completed his first novel, *The Dream Life of Balso Snell*—which would not be published until 1931—West was rather at loose ends professionally. He was still working at the hotel and writing fiction pieces, while trying unsuccessfully to manufacture and market candy and chili con carne.

Ironically it was West, not Perelman, who took inspiration from Susan Chester's lovelorn column. Very soon after the dinner meeting, he began work on a novel based on the letters that would become *Miss Lonelyhearts.* It would take him four years to complete and would establish his literary reputation.

Sid and Laura were married that same year. Tradition has it that the date was July 4, 1929, but their marriage certificate reveals that they were actually married on June 20.[20] Sid was twenty-five; Laura, eighteen. They moved into Sid's apartment at 64 West 9th Street and sailed for Europe two months later, on August 16. Their honeymoon was financed by Laura's parents.

While they were abroad, Sid's first book was published by Horace Liveright, Inc. (formerly Boni and Liveright). Entitled *Dawn Ginsbergh's Revenge,* it contained forty-nine pieces, most of which he had written for *Judge,* including "What It Minns to Be a Minnow," "Around the Shops with 'Babs' Perelman," "On Being Offered a Nickel to Run Along and Be a Good Boy," "How to Fall Out of a Hammock" and "Do Spark Plugs Think?"

A flamboyant, handsome Jew, Horace Liveright was a maverick in the publishing business, which for years had been dominated by conservative Gentiles from old families. According to Bennett Cerf, one of Liveright's partners, "there had never been a Jew before in American publishing, which was a closed corporation to the rising tide of young people described in *Our Crowd*. Suddenly there had burst forth on the scene some bright young Jews who were upsetting all the old tenets of the publishing business—and the flashiest of all was certainly Liveright."[21] A number of Jews in publishing, among them Alfred A. Knopf, disapproved of Liveright. They felt he was a poseur and reckless in his business dealings. Liveright's office—in a brownstone on 48th Street—was the scene of wild parties. Occasionally the irate husband of one of his many mistresses would storm into the vestibule, waving a pistol and threatening to shoot him.

Liveright published books that other publishers thought were too risqué, including Gertrude Atherton's *Black Oxen* and Warner Fabian's *Flaming Youth*. (Fabian was the pseudonym of Samuel Hopkins Adams, who wrote it mainly as a jest.) But his authors also included William Faulkner, Sigmund Freud, Ernest Hemingway, Eugene O'Neill, Sherwood Anderson, E. E. Cummings and Theodore Dreiser.

Unfortunately, Liveright made the mistake of becoming a theatrical producer, investing most of his money in shows. His choice of plays was poor, and he soon lost most of his fortune. In 1930, a year after publishing *Dawn Ginsbergh's Revenge*, he was forced out of the firm. It went into bankruptcy three years later.

Liveright died in September of 1933, at the age of forty-six. A few days before his death, a friend found him in his furnished room, trying to cover a hole in the sleeve of his blue serge jacket with some blue ink and cloth so that when he wore it his white shirt would not show through.[22]

But when *Dawn Ginsbergh's Revenge* was published, Liveright's tragic demise lay four years in the future. Sid and Liveright seem to have had a fairly friendly relationship, in contrast to Sid's subsequent quarrels with other publishers. A month before Sid and Laura were married, Sid gave Liveright an oil painting for his office with the hope that it "would bring him and his staff good luck."

Some of the pieces in *Dawn Ginsbergh's Revenge* satirized the sensational fiction Liveright loved to publish. In the lead piece, "Puppets of Passion, or A Throbbing Story of Youth's Hot Revolt Against the Conventions," Dawn Ginsbergh, like Mona Fentriss in *Flaming Youth*, is a restless, rebellious beauty who is bored by her distinguished suitors. She succumbs to love only when she meets Moe Feinbloom, a moronic iceman who is baffled when she kisses him on the mouth. Although callow in comparison to his later work, the piece employs a favorite Perelman literary device: the use of a series of non sequiturs that grow increasingly absurd and soon leave readers rubbing their eyes in disbelief:

> A knock on the door aroused Dawn from her lethargy. She hastily slipped it off and donned an abstraction. This was Dawn, flitting lightly from lethargy to abstraction and back to precipice again. Or from Beethoven to Bach and Bach to Bach again.[23]

That Sid got his start writing for a college humor magazine is evident in many of the other pieces; there are the inevitable jokes about Prohibition and students who attend Ivy League colleges. In "Love's Whirlpool," a flea is compared to a Yale student, except that the flea is "bright-looking."

Throughout Perelman's career one of his favorite sources of satire was advertising, about which he once said: "Great fatuous booby that I was, I imagined advertising would be destroyed from the outside. It won't; it's going to bubble and heave and finally expire in the arms of two nuns, like Oscar Wilde."[24] In *Dawn Ginsbergh's Revenge*, a woman, who is finally able to live a normal life after her blackmailer is killed by a flea bite on the kneecap, announces: "Now we own our own home, drive a Ford car, play the saxophone, read fifteen minutes a day and talk intelligently on any topic. I am a happy mother at last, and I owe it all to Bilge Reducing Gum, which I have chewed ever since I left primary school."[25]

In these pieces Perelman also introduced other typical conceits such as addressing the reader as if he were a child asking to be told a story: "But the oboes did not do the work either, for it is notorious that oboes never do work. That, kiddies, is why they *are* oboes." He was fond of ending a piece with the word for one of his favorite Jewish delicatessen foods: "Our part of the tale is finished. *Pastrami!*" In some of the stories, he possessed the uncanny ability to assume a female persona, writing sometimes as Babs Perelman, a fashion editor, or Constance ("Peaches") Perelman, "the most pulchritudinous girl in the whole U.S.A.," or Princess Abou Ben Perelman, a beautiful half-caste Armenian princess in the stronghold of the sultans.

Like Dorothy Parker, he had no love for A. A. Milne and displayed his dislike in the tale of a sea serpent whose ambition in life was to devour the creator of *Winnie the Pooh:*

> *He wants to eat that A. A. Milne,*
> *Whose writings are so quaint.*
> *I'm glad of that because they fill me*
> *With a tendency to faint.*[26]

In his later work, Sid invariably portrayed Laura as an amazon who towered over him physically and his children, Adam and Abby, as hellions who were always getting into mischief and making his life miserable. This was in part a comic pose, reflecting the sentiments of the superficial twenties, but in "Billiards and Their Prevention," he describes a real distaste for children. "I am 25 years old and hate children, in which respect I am different from billiards; although I cannot say for sure whether billiards hate children, as I never asked them."[27]

The lengthiest piece in *Dawn Ginsbergh's Revenge* is "How to Make Love," a parody on self-help manuals. The piece was illustrated with sentimental photographs of 19th-century couples. "How to Make Love" was divided into ten sections. The tips on lovemaking were unlike any others on the subject, for Sid dealt with Outdoors Love (which was further subdivided into Ocean Love and Pasture Love), Problems of Kissing with a Full Beard and Baseball Love. The author's cynicism was apparent in the very first paragraph:

> What is that Mysterious Force which hastens the breathing, makes the heart tender, the spirit brave, the impulses generous and the will strong? Yes, children, you are right—Scotch. But there is still another Force which does not retail in four-fifths quart bottles and is infinitely more expensive. This Force is called LOVE. In this series of articles we shall discuss various kinds of LOVE and the proper methods, grips, holds and punches connected with this fascinating pastime.[28]

In the Tenth Lesson, the final section, Perelman introduces Laura, his new bride, to the reader. Her career as a baseball player for the New York Yankees may have been suggested by her brother Pep's frustrated ambition to play the game well:

> In response to frequent requests from readers, we present, as the final lesson in this amazing series on the Art of Love, two photographs posed

by the author, Mr. S. J. Perelman and his wife, Princess Veronica of New Haven, a full-blooded Turk. These are the first authentic photographs of the well-known author and his "ball and chain" and were secured only after much urging.

. . . The story of the meeting of Princess Veronica and the author is a romantic one. The princess was formerly part of the harem of Sultan Abdul Humid II. Mr. Perelman, at that time an ace in the Lafayette Escadrille, chanced to fly over Turkey and saw the princess waving to him from a quandary. He was so impressed by her beauty that he abducted her and hid her in his ancestral home in Wales. Then, under the nom-de-plume of Charles Lindbergh, he flew back to America with Veronica secreted in the fuselage of the plane. The rest is history. Veronica, unfortunately, has splay feet, and her witty husband often remarks that she is of a splayful disposition. But she is a good wife to him and even earns an extra penny now and then shagging grounders for the Yankees in the outfield.[29]

The two photographs he mentioned were not of Sid and Laura; they were captioned "I Couldn't Resist You" and "When Dreams Come True." Sid selected the photographs and drawings in *Dawn Ginsbergh's Revenge*, many of which were influenced by Max Ernst and other Surrealist painters. A piece entitled "Report of the Perelman Beard Commission" was illustrated with drawings of mops and brushes.

There were three printings of *Dawn Ginsbergh's Revenge*, and the book sold approximately 4,600 copies, a respectable number for its day.[30] As Sid said later, "It was a curious little volume, bound in the horripilating green plush called 'flock' used to upholster railroad chairs."[31] The author's name was accidentally omitted from the title page. "I presumably was so overawed at the permanence I was achieving that I neglected to check this detail," he said.[32]

Two days after the book's publication, Liveright ran one of his catchy ads in the *New York Times*. Undoubtedly written by Sid, it read:

Learn about Perelmangitis (stitches in the side)
from Herr Doktor Professor S. J. Perelman
(Perelman of *Judge*)
in
**Dawn Ginsbergh's Revenge**
*Outrageously Illustrated*

60

With this, the first volume in the trilogy called *Swann's Way Down Yonder in de Cornfield*, S. J. PERELMAN makes his bow. Woven into its pattern is the incredible gaucherie of life in the straw hat mines of Dutch Guiana [sic]. The book itself was woven entirely under water by a small band of panama hat weavers.

One-time dean of the Chiropody School at Harvard, PERELMAN was thrown on his own resources at the age of 35. For years he has tramped the pampas known only as Trader Hornstein.

You will want to read this book out loud; you will want to shout about it from the housetops. With every copy of the book goes a free housetop. *This book does not stop at Yonkers!*

Priceless (*$2.00*)

Despite this advertisement, the book was not widely reviewed. Many years later Perelman refused to let his publishers reprint it, saying it was "too dated."[33] However, one person who received a copy from the Liveright publicity department adored it and enthusiastically endorsed it, writing a jacket blurb that said: "From the moment I picked up your book until I laid it down, I was convulsed with laughter. Someday I intend reading it."

His name was Groucho Marx.

# 4

# "I TOLD YOU I'D
# WAX ROTH SOME DAY"

## *(1929–1930)*

Sid and Laura spent their honeymoon in France, returning to the United States in September of 1929 to take up residence at Sid's apartment on West 9th Street. They had had a wonderful time abroad and immediately started saving money in hope of living there permanently.

At first they seemed happy together. Laura enjoyed going to the movies and attending parties given by Sid's friends. She shared his perceptiveness about people, and the two loved to dissect the personalities of the guests after a dinner party. She had a quick wit that Sid appreciated and, as time went on, an eye for the grotesque situation that stimulated his comic imagination.

In many respects the Perelmans' attitude toward marriage was typical of sophisticated young couples in the twenties and thirties. It was considered important to preserve one's privacy and sense of independence. Extramarital affairs were tolerated as long as they were casual and discreetly conducted. Sexual freedom proclaimed one's emancipation and need for diversion, while monogamous love was regarded as sentimental, confining and hypocritical.

This philosophy was to bring both Sid and Laura great unhappiness.

In 1930 Sid had decided to switch from writing for *Judge* to *College Humor*, a magazine based in Chicago. He would continue writing for *Judge* until the beginning of 1931, however. This change of jobs was crucial to his development, for during this period he began to write longer pieces in a more sophisticated style. "I was beginning to develop a sense of parody and of lapidary prose," he told William Zinsser.[1]

*College Humor* billed itself as "the magazine with a college education." In every issue there was an article about a well-known college or university and a pictorial section on interesting collegians. Corey Ford, Dr. Seuss, John Held, Jr., Don Herold, Donald Ogden Stewart, George Ade, Margaret Culkin Banning, Walter Winchell and Zelda and Scott Fitzgerald all appeared in its pages. Groucho Marx contributed a long satiric piece entitled "Beds."

Sid's first piece was an excerpt from his *Parlor, Bedlam and Bath*, a comic novel he wrote with Quentin Reynolds. It appeared in the July 1930 issue and was followed by a second excerpt the following month. During the next year and a half he had a piece in almost every issue. They bore titles such as "The Thrill Girl," "The Kiss Fool," "Lucy Libido's Lions," "Passion's Whirligig" and "Woman Bait." Several were satires on the sensation-seeking coed, the vapid actress or the downtrodden waitress who could not afford to go to college but succeeded in life anyway because she had a voluptuous figure. Usually the characters boasted outrageous names such as Garish Cooper and Ming Toy Epstein.

At *College Humor*, he continued to illustrate his pieces as he had at *Judge*. He had dropped the motif of two men, and many of his cartoons were now literal translations of well-known sayings or clichés. One caption, which read "I think I'll cast Pearl before swine," accompanied a drawing of a father shoving his baby daughter in front of some pigs. Another—" 'I told you I'd wax Roth some day,' shrieked Mrs. Roth"—was featured underneath a cartoon of a woman waxing her husband while a friend looks on incredulously.

Sid was irreverent about his own talents. His byline often read: "Plot and Landscape Gardening by Perelman," "Written on Swedish Health Bread by S. J. Perelman" or "Greased Wire Work by S. J. Perelman."

Sid's last article for *College Humor*, "Seedlings of Desire," appeared in the February 1932 issue. H. N. Swanson, the editor, stopped working for the magazine six months later, and *College Humor* suspended publication in March of 1934. It was the first in a series of humor magazines—*Vanity Fair, Life, Judge*, Norman Anthony's *Ballyhoo*— that were to go out of business in the next few years, victims of a change in national taste. As the Depression deepened, people turned away from humor. They wanted to read less trivial and more sober writing.

H. N. Swanson, who later became a successful movie producer and agent, remembers that it was he who suggested to Sid that since his captions were so long (often four to six lines) he might dispense with the cartoons and concentrate on writing longer pieces. "Very often over a beer or two, he would tell me some idea he was 'fooling around with,' " Swanson recalls. "I told him I would buy any he ever put on paper, without even reading them. In later years Sid said that line stuck in his mind and made him think he was a writer after all."[2]

Sid himself had reached a crossroad about his drawings. No longer certain whether he wanted to remain a cartoonist, he began experimenting with other artistic forms, in particular with collage, which was then popular in Europe. He also became interested in realism and took courses for a year at the Art Students League in New York, where he drew from a live model.

After he started working as a screenwriter for the Marx Brothers, he gave up his career as a cartoonist entirely. Many of his friends were professional artists, and over the years they tried to encourage him to resume his drawing. Some even presented him with drawing supplies, but he never bothered to use them.

Although he began to think of himself solely as a writer now, he had little faith in his ability. He still imitated the work of his favorite humorists—Stephen Leacock, George Ade, Ring Lardner—and later confessed to Dick Cavett that "I was such a shameless Lardner thief I should have been arrested."[3] Feeling that he would be unable to sustain a full-length piece of prose on his own, he decided to collaborate on a novel with Quentin Reynolds, who had become a reporter and sportswriter for the *New York Evening World*.

"Convinced that it would be an easy matter, we fashioned a kind of plot about a rich young man who lived in the Village and had limited interests: speakeasies and girls," Reynolds wrote. "My part was to type out the rough chapters; Sid's was to clothe them with his mad humor and decorate them with this sort of introduction:

> The storm at sea—In which our heroine breasts the waves and vice versa—Bertha writes Goethe a letter—Goethe writes Bertha a letter—They tear up each other's letters—Futility.[4]

The authors decided to call their book *Through the Fallopian Tubes on a Bicycle*, a title that even the liberal Horace Liveright thought was too risqué. Under the more sedate name *Parlor, Bedlam and Bath*, the book was first serialized in *College Humor* before being published by Liveright in 1930.

It was a summer of expectations. Both authors desperately hoped that the book would be a bestseller and bought by the movies. But sales were disappointing. Only 1,500 copies were sold—far fewer than *Dawn Ginsbergh's Revenge*—and the book did not earn back its advance. As for the movie deal, it failed to materialize, although Groucho Marx reportedly had expressed some interest in it. A year or two later, when Sid was working as a scriptwriter at Paramount, he looked up the reader's report on the novel. It said simply, "More bedlam than parlor or bath."[5]

The reviews generally were good. The *New York Times* commented: "With a shaky skeleton of a narrative, the authors have dedicated themselves to the sole purpose of being entertaining and they have succeeded brilliantly."[6] An anonymous reviewer in the *Saturday Review of Literature* had some reservations, however: "The book is good, though it falls occasionally into a bog. Essentially it is like nothing else that we know in spite of passages and attitudes that remind us of McEvoy, Sullivan, Stewart, Lardner, Benchley, Groucho Marx and Joe Cook. Anyone to whom this list is a roll-call of the well-beloved will be thoroughly delighted with Perelman. He is never really derivative, although it is plain where he went to school." The reviewer concluded that "a generation from now it will be largely indecipherable and thoroughly inane, but here and now it's grand good stuff"[7]—an astute judgment, for the book's humor is woefully creaky by modern standards. Its main interest lies in the fact that it remains Perelman's only attempt at a comic novel, unfortunately one that he couldn't quite bring off.

The characters are largely cartoons, and the plot so convoluted as to be almost incomprehensible. Whether this was Reynolds' or Perelman's fault—or the fault of the original 1917 farce, *Parlor, Bedroom and Bath*, by C. W. Bell and Mark Swan, on which it was based—is impossible to determine, but it should be pointed out that one of Sid's weaknesses whenever he tackled a form longer than the comic essay was his lack of narrative drive and sense of drama.

Of fascination, however, is the satire on twenties sexuality, with its emphasis on free love, coupled with cynicism about true love and commitment. When the characters in *Parlor, Bedlam and Bath* aren't drinking themselves blind, they are stumbling into bed with nameless strangers, presumably to proclaim the fact that they are fun-loving, independent spirits. This depiction of the amoral sex lives of his contemporaries was not another one of Perelman's flights of fancy, but rooted in reality—and his own experience. It reflected his and Laura's youthful attitudes toward sex and marriage.

*Parlor, Bedlam and Bath* celebrates the exploits of Chester Tattersall, the scatter-brained son of an improvident father. Following the death of his uncle Marmeluke, Chester inherits a great deal of money. Suddenly very rich, he quits his job as a clerk at the New York Telephone Company and devotes himself entirely to a life of pleasure. He spends most of his time in Greenwich Village speakeasies, and when he isn't inebriated, he seduces women. So casual are his affairs that he never bothers to learn the women's last names.

Eventually Chester's life catches up with him when he spends the weekend at the home of an old college friend, Rolf Weatherbee, and discovers to his horror that he has slept with most of Rolf's female relatives, including his wife Helen. Appalled by his life of excess, he decides to reform and get married, but, in another terrible twist of fate, soon learns that his fiancée, showgirl Cherry LaRue, has also enjoyed an intimate relationship with Rolf—in fact, she is his former wife. In time-honored twenties tradition, Chester tries to end his pain by jumping out a window, but fortunately lands on a ledge and isn't hurt. Cherry is unmoved by Chester's attempted suicide. After he sails out her window, she decides that it's time for her to go to bed and is about to retire when Chester's head reappears at the window:

> "Oh, it's you," observed Cherry. "I thought you were dead."
> "No, I was caught on a ledge. You didn't even care," he added reproachfully.
> "But I do care, darling," cried Cherry. "You can't know how I care!"
> He climbed back into the room. Somewhere between her chair and the window their lips met. The candle flared and then guttered out, the last petal fell from the rose on the bureau; but Cherry and Chester paid no heed. They had found their bluebird in the vale of heart's-desire.[8]

Years later Sid said that the failure of *Parlor, Bedlam and Bath* cured him of any ambition to write another comic novel. According to a friend, he refused to have a copy in the house.

Sid as a toddler. This photograph was taken at the Bellin Studios near the B. F. Keith Theatre in Providence, Rhode Island, where as an adolescent Sid would be introduced to the madcap humor of the Marx Brothers.
*Courtesy of Mr. and Mrs. Vincent Mason.*

Perelman's first cartoon for the *Brown Jug*, November 1921.
*Courtesy of Brown University Archives.*

"What does the expression 'in your odd minutes' mean, Bob?"
"Why, your odd minutes are those when you are not working."
"I should think your odd minutes would be those when you are working."

The *Brown Jug* staff, 1925. Perelman, the new editor-in-chief, is third from the right in the front row.  *Courtesy of Brown University Archives.*

IF WE CAN BELIEVE THE OLD STORIES ABOUT THE FREE-LUNCH COUNTERS
IN THE BAR-ROOMS

"It is not permitted any one, in the hours of study to speak to another, except in Latin, either in the College, or College Yard —"

"The conduct of the students with respect to morality and good manners, in the times of Vacation, shall be cognizable equally as when present at College —"

"The Steward shall be permitted to sell to the Students, in the times allowed for Recreation, Cyder, Strong Beer, Small Beer —"

"Any student passing by one of a class above him, shall take off his hat in a respectful and decent manner."

## EARLY LAWS OF THE COLLEGE
(From the Corporation Records of 1783)

### NATHANIEL VonWALLENSTEIN WEINSTEIN, New York N. Y.
#### "Pep"

From his seat in 28 U. H., "Pep" looks across at the Dean's office and smiles placidly, for he is an easy going, genial fellow. Addicted to reading the latest and best, he introduced "Jurgen" and "DeMaupassant" to us — for which we are truly thankful. He passes his time in drawing exotic pictures, quoting strange and fanciful poetry, and endeavoring to uplift Casements. He seems a bit eccentric at times, a characteristic of all geniuses. To predict his future would indeed be a hard task, so we'll leave the answer to the crystal and the astrologer. May his slogan always be "Honi soit qui mal y pense."

### SIDNEY JOSEPH PERELMAN
#### "Sid"
Norwood, R. I.

Mr. Perelman is our leading sophisticate, chief rooter for Huxley, and greatest admirer of Ezra Pound. He was a quiet and ingenious lower classman; but he has since fought the good fight against Babbettism, Sham, Hypocricy, and Mediocrity. All are supposed to quail before the vicious slashes of his pen and pencil. If we can judge from his ability to extract cigarettes from one and all, he will be a success in the world along with Mencken and Nathan.

Jug Board (1) (2) (3) (4); Editor-in-Chief (4); Liber Board (1) (2) (3) (4); Sphinx Club (3) (4); English Club (3) (4).

West and Perelman's yearbook pictures in the *Liber Brunensis*. West graduated from Brown in 1924, but Sid, who was poor at math, never received a degree.
*Courtesy of Brown University Archives.*

Two typical Perelman cartoons for *Judge*, 1925.
*General Research Division, The New York Public Library, Astor, Lenox and Tilden Foundations.*

## THE DOLLY SISTERS

"Yes, Danzig, it's interesting t(
think of the two skeletons hidden awa)
around here."
"What! Why—why, Plushface
where are they?"
"Inside of us, m' dear, inside of us.'

## GRADUATING FROM NIGHT SCHOOL

"Was your cousin driving fast before the crash?"
"Fast? He was driving so fast that the Pekingese on the seat beside him looked like a dachshund!"

Perelman in New York, c. 1925.
*Courtesy of Brown University Archives.*

Laura with Gherky in
Hollywood, c. 1930.

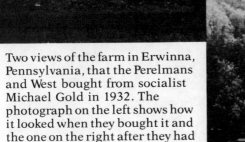

Two views of the farm in Erwinna,
Pennsylvania, that the Perelmans
and West bought from socialist
Michael Gold in 1932. The
photograph on the left shows how
it looked when they bought it and
the one on the right after they had
been living there for several years.

Kidding around with Nathanael
West, c. 1930.

Sid and Laura, and Laura and West at the Erwinna farm, c. 1932.

During the filming of *Monkey Business*, 1932. Counterclockwise from left to right: Groucho Marx, gagwriter Solly Violinski, Perelman, Arthur Sheekman and Will B. Johnstone.

West's jacket photo for *Miss
Lonelyhearts,* 1933.

Sid and Laura in a 1934
passport picture.

\*     \*     \*

When *Parlor, Bedlam and Bath* was published, Sid and Laura were again in Europe, having arrived at Cherbourg in the early part of June 1930. On this trip they went to Munich, St.-Malo and Paris, where they visited their friend Beatrice Mathieu, whom they had met on their honeymoon trip a year earlier. Beatrice covered Paris fashions for the *New Yorker*, and the Perelmans both thought she would make the perfect wife for Nathanael West. When Beatrice came to New York several months later, they introduced her to Nathanael. The two were instantly attracted to one another, and soon West began to talk seriously of marriage, telling Beatrice that he planned to come to Paris as soon as he got an advance on his new book. But West, who had difficulties making a commitment to any woman, began to stall about going abroad, and the relationship ended.

Sid and Laura had returned to Europe with the hope of living there permanently. But they had not saved enough money to support this venture, nor could they find work abroad. In early August they returned to New York and sublet an apartment on 92 Grove Street for the fall and winter.

That winter the Perelmans entertained a great deal. Among the frequent guests at their parties were Edmund Wilson and their neighbor, E. E. Cummings, who lived at 4 Patchin Place from 1923 until his death in 1962.

According to Sid's friend, writer James Lee, many years later Sid ran into Cummings late one night in Washington Square Park. The two men strolled along, and as they passed an apartment building at the edge of the park, Cummings stopped suddenly and stared at it. "What scenes of sordid domesticity do you think are being played out behind those lighted windows?" he asked. "Why, that's my apartment," Sid protested. "I know," Cummings replied.[9]

Nathanael West thought Cummings was crazy because he once sat on the floor of Siegel's Restaurant and "shouted all the dirty words he knew."[10] West's work on his new novel, based on the "Susan Chester" letters, was going slowly. He would not finish it until 1933. He let Perelman read the first four chapters of the book and became discouraged when Perelman said he felt they were too psychologically oriented.

In December of 1930, West became the manager of the Sutton Club Hotel at 330 East 56th Street, a job again arranged by a relative who owned stock in the corporation that owned the hotel. There, in between his managerial duties, he was able to continue work on *Miss Lonelyhearts*.

The Sutton, which was originally intended to be used as a woman's club, was not as well-patronized as the Kenmore. A number of rooms were always vacant, and West let his friends stay in them free of charge. When they weren't in Europe or out in Hollywood, Sid and Laura often stayed in the hotel, and so did Laura's mother, Anuta, after her husband died. Other guests included Edmund Wilson, Robert Coates, James T. Farrell and his wife, Erskine Caldwell, Quentin Reynolds and Norman Krasna. Lillian Hellman, whom Perelman met when she was employed as a reader at Liveright's and married to Arthur Kober, wrote *The Children's Hour* at the Sutton. Dashiell Hammett, unable to meet his bill at the expensive Hotel Pierre, managed to sneak out and into the Sutton dressed in all the clothing he owned. Thanks to West's largesse, he was able to finish his detective novel, *The Thin Man*. It became a bestseller and made him a rich man.

In discussing Nathanael West in "The Hindsight Saga," Perelman described the Sutton in attractive terms, glossing over its seamier side. It was not unlike an artist's colony, he said, a place where even the elevator man was writing a play and poets read their verse at teatime to lady librarians in the lobby. Other residents had a far different impression. John Sanford, who stayed there for five months, remembers the Sutton as being quite run-down. The clientele, he says, consisted mostly of tennis bums and prostitutes, who seemed to have had no trouble plying their trade even though the beds at the Sutton were very narrow and the sexes segregated on alternate floors.[11] Suicides were common. During West's tenure, a number of people killed themselves by leaping off the terraces.

Why did Perelman overlook this sordidness? Even though West had been dead for almost thirty years by the time he wrote about him, perhaps Sid still needed to portray him in halcyon terms because he felt some guilt about him. After all, West and Perelman had had similar professional aspirations; they regarded themselves as emotional and literary soul mates, in many respects mirror images of one another. Because their relationship was one of genuine fondness and mutual respect, competition between them was a thing they did not like to acknowledge. Yet, by 1930, their fortunes had reversed themselves. No longer was West the pampered, rich young man indulging every whim. Sid, who had had to struggle early in life, was now earning a good living, not at a nine-to-five job, but by his drawing and writing. At twenty-six, he had already had two books published. West, on the other hand, still labored in obscurity. Ironically, it would be Sid, not West, who could afford to return to Europe in the middle of the Depression. Yet West, who had hoped to get an advance on *Miss Lonelyhearts* so he could return to Paris, had sent a few chapters to Clifton Fadiman at Simon and Schuster and had been offered neither money nor a contract on his work.

In the late 1920s, there was still another development in Sid's career that would widen the professional gap between them.

One of the hits of the 1928–29 Broadway season was *Animal Crackers*, a comedy by George S. Kaufman and Morrie Ryskind that starred the Marx Brothers. Attending a performance with Laura, Perelman, who had never met Groucho Marx, sent him a note during intermission, thanking him for his "endorsement" of *Dawn Ginsbergh's Revenge*.[12] Groucho's response was typically quixotic. Through an usher he invited the Perelmans backstage after the show, then tried to shock them by breezing into his dressing room attired in his undershorts.

After getting dressed, Groucho told them that one of the networks had approached the Marx Brothers to do a radio serial.[13] Would Sid be interested in writing the script with Will Johnstone, a cartoonist for the *New York Evening World*? When Sid replied that he had never written a radio script, Groucho seemed unperturbed. Neither had Will Johnstone, he said. As a matter of fact, their lack of experience might be an asset, for as rank amateurs, they might possibly come up with something original.

Sid and Johnstone, who'd written *I'll Say She Is!*, a successful vaudeville show in which the Marx Brothers had appeared, spent the next few days trying to conceive a fresh comedy situation for the Marx Brothers that would appeal to radio audiences. The only idea they came up with was vague, something about the comedians stowing away in barrels aboard an ocean liner. They rapidly discarded it as being too silly.

Nothing more came to mind until a few days later, when Sid and Will were invited to a story conference with the Marxes over lunch at the Hotel Astor. This luncheon proved chaotic, with Groucho griping about the $240,000 he had lost in the stock market, Chico constantly jumping up to make phone calls to his bookie and Harpo more fascinated by the lady diners than conversation about radio skits.

At last, the talk turned to business matters, and Perelman and Johnstone had no choice except to present their only idea. Both expected a negative reaction, but to their surprise, Groucho, after a brief conference with Harpo and Chico, announced, "This is too good to waste on a radio show—it's going to be our next picture."[14]

# 5

# ENTER GROUCHO MARX

## *(1930–1932)*

In essence it was an experience no
worse than playing the piano in
a house of call.

S. J. PERELMAN, 1966[1]

Over the years Perelman's name has become inextricably linked with
that of the Marx Brothers. People who have never heard of him as a
writer display a sudden interest when they are told that he wrote
scripts for Harpo, Groucho and Chico Marx. Some say that Groucho
owed everything to Perelman and that Perelman singlehandedly created Groucho's comic persona. Perelman fans, attending a Marx
Brothers film, tend to laugh and nod knowingly every time Groucho
leers and makes one of his jaundiced wisecracks: Only Perelman, with
his genius for non sequiturs, could have thought up a line like that.

Sid should have been pleased by this adulation, but he never was.
In fact, as time went on, he began to deplore and play down his
connection with the Marx Brothers. In a sense they had been his
stepping-stone to fame, but it was a fame he didn't care for. He felt
that his work for the *New Yorker* and the plays he wrote for Broadway
were far greater achievements. Besides, the assumption that he singlehandedly created the style of four of the early major Marx Brothers
films—*Animal Crackers, Monkey Business, Horse Feathers*, and *Duck
Soup*—was untrue. He had worked on only two—*Monkey Business*
and *Horse Feathers*, and the scripts had been written in collaboration
with other writers and the brothers themselves. In later years, when
reporters asked him what it was like to work with the Marxes, he

71

usually retorted that they were "capricious" and "disorganized," as well as "boorish," "ungrateful" and "megalomaniacal."

Groucho was equally bitter about Perelman. In 1972, he told a reporter that Perelman "could write a funny line, but never a script. When he was writing for us, he was working with four other men. He thought he was the greatest writer in the world and didn't want to be identified with comedians . . . thought we were too low. After we became successful, he came out and said he wrote a great part of the Marx Brothers. This just wasn't true. We had good writers, but he wasn't one of them." At this point Groucho interrupted his harangue and added sweetly, "I had dinner with him in England about six months ago. I don't think he's as funny anymore."[2]

It was not always so. In the early days of their relationship, Sid would often stay with Groucho in Hollywood, and when Groucho came to New York, which he did frequently, he would call up Perelman and have dinner with him. Sid gave Groucho a photograph of himself, which he inscribed "To Groucho, in memory of our many campaigns together in the Sudan." The two men corresponded, usually to complement each other on some recent achievement. In his letters, Sid was fond of addressing Groucho as "Cuddles."

Groucho particularly liked Sid's *Westward Ha!*, which was published in 1948, and wrote him a letter praising it highly.[3] He was so enthusiastic about the book, an account of Perelman's journey around the world, that he even wrote his family doctor telling him to buy a copy.

Sid was touched by his old boss's enthusiasm. In a letter dated June 26, 1948, he replied:

Dear Groucho,

Your letter was a kind deed in a naughty world (a phrase I copped out of Bartlett's Book of Quotations years ago and have been trying to work in ever since). It was particularly heartening since it arrived at one of those moments of self-laceration that free-lance writers sometimes experience (never more than eight hours a day, however). In these rare moods the subject is given to regarding himself through the wrong end of a telescope and inquiring through his teeth, "Too proud to stay in your father's dry-goods business, eh? I told you that you'd rue the day." None of this, of course, would have happened had I actually stayed in my father's business, where my superb acumen would undoubtedly have made me the uncrowned king of the gingham trade. . . .[4]

In the late 1940s, when Sid was honored at a testimonial dinner in Beverly Hills, Groucho, who liked to make irreverent toasts, introduced him with these words: "Here is a man who has not let success go to his head—a man who is humble and unspoiled. He is as unassuming, as comfortable to be with as an old glove—and just about as interesting."[5]

In the same affectionate bantering fashion, Sid retaliated in April of 1952 in a piece he wrote for *Holiday*. Entitled "I'll Always Call You Schnorrer, My African Explorer," it described a visit to Hollywood, where Groucho was filming *A Girl in Every Port* for RKO. In the piece, Sid twits Groucho about his legendary stinginess, relating how Groucho, instead of offering him a place to stay, suggests that he sleep in an old jalopy on a used-car lot. When the two have lunch, there is much give-and-take about who will pick up the check, with Perelman having the last laugh a few days later at Romanoff's by signing Groucho's name to the bill after the comedian walks out, leaving Sid with the check.

Groucho dedicated his 1959 autobiography, *Groucho and Me*, "To These Six Masters Without Whose Wise and Witty Words My Life Would Have Been Even Duller: Robert Benchley, George S. Kaufman, Ring Lardner, S. J. Perelman, James Thurber, E. B. White."

Sid's piece about the Marxes, "The Winsome Foursome," published in *Show* in November of 1961, was far less flattering, but this did not seem to affect Groucho's feelings. As one who regularly insulted friend and foe, he was possibly thick-skinned about receiving insults from others. Brickbats were things he expected of his associates, especially if they were professional wits and had come of age in the twenties. Publicly, he continued to extol Sid's talents, commenting in *Variety* in 1964, "Women don't understand crazy humor such as that of Perelman or Benchley or even the early Marx brothers. I think our earlier films were funnier than the later ones, but they didn't gross as much as those in which we dragged in a story and a love interest."[6]

Four days after this piece appeared, Sid and Groucho met for lunch at the Connaught Hotel in London. It was not altogether a social occasion, for they were being interviewed by British critic Kenneth Tynan, who admired their work immensely.

"Side by side, when I entered the lobby, sat two middle-aged men with plenty of head visible through their hair," Tynan wrote. "Both wore tweed suits and striped shirts with button-down collars. Both had toothbrush mustaches, of which Perelman's was straw-colored and upswept, while Groucho's was close-cropped and grey. At 60, Perelman is Groucho's junior by nine years and you notice at once that he defers to his elder as a performer. Similarly, Groucho defers to Perelman as an intellectual. They are both New Yorkers and Jewish; Perelman was born in Brooklyn and Groucho on Manhattan's upper East Side."[7]

The two men talked about Jewishness and the success of Jews in American show business. Perelman thought it was due to the fact that Jews were immigrants trying to master English, and that much of their humor derived from the mispronunciation of common expressions. Groucho disagreed. "You taught me that," he told Perelman, "but then I was trying to be an intellectual." Groucho felt that American comedy was not so much Jewish as urban, which made it appeal to Jews, the majority of whom lived in cities.

The lunch was cordial. Sid and Groucho traded anecdotes about Fanny Brice, George Burns and Gracie Allen and reminisced about the West Side Writing and Asthma Club they had founded together in the thirties. Then they posed for photographs—the first, they believed, ever taken of them together.[8] In the photograph that appeared in the *Observer* several days later, Groucho is telling a joke, cigar in hand, while Sid seems convulsed by what he is hearing. They both appear to be having a wonderful time, although years later, shortly before his death, Groucho told one of his biographers, Charlotte Chandler: "I once did an interview with Sid Perelman for a London paper, and I think it was the dullest interview ever done with two men who were supposed to be funny because we were trying to outpunch each other. It's not funny to see people trying too hard."[9]

The luncheon at the Connaught was the last time Groucho ever spoke well of Perelman in public. In interview after interview in the late 1960s until his death in 1977, he expressed only contempt for the writer he had once greatly admired. "The best writers for us were George S. Kaufman and Morrie Ryskind," he told Burt Prelutsky of the *Los Angeles Times*. "The worst, strangely enough, was S. J. Perelman. He could write funny for the *New Yorker*, but not for the Marx Brothers."[10] In another interview with Robert Altman, Jon Carroll and Michael Goodwin, he zeroed in on what he felt was Sid's real shortcoming as a writer: "He wasn't a dramatist. He could write funny dialogue, but that's very different from writing drama. For that we needed a different kind of writer like Kaufman and Ryskind, who won the Pulitzer Prize for *Of Thee I Sing*."[11]

Groucho's final thoughts on Perelman were summed up in a brilliantly evasive statement in *The Grouchophile*, published a year before his death: "In recent years the press has concocted a feud between S. J. Perelman and me, but no such feud existed. Sid has often been asked about writing for the Marx Brothers, and I have often answered questions about his contributions to our films. What Sid and I both agree on is that he is a great writer with a brilliant comic mind that didn't always mesh well with the lunacies of the Marx Brothers."

What happened to change Groucho's mind? At the time of the later interviews, he was past eighty—deaf, feeble and a victim of several strokes. Physical deterioration had stripped him of what few inhibitions he had left, and perhaps he was at last able to give vent to a long-suppressed rage, made even more intense because it involved not only his artistic integrity, but that of his alter ego, the comic creation known as Groucho Marx. In fact, it seems plausible to assume that all the time Groucho was writing endearing dedications and exchanging impudent letters with Sid he was aware of the cruel gossip, the rumor that he owed a tremendous debt to a man whose literary genius and bizarre humor—even physical appearance—he had artfully mimicked. "I was doing this kind of comedy long before I met S. J. Perelman," he once said defensively.

Alistair Cooke remembers taking his daughter, Susy, to Groucho's one-man show at the Huntington Hartford Museum in New York in the early 1960s. Groucho sang funny songs, mostly written by Harry Ruby, a man many people thought was one of the funniest men who ever lived. That night Ruby accompanied Groucho on the piano. Groucho told the audience that Ruby looked like "a dishonest Abraham Lincoln" as Ruby just sat there, the butt of Groucho's jokes—many of which were Ruby's handiwork.

"When we went to the show, I had totally forgotten that about one or two months before, Groucho had given all his letters to the Library of Congress," Cooke says. "I was then the chief American correspondent for the *Guardian*, for which I had written a piece when the donation was announced. It was very friendly, very much a 'bully for Groucho' piece. But I added that there should be only one condition: if the Library of Congress accepted Groucho's letters and movie scripts, it also ought to take the letters of S. J. Perelman since Groucho Marx was a creation of S. J. Perelman and Groucho's letters were probably written by Perelman. It was a joke, but Groucho was remarkably unsusceptible to jokes on him.

"Susy and I enjoyed the show very much, and Groucho's frailty added to the absurdity of the songs. We went backstage, and he was in a flaming temper. He said, 'I ought to have you thrown out,' and I said, 'What are you talking about, Groucho?' I was really quite honestly innocent at that point until he said, 'I got that piece of yours sent from London about my work and the movies and Sid Perelman,' and he said, 'You know Sid Perelman never wrote a line of my letters.' He went on and on and on."[12]

Groucho, who himself had published humor pieces in *College Humor* and the *New Yorker*, may have been jealous of Sid's literary fame. Sid was lionized in the press while other writers such as George S. Kaufman, who had worked for the Marx Brothers and given Groucho his walk and his talk, were not given as much credit. Undoubtedly Groucho had tired of reading analyses of his films that attributed most of the best lines to Perelman, such as "I'd horsewhip you if I had a horse" from *Horse Feathers*, a line actually written by Harry Ruby.

Nat Perrin, who worked on a number of Marx Brothers films, feels that despite all of Groucho's cracks about Perelman's screenwriting talent, Groucho respected him enormously. Perrin feels that it wasn't so much that Groucho was anti-Perelman as that he wanted to make sure another of his writers, Arthur Sheekman, a very close friend with whom he had done several books, received as much credit as Perelman for his contribution to Marx Brothers films.

In fairness to Sid, it must be said he never claimed to have written most of the Marx Brothers films singlehandedly. In countless interviews, he was careful to set the record straight, disclaiming authorship for *Animal Crackers* and *Duck Soup* by stressing that the only two films he had worked on had been written in collaboration. When a reporter tried to quiz him on which lines he had written, he demurred, saying that it was so long ago he had totally forgotten.

In 1974, he told Howard Kissel: "The Marx Brothers movies were really community efforts. They themselves were so anarchic—they sought advice and help from every possible quarter. It's impossible to trace the actual authorship of those films."[13]

Groucho, of course, held sway over Sid right from the start. In 1931, he was one of America's top entertainers, a star with an entourage, a person in a position to say "It stinks" and have sycophantic writers try to make it right. For Perelman, an egotist who disliked taking orders, it wasn't so much Groucho's "capriciousness" and "ungrateful" attitude that he disliked as his dominance.

Groucho may also have been too much like himself. Sid had always had a poor self-image. He imagined himself shorter and punier than he was and was always conscious about a scar below one ear. He would never permit himself to be photographed from any angle that might reveal it. If Nathanael West—tall, well-built and handsome—was his idealized physical self, then Groucho, homely, short and nearsighted, represented the self-image he despised. It was as though he were looking at himself in a mirror, hating what he saw.

If their physical resemblance was startling, so were their personalities. Both were slight and dapper, with toothbrush mustaches. (Groucho, whose greasepaint mustache had been his trademark for years, grew a real one for his appearance on the radio version of "You Bet Your Life" in 1947; clean-shaven for years, Perelman grew a mustache in the 1950s.) Neither ate or drank to excess. Both were moody, temperamental, egocentric and unpredictable. They could be mean, petty, hostile, yet when the occasion demanded it, capable of disarming charm and dazzling wit. Both were intensely private, loath to reveal their inmost feelings, men who used their wit as a shield against a world they distrusted. "I am a serious man with a comic sense," Groucho once said. It could have been said by Sid.

Outwardly, though, their behavior was very different. Sid was shy and withdrawn, while Groucho was brash, fast-talking, a show-off who felt compelled to twist everything said to him into a joke at someone's expense. Yet many of Groucho's friends felt this was a facade; basically, he was shy and romantic, although he would rather have died than admit it.

Both Sid and Groucho were haunted by the specter of poverty. Neither spent a cent unless it was absolutely necessary. Perelman constantly worried about money. He rarely took cabs and seldom gave presents, while Groucho was always fearful he would be penniless in his old age. Whenever he dined at a fashionable Hollywood restaurant, he always parked his car several blocks away to avoid having to tip the parking lot attendant. Married (and divorced) three times, he was furious if his wives bought anything without his permission, and he refused to let his children take piano or ballet lessons because he considered them an unnecessary expense.

Both Sid and Groucho were hopeless Anglophiles, filled with a romantic yearning for England in the glorious days of Queen Victoria. Perhaps the precariousness and drabness of their parents' lives as immigrants drew them to this sentimental notion. Or perhaps by

77

identifying themselves with English culture, they hoped to forget their peasant origins. It is also possible that they felt the English, with their well-known tolerance of eccentrics, would be more accepting of their quirks and inconsistencies than the cruder and more conventional Americans.

But all this lay in the future on a cold winter afternoon in 1930 when Sid Perelman and Will Johnstone were rushed across the street from the Hotel Astor to the New York office of Jesse Lasky, boss of Paramount Pictures. There they signed six-week contracts at $500 dollars a week and made travel arrangements to go to Hollywood.

Getting to Hollywood proved almost as traumatic as work on the new Marx Brothers picture. Laura had broken her arm after falling on an icy sidewalk. Gherky, the Perelman schnauzer, couldn't be left behind and, once aboard the 20th Century, barked incessantly. According to Sid's later account, the dog was eventually banished to the baggage car, "where he ululated for three thousand miles and spread neurasthenia among the postal clerks."[14]

In Hollywood, Sid, Laura and Gherky (German for *cucumber*) stayed first at a hotel, but soon moved to an inexpensive apartment in a bungalow court and then to the Garden of Allah on Sunset Boulevard, a favorite haunt of movie screenwriters. Both Perelmans were depressed by Hollywood. "Hollywood Boulevard creates an instant and malign impression in the breast of the beholder," Sid later wrote. "Viewed in full sunlight, its tawdriness is unspeakable; in the torrential downpour of the rainy season, as we first saw it, it inspired an anguish similar to that produced by the engravings of Piranesi. . . . After a few days I could have sworn that our faces began to take on the hue of Kodachromes and even the dog, an animal used to bizarre surroundings, developed a strange, off-register look, as if he were badly printed in overlapping colors."[15]

Everyone in Hollywood went to bed at ten-thirty, he told Edmund Wilson, and there wasn't any place to go at night. Even restaurants such as the Brown Derby were empty after that hour, and he saw only a couple of people in them—among them Wilson Mizner, owner of the restaurant.[16]

His mood was not lightened by his first sight of the Paramount Studio, which reminded him of a factory, nor was he cheered by a meeting with Herman Mankiewicz, the caustic Teutonic producer of *Monkey Business*. Mankiewicz, a first-class wit and compulsive gam-

78

bler, had long ago shed any illusions about the Marx Brothers. "They're mercurial, devious and ungrateful," he told Sid. "I hate to depress you, but you'll rue the day you ever took the assignment. This is an ordeal by fire. Make sure you wear asbestos pants."[17]

Teet Carle, the former publicity director at Paramount, was then working as a unit publicist assigned to *Monkey Business*. He remembers meeting Sid shortly after Johnstone and Perelman arrived in Hollywood. Sid had shown Carle a copy of *Dawn Ginsbergh's Revenge*, not as a matter of ego, he said, but to show how he spelled his name. He pointed out Groucho's blurb on the dust jacket, telling Carle that Groucho's first submission had been "This book will always be a first edition," which he said he thought hilarious. But Horace Liveright had rejected the line on the grounds that if the book went into other printings, a buyer might mistakenly assume he did own a first edition.

"I was struck by the difference between Perelman and Johnstone," Carle recalls. "Sid was smaller, not so handsome, he wore heavy-lensed glasses and was much younger. Johnstone had wavy white—or maybe blonde—hair and was perhaps fifteen years older. He also was more reserved."[18]

Sid, Carle felt, was a likeable person who was easy to know. He was able to cope with working for the Marxes even when the studio moved them, with their secretary Rachel Linden, into Perelman and Johnstone's tiny two-room office, thereby forcing the two writers into tenementlike rooms that were directly above the office of some construction workers.

Sid was intensely curious about the stars with whom Carle had worked, especially Clara Bow, Richard Dix, Wallace Beery and Chester Conklin. Carle's professional relationship with W. C. Fields fascinated him, and he loved the publicist's story about how Fields, who could be difficult to interview, suddenly loosened up and talked for two hours. As much intrigued by strange names as Perelman, Fields had done a double-take when Teet Carle told him his first name was actually Cecil, a name he detested. Fields then confided that in his boyhood his family had called him by his middle name, Claude, which he also hated. He much preferred to be called by his nickname, Whitey.

Another person at Paramount who intrigued Perelman was the writer George Marion, Jr. At that time Marion was a very famous writer of titles for silent comedy features. He was so prolific that he was able to write titles for three films in two weeks.

Sid kept Carle well-supplied with stories about the Marx Brothers during the making of the picture, while Carle enlightened him about studio politics.

"One night Sid went to the fights at the Hollywood Legion with Groucho," Carle remembers. "He told me how, as a fighter named Danny danced out to start the opening round, Groucho yelled, 'Come on, Danny, give him a boxing lesson!' His opponent threw a punch and even before Danny had hit the canvas, Groucho yelled, 'And take one yourself!' Then there was the time Sid told me how the Marx Brothers' father, often at the studio, asked Harpo, 'Can I borrow your ducks tonight?' Harpo said, 'My tux, you mean? What for?' The old man (whom we all liked) answered, 'I've got tickets to a previous.' "

Perelman and Johnstone managed to complete the script of *Monkey Business* in little more than six weeks. They had only the vaguest idea of what they were doing but thought their script would sound professional if they put in a lot of technical terms. Wherever possible, they threw in words such as "dolly," "iris-out" and "Vorkapich shot" (a fast close-up that had been invented by the montage editor and film theorist at RKO and Paramount, Slavko Vorkapich). As Sid later said, "We thought in our innocence that all these instructions would act as a guide to the director. We wrote about 125 pages in this fashion."[19]

In February of 1931, as soon as the Marxes had returned from their engagement at the Palace Theatre in London, they summoned Perelman and Johnstone to read the script to them in their suite at the Roosevelt Hotel. The writers, who were the first to arrive, flipped coins to determine which one of them would read the script. Perelman won. He later claimed that his only acting experience had been a minor role in a high-school pageant based on the life of Pocahontas. At any rate, he was not an adept public speaker, and that night his nervousness was intensified by the perhaps deliberate tardiness of Groucho and his brothers.

After a forty-five-minute wait, the audience started drifting in . . . first, the Marxes' father, then Herman Mankiewicz with his brother Joseph, then a Paramount scriptwriter, three of the Marxes and their wives, their lawyers, dentists, accountants—and several dogs, including Zeppo's Afghans, who had devoured the upholstery of his car that afternoon, and Chico's wirehaired terrier, which immediately started fighting with the Afghans. Finally Groucho and his wife arrived.

There were at least twenty-seven people and five dogs in the room. As soon as they had all more or less settled themselves, Sid began reading the script, including all the technical terms. It took about an hour and a half. During the reading Harpo, the dogs and several people went to sleep.

"But Perelman went on reading," said Arthur Sheekman, Groucho's gag man. "Valiantly, I thought. I would have shot myself on page 25."[20]

After Sid had finished reading, there was a deathly silence. Finally Chico asked Groucho, "Well, what do you think?" Groucho took the cigar out of his mouth and said, "It stinks," whereupon all the guests, including the dogs, got up and left the room.[21]

Fully convinced that he and Johnstone would be fired the next day, Sid was surprised to learn that the Marxes thought the script might work if it was thoroughly overhauled. He and Johnstone spent the next five months rewriting it. They were joined by other Marx Brothers writers: Arthur Sheekman, Nat Perrin, J. Carver Pusey and Solly Violinski. The brothers also threw in suggestions, as did Herman Mankiewicz and Norman McLeod, the director.

One of Groucho's criticisms of Sid was that his humor was too literary and convoluted for a mass audience. It was during the making of *Monkey Business* that their lifelong battle began about whether screen comedy can ever afford to be intelligent or intellectual.

Groucho particularly objected to a love scene between himself and Thelma Todd, in which Sid had written that Groucho was to jump up and say, "Come, Kapellmeister, let the violas throb, my regiment leaves at dawn." Then he was supposed to parody a famous scene from the popular film *The Merry Widow* with Mae Murray. Groucho told Sid, "The trouble is that the barber in Peru won't get it," meaning Peru, Indiana. Perelman tried to convince him that the scene would reveal Groucho's genius for parody. But he could not convince Groucho, and the *Merry Widow* scene was deleted. Sid's "Come, Kapellmeister" line remained in the picture, however, and he confessed that whenever he saw *Monkey Business*, he felt a sense of triumph when he heard Groucho say it.[22]

Groucho's insecurity irritated Sid. Like many comedians, Groucho couldn't relax until he heard the audience laugh. He and the writers would work on a sequence for weeks until it seemed perfect. Then, a few days later, Groucho would say he was very worried about the scene and start tampering with it again, and Sid realized that he had probably run into someone, an agent perhaps, who in his own interest had made him doubt his writers' capabilities.

After Groucho's death, Sid said that the only person capable of awing Groucho was George S. Kaufman. The playwright's glacial personality and formidable reputation intimidated the comedian.

Even at the risk of displeasing Groucho, Sid was always trying to sneak recondite allusions into the script of *Monkey Business*, which Sheekman would then delete. Once Sid wanted to make a pun on the German *Morgen*, which means *morning*, and J. P. Morgan. "I think we draw the line at German puns," said Sheekman.[23]

Sid grew to dislike Sheekman and when later he started work on *Horse Feathers*, he wrote a friend that he hoped the gagman would not be too involved in the project. (Sheekman did work on the picture, however, although his contribution was uncredited.)

The only thing the second script of *Monkey Business* had in common with the first was that it was about stowaways on an ocean liner. Everything else was changed. This new version was written mainly by Perelman and Sheekman; Johnstone wrote the sight gags for Harpo, while Nat Perrin wrote the ones for Chico.[24]

With so many writers involved in the script of *Monkey Business*, it is impossible to know which writer wrote what line, although certain critics see Sid's hand at work in such lines as "lodge with my fleas in the hills" and "you must have been married in Rompers."[25]

Finally, after a few weeks of rehearsal on the sound stage, in which more gags and dialogue were added, *Monkey Business* reached the cameras in midsummer and was released in September of 1931. Depression audiences responded to its irreverence and unabashed spirit of insanity. It became one of the biggest hits of the season, breaking attendance records everywhere.

The picture begins on an ocean liner, where the four brothers are stowaways in barrels. ("The stowaways of today were the stockholders of yesterday," observes Groucho.) Discovered by the first mate when they start singing "Sweet Adeline," the Marxes are routed from their barrels and then proceed to dash about the ship, manhandling the other passengers. The film follows their misadventures as each brother sings a verse of a Maurice Chevalier song in a vain attempt to convince New York customs officials that he is indeed the singer, whose passport they have stolen. (When a customs official tells Groucho that his passport picture doesn't look like him, he snaps, "It doesn't look like you either.'') They attend a racketeers' ball and finally wind up in a barn, battling gangsters, while Groucho sits on the rafters, commenting on the action as if he were a radio sports announcer at a prizefight.

In general the critics were enthusiastic about the film, and many praised the writing. Mordaunt Hall in a review in the *New York Times* commented, ''This *Monkey Business* is, if anything, wilder than *Animal Crackers* and although it is perhaps not quite as expertly written, it is one constant round of merriment, utter nonsense, and wicked puns.''[26] This opinion was shared by Sid, who personally felt that *Monkey Business* wasn't as good a picture as *Animal Crackers*.[27] But Harry Evans in *Life* (then a humor magazine) believed that it was not merely the writing that gave *Monkey Business* its lunatic sparkle. ''With all due credit to the commendable efforts of these funny fellows [Johnstone and Perelman], we must add that we can thank Groucho for making the lines seem more original than they are.''[28]

Many students of the Marx Brothers have noted that certain sequences in *Monkey Business* bear a close resemblance to comic strips. This cartoonlike quality became part of the Marx Brothers' style, for as Louis Chavance pointed out in a few years after the picture was released, ''it is extremely significant that the first scenario written for them with special intention for the screen was composed solely by caricaturists. . . .''[29]

Of the Marx Brothers, Sid once said, ''I did two films with them, which in its way is perhaps my greatest distinction in life, because anybody who ever worked on any picture for the Marx Brothers said he would rather be chained to a galley oar and lashed at ten-minute intervals than ever work for these sons-of-bitches again.''[30]

But in October of 1931, he was not chained to a galley oar, but in New York, staying at the St. Moritz and waiting for the Marxes, Mankiewicz and other members of the writing team, which this time consisted of Johnstone and the songwriters Bert Kalmar and Harry Ruby, to come East so that they all could start working on the script for a new picture.

Sid had just completed the dialogue for a Winnie Lightner picture at Warner Brothers, but the studio refused to give him a six-month contract following his initial six weeks of work, preferring to have him work week-to-week.[31]

Sid hated Warner Brothers even more than he did Paramount. The regimentation was stifling. He had to be at his desk promptly at nine and could not leave until six. Phone calls were not permitted. Furthermore, the commissary closed immediately after breakfast, so that it was not even possible to vary the monotony by taking a coffee break.

The prospect of working with the Marx Brothers again did not appeal to him either. Their exhibitionism thoroughly disgusted him. According to Edmund Wilson, "Harpo told West and his sister to come into the dressing room, asking, 'Are you decent?' when he didn't have a stitch on. They 'took physical advantage' of people—Groucho terribly tiresome to talk to, gagging all the time, terrific vanity—Perelman finally had a showdown with him, said, 'That's not very funny!' about one of his gags—Groucho said, 'Oh, so you don't think that's very funny?' and gave him to damn well understand that he'd better think it was funny."[32]

When the Marx Brothers and their entourage finally arrived in New York, everyone sat around, trying to think up an idea for a picture. After much soul-searching, they agreed that the movie should have something to do with college life, although no one could be specific about the plot. Then they all returned to Los Angeles, with Sid going by boat via Cuba and Panama.

Its title taken from a 1928 Barney Google cartoon, *Horse Feathers* eventually emerged as a satire of college life, with the emphasis on athletics at the expense of education. Groucho plays Professor Quincy Adams Wagstaff, the new college president of Huxley College, who if he wants to keep his job must produce a winning football team. (The last game the college football team won was in 1888, and every year since then a college president has been fired.) After taking office, Groucho immediately breaks into a song, "Whatever It Is, I'm Against It," written by Kalmar and Ruby, and leads the faculty in a soft-shoe routine. He then instructs Harpo, the local dogcatcher, and Chico, whom he recruits in a speakeasy, to play football for Huxley. They are also to kidnap two rival team players until after the big game, but get kidnapped themselves, and the plot becomes increasingly convoluted.

Since neither the Marxes nor Kalmar nor Ruby had ever attended college, it is probable that Sid, who spent most of his college years writing diatribes against university policies, contributed much of the satire on academia in *Horse Feathers*. The very theme of the movie—athletics at the expense of education—was reminiscent of the fiery editorials he composed for the *Brown Jug*, in which he had proclaimed, "Millions for athletics, and not a cent for aesthetics." He may also have been responsible for one of the film's most hilarious scenes, in which Groucho asks two professors, "Where would this college be without football? Have we got a stadium?" "Yes," the professors agree. "Have we got a college?" quizzes Groucho. "Yes," say the professors. "Well, we can't support both," concludes Groucho. "Tomorrow, we start tearing down the college." The professors are aghast. "But, Professor, where will the students sleep?" "Where they always sleep. In the classrooms," retorts Groucho.

Then Groucho's secretary rushes into his office to tell him that the Dean of Science is impatiently waiting to see him. "The Dean," she tells Groucho, "is furious. He's waxing wroth." "Oh," replies Groucho, "is Roth out there, too? Tell Roth to wax the Dean for awhile."

These lines have always been attributed to Sid, who had used a similar play on words in a cartoon he did for *College Humor*, but whether he or another writer actually wrote the final film version does not matter. The spirit of *Horse Feathers* is pure S. J. Perelman. Only a man who was forced to endure four years in a place where he didn't fit in and that refused to graduate him could have made such devastating fun of it. And for that contribution alone, Groucho should have been grateful.

# 6

# LAURA

## *(1930–1932)*

People who met Laura Perelman in later life often compared her to a large wounded bird. This comparison was perhaps not accidental, for Laura felt happiest outdoors. She loved the willows and maples on her Pennsylvania farm and, like her mother and her brother, adored dogs. An avid hunter, West owned several pointers, but Laura's dogs were of a softer, more cuddly variety. A number of photographs depict her squeezing them tightly, as if she feared what would happen to her if she relaxed her grip. Among her dogs were Gherky, the standard schnauzer who accompanied her and Sid on their first trip to Hollywood; a dachshund; and Misty and Tartuffe, two magnificent standard silver poodles. It is also reported that Laura's lover Dashiell Hammett borrowed the name of one of her dogs, Asta, for Nick and Nora Charles's perky wirehaired terrier in *The Thin Man*.[1]

Like Laura Wingfield in Tennessee Williams' *The Glass Menagerie*, Laura loved fragile miniature objects. A wall closet in her living room in Bucks County was filled with over a hundred tiny china dogs and cats.[2]

After *Horse Feathers* was finished, Sid and Laura went back to Europe, returning to New York in September of 1932. Shortly after their return, Sid began work on a new revue, *Walk a Little Faster*. The Perelmans had spent most of their money in Europe and, to make ends meet, were living in a suite of small rooms at the Sutton Hotel that West let them use free of charge. In June of that same year they celebrated their third wedding anniversary. Laura was now twenty-one years old; Sid, twenty-eight.

In November, Laura began keeping a diary. This journal, which

86

she kept for only a month and which was written in a girlish hand in a school notebook, revealed a woman who was extremely unhappy. In secret despair over her feelings of futility, she considered a writing career, a nine-to-five job, sessions with an analyst, a love affair, and finally, suicide as possible solutions to her emotional problems. She had begun to drink heavily and feared becoming an alcoholic.

Undoubtedly Laura's depression may be partly attributed to the death of her father, Max, who had died that summer of bronchial disease. His death had devastated her brother, who had been horrified by the sight of his father in his coffin. The undertaker had rouged Mr. Weinstein's cheeks, shaved his thick eyebrows and dressed him in clothes he had never worn in life. To Nathanael he was almost unrecognizable. When he threw the first spadeful of dirt on his father's coffin, he felt "an awful jolt," he told Edmund Wilson.[3] What Laura felt must have been something similar, although she never mentioned it in her diary.

Laura's widowed mother, Anuta, was another problem. After her husband's death, she moved into the Sutton so she could live near Laura and Pep, who also maintained an apartment there. Grief-stricken and depressed, she spent most of the day in her room, complaining of noises in her head and monopolizing Laura's time.

In her diary Laura also revealed her longing for fulfillment and a sense of direction. She dreamed of becoming a writer, like her brother and her husband. Her journal is filled with ideas for movie scripts and short story titles such as "An Elephant to Ride Upon" and "Momentary Flowers." But she also confesses that every time she tried to write, a great lassitude overcame her.

"There is something terrifically wrong with me," Laura wrote. "I make believe it is physical (low blood pressure) but it's a mental laziness. I am convinced the only thing I could do would be something routine like work in a store. I tried to write and find I can't put myself to the labor of it. I need someone with a whip at my back."

Much of the diary was devoted to an analysis of her own and her brother's relationship to Sid. She felt that she and Pep were lethargic people who depended on Sid for their social contacts. "Louse that I am, I feel how dependent I am on him and do nothing about it. And now Pep leans on him. We are a strange family. Totally lacking in guts—*Soft* and all of us without friends," she wrote.

"These are supposedly our 'best years.' I am wasting mine *absolutely*. Maybe I will make a better old lady. The reason people think

87

I am twenty-eight is because I have the gayety [sic] of a person that age. I feel heavy and very often suicidal. I drink for that reason."

Sid was the one with verve and stamina, Laura noted sadly. Her brother, through his writing, had begun to break out of his lethargy while she couldn't seem to accomplish anything. "I cannot continue like this," she wrote. "Nat doing something is spoiling our relationship. Even if I were able to be a hausfrau I would tire of it. Maybe the farm would be a solution."

Laura's spirits improved whenever she went to Erwinna, in Bucks County, Pennsylvania, where she, Sid and West were contemplating buying an 83-acre farm near the Lehigh Canal from Michael Gold, the socialist author of *Jews Without Money*. In her diary, she recorded an automobile trip that she, West, Lillian Hellman and Gherky the schnauzer took to Bucks County on November 4, 1932. The group of young people borrowed a convertible and drove to the home of a young couple, Josephine Herbst and John Herrmann. Both were novelists, and West had become friendly with them after publishing an excerpt from Herrmann's novel *Foreign-Born*, in *Contact*, a short-lived magazine West coedited with William Carlos Williams and Robert McAlmon.

The Herrmanns lived in a 17th-century stone farmhouse that they rented very cheaply. Josie greeted her guests wearing a blue skirt and bright green scarf. "I couldn't help thinking of the 'Village,' and yet she looked all right," Laura observed in her diary.

Laura helped Herrmann prepare the lunch. After it was eaten, everyone started discussing literature, a topic she felt was out of place on a beautiful fall day. So she slipped away outdoors and picked some walnuts, surrounded by sheep grazing quietly on the lawn.

At the end of their visit, West drove Laura and Lillian Hellman back to Warford House, an inn in Frenchtown, New Jersey, where he was staying and attempting to finish *Miss Lonelyhearts*.[4] "We were sitting in the back and got very excited when Nat was driving," Laura wrote. "He goes so fast and it's bad on a curving country road. Not protesting but holding it in, I felt terrible."

After West left them, Lillian Hellman drove Laura the rest of the way to New York. But the trip back was ill-fated. On the way to Manhattan, Laura "lit a cigarette and put another one against it for Lillian. A spark flew in her lap and then the telephone pole came at us very slowly and I closed my eyes when the crash came and I heard the glass breaking. *Jesus Christ.* Don't step on the wires, they might be live wires. Don't step on the wires."

Fortunately, both women were unhurt, although the convertible West had borrowed was badly dented.

For the next few days, Laura felt jittery whenever she thought about the accident. To make matters worse, West and the owner of the convertible were furious about the damage. Laura's mother was sick, sitting alone and silent in the dark of her room, something she did when she felt unwell. In her diary, Laura noted that the only thing she had to look forward to was the Sunday opening of Sid's new revue, *Walk a Little Faster*, in Boston. But the trip would only be for three days, and she wondered "what in the hell will I do with myself" when she came back to the Sutton. The entry ends with a single word: "Mother."

Laura was still depressed on the evening of November 9. West, who had returned to the Sutton from Frenchtown, said something that greatly upset his mother. Then he went out for the evening, leaving Laura to calm her mother down. Sid, who was preoccupied with last-minute changes for *Walk a Little Faster*, came home for dinner but left immediately, leaving Laura alone and at loose ends.

Laura wrote in her diary that the only nice thing that happened all day was shopping at Klein's on Union Square, where she bought a Chanel dress for five dollars. (Klein's, a famous cut-rate clothing store, was so incredible she felt a movie should be written about it.)

That afternoon a male friend named Peter had asked Laura to go to the movies, but she had refused, a fortunate decision, she wrote in her diary, since Sid had decided to come home for dinner. Peter told Laura that he had seen Sid and a female friend of hers named Irma leaving the Brown Derby in Hollywood and "very righteously snubbed him."

"It's bad enough Perel doing it but Irma—where in the hell does she get off. They both think they own me," Laura wrote. Immediately she expressed a fierce desire to drive to Bucks County. "If I had some money of my own I would go off somewhere in the country with Alice maybe [probably fashion model Alice Shepard, Laura's friend who was dating West]. I would love not to see Pep, Perel, Lillian and Mother. I would love Gurky."

The following day she felt in better spirits. Perelman, she noted, was more attentive to her than he had been in a long time. He took her to a rehearsal of his revue and then with a friend to Tony's, a fashionable New York restaurant, where to her amazement they closed the place down. When they finally decided to leave, Sid and his friend were drunk and making insolent wisecracks to the doorman. Their banter at the doorman's expense upset Laura, who didn't like to "watch someone else ride a guy," so she left.

Many of the entries in Laura's diary are devoted to her conflicting emotions about her marriage. At times she viewed herself as weak and helpless, a woman despised by a cruel and unfeeling husband who yelled at her when she was drunk or wearing a dress he considered too low-cut. At other times, she regarded him as a charming man who deeply loved her. Boredom and lack of excitement, she felt, were their basic problems. Life had been too easy for them both. They had not been confronted with any severe crisis such as war, poverty, illness or a serious extramarital affair that might have brought them closer together. Laura wrote that she was jealous whenever Sid displayed an interest in another woman, not because he found that other person more attractive than herself but because he had found a new relationship to rekindle the sexual passion that had once existed between them.

In her opinion it was not Sid's infidelities that were ruining their relationship; it was his coldness and inability to sympathize with her, to give her what she needed emotionally. "Sid is definitely a cold person and he needs a *bomb*," Laura wrote. "Jealousy means nothing—I am jealous if he shows interest in someone else—but not because of the someone else—but jealous of his finding that someone else. Sid's emotions (the natural ones) are coked up from something. Maybe from a feeling of inferiority because he thought he was funny looking. It's a defensive reaction, as it has been, but now it *is* part of him."

Yet, Laura realized that one of the reasons that she remained deeply devoted to Sid was that he made her feel womanly. The men she had dated before her marriage seemed weak in comparison; with them, she had been forced to assume a more dominant role. With her husband, a man of strong convictions and ambition, she was quite the opposite—feminine, coquettish, easily reduced to tears.

At some point during this period Laura must have ventilated her feelings about her marriage to certain people. In Edmund Wilson's journal, written in the early thirties, there were several entries devoted to Sid and Laura, whom Wilson described as "smart and fashionably tapering, though with good full figure."[5] One entry reads:

> *Perelmans; Hollywood.* Jewish girl, very nice and intelligent, not fancy, who had lost her husband out there after three years—her theory that Jewish men thought themselves ugly, so had to keep proving to themselves what they could do in the way of getting Gentile girls—she thought you had to have a permanent relation with somebody but they would go crazy when they got out to Hollywood—any little dumbbell from Indiana—the Jewish situation very important out there—Thalberg and Norma Shearer had nothing for each other—Thalberg just wanted to show what he could do—Everybody scared—she'd seen prominent Jewish executives break chairs because their wives had used the wrong fork.—When she'd first gotten out there, some other woman had said to her: Oh, do save George Kelly!—who cared whether George Kelly was saved or not?—had no use for writers who went out to sell themselves and then groused about it. . . .[6]

The Boston opening of *Walk a Little Faster* was not the glamorous affair Laura had envisioned. In the early morning hours following the opening, Laura, dressed in a beautiful dress loaned to her by Alice Shepard, got drunk and berated Sid for what she felt was the poor quality of his sketches for the revue. She and Sid argued bitterly. Then, still wearing her beautiful dress, she flounced out of the hotel and wandered the streets for hours. Returning to the hotel near dawn, she woke up Alice Shepard, with whom Sid had disappeared at a party the previous night. "When I told her why I had come she misunderstood and thought I had a tiff about her and Perel. Then she had confessed that she had been receiving 'love pats' from Perel in the taxi," she wrote. "Up until now I have kept away from any of Perel's friends but not anymore. I told him I didn't like the idea."

Her return to the Sutton a few days later was even a worse letdown than she had imagined. Not only did she have a hangover, her throat was sore, she was menstruating and the night before she had had terrible nightmares. Only the thought of the fun she'd had in Boston with Courtney Burr, the revue's producer, and Evelyn Hoey, an actress in the show, made her feel a little better. "Courtney is a swell person and I had a lot of fun with him," she wrote. "Coming back here is terrible. This hotel, poor Fatty [Walter "Fats" Saunders, a college friend of Sid's], Pep and everything."

December of 1932, the month West finished *Miss Lonelyhearts* in

Frenchtown, was a time of even greater conflict and desperation for Laura. In her diary she prayed for the strength to be content with her life and obsessively dreamed of escaping to Erwinna. There were no entries for three weeks until December 19, the day she and Sid, with West as co-owner, purchased Michael Gold's farm for $5,500, making a down payment of $500, which they were partially able to raise by selling a baby grand piano they had in storage to the owners of the Sutton. On that day, Laura wrote in her diary: "I know that I could easily become a drunk, I also know that I can't (in the end) get on without Perel."

The final entry was dated March 11, 1933. No one knows why Laura abruptly stopped writing in her diary. Perhaps it was mere whim or boredom or very probably it was because she became involved with the new farm.

On March 6, President Roosevelt had closed the banks, and on March 9, when people were standing in line to withdraw their money, Sid and Pep—"my boys," as she sometimes called them—had driven to Erwinna with a toilet they wanted to install in the farmhouse. Laura was left with only a quarter in her pocket; Sid had only a few dollars in cash. Fortunately West was able to cash a few small checks in Erwinna, and Laura knew that they would also be able to charge their food at the Sutton.

Their precarious financial condition frightened Laura. *Walk a Little Faster*, which had run for several months on Broadway, was about to close, and the only job Sid could get was on the Fanny Brice–Royal Gelatine radio show. He was gone most of the day, writing material for the program. Once more Laura was left alone. She considered getting a job, but was convinced no one would hire her.

Laura decided not to see Courtney Burr anymore. The one time he took her out, they had both drunk excessively and Laura had stayed out so late, she was afraid her mother and Sid would notice. "When you get very drunk, nothing seems important (not even Perel) to you—especially Time," she wrote. "Drinking is swell fun but the business of pulling yourself together afterwards is so difficult especially among a gang of non-drinkers. The only thing that saves your life the next day is to have a drink. O . . . a cycle!"

Yet Courtney Burr continued to fascinate her. She toyed with the idea of writing a book about him. To Laura, Burr seemed a dashing and colorful person. He reminded her of Paul Gauguin when he left his wife and responsibilities and headed for Tahiti. A good title for her biography of him, Laura thought, would be *Gauguin in Carpet-Slippers*.

A very close friend of West's was sufficiently disturbed by the spectacle of Laura's anguish to write a book about it. In 1954, fourteen years after West's death, Josephine Herbst's novella, *Hunter of Doves*, was published to critical success in the international journal *Botteghe Oscure*. A haunting psychological study of West's relationship to Laura and Sid, it is considered by many West scholars to be possibly the most perceptive portrait ever written about the enigmatic West.

*Hunter of Doves* concerns a naive young man named Timothy Comfort who is working on a biography of his literary idol, Noel Bartram, who (like West) had been killed several years before in an automobile accident. He interviews Constance Heath, an artist who was Bartram's good friend, in the hope of gaining some insight into what Bartram was really like. Timothy's biography is authorized by Joel Baker, Noel's literary executor and close friend in college, who for many years has been married to Bartram's sister, Nora, that "tall, slim creature with the birdlike head who might have been his twin."

At first Mrs. Heath is reluctant to help Timothy Comfort—he seems far too prosaic to be entrusted with the task of unraveling Bartram's subtle and complex personality. Yet, during their conversation and at the conclusion of their interview, her memories are unleashed. Painfully, she explores both her own and her writer-husband's friendship with Bartram as well as his relationship to Nora and Joel Baker in a series of revealing flashbacks.

Like Laura, Josephine Herbst was struck by Sid Perelman's (Joel Baker's) peculiar detachment:

> I was seeing Joel Baker in the elevator, late at night, in that hotel where Noel had an apartment on the top floor. I knew the Bakers lived in the same hotel but I had never met either of them. Going up late one night, I saw this man standing in the elevator, with a dog, a big-muzzled dog with a handsome beard, and the man shrunk back into a corner, aloof and apart, apart from himself, you might say, simply cut off from the world. He had the dog on a leash, and, in a sense, he had himself on a leash. There might have been three of them in the place, not two. I knew it was Baker; I recognized the dog that had once been in Bartram's place when I was there. The man stood so far away, though he was only two feet from me, his aloof face as haughty as something engraven on an old tomb. I don't know why I liked him, instantaneously, but I did. Not a

handsome face, but oddly ugly, implying a kind of central intensity that is, for me, the greatest attraction there is. But then they all had it— Baker, Nora and Bartram. I looked at him but he didn't deign to look at me, that is, not directly. Out of a corner of his eye, he was sort of sizing me up. And I liked that, too; anything is better than being ignored. Without curiosity, what are we? Mere muffins.[7]

In contrast to the distant Joel Baker, Noel Bartram (Nathanael West) is portrayed as a gentle, softspoken young man with a taste for Brooks Brothers clothes, British cars and hunting, even though he was a poor marksman and at the end of his life shot doves, the only birds that did not elude him. Like his sister, Nora, Bartram had terrible conflicts that threatened to overwhelm him. Although he had managed to break loose from a hard-driving family of businessmen and a quietly dominating mother, The White Queen (Anuta), who disapproved of his artistic ambitions, and had actually finished a novel, he had paid a price for his adulthood. In Mrs. Heath's opinion, Noel Bartram's "triumph over his lethargy, Bartram's entry into his own real world, cut him off from some source. His family did not matter, his mother's great soft mutterings did not matter. But his sister, that mattered, and in some curious, involved way he was no longer the solid friend of her husband, but a rival. Oh, a most modest rival for it was a bore to most of their friends, Bartram's admiration of his brother-in-law's witty works. Bartram was always quoting Baker. He might have been his younger brother for all that they were practically the same age."[8]

But it was his sister Nora (Laura), "this softer shadow of his own nature," who obsessed Noel:

His grief was Nora, young Nora, whose strange behavior eluded him, tortured him. She drank; no one knew how much. That pearly skin might be desert sand. Some terrifying deep thirstiness parched her long slender body. With pride he insisted that if she drank a lot, no one would know it. She was not one of the unseemly women who turn boisterous. At any moment, she could walk a chalk line, could turn a face, pure and unflushed, toward anyone, carry on a conversation in polite, self-contained syllables. But at some moment, unforeseen, she disappeared. At these infernal parties, she might leave the room without his noticing it. Soon an odd feeling that something was not right made him hunt every corner. Once he had managed to slip out and to follow her as she had walked swiftly as to some certain destiny in the empty dark of three o'clock in the morning. But at the moment when he hoped to catch up with her, she had picked up a cab when there was not another in sight for pursuit. Where did she go?⁹

When Mrs. Heath and her husband first meet Noel Bartram at the New York hotel where he is manager, as they leave the room, Mrs. Heath notices "a pair of long black suede gloves, one draped on the arm of a chair and one dropped to the floor with its fingers lightly spread as though to break a fall. The black gloves and her image of the probable woman who had dropped them filled her painter's mind with thoughts of a possible Toulouse-Lautrec female."¹⁰

Several months after Timothy Comfort's visit, Mrs. Heath runs into Joel and Nora Baker in a New York bar. She has not seen them for many years. With them is Timothy Comfort, whose qualifications as Bartram's biographer, Joel confides to her, he is seriously beginning to question:

Beyond Baker, she could see Nora's bowed head with the sleek glossy wing of hair drawn up under a little hat. Though Mrs. Heath knew she was no longer the slim elusive girl but a solid matron with two growing children, the view she had of her, shut off as she was by Baker, was of old symbols and signs of the young Nora. That wing of hair, those gloves! For the long black suede gloves lying along the counter might have been the identical pair Mrs. Heath had witnessed the first day she had visited Bartram in his hotel. The fingers of this pair, curled, abandoned, suggested now, as they had then, some chanson-singer in a French café. And the hand, the long hand with the green emerald ring, might have belonged to the young Nora who had bewitched her brother.

The phoenix-forms of the past were so insistent that once more she was back in the living room at Bartram's house, for the moment called to life by the emerald ring. Once more she was seeing the brother and sister as she had come upon them one summer day, when, as she stepped into the shadowy room, they had appeared to be as freshly dipped in some cool, watery light. Though she did not know, then, that it was to be the last time she should ever see them together, she had felt it as some special occasion. Lolling in two chairs, facing a glass table upon which rested two mellow drinks and two immaculate iced cupcakes, they might have been listening to some enchantment beyond any that could be conjured up by the Mozart record they were actually playing. The White Queen was invisible. Baker was off chasing some light of love and the night of Nora's adventuring had led her this time straight to her brother. They were so given over to their private view that Mrs.

95

Heath, after a few awkward comments about the weather, had made
some excuse to slip away. Bartram had come to the door with her,
smiling not for her, but out of his own happy jubilation. His sister barely
moved her head in farewell and lay stretched in her chair, in a trance
of ease, extending two slippered feet in green snake skin that made of
her body in its frail white dress an attenuated blossom. . . .

In the loneliness that close proximity to the happiness of others brings,
Mrs. Heath felt for the absent Baker. He was beyond the reach of the
enchanted music and on the summer road she felt for him as one outcast
feels for another.[11]

When *Hunter of Doves* was published, Sid and Laura made no
public comment. It is rumored, however, that privately they were
deeply offended by Miss Herbst's portraits and her interpretation of
their relationships with West. The question is still being debated by
friends of the trio: How did Perelman really feel about West and was
the early failure of his marriage influenced by the obsessive closeness
that Laura and her brother had for one another? No one ever dared
ask the question during Sid's and Laura's lifetime and no one can
answer it now, since all the people involved in this enigmatic triangle—so full of subtle complexities that lead down shadowy corri-
dors of questionable memory—are dead.

# 7
# "A DREARY INDUSTRIAL TOWN"

## (1932–1934)

Hollywood is a dreary industrial town controlled by hoodlums of enormous wealth, the ethical sense of a pack of jackals, and taste so degraded that it befouled everything it touched.

S. J. PERELMAN, 1963[1]

Both Sid and Laura had nothing but contempt for Hollywood when they worked there. But the older Sid got, the more glamorous Hollywood became. He was truly nostalgic about it.

ALLEN SAALBURG[2]

Courtney Burr, the man Laura found so intriguing, was a millionaire stockbroker who had become a theatrical producer after losing his money in the stock market crash. At first, his plays were unsuccessful. One of his shows netted him only fourteen dollars, and his 1932 production of *Hamlet* with Norman Bel Geddes closed after three weeks. Undaunted, Burr decided to produce a revue, *Walk a Little Faster*, starring the bewitching Canadian comedienne Beatrice Lillie and vaudevillians Bobby Clark and Paul McCullough. Burr's millionaire friends, Jock Whitney and the Astors, helped raise the money. Sid Perelman was hired to write some of the sketches.[3] Vernon Duke and E. Y. Harburg did the music and lyrics, respectively, and Albertina Rasch the choreography. The production was conceived and designed by Boris Aronson and directed by Monty Woolley, Burr's friend and former classmate at Yale.

Sid had written for revues before. He contributed a sketch, "His Wedding Night," to the *Third Little Show*, which opened at the Music Box Theatre on June 1, 1931, and ran for 136 performances. That

97

show also starred Beatrice Lillie, who sang Noel Coward's "Mad Dogs and Englishmen" while seated in a rickshaw against a tropical setting. But as one critic noted, "S. J. Perelman's 'His Wedding Night,' a lunatic creation, is one of the high moments of the entertainment."[4]

*Walk a Little Faster* proved a very different matter. Every time Sid wanted to change a line in one of his sketches, he had to have the revisions approved by the various lawyers, managers and backers involved in the production. Always quick to take umbrage, he did not conceal his irritation, and many years later Vernon Duke wrote that Sid had reminded him of "a bespectacled black panther in a Brooks Brothers suit."[5] The Boston opening at the Majestic Theatre added to his frenzy. Sets failed to materialize, stagehands could be seen still moving props and furniture when the curtain went up and several actors in the show never appeared on stage at all.

Despite these misfortunes, Boston audiences adored the show, especially Vernon Duke's beautiful "April in Paris," which was sung by Evelyn Hoey and danced against a striking Aronson set of a Parisian café.

Unimpressed by the applause, Burr quixotically decided that the revue needed a thorough overhauling before it opened in New York. Without telling the authors, he telephoned his friend E. Ray Goetz, a successful songwriter, and told him to come to Boston to do the necessary revisions.

Burr and Goetz spent the weekend holed up in Burr's lavish hotel suite. When Perelman, Duke, Harburg and Aronson went to the theater a few nights later, they found that all the best sketches and songs had been lumped together in Act One. According to Vernon Duke, he and his colleagues were aghast at the changes and, as soon as the act ended, dashed for the nearest exit. "Out in the fresh air we stared at one another. Aronson shaking his head unbelievingly, Perelman's bespectacled black-panther face wearing a typically savage scowl," Duke wrote. "Knowing that all the 'weak sisters' were dumped into Act Two, no doubt with the assumption that the audience, shattered by the first act's magnificence, would, by then, swallow anything, we couldn't face the actors about to be slaughtered in the line of duty and betook ourselves to a neighboring bar. At 10 p.m. we emerged, unable to stand the suspense any longer, and were equally unable to re-enter the theatre; masses of people were pouring out of the Majestic, looking sulky and dejected, and blocking all the entrances. Our first guess was that the paying customers, crushed by the horrors of the second act, left in protest, but that was not the case. Goetz' strategy was simply to cut out five of the more offensive items, without replacing them; thus the curtain went down at 9:50 p.m. (instead of the 11:45 of the opening night's performance) and the audience saw the shortest revue in theatrical history. The original routine was restored on the next evening, Mr. Goetz leaving Boston by an early train."[6]

*Walk a Little Faster* opened to mixed notices on December 7, 1932, at the St. James in New York. Robert Benchley, then drama critic of the *New Yorker*, found the revue more sparkling than the Folies-Bergère, which he had seen the previous week in Paris. "As for the sketches in the two shows, the American offerings, written for the most part by S. J. Perelman and R. MacGunigle, are not only funnier no matter what your nationality, but rank as among the cleanest seen even on this side of the Atlantic for some time."[7] But Brooks Atkinson of the *New York Times* found the sketches "mostly silly," and the show "a timid brew of turns and songs."[8] Richard Lockridge of the *New York Sun* felt that it was only Bea Lillie's comic genius that made "Scamp of the Campus," in which she impersonated a madcap coed of 1906, a highlight of the show. "Bea Lillie, in outlandish clothes, is the bright spark which almost sets alight an effortful sketch by S. J. Perelman which has otherwise only a parade of old slang to recommend it."[9]

The authors made no money from the show, even though it ran for 119 performances. Vernon Duke reported that after every Saturday matinee, one of the backers' representatives would appear at the box office to collect the backers' share of that week's receipts. After the cast and orchestra were paid, nothing was left for the authors, although eventually Burr was forced to give them all a cash settlement.

In the next few months Sid divided his time between commercial writing and pieces of a literary nature, a pattern that would remain more or less set for the rest of his life. He contributed material to Fanny Brice's radio show, as well as a piece called "Scenario" to *Contact* magazine. More bitter than humorous, "Scenario" was a brilliant patchwork of inane conversations that Sid had overheard in Hollywood between producers and writers, mixed with clichés from some of the banal films he had worked on. As time went on, many literary critics came to regard it not only as Perelman's most important single piece, but also as an influence on West's *The Day of the Locust*. It began:

Fade in, exterior grassy knoll, long shot. Above the scene the thundering measures of Von Suppé's "Light Cavalry Overture." Austerlitz? The Plains of Abraham? Vicksburg? The Little Big Horn? Cambrai? Steady on, old son; it is Yorktown. Under a blood-red setting sun yon proud crest is Cornwallis. Blood and 'ouns, proud sirrah, dost brush so lightly past an exciseman of the Crown? Lady Rotogravure's powdered shoulders shrank from the highwayman's caress; what, Jermyn, footpads on Hounslow Heath? A certain party in the D. A.'s office will hear of this, you bastard. There was a silken insolence in his smile as he drew the greatcoat about his face and leveled his shooting-iron at her dainty puss. Leave go that lady or I'll smear yuh. . . . It's right up the exhibitor's alley, Mr. Biberman, and you got to hand it to them on a platter steaming hot. I know, Stanley, but let's look at this thing reasonable; we been showing the public Folly Larrabee's drawers two years and they been cooling off. Jeez Crize—it's hisTORical drama, Mr. Biberman, it'll blow 'em outa the back of the houses, it's the greatest thing in the industry, it's dynamite! Pardon me, officer, is that General Washington? . . .[10]

"Scenario" forcefully expresses Perelman's contempt for Hollywood and its materialistic values. Undoubtedly, his feelings were influenced by a fresh exposure to the movie industry, for in 1932, again needing money, he returned to California, as he would many times during the thirties and early forties, working on a succession of mediocre films for a variety of film studios. Meant to divert Depression audiences—and later a nation at war—most of the films he worked on seem like quaint antiques by today's standards. Many were comedy melodramas involving gangsters, a popular motif at the time. Certainly none of them ever attained the stature of *Monkey Business* or *Horse Feathers*. Mainly B pictures, they passed quickly into oblivion—usually with quite poor reviews attached—and are seldom seen today, either in revival houses or on television late-shows.

In Hollywood, Sid soon secured a scriptwriting assignment at RKO for a film entitled *Hold 'Em Jail*, dubbed a "slam bang farce." Its cast included Bert Wheeler, Robert Woolsey, Edna May Oliver—and Betty Grable in a minor role. Wheeler and Woolsey played a couple of stupid salesmen who land in jail after being framed by a gangster and are recruited by the warden, a football enthusiast, for the prison football team. Undoubtedly Sid's association with *Horse Feathers*, another football farce, had something to do with getting the assignment.

*Hold 'Em Jail* was not a success, nor were most of the pictures

Perelman worked on during those years. His next writing assignment was for *Sitting Pretty*, a musical starring Jack Oakie, Ginger Rogers, Thelma Todd and Gregory Ratoff. Perelman worked with a collaborator, Jack McGowan, whom he heartily disliked, later calling him "a beefier forerunner of Archie Bunker" and "the second most odious person" he knew in Hollywood.

In their spare time Sid and Laura had been working on a play together—one they had conceived during their honeymoon in Paris. They finished it on a second trip to Paris and showed it to Courtney Burr, who was still producing shows and had just had a hit musical—*Sailor, Beware!* Burr agreed to produce it—and it opened at Henry Miller's Theatre on December 5, 1933.

Entitled *All Good Americans*, it was set in Paris and concerned the American expatriates who frequented the Dôme and Jimmy's Bar. Hope Williams played Julie Gable, an American fashion writer, and Fred Keating the debonair barfly with whom she falls in love. Cast in a minor role as an accordion-playing young man from America was a recent graduate of Princeton, the twenty-one-year-old James Stewart (picked for the part because he happened to play the accordion). It was his first acting role on Broadway.

On opening night the atmosphere was gala—for on that same day the Eighteenth Amendment had been repealed and Prohibition was ended. Wine flowed freely. Ethel Barrymore was there, as were Irving Berlin and Moss Hart, Tommy Manville and Mrs. Adam Gimbel, resplendent in a black velvet gown and silver fox cape.

But the play charmed no one. The glamorous audience found it tepid and the reactions of the critics ranged from lukewarm to icy. It closed on January 8, 1934, after a run of five weeks. It was performed for charity in July of that same year, with Robert Taylor and Betty Furness in the cast. Both were juvenile players at MGM, which had purchased the film rights to the play for $20,000. The film, for which Wells Root wrote the screenplay, also opened in July of 1934. Entitled *Paris Interlude*, it was a heavily embroidered version of the Perelman original. But critically and financially, the film was no more successful than the play. Wrote Richard Watts, Jr.: "Numerous plot complications and a huge romantic seriousness now take the place of the slightly laborious epigrams of the stage version but really the differences are not so important as to be of any vast note. For *Paris Interlude* is just about what it was originally, a thin and unconvincing cartoon, attempting rather laboriously to recount the antics of a group of presumably witty and daring American expatriates."[11]

In the midst of these ups and downs, Nathanael West's novel, *Miss Lonelyhearts*, was published by Horace Liveright, Inc. Reviews were excellent, but a few months later, the firm went bankrupt, and only a few copies were sold. West, who desperately needed money, was overjoyed when he learned that 20th Century–Fox had bought the movie rights for $4,000. The money enabled him to quit his job at the Sutton and devote his full time to writing.

In July of 1933 he followed Laura and Sid to Hollywood, landing a job at Columbia Pictures as a junior screenwriter on a week-to-week basis. His salary was $350 a week. According to Tom Dardis, "Most of Columbia's output at this time was of the grade-B variety, the films shown at the bottom half of a double bill. West was not starting at the bottom in Hollywood, but he was close to it."[12]

West completed two screenplays, *Beauty Parlor* and *Return to the Soil*, which were never produced. He was let go after seven weeks and returned to Bucks County, where he immediately began work on a third novel, *A Cool Million*. Not until 1936 did he work again as a screenwriter.

West worked for the minor studios but Sid was in a much higher echelon. His salary of $600 a week was almost twice West's salary at Columbia, and the pictures he worked on featured more important stars. During the thirties and forties, he wrote mainly for the "majors"—Paramount, RKO, 20th Century–Fox and MGM. Only briefly did he work for one of the "little two" studios—Universal, which let him go after two days on the job.

In 1935 Sid and Laura went on salary as a writing team at MGM and were paid $1,000 a week.

Although Perelman was well paid for his film work in comparison to the money he earned from magazine writing, he had difficulty accepting the fact that he was financially dependent on the film industry. He continually raged against its vulgarity and stupidity. West, on the other hand, appears to have made his peace with Hollywood. As John Sanford told Tom Dardis, "he knew that he was buying time for other things" and was grateful for the chance to work at all.[13]

But Hollywood, for both men, was a gold mine of material. West's last novel, *The Day of the Locust*, is still one of the best books about

Hollywood ever written, and some of Perelman's funniest pieces are about the movies and the bizarre people involved in them, and his own fantastic adventures as a teenage moviegoer and later a professional screenwriter.

Perelman's movie work was also buying him time for other things. In July of 1933, he contributed a short piece, "Nathanael West: A Portrait," to a critical symposium devoted to *Miss Lonelyhearts*, which appeared in *Contempo*, a small literary magazine published at Chapel Hill, North Carolina. William Carlos Williams and Josephine Herbst were among the other contributors.

Perelman's portrait of West was as follows:

Picture to yourself a ruddy-cheeked, stocky sort of chap, dressed in loose tweeds, a stubby briar in his teeth, with a firm yet humorous mouth, generous to a fault, ever-ready for a flagon of nut-brown ale with his cronies, possessing the courage of a lion and the tenderness of a woman, an intellectual vagabond, a connoisseur of first editions, fine wines and beautiful women, well above six feet in height and distinguished for his pallor, a dweller in the world of books, his keen grey eyes belying the sensual lip, equally at home browsing through the bookstalls along the Paris quais and rubbing elbows in the smart literary salons of the Faubourg St. Honoré, a rigid abstainer and non-smoker, living entirely on dehydrated fruits, cereals and nuts, rarely leaving his monastic cell, an intimate of Cocteau, Picasso, Joyce and Lincoln Kirstein, a dead shot, a past master of the foils, dictating his novels, plays, poems, short stories, epigrams, aphorisms, and sayings to a corps of secretaries at lightning speed, an expert judge of horse-flesh, the owner of a model farm equipped with the latest dairy devices—a man as sharp as a razor, as dull as a hoe, as black as the raven's wing, and as poor as Job. A man kind and captious, sweet and sour, fat and thin, tall and short, racked with fever, plagued by the locust, beset by witches, hag-ridden, cross-grained, a fun-loving, serious minded dreamer, visionary and slippered pantaloon. Picture to yourself such a man, I say, and you won't have the faintest idea of Nathanael West.

To begin with, the author of *Miss Lonelyhearts* is only eighteen inches high. He is very sensitive about his stature and only goes out after dark, and then armed with a tiny umbrella with which he beats off cats who try to attack him. Being unable to climb into his bed, which is at least two feet taller than himself, he has been forced to sleep in the lower bureau of a drawer since childhood, and is somewhat savage in consequence. He is meticulously dressed, however, and never goes abroad without his green cloth gloves and neat nankeen breeches. His age is a matter of speculation. He claims to remember the Battle of the Boyne and on a fine night his piping voice may be heard in the glen lifted in the strains of "For she's my Molly-O." Of one thing, we can be sure; he was seen by unimpeachable witnesses at Austerlitz, Jena, and Wagram, where he made personal appearances through the courtesy of Milton Fink of Fink and Biesemyer, his agents. What I like about him most is his mouth, a jagged scarlet wound etched against the unforgettable blankness of his face. I love his sudden impish smile, the twinkle of those alert green eyes, and the print of his cloven foot in the shrubbery. I love the curly brown locks cascading down his receding forehead; I love the wind in the willows, the boy in the bush, and the seven against Thebes. I love coffee, I love tea, I love the girls and the girls love me. And I'm going to be a civil engineer when I grow up, no matter WHAT Mamma says.[14]

One might be tempted to analyze this piece line by line, looking for clues to the personality of the "real" West or the "real" Perelman, for that matter, as several scholars have, except for the fact that it is one of those elaborate literary jokes that were so popular in the 1920s. Sid always had trouble writing seriously, even when the subject was his best friend and the occasion a solemn one, a critical symposium devoted to a novel West had labored on for years. Although undoubtedly there is some truth in the observation that this piece reveals West's contradictions—the clash in him between the romantic dreamer and the disillusioned realist—it must be stated that if these were West's conflicts, they were Arthur Kober's, too, for several years later Perelman used almost the same words to begin a profile of the playwright. Questions of self-plagiarism aside, "Nathanael West: A Portrait" remains one of Sid's most important pieces, illustrating how wordplay and parody, not self-revealing emotions, were the foundations of his humor and personality.

It was perhaps inevitable that Perelman and West should collaborate, and in the summer of 1934, they wrote a play together, a broad satire on publishing and pulp writers. Its heroine, Diane Breed Latimer, who writes bestselling cheap fiction, was based on their old college professor, Percy Marks. The play's title, *Even Stephen*, was taken from the title of the poem that Laura had written while she was at Pembroke. If the theme of *Even Stephen* sounds more like Perelman than West, it is because West deferred to Perelman as an artist. He considered him a genius and once said to playwright Joseph Schrank, who was his neighbor in Erwinna, "I think his stuff is going to live." When Schrank replied, "I think your books have a greater chance," West acted greatly surprised.[15]

Perelman and West had high hopes for their play, but it was never produced. That summer they also talked of writing a novel together, but the Perelmans went back to California before anything could come of it. The two men never collaborated again.

# 8

## "STRICTLY FROM HUNGER"

### *(1935–1940)*

Nathanael West, with his unique talent, may not have been an ideal collaborator for Sid, but Laura was more than eager to take his place. Like her brother, she was quick to spot the offbeat and bizarre. She was also bored, in need of something to do. Sid was making a name for himself. He was mingling with sophisticated and famous people, while she had neither children nor a job. Although a flop, *All Good Americans* had given her the sense of direction she desperately yearned for. It had been an opportunity to test her artistic talent. No longer was she frittering away her time in idle pursuits. Like her husband and brother, she was a creator, too.

In the 1930s there were many husband-and-wife writing teams in Hollywood. Among them were Perelman's good friends, Dorothy Parker and Alan Campbell. There were also Frances Goodrich and Albert Hackett, who wrote the Thin Man movies together. Financially, there were certain advantages to husband-and-wife teams. Sid, working alone, made $500 to $600 a week, while he and Laura as a team could command twice that amount.

In 1935 Sid and Laura got their first assignment. The film was *Greenwich Village*, and its producer was Irving Thalberg, the legendary "Boy Wonder" who was then the creative czar of MGM. *Greenwich Village*, which was never made, was one of his last projects. He died a year later at the age of thirty-seven.

Dark, intense and fiercely egotistical, Thalberg was much admired by Groucho Marx and Anita Loos—but Perelman disliked him. For one thing, Sid found his views on life and filmmaking too simplistic and moralistic for his taste. He also hated the fact that Thalberg had

106

tried to crush the newly formed Screen Writers Guild. "The writer is a necessary evil," Thalberg had stated. (Perelman later wrote in his piece about the producer, "And Did You Once See Irving Plain?", "the assertion that he said 'weevil' appears to have no foundation in fact.")

While the Perelmans were in his employ, Thalberg kept shilly-shallying about the type of picture *Greenwich Village* should be, and Laura and Sid were let go after four months of thumb-twiddling and false starts. "Unfortunately," Sid recalled, "we never got a clear reading from Mr. Thalberg about whether he wanted La vie de Bohème or another Rip Tide: The Story of a Woman's Conflicting Emotions or a singing disaster film like San Francisco, so in the end as the Tarot pack accurately predicted, we went back to Bucks County and he to Elysium."[1]

As a team, Sid and Laura had a bit more luck at Paramount, where they wrote *Florida Special*, a mystery comedy in the style of *Grand Hotel*, which was released in the spring of 1936. It took place on a train and starred Jack Oakie. Two other writers were also involved on the project, but the results, it seems, were not too impressive. *Variety* noted: "It took four people to turn it out and from a literary point of view they have done a slovenly job, but the yarn is packed with belly laughs, mostly on the wisecracking order."[2]

In 1935 Sid was teamed up with several writers at 20th Century–Fox on a screen adaptation of a musical comedy that had been a big hit in England, *Nymph Errant*, from the novel by James Laver. According to Lester Cole, he and Sid hated the original show and felt it would work on the screen only if it were totally revamped. But every time they broached the subject to Buddy De Sylva, the producer, they were told that the head of the studio, Winfield Sheehan, adored the story just as it was. If they wanted to keep their jobs, they were not to change a line.

The writer Samson Raphaelson was also working at the studio. Raphaelson had just had a hit play on Broadway, *Accent on Youth*. Cole, Perelman and Raphaelson often lunched together, and Raphaelson's constant bragging about the film script he was working on got on Sid's nerves—or perhaps it was the fact that *All Good Americans* had been a flop while Raphaelson's play had been a hit.

Cole and Perelman's office was directly below that of the scenario editor in charge of screenwriters, Colonel Jason Joy. One day, a cap fell off the steam pipe that ran between the two offices, and Cole and

Perelman were able to overhear everything Joy said. Several days later, they heard Joy boom out, "Raphaelson's script is no good? You want me to fire him?"

Perelman and Cole leaped from their typewriters and dashed down the hall to Raphaelson's office. With a certain amount of sadistic pleasure, Perelman told Raphaelson that he had just heard his script was lousy and perhaps he should look for another line of work. As Raphaelson sat staring at him incredulously, the phone rang. It was Joy telling him he had just been fired. Stunned, Raphaelson demanded to know how Perelman and Cole had gotten the news ahead of time, but they refused to divulge their source.

A few days later, Cole and Perelman learned, via the steam pipe, that the studio bigwigs had also found their script unacceptable and were about to give them the axe. Rather than be subjected to this humiliation, they raced to De Sylva's office and quit on the spot.[3]

Lester Cole remembers that some years later he ran into Buddy De Sylva, who told him that Winfield Sheehan had been aghast when he read his and Perelman's script. "Who dared to change not only the lines but the whole goddam story?" Sheehan demanded. "Buddy, who knew we had followed the script, much as we disliked it, brought him the original libretto of the musical he had bought," Cole wrote. "It was only after looking at it that he realized that, perhaps a little drunk, he had given his London man the wrong title, and he had bought the wrong musical. Embarrassed, he swore De Sylva to silence. The project was coffined and quietly buried."[4]

The Screen Writers Guild had been created in 1933 to better the working conditions of screenwriters. Several of Perelman's good friends—Dashiell Hammett, Lillian Hellman, Frances Goodrich and Albert Hackett—were among the founders of the Guild. Sid, Laura and West were active members, with Laura serving on the Guild's executive board. In April of 1936, a bitter dispute occurred involving the Guild, which had asked for legislation to protect the way in which an author's material could be used. The film producers struck back by creating their own organization, the Screen Playwrights, which was actually controlled by Jack Warner, Irving Thalberg and Louis B. Mayer. They threatened to blacklist all the writers who would not resign from the Guild. In effect, the Guild was crushed, and it was not until a year later that the newly created National Labor Relations Board decided that the producers had joined in a conspiracy to suppress the Guild. Two years later elections were held to determine which organization should legitimately represent writers. Screen Playwrights resorted to all kinds of questionable tactics to ensure that its side would win, such as getting people to vote who weren't screenwriters—among them Jean Harlow's mother, even though Mayer claimed she had written the script for one of her daughter's films.

But Screen Playwrights was overwhelmingly defeated in the August 8, 1938, election, and the Screen Writers Guild won the right to be the collective bargaining agent for screenwriters in eighteen movie studios.

Sid staunchly supported the actions of the Guild. When he learned that James K. McGuinness, Irving Thalberg's spokesman in the dispute, was contributing a piece to the *Kalmar and Ruby Songbook*, to which he had contributed a piece on Harry Ruby, he wrote an irate letter to Bennett Cerf at Random House, demanding that his own piece be withdrawn. Cerf pleaded with him to change his mind, but Sid was adamant. His piece on Ruby was omitted from the collection.[5]

Sid usually spent the summer in Bucks County, but that year he stayed in town to finish a musical version of S. N. Behrman's *Serena Blandish* (based on the Enid Bagnold novel, *A Lady of Quality*) for Vincente Minnelli. For some obscure reason Minnelli envisioned *Serena Blandish* as an all-black production, with Lena Horne playing Serena, Ethel Waters the countess and Cab Calloway as Lord Ivor Cream. Although Sid was unenthusiastic about such a version, he managed to finish the script. It was never produced, since Minnelli realized that it would be too costly to stage.[6]

Minnelli became the subject of one of Sid's unorthodox profiles. When his publicity representative, Eleanor Lambert, read it, she sent Minnelli a telegram, demanding that he tell the editors of *Show* magazine to withdraw the profile. She was afraid people would believe it was true, and it would ruin Minnelli's career. Minnelli read the profile a few days later. It began:

> One sweltering summer's day a dozen years ago I had dropped into the main reading-room of the New York Public Library. I was deep in Bulfinch's *Age of Fable*, busily shading the illustrations of Greek and Roman divinities with a hard pencil and getting some truly splendid effects when I became aware that a strange individual had entered the room. He was apparently a foreigner, for he bore in his lapel a green immigrant tag reading "Ellis Island—Rush." His clothes were flapping

hand-me-downs greasy with travel, and altogether, he was as extraordinary an unhung horse-thief as you would encounter outside a gypsy encampment.[7]

Minnelli loved it. He wired Eleanor Lambert: "Piece stands as is. All my life, I've been trying to achieve that reputation."[8]

That summer of 1936 Sid and Laura were awaiting the birth of their first child after seven years of marriage. On October 19, a son, Adam, was born, whom Sid jokingly described to I. J. Kapstein as looking "like neither of us as much as like Pep—which conjures up some pretty interesting speculations."[9] He wrote Kapstein that Laura "had an easy time and insists on raising a brood"—his own feelings on the subject were not mentioned. However, he appears to have been amenable to Laura's wishes, for a year and a half later, a daughter, Abby Laura, was born.

Following Adam's birth, the Perelmans moved back to their East 56th Street apartment, where Sid continued to write for the *New Yorker*. He collaborated with Beatrice Mathieu on a play. In March of 1937, he wrote Kapstein that they had completed the first two acts. But the play remained unfinished and no draft of it exists.

Writing for the *New Yorker* had become a steady source of income at last, for Sid now had an arrangement with Harold Ross and Gus Lobrano to provide the magazine with a set number of pieces a year. The contract gave him great pleasure for, as he told Kapstein, the comic essay was his favorite form of literary creativity and the only kind of writing he enjoyed.

His first piece had appeared in the magazine in the December 13, 1930, issue. Entitled "Open Letter to Moira Ransom," it was based on a newspaper item he had read in which a woman reported that the strangest sight she ever saw was a drunken man kissing the statue of a horse in a fountain. According to Perelman, he was the man she had seen:

Dear Miss Ransom:

Things have come to a pretty pass indeed when a taxpayer can't step into a park without a covey of spies like yourself skulking in the shrubbery. So *you* were the sallow girl in the Russian pony coat I saw when I came out on the Pratt Street side. Not that I would sully *my* lips asking

110

what you were *doing* in Barlow Park that night. I suppose you were sitting up with a sick rhododendron. Humph! . . .

Sid's first editor at the *New Yorker* was Gus Lobrano, a gentle, unpretentious man who preferred bowling to literary discussions. Sid liked and respected him. Like Sid, Lobrano had a dry wit and was a fastidious dresser. Their relationship seems to have been unmarred by the resentments and financial disputes that marked many of Sid's other professional dealings. He enjoyed writing for the *New Yorker*, he said, because of its "respect for the word" as well as its civility to writers. He also liked the fact that the editing of his pieces was usually minor and the changes made only with his permission. Once, as Israel Shenker recalls, Sid received a phone call from William Shawn, who edited his work following Gus Lobrano's death, asking if Sid minded changing a dash in a certain line to a semicolon. Perelman replied that he preferred the dash. The dash remained.[10]

Socially Sid mingled very little with the *New Yorker* staff. He never worked on the magazine's premises. Instead for many years he rented a room he called his "web" on the third floor of a seedy walk-up on Sixth Avenue between 13th and 14th Streets. Spartanly furnished with two rocking chairs, a desk, a camp bed and typewriter, the room had one window that faced a blank wall. "There is no sky to distract me," he told his close friend Philip Hamburger.[11] The walls were decorated with a watercolor of Paris by Stuart Davis and photographs of three men he greatly admired—Somerset Maugham, Gus Lobrano and James Joyce. In later years he added a pedestal crowned with the top hat David Niven had worn as Phileas Fogg in *Around the World in 80 Days*.

Sid wrote very slowly. Writing, for him, was a painful, laborious process, no matter what the medium. He worked as hard on a worthless screenplay as on a piece for the *New Yorker*. "I'm a bleeder," he liked to say, explaining the fact that in two and a half weeks he was seldom able to produce more than 2500 words. He kept regular hours— writing from ten to six, six days a week. "When he was working on something, he was a martinet about his time," recalls Louise Kerz, a friend. "I remember calling him once, and he said, 'I'm in the middle of a sentence and I'll call you back when I finish,' and he didn't call me back until the next day. I said, 'Have you finished the sentence?' and he said, 'I just finished that sentence.' "[12]

He considered it a rare day when he finished a page of copy. Once he described writing as "wading through a swamp without high rubber boots." He liked to boast perhaps with tongue-in-cheek that he customarily wrote thirty-seven drafts of an article. "I once tried thirty-three, but something was lacking, a certain—how shall I say?—*je ne sais quoi*. On another occasion, I tried forty-two versions, but the final draft was too lapidary."[13]

Another friend, Professor Constance B. Hieatt, professor of English at the University of Western Ontario, wrote: "Sid's method of revision went miles beyond what most of us do . . . I remember once looking at a sheet of paper he had left in his typewriter. It was two whole pages of nothing but one sentence, each time changed just a little bit. He double-spaced when he got to the end of the sentence, then tried again. Nor was this a major work; as I recall, it was a script for a skit of some kind to be used at the New York World's Fair."[14]

Sid often liked to hone and refine a story verbally before he wrote it. Many of his pieces started out as entertaining anecdotes at cocktail parties. Several of his friends recall his trying out in anecdotal form some humorous piece he was currently working on to test their reactions.

Every day Perelman read newspapers from all over the world, hoping to find a bizarre item that might inspire his strange and wonderful imagination. His friends were instructed to be on the lookout for peculiar names or newspaper clippings that described ridiculous fads or fantastic extravagances.

Lacking a suitable target for his humor, he might deliberately subject himself to a boring or disastrous situation with the hope of deriving some interesting material from it. Once he and Laura took an eight-day cruise of Lake Okeechobee in Florida. They had nothing in common with the other passengers, who mostly discussed the commercials they had seen on television. The trip was deadly dull, but Sid got a funny piece out of it.

Sid always believed that humor was too effervescent to be dissected. He did not like to analyze what made something funny nor did he believe that comic writing could be taught. He was convinced that humor had to be based on reality, moreover, which was why he often used newspaper articles as a point of departure. "There's nothing so tiresome as nonsense piled upon nonsense," he said.[15]

He liked to stress that as a humorist he had "no purpose beyond the function to entertain,"[16] although at other times he contradicted himself, saying that humor's function was to deflate pretentiousness and expose man's follies. By its very nature, humor was an angry business. "Generally speaking, I don't believe in kindly humor—I don't think it exists," he once said in an interview. "One of the most shameful utterances to stem from the human mouth is Will Rogers' 'I never met a man I didn't like.' The absolute antithesis is Oscar Wilde on the fox-hunting Englishman: 'The unspeakable in full pursuit of the uneatable.' Wilde's remark contains, in briefest span, the truth, whereas Rogers' is pure flatulence, crowd-pleasing and fake humility."[17]

He preferred to be thought of as a writer, not a humorist. "The humorist conjures up a picture of a man with his hat brim flopped up and a cigar in his face, popping one-liners, as they're called, you know. I don't think that's my exact stance. I try to write as well as I can on light subjects."[18]

Sometimes accused of being too literary and arcane, he refused to simplify his style to attract a wider audience. "People who like my work have to understand words and their juxtaposition as well as the images they create. It's very hard to make a person laugh who doesn't have inside him the words I use. My humor is of the free association kind, and in order to enjoy it, you have to have a good background in reading. It's a heavy strain for people who haven't read much."[19]

Many people assumed that with Sid's incredible literary talents, he yearned to write a masterpiece. But his greatest ambition seems to have been to write a commercial hit. Numbers of his friends stress the fact that he wrote only when he needed money. Says Heywood Hale Broun: "Sid didn't write for pleasure or posterity. After he received a good deal of money for a television show, 'Malice in Wonderland,' he did not write for six months."[20]

In July of 1937, Random House published *Strictly from Hunger*, a second collection of Perelman's comic pieces. It was dedicated to his son, Adam, and contained twenty-one pieces from the *New Yorker*, *College Humor*, *Life*, *Judge* and *Contact*. Sid was paid a $300 advance against royalties.

Two of the funniest pieces in the collection were "A Farewell to Omsk," a parody of Constance Garnett's translation of Dostoevsky, and "Waiting for Santy," a satiric takeoff on Clifford Odets' popular left-wing play, *Waiting for Lefty*. Santa Claus was described by his gnomes as "a parasite, a leech, a blood-sucker—altogether a five-star nogoodnick! Starvation wages we get so he can ride around in a red team with reindeers."[21] Odets did not think it was funny.

The book received the personal attention of Bennett Cerf, editor-in-chief of Random House, and Saxe Commins, its senior editor. To judge by the jocular correspondence between Cerf and Perelman, Sid had found a publisher very much to his liking, and although their relationship deteriorated as time went on, its initial mood was genial. Sid complimented Cerf (whom he later called Barnaby Chirp in his comic essays) on the appearance of the book, which he found "restrained and dignified" in contrast to Liveright's flamboyant treatment of *Dawn Ginsbergh's Revenge*. He was pleased with Cerf's meticulous attenion to details. They exchanged jokes and kidded each other about sex and their lives as gentlemen farmers. Cerf, who prided himself on his urbanity and wit, tried to outdo Perelman, and Sid retaliated in kind.

*Strictly from Hunger* received a bad review from Robert Van Gelder in the *New York Times*, but other critics loved it. Charles A. Wagner in the *New York Mirror* noted: "There are of course many reasons why a reviewer cannot read a book, but it is a rare occasion indeed to come upon one which cannot be read because the tears of laughter fall so freely that our glasses blur up hopelessly."[22] In the *New Republic* Miriam Borgenicht wrote: "Occasionally it falls into the banal by way of literary exercise and quips whose point can be guessed before they turn the corner; more often (as in Red Termites, the travesty on red-baiting), it reaches peaks of comic distortion which cover really fine satire. Taken in one gulp, all this waggishness is likely to put a strain on even the most faithful Perelman addict. But absorbed in judicious teaspoonfuls, it is calculated to disturb the sanity of any reader."[23]

But the best reaction of all was contained in the introduction Robert Benchley had written for the book. ". . . Perelman took over the *dementia praecox* field and drove us all to writing articles on economics for the *Commentator*. Any further attempts to garble thought-processes sounded like imitation-Perelman. He did to our weak little efforts at 'crazy stuff' what Benny Goodman has done to middle-period jazz. He swung it. To use a swing phrase, he took it 'out of the world' and there he remains, all by himself."

Perelman must have particularly liked the comparison to swing music, since he and Laura were jazz aficionados and great admirers of Goodman. One of their favorite pastimes was to go to the Pennsylvania Hotel and listen to Goodman's band. After the performance Goodman would often invite the Perelmans to his hotel room, where he would play them his recordings and they would dance. Sid wrote to I. J. Kapstein that "listening to things like *Whisperin'*, *Bugle Call Rag* and songs of that vintage carries me back to dim parlors adjacent to Candace Street Grammar School where we used to do the camel walk with immature hussies in formfit sweaters."[24]

The sales of *Strictly from Hunger* were, as Cerf wrote Perelman, "nothing to brag about."[25] He attributed this to the hot weather that had blanketed the country that summer. Sales were decent in Hollywood and New York, but nowhere else, Cerf said, and he ended his letter by suggesting that perhaps they would improve if.Perelman could get involved in a scandal with a movie star, an allusion to George S. Kaufman's headline-making liaison with movie actress Mary Astor.

Some time later, when Sid's friend Stanley Rose, owner of a bookstore on Hollywood Boulevard, was having financial problems, Perelman wired Donald Klopfer at Random House, asking him to send all his royalties from *Strictly from Hunger* to Rose. If they amounted to less than $250, he asked Klopfer to make up the difference, saying he would later cover the debt.[26]

Klopfer wired him back that since its publication almost a year ago, *Strictly from Hunger* had earned only twelve dollars in royalties.

In October of 1937 Sid and Laura were back on the MGM payroll. Irving Thalberg was dead, and they were starting afresh with a screenplay for the Nelson Eddy–Jeanette MacDonald picture, *Sweethearts*. Although Eddy and MacDonald had already made four pictures together, *Sweethearts* was their first in Technicolor. Miss MacDonald was apprehensive about the public's reaction. "I'm nervous," she confided to Regina Crew of the *Journal-American*. "I don't know how they'll like me in Technicolor. Maybe my cheeks will be too, too pink, my lips too red, my eyes and hair strange and unfamiliar."

The producer of *Sweethearts* was Hunt Stromberg, a handsome Kentuckian and slovenly dresser. Perelman found him almost as difficult as Irving Thalberg. The only way he and Laura were able to endure his endless story conferences was to watch his shoelaces untie themselves as he paced back and forth, vainly trying to light one of his expensive pipes. Sid's miseries were compounded when Laura, who was again pregnant, was unable to continue working, and their salary was cut to $500 a week.

To Laura's surprise, she was replaced by two people—Dorothy Parker and Alan Campbell. Perelman had met Dorothy in 1932, at a cocktail party given by Courtney Burr. Dressed in a chic black Lanvin frock and long gloves, she had been quite drunk, and after Burr asked his guests to suggest titles for his new revue, she had lashed out at Sid when he told her that the two titles she suggested—"Pousse Café" and "Aces Up"—lacked punch. Perelman vowed that the next time they met he would "skewer her with one of her own hatpins."[27] But he was totally charmed the day after the party when she sent him a dozen roses with a note of apology.

In time the foursome became good friends. The Campbells visited the Perelmans at their farm in Bucks County frequently and fell so in love with the area that they bought a farm of their own in nearby Pipersville in 1934.

At their story conferences for *Sweethearts*, Dorothy Parker would sit knitting what Perelman described "a gray artifact seven feet long that looked like a staircase runner,"[28] while Alan did most of the talking. Every so often Stromberg would stop pacing and pontificating and ask Miss Parker her opinion of the script's progress, and she would look up from her knitting and reply rather breathlessly that she thought it was "marvelous."

One day, while Stromberg was trying to light his pipe, a match flew into Miss Parker's chair, setting it on fire. Fortunately, she wasn't hurt, although no one knows what became of the "artifact."

In the end, only Dorothy Parker and Alan Campbell received screen credit for *Sweethearts*. Sid and Laura didn't object, for although the public agreed that Jeanette MacDonald's red hair looked wonderful in Technicolor, the critics blasted the picture. One reviewer wrote that the plot "was so sweet that it practically breaks out with diabetes."

At MGM, Sid lunched with the Campbells every day. He also ate with Herman Mankiewicz, Robert Benchley, Donald Ogden Stewart, Edward Chodorov and F. Scott Fitzgerald, who was writing a screenplay for Erich Maria Remarque's *Three Comrades*. Perelman noticed that while some of the other writers took lunches of two or three hours, Fitzgerald never took more than half an hour and drank only

7-Up. To Perelman's amazement, many people at the studio didn't have any idea who he was.

In later years Sid said that the importance of literary friendships in his life could not be overestimated.[29] In New York and Hollywood he had many friends among writers and later in England he was friendly with Maugham, T. S. Eliot, Chaim Raphael and Norman Lewis. Although he was never a part of the Algonquin Round Table and scorned their brittle, wisecracking repartee and the elaborate word games the group was addicted to, he was personally fond of George S. Kaufman, Robert Benchley, Marc Connelly and Dorothy Parker.

Through the many years of their association, Sid and Dorothy Parker had an off-again, on-again relationship. One of their misunderstandings started when the Campbells invited Sid and Laura to dinner at their Pipersville farm. As they drove up, the Perelmans were shocked to see that three enormous Norway maples in front of the house had been chopped down. When Sid asked why, Alan informed him that they had cut off the light from the house.

Sid, who knew the name of every type of tree on his property, was aghast. "You must have needed the wood awful bad," he said.

Dorothy and Alan did not think his remark was funny. Dinner was strained, and they did not speak to him for a couple of years after the incident.

Realizing that the feud had grown to ridiculous proportions, Sid eventually invited the Campbells to a dinner party at his house. He also invited two other guests, one of whom was an ardent fan of Dorothy's. After the evening was over, Sid asked Dorothy what she thought of the man. "She said," Sid reported, " 'You must have needed the wood awful bad.' " Sid thought this was so funny he "screamed with laughter. But that mysteriously angered her, and they didn't speak to us for another whole year."[30]

Yet even in Dorothy Parker's last difficult years, when she was so drunk and vituperative that most of her friends had abandoned her, the Perelmans remained basically loyal to her. On her seventy-second birthday they invited her to their apartment for drinks, and when she died one year later in 1967, Sid attended her brief service at a Manhattan funeral home. A violinist played Bach's Air for the G String, a title Dorothy always thought was funny, and Zero Mostel and Lillian Hellman delivered brief eulogies. "I'm sure Dorothy's foot was tapping even through as short an exercise as that because she had a very short fuse," Sid quipped.

Of all the male writers Sid befriended, he said he knew F. Scott Fitzgerald the best. He and West often visited Fitzgerald on the Edward Everett Horton estate at Encino, California, where Fitzgerald was living. Spending part of the time with him was Sheilah Graham, the Hollywood columnist, about whom Sid later said, "Well, it seems that while cleaning out a thimble she discovered still more revelations anent that tortured spirit Scott Fitzgerald." On these evenings with Fitzgerald, the three men talked about the Screen Writers Guild, and West, who was active in the Guild and several left-wing organizations, urged Fitzgerald to participate in some of these activities. Fitzgerald demurred. He felt that a writer should express his political opinions only in books.[31]

Fitzgerald was impressed with both Perelman and West's writing. When West applied (unsuccessfully) for a Guggenheim Fellowship, Fitzgerald wrote him a letter of recommendation. After *The Day of the Locust* was published, he wrote Sid that the novel "has scenes of extraordinary power—if that phrase is still in use. Especially I was impressed by the pathological crowd at the premiere, the character and handling of the aspirant actress, and the uncanny almost medieval feeling of some of his Hollywood background, set off by those vividly drawn grotesques."[32]

On a more intimate note, when Adam Perelman was born, Fitzgerald recommended the nurse who had taken care of his daughter, Scottie. And in 1939, he bought Perelman's Ford.

In his notebook he jotted down the following observations of Perelman and West:

> Sid Perleman [sic] is effete—new style. He has the manners of Gerald Murphy and almost always an exquisite tact in prose that borders on the precieuse. I feel that he and I (as with John O'Hara and the football-glamor confession complex) have some early undisclosed experience in common so that at this point in our lives we find each other peculiarly sympathetic. We do not need to talk.
> Sheilah noted his strange grace doing his interpretation of "Slythy" in the Charade the other night.
> I like his brother-in-law West. I wonder if he's long-winded as a defense mechanism. I think that when I am that's why. I don't want to be liked

or to teach or to interest. That is my way of saying "Don't like me—I want to go back to my dream."

I know Nat through his books which are morbid as hell, doomed to the underworld of literature. But literature. He reminds me of someone. That heaviness. But in no other person it could be got used to—in Nat it has no flashes except what I see in his eyes, in his foolish passion for that tough and stupid child Mc———. Sid knows what I know so well that it would be blasphemy to put it in conversation.[33]

The Perelmans and West also saw a great deal of Dashiell Hammett and Lillian Hellman. Hammett was working as a screenwriter, and Hellman as a manuscript reader, at MGM. "The five of us, and a few others, stayed close together," recalled Miss Hellman, "not only because we liked each other, but because we were in what was called 'the same salary bracket.' Then, and probably now, if you were a writer who earned five hundred dollars a week you didn't see much of those who earned fifteen hundred a week."[34]

Once, Hammett, who slept around a great deal, contracted gonorrhea. He wrote Lillian, who was back East:

Last night I ran into Sid . . . in the Brown Derby, brought him home with me, gave him some Bourbon, and wound up by doing a little pimping for him. God knows I'm doing my best to keep celibacy from rearing its ugly head in Hollywood! But something's got to be done to keep the gals moderately content while I'm out of order.[35]

Hammett and Laura were sexually attracted to one another and had a week-long affair. Albert Hackett told interviewer Steven Marcus that as a practical joke Hammett once hired a call girl to disrobe in his bathroom, "and Sid went to the bathroom and gee, he was gone a long time, and then Laura Perelman and whoever went up there and caught them flagrante delicto. That was a story. It ended with Laura going off to San Francisco with Hammett, I remember that, they were gone for days, and there was hell to pay all around."[36] According to Hammett's biographer, Diane Johnson, the affair had "deeply upset both Perelman and Hellman who had remained friends but stayed off that one topic."[37]

Laura's affair with Hammett appears to have been merely a brief encounter. As intensely private as her husband, she never referred to her relationship with him in later years. Although she undoubtedly found Hammett attractive, her running away with him to San Francisco was perhaps her way of punishing Sid for his numerous infidelities, which she tried to condone but secretly resented. Once, many years later, Laura cryptically told a friend that "the man I loved died." The friend thought she meant Hammett, but Laura also could have been referring to her brother Nathanael, to an unknown lover or perhaps symbolically to Sid, who had disillusioned her early in their marriage.

Laura's 1932 diary mentions Hammett only once, but his name comes up in connection with a man called Peter. "Peter called—I dreaded it, Dash gave him the address in spite of my telling him not to." In another entry, Laura writes, "I am 21 now and the two big loves of my days so far are both unsuccessful. Kleban was definitely a failure and with Perel—we are just shambling along with our pocket shamblers." In Laura's diary, Hammett is not among the men she fantasizes about. In fact, contrary to Josephine Herbst's fictional portrait of Laura as a sexually driven woman, there is no concrete evidence to support her theory.

In any event, Laura's relationship to Lillian Hellman remained more or less unchanged following the Dashiell Hammett episode. Sid, rather than Laura, seems to have been the target of Lillian's wrath. It is reported that she was so mad at Sid for telling her about the affair when he returned East that she wouldn't speak to him for an entire year. Lillian's rage was understandable, since the episode was the second contretemps she had lived through with the Wests. She had fallen in love with Nathanael, but he had proved indifferent.

Yet the two women remained friends and enjoyed drinking together for many years.

Privately, Lillian took a dim view of the Perelmans' marriage and felt at the time of their wedding that "it wouldn't last the weekend."

In 1938, about the time Hitler took over Austria, Sid and Laura again were in Hollywood, working on screenplays for two Paramount pictures, *Ambush* and *Boy Trouble*, both released in 1939. Perhaps because they were the only writers on these two films, the screenplays were better than those for films they had worked on with other collaborators. Based on a story by Robert Ray, *Ambush* was a melodrama about a meek man who was actually a bank robber. In an unusual bit of casting, Ernest Truex, long known as a light comedian, played the cold-blooded killer, while Gladys Swarthout, the Metropolitan Opera star, played her first dramatic role as a stenographer who unwittingly gets involved with the bank robber and his gang. *Time* called *Ambush* "A Grade B production which was one of the best shows of 1939,"[38] and several critics praised the screenplay. The *Sun* noted that not only was it tightly written, but that "the wit of the dialogue relieves the implausibility of the narrative."[39]

*Boy Trouble* was a heartwarming, homespun drama about a child-hating father whose wife brings home two energetic boys from an orphanage. The cast included Charles Ruggles and Mary Boland. Donald O'Connor and Billy Lee played the two young boys. Again the film got good reviews. *Variety* said "it steps out of the modest productive groove to surprise in its class. It will find welcome on any neighborhood program and may even travel in faster company where homespun entertainment is relished."[40]

Sid's fame as a humorist was growing. Despite his shy, diffident manner in public, he was thought of as "a personality," and in 1939—the year of the Munich pact and the invasion of Czechoslovakia—WOR, a New York radio station, asked him to be master of ceremonies on a radio quiz show, "Author, Author!" The other authors included Ellery Queen, Carl Van Doren and Ruth McKenney, whose book *My Sister Eileen* was a current bestseller and whose real sister Eileen would soon become the wife of Nathanael West. Each author was given a brief comic or dramatic sequence and asked to fashion an impromptu plot based on it. The idea sounded wonderful in theory, but critics found the show's humor forced. *Variety* noted: " 'Author, Author!' attempts 'Information, Please' humor along different lines and misses fire . . . S. J. Perelman, an established humorist, is the m.c., and apparently thinks that calling one of his guests 'a rat,' or some such flattering term, gets laughs. His guests, in turn, call him 'a rat.' It's unfunny."[41]

The show brought Sid publicity but little money. Again in late November, shortly after France and England declared war on Germany, he and Laura returned to Hollywood. This time they decided to drive cross-country with Adam and Abby, the children's nurse Lula, as well as the family dog. The endless driving, indifferent food and inadequate accommodations got on everyone's nerves. It was with a sense of relief that Sid deposited the children and their nurse at West's home in Los Angeles and took the dog to a kennel, while he and Laura spent a few days at the Hotel Hollywood Knickerbocker. West was then working as a screenwriter at RKO. His mother, Anuta, lived with him.

Sid had never cared much for his mother-in-law, feeling that she was a cold-hearted woman who only considered him and West successes if they made lots of money. Many of West's friends felt that West remained a bachelor because every time he became seriously interested in a woman, Mrs. Weinstein squelched the romance. She had grown quite deaf, but none of the hearing aids the Perelmans brought her seemed to work. Laura appears to have had a love-hate relationship with her mother. She called her often, but usually their phone calls ended in an argument. Yet Mrs. Weinstein was a wonderful grandmother to little Adam Perelman. According to a friend, she treated him "like a little prince," and the boy was devoted to her.

Soon after their arrival in Hollywood, the Perelmans rented a house on Angelo Drive in Beverly Hills for three months and enrolled Adam in a nursery school nearby. They set out to look for work. It took them eight weeks, but finally, in late January of 1940, they were hired by James Roosevelt to work on his first picture for United Artists. The film was titled *The Bat*, and the Perelmans ground out over a hundred pages of screenplay in three weeks. Their efforts were wasted, for the picture was shelved, and Roosevelt's company, according to the trade papers, became involved in other projects.

That winter Sid and Laura saw a lot of Dorothy Parker and Alan Campbell, who were living at the Garden of Allah. The Campbells liked to spend the evening drinking what Perelman called "creolin" cocktails and seldom got around to eating until eleven or twelve at night, a habit that annoyed Perelman, who was never much of a drinker. He asked them if dinner could not be served earlier, but their only response was to exchange nasty comments about him.

The Campbells' habit of involving the Perelmans in their marital problems also irked him. Dorothy and Alan were each prone to taking Sid or Laura aside and telling each one how much they loathed one another. Privately Sid had little use for Alan Campbell, who had an effete manner and a voice he described as being "in the upper register." Behind his back he referred to him as "Just an Old Scold," and wrote a friend he was on the verge of "hitting him with a Mack Truck practically every time I see him."

All his life Perelman had despised homosexuals, referring to them as *feigelich*. That winter he wanted to stop seeing the Campbells, but every time he broached the subject to Laura, she talked him out of it, perhaps because she found the Campbells good drinking companions.

According to a friend who knew both couples well, Sid Perelman regarded Dorothy and Alan as gossipy, bitchy people. He felt that every time he and Laura went to the Campbells, they were drawn into bitchy behavior themselves, which they later regretted. "But they, too, were very gossipy, although not as bitchy and malicious as Dorothy and Alan," the friend added. "They were always picking up on little things that people had said to them and analyzing them."

In February, Sid mailed Bennett Cerf a new collection of twenty-four pieces he had written for the *New Yorker*, the *New Masses* and *Broun's Nutmeg*. He wanted to call the new collection *Look Who's Talking!*, a title Cerf liked, although he thought that the new collection was not as good as *Strictly from Hunger*, which had more "variety," "belly laughs" and "dialogue." Cerf offered Sid the same royalty terms as before, but said that he would prefer not to pay him an advance. If he insisted on one, he would pay him $250. Cerf ended his letter by saying, "I hope you don't mind my being absolutely frank about this matter. All of us know by bitter experience just how well these books of selections sell, particularly when 80% of the material comes from one magazine. There is no use kidding ourselves. I wish you'd take a crack at a novel one day."[42]

In his reply, written less than a week later, Sid pointed out to Cerf that *Look Who's Talking!* should have better sales than *Strictly from Hunger* because he was beginning to develop a large coterie of readers in the *New Yorker*, as well as receiving lots of publicity as the m.c. of "Author, Author!" As for the advance, it was mandatory that Cerf give him one, preferably for $300, which was what he had received for *Strictly from Hunger*. He needed the money, as the movie business wasn't half as lucrative as he thought it would be.[43]

Cerf capitulated, and several days later, Sid received the following note from Donald Klopfer: "I am enclosing two contracts for your signature, having given in on every point that your hard-hitting, clever Yankee mind was able to devise. The 300 bucks is yours, although I hate to part company with any money. Tradition, you know."[44]

Although Sid, when he was in the mood, could be charming and entertaining socially, in business he was a very different sort of man. He could be a tough bargainer, suspicious to the point of paranoia, and rude and high-handed in his dealings, although when one considers the paltry sum of $300 for this brilliant new collection, one must sympathize with his attitude. Later he was paid more generously, but during the course of his literary career, he changed publishers many times both in the United States and in England. With one or two exceptions, he appears to have found all his publishers unsatisfactory. Undoubtedly he was always looking for the big killing, the bestseller that would ensure his financial future, and when his publisher of the moment could not deliver it, he felt cheated and taken advantage of. On the other hand, many of his editors found him to be less than the ideal author. He was not above making a deal with one publisher when he had an unwritten agreement to be published by another.

After *Strictly from Hunger*, Perelman's disappointment with Cerf and Random House became more and more apparent. He kept writing Cerf detailed letters about promotion, advertising and the reviewers he wanted his new book to be given to. Robert Van Gelder, who had lambasted *Strictly from Hunger* in the *New York Times*, must not review the new collection, he wrote. Instead the book should be given to Charles Poore.[45]

He also asked Cerf to send the galleys of *Look Who's Talking!* to Dorothy Parker, F. Scott Fitzgerald and Alexander Woollcott for special endorsements. He had heard that Woollcott had told Dorothy Parker that Perelman was the only humorist who made him laugh aloud. Galleys were sent to all three, but only Woollcott responded with a rather tepid endorsement: "My dear Mr. P: I have read *Look Who's Talking!* with great relish. You make me laugh, which in these times is quite a feat."[46]

Six months later Perelman wrote Cerf that he had seen Dorothy Parker recently and that she had told him she had sent Cerf an enthusiastic blurb for the book which had not been acknowledged. Sid accused Cerf of being ill-mannered and negligent in not using any of his friends' blurbs on the book jacket.[47]

Cerf promptly wrote back, saying he had never received an endorsement of any kind from either Fitzgerald or Parker, and that Woollcott's blurb had been much too weak to be used on the jacket. He reminded Sid that when Random House received blurbs, "we have enough sense, not to mention ordinary good manners, to acknowledge them."[48]

Cerf was undoubtedly telling the truth. For not only did Dorothy

Parker like to eat her dinner at midnight, she also had the habit of telling her friends that she had done them a favor when she hadn't done anything of the kind.

In the spring of 1940, while they were waiting for *Look Who's Talking!* to be published, Laura and Sid went back to MGM to work for Edgar Selwyn on a screenplay for *The Golden Fleecing*. They hated the script, which was dull, and they hated being back at the studio. Laura wrote to a friend that every day Sid wanted to quit and every day she managed to talk him out of it.

Money again was the only reason they stayed. *The Golden Fleecing* was another one of those stories about a meek hero who becomes involved inadvertently with mobsters. Lew Ayres and Lloyd Nolan played the hero and the mobster, respectively. The reviews were discouraging. *Variety* noted that "the picture was handicapped by inept direction of a weak script" and the *New York Times* felt that while the idea had "comic possibilities . . . the scenes are monotonously paced and even Mr. Ayres's querulous performance becomes exasperating after a while."[49] Once again the Perelman writing team had done their best but their efforts had come to nought. All the sacrifices, the draining of energy, the travel and the inconveniences paid off only in discouragement and two checks that were quickly spent.

In April, they were again out of work. They longed to return to the farm in Bucks County but felt they should look for assignments in Hollywood. The winter had been severe, and Laura worried about the trees on their property.

No assignment showed up and in June they went back East by train. They hoped to spend the whole summer in Pennsylvania. Perelman wrote to his friends, Ruth and Augustus Goetz, who also owned a house in Bucks County, asking them to have a local carpenter knock down a wall on the second floor of his house to give the children more room.[50] He wrote that life in Hollywood was far too stifling for kids and maybe a summer spent in Erwinna would be good for them.

And maybe for himself, he might have added. He had gone to the Coast to make money but once more the trip had been a fiasco. He had to find a project that would test his abilities, bring him a lot of money and free him from the endless round of shuttling back and forth from New York to Hollywood. Perhaps *Look Who's Talking!* would do it. Recently he had written Bennett Cerf, trying to persuade him that an early publication would be to everyone's advantage, as many readers were turning to humor to take their minds off the war steadily escalating in Europe. Cerf was amenable, and the publication date was moved up to August.

*Look Who's Talking!* contains some of Perelman's best writing and reveals him at the peak of his literary power. Among its gems are "Somewhere a Roscoe," a takeoff on pulp detective fiction. It begins:

> This is the story of a mind that found itself. About two years ago I was moody, discontented, restless, almost a character in a Russian novel. I used to lie on my bed for days drinking tea out of a glass (I was one of the first in this country to drink tea out of a glass; at that time fashionable people drank from their cupped hands). Underneath, I was still a lively, fun-loving American boy who liked nothing better than to fish with a bent pin. In short, I had become a remarkable combination of Raskolnikov and Mark Tidd.

Also in the collection was "Frou-Frou, or the Future of Vertigo," a rollicking satire on Diana Vreeland's famous "Why Don't You?" column in *Harper's Bazaar*. Miss Vreeland's column, which she started writing on a free-lance basis in 1936, was like no other advice column ever written. Mixing snobbishness and exotic fantasy, it asked its readers such questions as "Why don't you turn your old ermine coat into a bathrobe?" and "Why don't you rinse your blonde child's hair in dead champagne, to keep its gold, as they do in France?"

Perelman's answer to this last outlandish suggestion was swift and to the point. He wrote: "After a quick look into the nursery, I decided to let my blonde child go to hell her own way, as they do in America."

Although not the bestseller Sid had desperately hoped for, *Look Who's Talking!* sold 2,000 copies in two months—far more than his previous two books had sold. In fact, Cerf was already planning a second printing. Reviews were good. *Time* compared his humor to hot jazz, surrealist painting and the deranged poetry of Rimbaud. It said his prose was "hard, sharp, bright and cold as a display of surgical instruments" and predicted that if Perelman continued "at the level of his last two books, he will have to be spoken of as one more greatly endowed U.S. author (Twain, Lardner, Crane, Melville, Wolfe, Faulkner, Fitzgerald, Hemingway) who never quite became what seemed to be in him to become. But like all of those he will have delivered enough."[51]

Still, mere accolades were not quite enough for Sid's driving ambition and need for money. What he felt might solve his problem was writing plays. One successful play—one staggering hit—would make all other writing unnecessary. So on their return to Hollywood he and Laura plunged into a play, a comedy melodrama, *The Night before Christmas*. Fired with enthusiasm, they sent the finished product off to George S. Kaufman, their Bucks County neighbor, hoping he would like it and produce it on Broadway. In December, they received the following reply:

"I was all set for a comedy from you people," Kaufman wrote, "and perhaps disappointed for that reason. I think you have done a workmanlike job. But the subject matter does not happen to be my dish. This is just a personal reaction and not to be taken too seriously. Thanks a lot and where shall I return the script?"[52]

# 9

# TRAGEDY

## (DECEMBER 22, 1940)

Our farewell to him at the farm, where he was starting to woo his muse with a few Spartan adjuncts like an inkhorn, a 14-gauge shotgun, and a blooded pointer, took place in an atmosphere of mingled resignation and hope. It seemed a cruel irony to be cheated of the rustic joys we had labored to achieve, and yet, if we were ever to enjoy them, a spell in the Hollywood deep freeze was unavoidable. As for West, his mood was jubilant; he was through forever with the hotel business, with the neurotics, drunks, and grifters he had been called on to comfort and wheedle. He had two tangible licenses to hunt and to fish, and one, invisible, to starve as a free-lance writer. We toasted his future and ours with a gulp of forty-rod, and bidding him Godspeed, turned our faces to the setting sun.

S. J. PERELMAN,
"Nathanael West," *The Last Laugh*

In the spring of 1935, Nathanael West returned to Hollywood. Again he desperately needed money. *A Cool Million*, his third novel, had been both a literary and commercial failure, remaindered six months after it was published.

It was a bad time to be in Hollywood. Screenwriting jobs were scarce, and West could not find work. He had to borrow money from Perelman. To economize, he lived in a run-down hotel called the Pa-Va-Sed near Hollywood Boulevard. It was an unbearably hot summer, and there were brush fires almost every night in the hills. West was sick most of the time, suffering excruciating pain from both gonorrhea and a congested prostate gland. Morphine was prescribed to relieve the pain, but West took more than the recommended dosage. Perhaps it was the effects of the drug—or perhaps it was his own vicissitudes—but his moods fluctuated wildly. The letters he wrote to Perelman during that hot, dry summer seemed like those of a man on the verge of a nervous breakdown. He felt guilty about the money he had borrowed from Sid and saw himself as a failure.[1]

Idle and unemployed, West passed the time talking to the grips, stuntmen, unemployed comics and prostitutes who lived at the hotel. The seamier side of Hollywood life—the world of pimps, gamblers and drug addicts—had always fascinated him. Once again, he toyed with the idea of compiling a dictionary of prostitute slang in his spare time.[2]

Finally, in early January of the following year, he got a job with Republic Studios, the least important of the independent film companies, at a salary of $200 a week.[3] Several months later his salary was raised to $250 a week, which was still one hundred dollars less than he had been making at his job at Columbia Pictures. But West was grateful. Even though he was working for "Repulsive Productions," as Republic was known in the trade, he had a job and could begin paying back his debt to his brother-in-law.

Like the Perelmans, West soon developed a knack for writing a screenplay quickly. During the two years he was at Republic, he wrote close to a dozen film scripts, including *Born to Be Wild, Ticket to Paradise, Follow Your Heart* and *The President's Mystery*. In the hope of getting a higher salary, he left Republic in January 1938 and was rehired by Columbia Pictures. They let him go fairly soon, and after four months of unemployment, he found work at RKO, the smallest of the major studios, at the same salary he had made at Republic.[4]

At RKO, West wrote B pictures. His first film, *Five Came Back*, written with Dalton Trumbo and Jerry Cady, surprised everyone in the film industry by being a hit. But West did not want to be stereotyped as a successful writer of B pictures and returned East to work on a new novel about Hollywood and the Pa-Va-Sed, which he planned to call *The Cheated*. While he was working on it, he collaborated with his Erwinna neighbor, Joseph Schrank, on a play, an antiwar comedy, *Good Hunting*. Schrank had written a hit play, *Page Miss Glory*, and was a screenwriter at MGM. West hoped that *Good Hunting*'s success would enable him to quit the movie business and devote his full time to serious writing. But *Good Hunting* opened shortly after the Munich crisis and the dismemberment of Czechoslovakia; it closed after two performances.

Unfortunately West had invested all his savings in the play. Broke once again, he returned to California and was able to pick up work quickly, at Universal, where he was employed at a salary of $350 a week. At Universal, he collaborated with Whitney Boulton on *The Spirit of Culver* and *I Stole a Million*, based on his friend Lester Cole's original story. *I Stole a Million* got good reviews and was financially successful. By coincidence, it opened at almost the same time as *Five Came Back*, and suddenly West was very much in demand as a screenwriter.[5]

West finished his new novel, which he eventually retitled *The Day of the Locust*, in the early part of 1938. Saxe Commins, Sid's editor at Random House, suggested that West send the novel to Bennett Cerf. Cerf liked the book and agreed to publish it if West would make certain changes. He offered him $500 against royalties and an option on his next two books.

Although West agreed to the changes Cerf suggested, he, like Perelman, would soon be at odds with his publisher. He disliked the dust jacket copy and the catalogue copy, which he felt were misleading, and especially objected to the jacket, which he thought garish and cheap.[6]

*The Day of the Locust*, which was dedicated to Laura, was published in May of 1939. Although many of the reviews were excellent, the book sold only 1,480 copies, and Cerf later wrote West, "By God, if I ever publish another Hollywood book, it will have to be 'My 39 Ways of Making Love by Hedy Lamarr.'"

*The Day of the Locust* is the story of people on the fringes of the movie business—the extras, stunt men, all the ordinary people who have descended on Hollywood in search of fame and glamor. Most of them have become "savage and bitter, especially the middle-aged and the old, and had been made so by boredom and disappointment." Its narrator is Tod Hackett, who, like West, had a "large, sprawling body," and a personality that reflected the author's dichotomies. He, too, was "a very complicated young man with a whole set of personalities, one inside the other, like a nest of Chinese boxes."

Certain critics of West's works feel that he did not write autobiographically. In a strict sense this is probably true. One looks in vain for realistic portraits of his family and friends. Yet his depiction of sexuality and marriage in his two major novels, *Miss Lonelyhearts* and *The Day of the Locust*, suggests that West was well aware of his sister and brother-in-law's unhappy marriage and that even though

130

S. J. PERELMAN

he did not write about them per se, he projected their restlessness, loneliness and compulsive infidelity onto some of his fictional characters. West's men and women are sophisticated, jaded people who are constantly seeking sexual adventures to relieve the boredom of their marriages and bolster their faltering egos. But philandering brings them no pleasure or relief. On the contrary, sex in West's novels is always portrayed as destructive, repellent and joyless.

People who knew West, Perelman and Laura socially were impressed by their closeness. A cousin of Laura's says they were "inseparable" as young people. Thus it is not surprising that triangles abound in West's two major novels. These triangles invariably consist of two men and one woman. One man is the observer of the other two people's conflicts, until he becomes hopelessly ensnarled in his own confused longings and passions and is either killed or emotionally shattered.

West himself shied away from intimacy and commitment and often chose to sleep with prostitutes rather than become deeply involved with women of his own background and sophistication. To commit oneself to one person, to love deeply, was to surrender oneself to the seemingly endless cycle of betrayal, humiliation and suffering in which Perelman, Laura and so many of their sophisticated married friends were trapped. Perhaps it was no accident that when Tod Hackett in *The Day of the Locust* wanders around the sets in the studio, he sees "a Greek temple dedicated to Eros. The god himself lay face downward in a pile of old newspapers and bottles."

A profound despair at man's inability to alleviate human misery permeates West's writing. His complicated relationship with his sister may have come into conflict with his feelings of devotion to Perelman, who was not only his best friend but a man whom he admired greatly as an artist and whose literary judgment he relied on.

But then, miraculously, toward the end of his life, he seems to have been able to shake off the miasmic Perelman influence as well as his mother's merciless domination. He fell in love.

Eileen McKenney was the sister of Ruth McKenney, a journalist who had detailed their adventures in Greenwich Village in a series of articles for the *New Yorker*, which became a bestselling book, *My Sister Eileen*, in 1938. West and Eileen met at the home of Lester Cole in October of 1939. "He had no permanent relationship with a woman, and it bothered him," Lester Cole says. "He tried many, many tried him, nothing lasted . . . And then it happened. Ruth McKenney, an

131

old friend, who had the year before written the bestseller, *My Sister Eileen*, was out for a visit to Hollywood, probably in regard to the sale of the dramatic rights. With her was her husband, Richard Bransten, and of course we invited them and Pep to dinner. How it happened I don't know, but Ruth failed to mention that her sister Eileen was there and coming with them. Imagine our surprise and delight when Eileen and Pep looked at each other, a long, inquiring unmistakable look. . . ."[7]

Two months later West proposed marriage. He and Eileen were married on April 19, 1940, in Beverly Hills. Sid was best man.

In certain respects, West's marriage was similar to Perelman's. Eileen was ten years his junior, as Laura was seven years younger than Sid.

In her short stories, Ruth McKenney portrayed her younger sister as a bubbly, charming extrovert who was very attractive to men. The real Eileen appears to have been quite different, a sad, vulnerable young woman who as *New Yorker* editor St. Clair McKelway told Jay Martin, "made little of herself, definitely felt inferior" and was "sentimental and emotional."[8]

West was Eileen's second husband. She had been married briefly to Morris Jacobs, who worked in radio. Shortly after their marriage, she became pregnant and, after separating from Jacobs, gave birth to a son, Thomas Patrick, whom Ruth helped her take care of in a rented house in New Milford, Connecticut.

In 1939, after terminating an unhappy love affair with St. Clair McKelway, Eileen moved to Hollywood. She worked at the Walt Disney Studios in the promotion and story departments. In Hollywood, she drifted from one man to another, yet her love affairs with a number of well-known men seem to have brought her no happiness. She felt guilty about sleeping around and worried about her son, who seemed disturbed and far too dependent on her. Like Laura, she drank too much. It was rumored that she tried to commit suicide. "At any rate, it was a very desperate life, a very sad case," Boris Ingster, who worked with West at RKO, told Jay Martin. "And all of Ruth's stories notwithstanding—although all that kind of joy bubbled up—[by 1939] the bubble was hollow—there was nothing gay about it."[9]

In *Hunter of Doves*, Josephine Herbst described Noel Bartram's fiancée as "a wisp, a sort of Doppelgänger of his sister . . . who seemed no more than a drawing on a slate scrawled by Nora and by Nora rubbed away."[10] At a party given to announce Noel's engagement,

Joel Baker and Noel's fiancée disappear. But Bartram, in the Herbst novella, like his counterpart in life, is not upset by his brother-in-law's philandering. "And wasn't it curious, too, that Bartram did not so much as censure his friend except in playful terms that only half-concealed actual pride?"[11]

Ordinarily, one would expect the marriage of two people as neurotic as Eileen and West to be a complete disaster. But their relationship by all accounts seems to have been a happy one. Like Laura, Eileen considered West a greatly gifted man. "She was an admirer of his writing, which of course was essential for perfect companionship," Lester Cole says.[12] And West seemed delighted to play father to Eileen's son, whom he now spoke of as "my child."[13]

Soon after their marriage, West expressed an interest in buying another house in Bucks County, and Sid wrote Gus Goetz, asking him to let him know if he heard of anything for sale.

On December 21, 1940, F. Scott Fitzgerald died of a heart attack in Hollywood. A day later, the Wests were driving home from a hunting trip to Calexico, Mexico. West was at the wheel, Eileen beside him in the front seat and Julie, one of their hunting dogs, was in the back of the car. Usually West let Eileen drive, but recently he had grown tired of his friends' wisecracks about his poor driving. That day he insisted on driving the car himself.

Near El Centro, California, there was a stop sign at an intersection, but West evidently failed to see it. A Pontiac sedan was approaching the intersection, and it smashed into West's station wagon as West hurtled past the stop sign. In the collision, Eileen and West were thrown from the car, West onto the highway, Eileen into a ditch. The driver of the Pontiac and his wife were injured, but not critically, and their infant daughter was unhurt.

An ambulance arrived, but it was much too late. Eileen died of a skull fracture on the way to the hospital, West in the emergency room of a skull fracture and cerebral contusions.

West was thirty-seven years old; Eileen, twenty-seven. They had been married nine months.

For Sid and Laura, nothing would ever be the same.

# PART TWO

1940–1970

# 10

# AFTERMATH

## (1940–1943)

As soon as Sid learned of the accident, he flew to California; Laura—grief-stricken and in shock—remained in Erwinna. At the Wests' North Hollywood home, he found things in a state of chaos. Various acquaintances of West were taking advantage of the situation and walking off with the couples' clothes and furniture. In the house were Christmas gifts the couple had wrapped,[1] and an unfinished letter to Sid and Laura about their play, *The Night before Christmas*, lay in West's typewriter. It was probably the last thing West wrote.[2]

On the evening of December 26th, Sid returned to New York on the Super Chief with the Wests' bodies. Sheilah Graham was on the same train with the body of F. Scott Fitzgerald, which was being taken to Baltimore for burial. Although fond of West, Miss Graham had disliked Eileen ever since she had accused Fitzgerald of caring only for the rich. "My attitude was so hostile toward Eileen—although previously we had been friends—that she took her husband away early from our small party," Miss Graham later wrote. "I was annoyed that she dared to die with Nat in a car crash near Encino within the same 24 hours as Scott. They would be going into the unknown together, and if anyone went with Scott, it should have been Zelda, or me—more me I thought at the time, but now I would say Zelda."[3]

A funeral service was held for West and Eileen at the Riverside Chapel in New York City. Eileen was cremated, and her ashes placed in West's coffin, which was buried at Mount Zion Cemetery in Maspeth, Queens.

Several days later, the Perelmans discovered that West's pointer, Julie, had somehow survived the crash. She had been found limping along the road near the scene of the accident. She'd been badly cut by splinters of glass, and the man who had found her had taken her to a veterinarian. He wanted to keep the dog, but the Perelmans successfully petitioned the court to make him give her to them.[4]

For Sid and Laura, seeing West's beloved dog romping about their farm might have brought some kind of solace. But Laura never fully recovered from her brother's death. "Pep's death demolished her," a friend says. "It was the greatest grief of her life." Christmas, which she and Sid always celebrated with a tree and stockings for the children, would always be an especially painful time for her.

Although undoubtedly affected by the death of Eileen and West, Sid seems to have been able to maintain his habitual sangfroid. With one exception, the letters he wrote shortly after the accident give no hint of sadness or depression, nor do they refer to the tragedy in any way. Perhaps he felt that West, who disliked sentimentality, might find any reference to grief distasteful, or perhaps like many supersensitive men of genius, he avoided harsh reality, preferring to live instead in a dreamland of romance, an adolescent fantasy world where death and horror do not exist. He might also have felt that as an artist and head of his family, he must preserve all his creative energy for his work, closing his eyes to experiences that might drain him emotionally.

In any case, the only available clue to the profundity of his grief lies in a letter he wrote less than a month after the accident to West's friend, John Sanford, who had asked him to write a tribute to West for *Clipper* magazine. Sid declined. He wrote Sanford: ". . . I am really so very close to the whole thing that I believe almost anyone who knew Pep well would be better equipped. I haven't any perspective about him, just a dull sense of unreality and shock which I am afraid will be a long while in disappearing."[5]

Later, in the 1950s, he wrote a piece for the *New Yorker*, "Calling All Addlepates," which seems strange, considering the subject matter. Perelman based it on a *New York Times* report stating that since daydreaming was considered the major cause of all super-highway car accidents, the Institute of Traffic Engineers had recommended that special band radio programs, devised by psychologists to keep drivers alert, should be made available to motorists on turnpikes.

Perelman poked fun at the recommendation, but his takeoffs on the possible radio shows the psychologists might devise were limp and without sparkle. Perhaps deep in his subconscious West's gory death at the wheel still troubled him, even though he might have thought he had gotten over it enough to approach the subject obliquely.

Practically, Perelman still continued to look after West's affairs. With fierce devotion he guarded West's literary interests. According to reports, one of the reasons he eventually severed relations with his own publisher, Random House, was his disappointment over the way they handled West's last book, *The Day of the Locust*.

As the years went by and West's novels were hailed as masterpieces by the critics, Sid's guardianship became even more stringent. Suddenly West was a writer who fascinated the reading public—people wanted to know about him. Writers were clamoring to write critical studies and biographies of him. Many had excellent credentials or came highly recommended, but Sid dismissed their requests with more than a touch of paranoia, saying they were parvenus who wanted only to advance themselves at West's expense. Undoubtedly he thought he was protecting his brother-in-law's troubled life from scrutiny, but he may also have been protecting himself and the secrets of his own marriage.

Work had always been Sid's salvation. In the months following West's death, he busied himself with a number of projects. These included his quota of articles for the *New Yorker*, a new collection of essays for Random House and a return to work on the new play, *The Night before Christmas*, that he and Laura desperately hoped would be a hit.

At Erwinna, Sid wrote in an old pigpen which he had converted into a study. West had written *A Cool Million* there. One of West's wooden duck decoys, of which he had had a sizable collection, rested on the desk. On the walls was West's collection of Audubon prints. Outside the window Sid could see the tulip tree that he and West had planted years before. As he wrote John Sanford, who was planning to dedicate a new book to West, "it's good to think that your dedication and this tree will remain to recall him."[6]

Money as always was a pressing issue. He began telling friends "the family bank balance [had] shrunk to a wizened condition only approached by my genitalia." His expenses were heavy during the

139

time of West's funeral, and he had to borrow $150 from Random House against his royalty account.[7] He and Laura finished their play— a farce about some burglars who take over a luggage shop at Christmastime so they can tunnel their way into a bank vault next door— but they could not count on its being produced. Shortly after the first of the year, Leah Salisbury, their agent, had sent it to Al Lewis, the producer, but he turned it down, telling Leah that although the Perelmans possessed extraordinary talent for theatrical writing and he was sure they would eventually write a smash hit, the play was really only a collection of funny anecdotes with no point of view or plot line.[8]

Courtney Burr liked it and agreed to produce it. After successful try-outs in Princeton and Boston, it opened at the Morosco Theatre on April 10, 1941. Ruth Weston starred as the coquettish owner of a lingerie shop, and Forrest Orr played Otis J. Faunce, the mastermind of the mob.

The 1940–41 Broadway season boasted an unprecedented number of hits. In fact, theatergoers were hard-pressed to decide which show to attend first. Should they see Gertrude Lawrence in Moss Hart's *Lady in the Dark* or Lucile Watson, Mady Christians and Paul Lukas in Lillian Hellman's *Watch on the Rhine*? Other tempting choices included Ethel Barrymore in Emlyn Williams' *The Corn is Green*, Peggy Conklin and Albert Hackett in Owen Davis's *Mr. and Mrs. North*, Vivienne Segal and Gene Kelly in John O'Hara's *Pal Joey* and Shirley Booth and Jo Ann Sayers in *My Sister Eileen* by Joseph Fields and Jerome Chodorov, who had based their play on Ruth McKenney's stories.

Although the competition was formidable, *The Night before Christmas* might have been a hit if it had had a strong central story. But Al Lewis's judgment had been correct—the play had no narrative drive—and the critics picked up on this weakness. Almost uniformly they panned the show. John Mason Brown wrote that the Perelmans "have done little more than make a tentative preliminary sketch of the play they meant to write." Although Wolcott Gibbs, drama critic of the *New Yorker*, devoted half of his review to extolling Perelman's talent, calling him "the greatest living exponent of the free-association method as applied to humor," he was also forced to admit that *The Night before Christmas* "isn't quite the play we hoped it was going to be . . . The authors are wonderful at thinking up isolated bits and pieces of fine nonsense but, unlike the same material in the hands of

Mr. Kaufman or Mr. Abbott, these are never made a structural part of the play, essential to its movement."[9]

Nearly all the critics agreed that the play's best feature derived from the playwrights' amusing use of underworld slang and was at its worst when it tried to be sane or sentimental.[10] Like George S. Kaufman, Perelman found love scenes tedious, and as Wolcott Gibbs pointed out, it was "as if he had written them off rather rapidly, conceivably on a train." The acting and directing also struck many reviewers as inept and slow-footed, lacking the kind of pace that comedy demands.

*The Night before Christmas* closed on April 27, 1941, after a run of twenty-two performances.[11]

Deeply discouraged, Sid must have been gratified by William Saroyan's belated support. In an article in the *Sunday Herald Tribune* appearing on the day the play closed, Saroyan commented on the Drama Critics' Circle Award:

> I wish they had made the award to these plays, without order: "Watch on the Rhine," "Pal Joey," "Native Son" and for good reasons, "The Night before Christmas." The reasons are that this play is new theatre— the error was that it was presented as if it were old theatre. Perelman should have staged the play. Writers like that have got to understand that the stage is the medium of expression and communication when one writes a play. This is going to be a natural development of method in the American theatre.[12]

Some people thought that *The Night before Christmas* would make a good B picture, and Leah Salisbury, eager to salvage what she could from its demise, tried to sell the film rights to Abbott and Costello, W. C. Fields, Wallace Beery, Edward Arnold and the Marx Brothers. The Perelmans sent personal telegrams to Fields and Beery, but neither was interested in buying the property.

One of Leah's friends was Gladys Robinson, wife of actor Edward G. Robinson. Evidently Mrs. Robinson was instrumental in picking her husband's scripts and shortly before the play closed, Leah wrote her a letter, suggesting that *The Night before Christmas* would make a wonderful vehicle for Robinson. In her letter Leah stressed that the part of Faunce, the mobster, would be a natural for her husband, who was famous for gangster roles, but that Mrs. Robinson must act quickly before Paramount, which had financed half the play, snapped up the film rights.

This ploy succeeded. Very soon thereafter Gladys Robinson sent Miss Salisbury a telegram stating that Warner Brothers wanted to buy the play for her husband.

Retitled *Larceny, Inc.*, the movie was released in April 1942. Produced by Hal Wallis and directed by Lloyd Bacon, it featured several performers who later became well-known. Among them were Broderick Crawford, Jackie Gleason, Jack Carson, Anthony Quinn and a blonde comedienne named Jane Wyman.

Critically, *Larceny, Inc.* met pretty much the same fate as the play on which it was based. Although the Perelmans had nothing to do with the screenplay, reviewers complained that the movie version had the same faults as *The Night before Christmas*.

Unlike most of the films Sid and Laura wrote in the thirties and early forties, *Larceny, Inc.* is occasionally shown today, largely because of the many actors in the cast who were in the early stages of their careers and also because certain critics regard it as one of Robinson's funniest films.[13]


In November of 1941, the Perelmans were back in Hollywood, hard at work. Represented formerly by Sam Jaffe, they had a new agent, H. N. Swanson, who had edited *College Humor* and was now working in association with Leah Salisbury. As soon as they arrived in Hollywood, Swanson landed them an assignment to work at Columbia Pictures on an original musical for Gregory Ratoff. Sid hated the treatment they wrote, calling it "purest cat vomit" and "a cesspool of a script." This job was complicated by the fact that Ratoff was directing two other pictures at 20th Century–Fox and seemed to have no idea—or even interest—in their musical. On the personal side, Sid found Hollywood as distasteful as ever. He was disgusted by the movie colony's apparent indifference to the war and complained to a friend that people seemed more interested in discussing some deal than in what was happening at the front.

Dorothy Parker and Alan Campbell were also in Hollywood, staying at the Garden of Allah. Alan was working on a film with Helene Deutsch; Dorothy was collaborating with Herman Mankiewicz and Jo Swerling on a projected life of Lou Gehrig. The Campbells' quarrels were incessant, and Dorothy was drinking so heavily she had to be admitted to a sanatorium. She threatened to divorce Alan and go back East, but the Perelmans, again playing the role of peacemakers, persuaded the couple to patch things up, and Dorothy returned home after being discharged from the sanatorium.

Many of Perelman's essays for the *New Yorker* contained playlets, and when Sid returned East, he revised several of the funniest ones into dramatic form in the hope that he could sell them as revue material. Leah Salisbury circulated these for him. They included a reworking of "Tomorrow—Fairly Cloudy" and "Thunder over Hollywood," but Billy Rose, Harry Kaufman and Philip Loeb were uninterested.

Sid was somewhat more successful in selling original material to comedians. Larry Adler, a young, slender harmonica virtuoso who played frequently on the radio, had decided to revamp his nightclub act and to include some banter between numbers. In the spring of 1942, he engaged Perelman to write material for him.

Sid wrote six spots for Adler, of which the third, delivered just before Adler performed "Daddy," is a good example of his work in the genre:

Thank you. You may not think an obscene little instrument like the harmonica has a long and distinguished history, but people often come from as far as ten feet around to ask me about it. The first reference found to the harmonica in this country is in Falcorni's travel diary of his trip to America in 1837. (I personally have never read it—I have better things to do.) On May 16th Falcorni wrote from Cincinnati: "Last night a whole cucumber lodged in my throat and I tried to dissolve it with whiskey. Today I have a very bad hangover, and to make matters worse, some creep in the next room is playing the harmonica." Obviously Falcorni didn't know what he was talking about, as the harmonica wasn't perfected until twelve years later. The next reference we find is from Mrs. Gasket, whose notorious affair with Lundigan, the Belfast Thrush, is described by Arthur Citron in *Thirty Years a Clusk*. Mrs. Gasket saw a harmonica in Savannah and threw a handkerchief over it, but it vanished. Mrs. Gasket also vanished, though a woman answering her description was later seen in a Turkish bath on 45th Street. She had a cucumber lodged in her throat and was attempting to dissolve it with whiskey. The earliest reliable authority, though, is believed to be Pfalzheim, circa 1885, who says: "Discovered a harmonica today in my laundry." Pfalzheim was one of those types who were always going around

143

discovering things of this sort. One of the things he didn't discover, however, was the boil in the middle of his back which afterward laid him in his grave. Boy oh boy, that little pimple certainly made a monkey out of Pfalzheim.

As far as we know—and we know practically nothing—the principle of the harmonica was evolved by a man in New Jersey named Tolstoy (Jack Tolstoy, not the famous novelist of the same name). Tolstoy found that by stretching tissue paper across a bedspring and blowing through it, you could go crazy in a very short space of time. The only trouble with the invention was that it was too bulky. People wanted a small portable contraption they could bring around to parties, something that would drive other people crazy as well. Out of this need grew the accordion, which is really the parent instrument of the harmonica. The accordion had three distinct offshoots: on one side the concertina and the harmonica, on the other a man named Frisbie who lives in Corpus Christi, Texas. I myself happen to be something of a virtuoso on both the accordion and the concertina, and to tell the truth I'm not so bad on Frisbie either. Matter of fact, those who have heard me play Frisbie claim I can practically make him talk, which is more than *Mrs.* Frisbie can do. She says he just sits there behind his newspaper, like the cat got his tongue.

And now that you have a working knowledge of the history and development of the harmonica that Deems Taylor would give his left baton for, to say nothing of a blinding headache, I'd like to play a stave or two. Here is a quaint 18th-century tune as fragile and lovely in its way as a bit of Dresden china. Ladies and gentlemen—"Daddy."[14]

Unfortunately, Perelman had an altercation with Adler about the fee. Adler claimed that he had used very little of the material in his nightclub tour, contending that audiences found him far funnier when he ad-libbed.[15]

Sid was furious when he learned this. Adler's complaint was the same as that of Groucho Marx—that Perelman's language was too highly flavored and literary to be mistaken for natural, ad-libbed dialogue. In an irate letter to Leah Salisbury, Sid accused Adler not only of being too inept a comedian to carry off his material but also of lying to him when he said he wasn't using his spots. He instructed Salisbury to tell Adler to stop using his material immediately and to pay him for the times that he had used it.[16]

However, Sid was too involved in other projects to brood over Adler's slight. He was beginning a series of twenty-six articles for the *Saturday Evening Post*, entitled "A Child's Garden of Curses, or The

Bitter Tea of Mr. P," as well as preparing a new collection of essays for Random House, *The Dream Department*. Again he received a $300 advance against royalties.

Dedicated to the memory of Nathanael West, *The Dream Department* was published in February of 1943. It had a jacket by McKnight Kauffer, an Englishman who had done some jackets for Modern Library titles and whom Sid regarded as one of the two or three great poster artists and designers of his time. As with his previous collections, the book featured pieces that had mostly been published in the *New Yorker*. Among other subjects, they dealt with dentistry, ladies' underwear, the love life of Paul Gauguin and Perelman's Bucks County neighbors, Kaufman and Hart. The two playwrights had become so successful they were being asked to appear in advertisements. An ad for Schrafft's Restaurant had featured "family album" style photographs of them, above the legend: "From Schrafft's Album of Distinguished Guests."[17] The idea of trying to convince people that if they came to Schrafft's, a family restaurant, they would see celebrities by the score so tickled Perelman that he wrote a satire about it, "A Pox on You, Mine Goodly Host:"

> Buoyant the advertisement had been, but I was frankly dazzled by the scene which confronted me. The foyer, ablaze with lights, was peopled by personages of such distinction as few first nights attract. Diamonds of the finest water gleamed at the throats of women whose beauty put the gems to shame, and if each was not escorted by a veritable Adonis, he was at least a Greek. A hum of well-bred conversation rose from the throng, punctuated now and again by the click of expensive dentures. In one corner Nick Kenny, Jack Benny, James Rennie, Sonja Henie and E. R. Penney, the chain-store magnate, were gaily comparing pocketbooks to see who had the most money. . . . As far as the eye could see, at tables in the background gourmets were gorging themselves on chicken giblet-and-cream cheese sandwiches, apple pandowdy, and orange snow. One fine old epicure, who had ordered a sizzling platter without specifying what food was to be on it, was nevertheless eating the platter itself and smacking his lips noisily.[18]

*The Dream Department* was received enthusiastically, and many reviewers were now calling Perelman "the funniest man in America." However, Diana Trilling in the *Nation* felt obliged to point out what she considered two major weaknesses of his humor: His endings were not as skillful as his beginnings; and his pieces, "like most occasional humor, [were] less amusing in mass than . . . taken at one time."[19]

*Time* pointed out: "They are, as Perelman's pieces have been for some years, overformularized; yet even at their most manufactured, they have a surface and a perfection of rhythm which little contemporary prose can touch. At their best, they stand with the best of Ludwig Bemelmans and of James Thurber as a shocking commentary on most of the nominally more solid and earnest books being written in English."[20]

The fake autobiography was a favorite device among humorists of Perelman's time, and following the *Time* review of *The Dream Department*, Sid was inspired to do a takeoff on a typical *Time* summary of his life:

> Button-cute, rapier-keen, wafer-thin and pauper-poor is S. J. Perelman, whose tall, stooping figure is better known to the twilight half-world of five continents than to Publishers' Row. That he possesses the power to become invisible to finance companies; that his laboratory is tooled up to manufacture Frankenstein-type monsters on an incredible scale; and that he owns one of the rare mouths in which butter has never melted are legends treasured by every schoolboy.
>
> Perelman's life reads like a picaresque novel. It began on a bleak shelf of rock in mid-Atlantic near Tristan da Cunha. Transplanted to Rhode Island by a passing Portuguese, he became a man of proverbial strength around the Providence wharves; he could drive a spike through an oak plank with his fist. As there was constant need for this type of skilled labor, he soon acquired enough tuition to enter Brown University. He is chiefly remembered there for translating the epigrams of Martial into colloquial Amharic and designing Brooks Bros.' present trademark, a sheep suspended in a diaper. . . .
>
> Retired today to peaceful Erwinna, Pa., Perelman raises turkeys which he occasionally displays on Broadway, stirs little from his alembics and retorts. Those who know hint that the light burning late in his laboratory may result in a breathtaking electric bill. Queried, he shrugs with the fatalism of your true Oriental. "*Mektoub*," he observes curtly. "It is written."[21]

If his electric bill was high, it was because he was hard at work on a new musical, which would not be a "turkey," but a solid hit.

# 11

## ONE TOUCH OF VENUS

### (1943)

A hush fell over the audience, and had to
be removed by the ushers.

S. J. PERELMAN
"Seedlings of Desire," *The Best of S. J. Perelman*

Ironically, the property that would liberate Sid temporarily from
Hollywood was an out-of-print novella by the English writer F. Anstey. Entitled *The Tinted Venus*, it told the story of a statue of Venus
that falls in love with a mortal who accidentally brings the goddess
to life.

Aline Bernstein, the stage designer, was charmed by Anstey's fantasy and thought it would make a good musical. She gave a copy of
the novella to her friend, Kurt Weill, who was searching for another
vehicle after his success with *Lady in the Dark*. Her instinct was correct. Weill adored the book and convinced Cheryl Crawford, the producer, who had recently staged a successful revival of Gershwin's
*Porgy and Bess*, that it should be her next show.

Miss Crawford got to work quickly. She hired Sam and Bella Spewack to write the book and Ogden Nash, the well-known poet, to
write the lyrics. Everyone felt that Marlene Dietrich would be perfect
for the role of Venus. But Miss Dietrich would not commit herself.
Every time Cheryl Crawford and Kurt Weill visited her elegantly
furnished Hollywood home and started to talk about the show, she
began playing her favorite instrument, the musical saw. Years later
Miss Crawford observed: "I was accustomed to many varieties of
eccentric behavior from stars, but I must confess that when Marlene

147

placed that huge saw securely between her elegant legs and began to play, I was more than a little startled. It was an ordinary saw about five feet high and was played with a violin bow. We would talk about the show for a while, then Marlene would take up the musical saw and begin to play; that, we soon found out, was the cue that talk was finished for the evening."[1]

Eventually, Miss Dietrich agreed to play Venus. Unfortunately, as soon as she was signed, Cheryl Crawford discovered that the Spewack script wasn't very good and she would have to hire another writer. "Ogden suggested Sid Perelman, an idea that appealed to us," Miss Crawford recalled. "Ogden and Sid had known each other for some time and were friends. But we agreed that the only fair thing to do was to tell Bella our decision before we involved anyone else."[2]

Bella Spewack fainted twice when informed that she and her husband had been fired. When she recovered, she was furious and never spoke to Cheryl Crawford again.

Sid was delighted when he learned that Nash had suggested him as a replacement for the Spewacks. He and Nash had worked together briefly at MGM in 1936 on Dale Carnegie's *How to Win Friends and Influence People*. The script was a hopeless mess but the two men soon discovered they had many things in common. Both had become writers after pursuing careers in other fields. Nash had taught for a year at St. George's School in Newport, Rhode Island, before coming to New York and getting a job as a bond salesman. After working in the advertising department of Doubleday, Page and Company, he became a manuscript reader for another publishing company prior to joining the staff of the *New Yorker*.

Older than Perelman by two years, Nash also favored steel-rimmed glasses and conservative, well-cut clothing. He, too, had gone to Hollywood in the early thirties and hated every minute of it.

Since Nash had attended Harvard for a year, he and Sid were able to use the Harvard Club as a place to work. They ground out an entirely new version of the play in the same room where Robert Sherwood had written several of his plays.

A fantasy is an especially difficult form to pull off, but everyone who read the Perelman-Nash script agreed that they had succeeded brilliantly. Out of Anstey's slender idea they had fashioned a charming story in which a statue of Venus, owned by a wealthy art dealer, comes to life when Rodney Hatch, a prosaic barber from Ozone Heights, slips on her finger the ring he has just bought for his fiancée. The fates decree that Venus must marry the man who reanimates her, though the barber loves the shrewish woman to whom he is engaged. Venus gets rid of her rival by exiling her to the moon. But she finds life with the barber in Ozone Heights mundane, and the play ends with her decision to return to her immortal status.

Marlene Dietrich hated the new version of the script. She told Cheryl Crawford that she could no longer even consider the role as the play was now "too sexy and profane." As the mother of a nineteen-year-old daughter, she felt that it would be unseemly for her to display her legs on stage. Nothing anyone could say would make her change her mind.[3]

Other leading ladies were considered—Gertrude Lawrence, Lenora Corbett and the ballerina Vera Zorina, who had recently starred in a Broadway show with a similar theme, *I Married an Angel*. None was suitable. One day Miss Crawford got a call from the agent Audrey Wood, saying that one of her clients, Mary Martin, was available and would like to read for the part. Miss Martin had been a hit several years before in her Broadway debut when she sang "My Heart Belongs to Daddy" in the Cole Porter–Vinton Freedley musical, *Leave It to Me*. After that she had gone to Hollywood and made several films before coming back East to star in another Freedley musical, *Dancing in the Streets*. The show had closed out of town, and Miss Martin was looking for a new vehicle. Although she longed to play the part of Venus, she was not quite sure that she was beautiful and statuesque enough to play it. She felt that her neck was too long and her figure too petite. Her husband and manager, Richard Halliday, tried to change her mind by taking her to the Metropolitan Museum in New York. "So he took me to that huge place, led me to where the statues are, and said, 'Look, this is a Venus.' We must have seen fifty varieties: tall ones, short ones, even one who was noticeably broad of beam. All were marked 'Venus,' " Miss Martin recalled. " 'You see?' Richard asked. 'Each sculptor has his own idea of Venus. They aren't all Venus de Milo.' "[4]

Kenny Baker, who had achieved success as a radio and film singer and actor, was chosen to play the part of the barber. Elia Kazan was the director. An alumnus of the Group Theatre, Kazan had played leading roles in Group productions, including *Waiting for Lefty* and *Golden Boy*. Although he had directed several plays, he had never directed a musical comedy. Agnes de Mille was choreographer. A niece of Cecil B. de Mille and granddaughter of the political economist

Henry George, Miss de Mille, herself a dancer, was well-known for her inspired ballet of cowboy life, *Rodeo*, and her carefully crafted choreographic work in the musical *Oklahoma!* Premiere danseuse of the show was Sono Osato, an exquisite woman of Japanese descent whose remarkable dancing in *One Touch of Venus* helped make it such a huge success.

Recalled Miss de Mille, "Perelman lived down on Washington Square, and we used to meet each other out walking, and I remember just before my husband Walter sailed for overseas for the duration, I think we met in the park, and he gave me a lovely book. He was charming, a rather rare thing. And then he gave me a signed book of his stories. We had known about him, Walter and I. We used to read him aloud screaming with laughter."[5]

Mainbocher, the couturier, designed Mary Martin's gowns. He had never done theatrical costumes before and initially refused the job. But Miss Martin changed his mind when she sang one of the songs, "That's Him," at a private audition in Kurt Weill's apartment. "As Kurt played the introduction . . . I picked up a little chair and carried it over right in front of Main. I sat on it sideways and sang 'That's Him' right smack into those kind brown eyes. . . . When I finished, Mainbocher said, 'I will do your clothes for the show if you promise me one thing. Promise me you'll always sing this song that way. Take a chair down to the footlights, sing across the orchestra to the audience as if it were just one person.' And that's how 'That's Him' was sung for the next two years."[6]

Mary Martin's fourteen gowns for *One Touch of Venus* cost between $15,000 and $20,000, an exorbitant sum for those days. They were worth the expense, however. Every time she appeared on stage in one of Mainbocher's creations, each with a pink silk lining to make her look like Venus on the half shell, the audience burst into wild applause. Photographs of the star wearing Mainbocher's creations appeared in *Harper's Bazaar*, *Vogue* and *Life*.

"Mainbocher taught her about taste, and she was smart enough to learn," recalled Agnes de Mille. "He realized that she had a very long and very beautiful neck so he revealed it and then tied a little black ribbon around it to accentuate it and he found out that she had good shoulders and a beautiful carriage and all of this was stressed and he really engineered those dresses on her in a way with halters and whatnot that were designed for her body, her muscles, her back, and she looked perfectly elegant."

Although Sid could have some very acidulous things to say about the actors and actresses appearing in his plays, he had nothing but praise for Mary Martin, as a person and as a performer. "I never knew an actress with less temperament," he told *New York Times* reporter Theodore A. Goldsmith. "She has the quality that the French call *sérieuse*, a devotion to her work that you wouldn't expect to find in a girl whose performance is as light and blithe as Mary's."[7]

His relationship with Elia Kazan was less smooth. According to Agnes de Mille, Kazan "was not so polite about the book, which was his special province. The authors complained, with some reason, that he distorted their intention.

" 'Their plot!' he moaned with his head on my shoulder. 'Their plot! They have asked me to study their character development! Oh, my God!' and he leaned, rocking with laughter, against the walls of the outer lobby and wiped tears from his eyes.

"This was not quite fair. The plot was, as Ogden Nash said, as substantial as *Puss in Boots*. They wanted style and fantasy. Style is a very tricky business, and the realistic method of the Actors Studio, in which Kazan had trained, proved no help. Our particular brand of nonsense needed a technique as developed and ritualistic as Noh dancing. The authors, nonetheless, behaved like gentlemen and were friendly throughout."[8]

Nash and Perelman also felt that Kazan's "visual sense was not well developed." Cheryl Crawford remembers that "Sid and Ogden had a little run-in with Gadge [Kazan's nickname] over a scene in a bus station. We were all watching the rehearsals in New York prior to the Boston opening, and Gadge stopped rehearsal. The actors were suspended in the middle of the scene, and there seemed to be some great difficulty. Gadge began to stride up and down, scratching his chin, deep in thought. After about fifteen minutes of this, Sid and Ogden began to get nervous and went up to him. This was not a good idea; Gadge was somewhat impatient of interruptions. But Ogden and Sid asked him what the trouble was. After ignoring them for a few minutes, he said: 'Well, I'm trying to think of some business for this scene.'

"Pointing to the script, they said, 'There is over a half page of single-spaced business description for that scene in the script.'

"He stared at the script and turned on them, exclaiming, 'That chicken shit. I never read that. What do you think my business is in being here? I'm the director; I have to think of the business. I never read that kind of thing!' Ogden and Sid retreated abashed to the shadows."[9]

Elia Kazan found Perelman to be a remote and rather morose individual. He says that if Perelman felt that he did not have an eye for the visual, he never voiced that criticism to him personally. In fact, Mr. Kazan says that the first time he ever heard about Perelman's complaint was thirty years later, when Cheryl Crawford's memoirs were published.[10]

By nature a pessimist, Sid was convinced that the show would be yet another "turkey." His presentiments were confirmed at the first dress rehearsal in Boston. Howard Bay, the scenic designer, had draped the top of the stage and the proscenium arch with a gray velveteen drape, which reminded Perelman, as he told Cheryl Crawford, of "an enlarged prostate gland."[11] Some of the costumes, designed by Paul du Pont and Kermit Love, were equally uninspired and needed to be redone before the play opened in New York.

But the worst contretemps occurred on opening night in Boston. Mary Martin was missing from the major ballet in the show, "Venus in Ozone Heights." "The chair on which she was supposed to be seated remained empty while the dancers pivoted around, gestured and grimaced toward nothing whatever," recalled Agnes de Mille.[12] Evidently, during the preceding fadeout, an inexperienced stagehand had moved the flat containing all of Miss Martin's changes of costumes to the wrong side of the stage. "She had searched frantically for her clothes, begging someone to find them. But the stagehands were too flustered to help," remembered Cheryl Crawford. "Mary had to run all the way across the back, as the stage was in full light. Panting and nearly naked she finally located her costume."[13] Then she appeared on stage just before the finale and sat down in her chair and began playing her scene with Sono Osato as if nothing had happened. The audience was totally mystified.

Although many of the Boston reviews were good, everyone agreed that much work had to be done before the show premiered in New York. Perelman, Nash, Weill and De Mille felt so strongly about the costumes and scenery that they threatened to go back to New York unless they were changed. Finally, Cheryl Crawford gave in to their demands; Jack Wildberg, her associate producer, borrowed $25,000 from Lee Shubert to pay for the necessary changes.

There were problems with the libretto as well. Perhaps Perelman's greatest failing as a dramatist was his inability to grasp the difference between humor that was spoken and humor that was read. In Boston, this difficulty surfaced markedly. Many lines that were supposed to get laughs were falling flat.

"George S. Kaufman, who was in Boston working on a show at the time, used to expound with eloquence, charm and sense about the difference between writing and writing for the theatre," Cheryl Crawford wrote. "He would wander in and watch the show from the back now and then during our run. One evening he took Paula Laurence [who played the second lead] to dinner and when he started talking about his favorite subject, Paula, who despaired that some of her funniest lines weren't getting laughs, asked him to do her a great favor: take Ogden and Sid out for a drink and give them the benefit of his theory about the difference between the two literary enterprises. He promised that he would within the next few days. When nothing happened in the show to indicate that George had gotten his point across, Paula asked him if he had talked to Sid and Ogden. He replied that he had and they seemed to understand very well. The next day Sid and Ogden had the occasion to take Paula aside to tell her about his talk with George. Each one of them thought that George was talking about the other, so neither of them did anything."[14]

Undoubtedly Sid resented the playwright's suggestions. His relationship to Kaufman seems to have alternated between good-natured kidding and envy. On the one hand, he delighted in telling the story about the time a real estate agent was showing Kaufman his farm in Erwinna just at the moment when the former owner, Michael Gold, who was teaching his relatives how to use a shotgun, accidentally shot his brother in the instep. Kaufman fled the scene, and it was many months before he could be induced to return to Bucks County to look at property. On the other hand, Sid was both envious and scornful of Kaufman's success as a playwright. One of his most amusing pieces, "Shubert, Shubert, I've Been Thinkin' " (collected later in *Vinegar Puss*), made fun of Kaufman and Edna Ferber's *The Land is Bright*, in which they used at least three separate sets of servants to "tirelessly dish out exposition":

BRIDGET (*flicking a feather duster over the furniture*): Divil an' all, 'tis the beast of burden Oi've become, runnin' upsthairs and down constantly tindin' to the requirements of me employers, the Burleigh Shostacs, as shure as me name is Bridgid, their devoted maid of all wurrk. A hundred and sivinty rooms to take care of; begorra, it kapes a body busy from dawn till dark. Oi'd have give me notice long ago if th' master wasn't such a swate soul, for despite his rough extherior and brusque ways, 'tis the grand ould gintleman he is, and the same applies to Mrs. Burleigh Shostac, though in lesser degree. As for their two childer, Whitney an' Brenda, Oi don't know phwhat's goin' to become of thim, indade Oi don't. Th' young felly's been aroistherin' around till all hours with fly chorus gurrls, refusin' to take his rightful place at the helm of th' vast Shostac industrial empire, and they do say Brenda's head over heels with Grimes, th' new coachman, wurra wurra. *(She exits, shaking her head; a moment later, Uncle Cudgo, the butler, enters, bearing a feather duster.)*

CUDGO *(ruefully scratching his grizzled poll)*: Lawkamassy, heah's a purty kittle ob fish, as sho's mah name is Uncle Cudgo dat's been de devoted family retainuh nigh on fo'ty yeah. Seems lak young Miz Brenda, which Ah done dandle on mah knee as a pickaninny, jist elope wif dat no-'count coachman Grimes, an' to make mattuhs worse, Whitney he gone blind fum drinkin' bad likker. De news done affeck de ole lady's ticker an' she peg out soon aftuh, closely followed by ole Mistuh Shostac, whut succumbed fum a sudden chill he cotched while horseback ridin'. Dis suttinly been a day jam-packed wif incident. *(Bridget re-enters. Her eyes flash fire as she sees Cudgo.)*

BRIDGET: Whisht, ye ould crow, g'wan with yiz! Don't yiz know Oi'm in charge of th' exposithory dialogue?

CUDGO *(blazing)*: Drat yo' impudence, young 'ooman. Ah's been raisin' de curtain an' 'stablishin' de premise ebber sence de plays ob Dion Boucicault, an' Ah ain' gwine countenance no sass fum po' white trash!

*One Touch of Venus* opened at the Imperial Theatre in New York on October 7, 1943, to an advance sale of $100,000. The reviews were generally favorable, and everyone connected with the show knew it was a hit. Although the critics almost unanimously praised Mary Martin, Agnes de Mille's ballets, Sono Osato's dancing, Kurt Weill's music and Mainbocher's gowns, they were divided in their opinion of the book and lyrics. Howard Barnes of the *New York Herald Tribune* said, "When the book is inspired, it is always first-rate. Perelman and Nash have put over some old chestnuts in the humorous line and they are genuinely funny...."[15] And *Newsweek* noted that "everything ... has been arranged by the team of Nash and Perelman with good taste and smart showmanship,"[16] while Louis Kronenberger of *PM* observed that the authors "at their best have delivered themselves of subtler wit than has probably ever graced a musical comedy before."[17]

But John Chapman of the *Daily News* disagreed, saying that the chief shortcomings of the show "were a lack of pace and a surprising lack of humor in the book,"[18] failings he felt could be remedied if Nash and Perelman did additional work. Wolcott Gibbs of the *New Yorker* was even more critical. He wrote: "As far as I can tell, the actual facts are about like this: *One Touch of Venus* isn't another *Oklahoma!* by a couple of country miles, contrived charm not being exactly the same thing as sunny inspiration; the humor provided by Ogden Nash and S. J. Perelman, who are responsible for the lyrics and the book, is neat and expert, but it hasn't the distinguished peculiarity you might have expected and my chum Kronenberger of *PM* to the contrary, it isn't really subtle enough to dazzle Proust."

Another sour note about the quality of the show's book was sounded by John O'Hara, whose musical, *Pal Joey*, Sid had panned. Shortly after *One Touch of Venus* opened, he wrote a friend: "Perelman's show got pretty good notices, but he didn't, which suits me right down to the earth as he said when *Pal Joey* opened that 'it just proves only a Frenchman can write about that situation.' "[19]

Sid had never aspired to write a play of lasting literary value. What he had always hoped to do was write something that would make him a great deal of money; in that respect *One Touch of Venus* fulfilled his personal aspirations. It played for 567 performances before going on the road, and the average weekly box office receipts were $35,000— a lot of money in any day.[20] Furthermore, Mary Pickford and Lester Cowan purchased the film rights for a sum approaching $750,000. After more than twenty years of trying to scrape along as a writer, Sid could at last afford to write on his own terms.

Now that he was the author of a hit musical, Hollywood was trying to lure him back with tempting offers. H. N. Swanson kept asking him to write a costume picture for Bob Hope . . . a comedy with Sally Benson . . . a Danny Kaye film. His asking price—without Laura— was now $1,250 a week, and Swanson and Leah Salisbury were sure they could get even more for him. The executives of one studio, desperate to get him and Nash as a team, sent each of them the same telegram: "Your partner has signed up with us for a long term. How about you?'' But their ruse backfired; Perelman and Nash were working in the same office when the telegrams were delivered.[21]

Even if they hadn't been, Sid would have refused. To him, Hollywood represented compromise, cheapness and ennui. What he wanted to do was stay in New York and work on an idea he was sure would be another hit.

# I2

## PERSONA

### (1944–1947)

I don't regard myself as a happy, laughing kid. What I really
am, you see, is a crank. I deplore the passing of the word
"crank" from our language. I'm highly irritable, and my senses
bruise easily and when they are bruised, I write. It's a strange
way for an adult to make a living, isn't it?

S. J. PERELMAN
to Jane Howard, 1962[1]

Like many humorists and comedians, who must labor every day to
make people laugh, Sid was not particularly funny in person. In fact,
he was quite the opposite. Deeply serious, acutely sensitive and vulnerable to criticism, he was, as he grew older, increasingly irascible
and subject to prolonged bouts of melancholia.

People who met him for the first time were usually struck by his
shy, reserved manner and taciturn behavior. He seldom made wisecracks to strangers, nor did he indulge in idle conversation to put
newcomers at their ease. At large social gatherings he could seem
very uncomfortable and would withdraw into himself and not say a
word. Paradoxically, when he next encountered the same group of
people, he might prove a marvelous raconteur, animated, sparkling,
witty, holding the whole group in thrall.

The memories of Sid's friends reflect the enigma of his personality.

Caskie Stinnett, former editor-in-chief of *Holiday* magazine: "He
was a very small man physically. He held himself very straight. His
face was very grave. He did smile and occasionally he'd laugh, but
this was unusual for Sid. He was not an easily amused person. He
had an enormous dignity which could be confused with shyness. But

157

there was a diffidence there. He had a very definite idea of what was right and wrong, and he could be offended easily."[2]

Philip Hamburger, a staff writer at the *New Yorker*: "He was very complicated and very private. He was so tremendously complicated. You could know Sid well and not know a great deal about him. Underneath his debonair facade was a deeply shy person. He played many different parts. He dressed the part and played the part of a boulevardier, a bon vivant."[3]

Paul Theroux, the writer: "I think that personally, although he was a complicated man, he was one of the friendliest, most balanced social writers that I have ever known. . . . His clothes were dapper without being obviously so. His style covered up the tensions underneath as it did in his writing. Behind the style was a very enigmatic man."[4]

Leila Hadley, a travel writer: "A lot of people thought that Sid was remote and untouchable. He always had a wall. He was always very well-mannered. He was always meticulously clean, neat, tidy and organized. I . . . never [saw] Sid anything but impeccably dressed."[5]

William Zinsser, writer and executive editor of the Book-of-the-Month Club: "He spoke beautifully. He spoke the way he wrote, which is not often the case. His sentences came out perfectly formed, with the recondite reference and the surprising allusion, and the precise social historian's detail, so he obviously thought very carefully. He was one of the last custodians of good conversation . . . of speech. His mind worked very precisely in conversation."[6]

Mrs. Robert Coates, widow of the writer Robert M. Coates: "He was a very romantic person basically. He protected himself against sentiment with wit and self-denigrating humor."[7]

Robert Gottlieb, editor-in-chief of Alfred A. Knopf and one of Sid's editors at Simon and Schuster: "He was very charming and very affable and a wonderful raconteur, a very amusing man, fun to be with, but in my view, a deeply self-involved, selfish and angry person, like many great humorists. . . . He ran away from trouble. He ran away from real emotional or psychic engagement. He was impeccable, but he was not generous."[8]

Frank Metz, art director of Simon and Schuster: "He was very tortured, insecure. I think he was a very difficult man to live with. I think he was vain. As they say in Yiddish, he had a lot of *mishegoss*. I think he was not a giver, but more of a taker. I think it must have produced a lot of strain on his wife. He was not an easy, likeable person and certainly I don't think he was an ideal father by any stretch of the imagination."[9]

Mike Ellis, former director of the Bucks County Playhouse: "Sid was a marvelously funny man when he was the center of attention. He was not a funny man in terms of sitting around a table with ten people. But if there were ten people sitting around a room and you wanted him to tell a story, he was a funny, funny man. It took some doing to get him 'on,' however."[10]

Louise Kerz, theater historian: "He kept his private life private and he kept it quite compartmentalized. There would be whole groups of people who wouldn't know about each other in his life."[11]

Allen Saalburg, the artist: "Sometimes I had the feeling that he was completely cold, but I don't know if that includes love affairs or not. . . . It was hard to know with a fellow like Sid if any love exists."[12]

Betty White Johnston, a screenwriter for the Marx Brothers: "I think he was a great person. I think a lot of people didn't know how really good he was inside."[13]

Heywood Broun published several of Perelman's essays in *Broun's Nutmeg*, a sophisticated—and shortlived—country newspaper he edited and published in the late 1930s out of his home in Stamford, Connecticut. Although widely quoted in leading newspapers, Broun's eight-page tabloid was published mainly for the amusement of its contributors who in addition to Broun and Perelman included Deems Taylor, Quentin Reynolds, John Erskine and Gene Tunney, who had long retired from boxing.

Broun met Sid when he was a guest on Perelman's radio show, "Author, Author!" They became fast friends. Broun's son, Heywood Hale Broun, also greatly admired Sid, who was the only one of his father's friends he got to know well.

When young Broun was drafted and sent overseas, Sid and Laura sent him packages of food and books. They did everything they could to make his life in the army easier, and so he was not prepared for the way they treated him when he returned to the United States. "When I got out of the army, I ran into for the first time Sid's strange mental problem, his up and downness, which was mingled with a little paranoia as dressing to his manic depression," he says. "I guess that I was out of the army for three or four weeks when I ran into him. He and Laura then lived on Washington Square North. . . . The

159

two of them received me like some remittance man who had broken his word and come back from Australia."

Through mutual friends the distressed younger man learned that Sid had decided that Broun probably considered him too old to be his friend. "Emboldened by this, I called him and we had a kind of fairly steady luncheon relationship . . . when he had the studio on 12th Street," Broun recalls. "I had lunch with him pretty near every week, and every now and then I would get a phone call from Laura, saying 'He's in the depths, please call and ask him to lunch, and for God's sake, don't say I told you to call.' So I would call and say how about lunch and those were the tough lunches, where you would try to amuse him and tell jokes and get weak smiles back and it was very hard going, but I was fond of him."[14]

A friend of Perelman's who wishes not to be identified says: "He was a very strange man. I would presume to say if I were a psychiatrist that he had very serious problems. He went into acute depressions which lasted sometimes for weeks, where he simply sat, staring into space and not saying a word, or coming up to the house, sitting there, with people milling all around him, absolutely mute. In the manic phase where he was bubbling over with witticisms, his conversations and dialogue were gems, whether it was over a pastrami sandwich or the result of some other more serious situation."

A woman friend of Perelman's remembers him as being enthusiastic and ebullient one minute and downcast and miserable the next. She says that he once chatted gaily over the phone about the wonderful plans he had made for them both that evening. When he arrived at her house several hours later, his mood had changed totally. He sat silent and morose all that evening and offered no explanation for his lack of communication.

Like Broun and the young woman, Sid's other friends were often puzzled by his erratic moods and mercurial behavior. He could see someone for years and then, without explanation, break off the relationship. The friend would never know what had caused his displeasure.

"Sooner or later you would become 'one of the bad guys,' " a friend recalled. "You never knew what you did to arouse his anger. But suddenly he no longer considered you his friend."

A woman who was his neighbor in Bucks County said: "He was seldom abrasive to anyone's face. He would often rewrite events to suit himself so that he was in the right."

A man who knew him very well said: "He could be perfectly charming to someone, and then as soon as they left the room, say something scathing about them."

I. J. Kapstein and John Richmond, who knew Sid well in his early twenties, do not recall these quixotic shifts of mood, though other classmates remember him as being depressed in college. In any event, his depressions occurred more frequently as he grew older. They could have been triggered by Nathanael West's death. Yet whether induced by that tragedy or by overwork or a biochemical change, his depressions could be incapacitating—so severe that they sometimes prevented him from writing for as long as a year.

"He was quite depressive and you would know it because the articles stopped appearing in the *New Yorker* and then when they started coming out again, you would know he was over the depression," says one of Perelman's physicians who wishes to remain anonymous. The doctor did not elaborate on Perelman's treatment, but several of Sid's friends speak of his having been given shock treatments on at least two occasions, one just after World War II and the other in the 1960s, on an outpatient basis at Columbia-Presbyterian Hospital. Whether these treatments or Lithium helped alleviate his condition is moot, since his medical records have not been made public, but according to reliable sources, as he entered his sixties, Perelman seemed to grow calmer and less prone to the devastating symptoms of his middle years. A friend says that Laura, before her death in 1970, told her that Sid was "on medication both for the manic part and the depressive part of his troubles." According to this same friend, Sid's mental condition "wasn't terribly visible very often on the surface. But if you knew him, it was quite obvious, and Laura said the medication had helped him a great deal in both respects. But in some ways it made him not as affable to other people as he had been when he was in a manic state. You could tell by reading some of his pieces, but it was never terribly blatant. He was just very, very cheerful."

Although Sid stayed married to Laura until her death, their relationship was marred by frequent infidelities. This was partly due to the sophisticated worlds of Hollywood, the *New Yorker*, Broadway and even Bucks County in which they circulated. Adultery was common among their creative friends and acquaintances: Husbands exchanged wives and friends betrayed friends, sometimes out of lust but more often out of boredom. But in the Perelman household there

161

seems to have been more frenzy and deeper disillusionment than were common in their circle. They stayed together and yet created an uneasy home life, a constant sense of tension that could not have made their children happy. Both tried to be good parents—yet the strains and disruptions of Sid's hectic professional life plus their own tortured relationship were much too demanding for serene domesticity. Under pressure, Sid would fly into fits of terrible rage—or subside into gloom for days at a time. Desperate for escape, but powerless to find it, Laura would resort to drink and a few hours of oblivion.

"Adam and Abby were ignored children," says a friend who often saw the family when they spent part of the summer on Martha's Vineyard. "The children were left alone together on the beach all day—day after day—while Sid and Laura were chatting, drinking, being social."

Although many people found Laura a much more likeable person than her husband, others felt that in her own way she was as remote and self-absorbed as he. "She was so lackadaisical, not given to expression or emotion either. There wasn't much love in that family at all," says a man who knew her well.

In his humor Sid liked to give the impression of a frustrated husband who would have been a great success with women if he weren't so homely and his wife so jealous. This, of course, was a false image. He had many affairs, which Laura pretty much condoned, although according to several friends, as time went on, they caused her great anguish, perhaps because he would temporarily find the elusive love she herself was restlessly seeking.

At some point Laura seems to have given up her own dreams of being a writer. Like many frustrated upper middle-class matrons, she devoted herself to running the household, socializing with friends and participating in school and charity functions. She began to paint pictures as a hobby, and what talent she possessed as a writer was now channeled into nurturing her husband's career. If she came across a funny item in the newspapers, she was quick to point it out to him. And she knew how to boost his morale miraculously when he became depressed about his work. "She became almost like his mother, calling me up and asking me to have lunch with him, and I'm sure I was not the only one she called," says Heywood Hale Broun. "She was trying to take care of him."[15]

"Laura always worried about Sid before he seemed to get better," a friend says. "She was always worried when he was working in a little room that he had on Sixth Avenue by himself. She would go down and see him to make sure that he was all right, that he hadn't killed himself or something like that. She was very fond of him."

Sid's affairs sometimes lasted for years, and sometimes they were merely brief infatuations. As a young man, he seems to have more or less confined his infidelities to friends of Laura's or Nathanael West's girlfriends, which suggests he may have felt that he was outsmarting Laura and her brother. "Sid told me that he started cheating on Laura the second day of their marriage," one of his mistresses has said. One wonders why he felt compelled to jeopardize his marriage when it had only begun, especially when his wife was a beautiful young woman of eighteen.

As he grew older, he pursued almost "every good-looking woman he met." These included actresses in his plays, shapely showgirls who were plentiful in the twenties and thirties, the wives of friends in New York and Bucks County for whom he would suddenly develop a schoolboy crush, as well as women he met when he was working in Hollywood studios or pickups he encountered on trains and planes. Beautiful women were his passion. He could not spot a stunning girl at a party or restaurant without wangling an introduction. "With beautiful women he would change chemically in front of your eyes," says a friend. "He would turn into a kind of Groucho Marx character."

"I am what Puritans scornfully call a womanizer. It's sort of a lay preacher," Sid wrote in *Eastward Ha!*

Sid's approach to women was complex. It ranged from an air of Heathcliffian gloom to the sexual high jinks of the Marx Brothers. Like Harpo, he did not hesitate to fondle the breast of some young lady he'd just met. Yet he could also play "the perfect gentleman," all shy good manners and courtliness. Underneath this contradictory behavior lay an obvious insecurity, possibly originating in despair at his unimpressive appearance.

How successful he really was with women is unknown. Some of Sid's friends are under the impression that he had hundreds of affairs; others that he was "a paper lover," whose seductions for the most part were conducted in his imagination. One of his passions was writing women wildly sexy letters. They are brilliantly witty and deliberately titillating—and give the reader the impression that Sid and the lady in question are having a passionate love affair. But this was not always the case. Many of the letters were written to women who were merely good friends, or involved with other men or on the verge of being married. Torrid letters were a romantic conceit on his part, a self-deluding image of himself as a boulevardier that he felt he needed to cultivate because people expected it of him. "As a comic writer, you develop 'a persona' for yourself," he told a reporter once, "and that is what turns into yourself. I don't know who the real 'you' is."[16]

Even Sid's lovers disagree about the extent of his womanizing. One woman, who had been intimate with Sid for many years, said, "He always had to have some girl," while another claimed that Sid's image as a Lothario was mainly fabricated and that there were far fewer women in his life than he led people to believe.

"Even if the relationship was not going on behind closed doors, he liked to have people think it was and that he was a ladies' man," says a beautiful young woman whom Sid took to many parties in the seventies. Although her presence aroused speculation, she, like many other women with whom his name was linked, insists that she was never physically intimate with him.

With women who were actually his lovers, Sid was known to be romantic and solicitous, showering them with compliments and doing them favors. If they were writers, he would offer them helpful suggestions about their work; if actresses, he would do his best to get them a job. His only flaws were his periods of dejection and despair (which he tried to explain to them as being only temporary and having nothing to do with them) and his tightness about money. And at least one woman found it odd that he had no appreciation of classical music, preferring jazz and popular tunes. "It surprised me that he only listened to WPAT, a popular music station, on the radio," she said. But these faults were minor ones; his lovers valued Sid's genius and wit, as well as his discretion, for he never revealed names or details of his relationships to friends. Ultimately, however, his natural reserve and detachment prevented him from remaining intimate on a close, day-to-day basis with any woman. He might appear to be on the verge of a commitment, but inevitably some domestic or professional obligation, or a trip to the far ends of the earth, would intervene conveniently.

Whether he genuinely loved Laura and wanted to stay married to her or dreaded the cost, scandal and certain disruption a divorce would cause is a tantalizing question. Although both he and she seem to have contemplated divorce on many occasions, they never instituted proceedings.

Perhaps Sid's obsession with beautiful women went back to his lonely youth and adolescence, when he had escaped from his drab life on the chicken farm to sit in picture palaces and watch such silent-screen beauties as Jetta Goudal and Louise Brooks playing their parts. The stars had long since grown old and faded, but his devotion to them never wavered. "He just adored old movie stars without knowing them. They put him in an entirely different mood," recalls Allen Saalburg. "His tone would change, and you could imagine there might be a tear or two in his eye. He became very sentimental, which god knows he wasn't. They were all treated with such romantic fervor. He was a changed person. Something good came over him in those times."[17]

Women were not the only recipients of Sid's mischievous—and salacious—letters. He would often end a letter to an editor by asking him what his "prospects for nooky [were] that winter" or urging a male friend to make sure that "the wick is regularly dipped in the soothing natural oils." Once he wrote a letter to one of the most distinguished editors in the history of publishing, informing him that he "was coming into the office to tender you a quick feel. Or, if you prefer, a leisurely one." The editor was vastly amused.

Sid also loved to write his friends hilarious descriptions of odd sexual practices he had discovered. One of his favorites was about a Dutch or German physician named Dr. Jacobus, whom he had read about in a book called *The Cradle of Erotica*. This doctor traveled around Malaya, measuring what Sid liked to call "everyone's whangee cane." The largest that Dr. Jacobus discovered—Sid gleefully reported—belonged to a Sudanese policeman. Once, he was reading a magazine and came across an underwear advertisement in which a rather demented-looking gentleman was measuring a pair of jockey shorts. He tore it out and sent it to a ladyfriend with a note: "Could this be Jacobus?"

Despite his uninhibited fantasy life, Sid decried today's emphasis on sex. He despised writers, male and female, who used four-letter words and blatant sexual descriptions in their work; women who wore men's pants and jackets and hid their hair under tweed and leather caps; and full frontal nudity in films. "The whole idea of full frontal nudity they've gotten to is the absolute opposite of sex," he once said. "The mystery is so much a part of the process. It has been said, often by myself, that the flash of garters in the cancan is far more exciting than frontal nudity because it's the reserve that tickles."[18]

During World War II Sid feared that he would be drafted. He couldn't imagine himself marching around with a gun, which was odd according to Heywood Hale Broun, as he was "a great romantic." Right after Pearl Harbor he trained for six weeks as a medical assistant so that if he were drafted, he would be inducted into the medical corps.

Meanwhile he and Laura were very active in the war effort. When she wasn't taking care of the children, Laura wrote sketches for the American Theatre Wing's "Lunchtime Follies." Sid went on an extensive war bond tour for the Treasury Department from 1943 to 1945. With him as fellow speakers were such writers as Edna Ferber, Louis Bromfield, Glenway Wescott, Kathleen Winsor and Colonel Frank Kurtz, the much decorated combat flyer whose plane *Swoose* was the only one of thirty Flying Fortresses to survive the first American campaign against the Japanese in the South Pacific. On one rainy day in Dallas, when Sid was standing in a receiving line, a woman came up to him, seized his hand and proclaimed, "The rains came— and so did you!" Perelman did not have the heart to tell her he wasn't Louis Bromfield, author of *The Rains Came*.

In 1944 Sid published a new collection of his *New Yorker* pieces, many culled from previous collections. It was called *Crazy Like a Fox* and consisted of forty-six essays. Bennett Cerf gave him an advance of $500 against royalties—a marked step upward from his former advances—and the book was a bestseller, selling 25,000 copies within a few months of publication. A reprint edition of an additional 30,000 copies was planned, and Cerf talked about bringing out a Modern Library edition, offering double his usual royalty rate.[19]

Sid gained a new champion—short story writer Eudora Welty. In her *New York Times* book review, she had nothing but praise for Perelman's humor. "It is highly complex, deviously organized, the work of some master brain being undoubtedly behind it—and is more like jiu-jitsu than any prose most of us have ever seen."[20]

In that same halcyon year, Sid started work on a new musical with his friend Al Hirschfeld, the theatrical caricaturist for the *New York Times*. Although Hirschfeld was not a playwright, the two men were drawn into a collaboration by their similar attitudes toward humor and their love for the theater. Their musical was to be a lighthearted lampoon of the future, depicting certain preposterous events that occur in 2076 when a time capsule dug up on the site of the World's Fair of 1939 makes mild-mannered tree surgeon Solomon Bundy heir to shares of the Futurosy Candy Corporation.

A year and a half later, in August of 1945, Perelman wrote Saxe Commins from Martha's Vineyard, where he and his family spent part of every summer, that after two rewrites he had finished the script.

He had high hopes for this musical, first called *Futurosy* and then *Forty-Five Plus*. Even before its production he counted on its being sold to the movies as a vehicle for Danny Kaye. But *Sweet Bye and Bye*, as it was eventually called, was a doomed project. At least three producers, including Cheryl Crawford, George Heller and Shepard Traube, agreed to produce it, but at the last minute backed out because of casting or financial problems.

Ogden Nash had agreed to write the lyrics, and in April 1945 he and Sid went to Hollywood to try to talk several actors into appearing in the show. Their efforts failed. Aware that practically every producer in New York had turned down *Sweet Bye and Bye* and it had a slim chance of production, Sid desperately wanted a writing job in Hollywood again. By May of the following year, he was berating H. N. Swanson for neglecting his movie interests. Why wasn't his agent getting him an assignment? When he hadn't needed work, there had been plenty of offers, but now, ironically, when he was available, producers were silent. Swanson wrote back that the postwar years were a bad time in Hollywood. Many established writers had been laid off, since there was an immense backlog of pictures still waiting to be released.[21]

Teaming himself up with Ogden Nash might provide a solution to his financial problems, but Nash's price was now $2,000 to $2,500 a week, and Sid was asking only half that amount. To save face, he would have to ask the same salary as Nash—which would then price them right out of the market.

Even with their salary discrepancies, Swanson kept trying to get them work as a team—on a new Deanna Durbin musical, *Up in Central Park*, and Paramount's *A Connecticut Yankee in King Arthur's Court*, which eventually starred Bing Crosby. But nothing panned out, and then Nash signed up for a new musical on Broadway and wouldn't have been able to go to Hollywood even if Swanson had found them something. Swanson began promoting Perelman alone or teamed with Laura. Still, no one wanted them—alone or together.

There were other disappointments for his ego and bank account. The English production of *One Touch of Venus* had fallen through when Mary Martin decided to do a play by Noel Coward. In Hollywood Mary Pickford and Lester Cowan, who had bought the movie rights, were stalling about making the film and talking about selling the property to one of the major studios. But as they informed Perelman, Nash and Kurt Weill, the only terms under which another studio would buy it would be if the authors relinquished their percentages in the property and accepted a flat sum for giving up their rights, which they had no choice but to do.

Produced by Lester Cowan for Universal International, *One Touch of Venus* was finally released in 1948. It starred Ava Gardner as Venus and Robert Walker as the young barber. The screenplay was written by Harry Kurnitz and Frank Tashlin. Only three of the original Kurt Weill songs were used, and these were given new lyrics. The film version lacked the charm of the original musical, and as Bosley Crowther wrote in his review, "A second-rate brand of slapstick has replaced the gossamer style. And the beauty and grace of Mary Martin are missed in Ava Gardner's lankier form . . . somehow we can't get over what a staggering expense was here made of a wonderful opportunity. Result: a cheap, lackluster farce."[22]

*Sweet Bye and Bye* went the rounds for several more years. Finally, in 1946, it was produced in New Haven by Nat Karson. According to Vernon Duke, who did the score, Karson was "better known as a scenic designer than a producer." His major credit appears to have been a production of *Hamlet* at Elsinore. The cast was headed by Dolores Gray, a talented young musical actress; Gene Sheldon, a vaudeville banjoist and comedian; and Walter O'Keefe, who had a popular radio show on which he would recite the lyrics of popular songs against a musical background. Boris Aronson, who had worked on previous Perelman shows, did the impressionist futuristic scenery and costumes. The dances were by Fred Kelly, Gene Kelly's brother.

From the beginning, the show was marred by ineptitude, especially in regard to the casting. Actors were hired who couldn't sing, and there were personality clashes among the principals. But the major problem seems to have been Nat Karson himself, who was a kind man personally, but not a strong enough figure to bring the production together.

*Sweet Bye and Bye* was folk singer Tom Glazer's first major Broadway show. He played a tramp, and he remembers the experience as chaotic.

"I was terribly confused. We had no direction. . . . Nobody told me whether I was doing anything right or not, and I couldn't understand that either. . . . It was very chaotic, and I noticed the other members of the cast thought so too. I remember that all the kids in the chorus and the principals—all they were hoping for was to be seen in New York whether the show was a hit or not. What I wanted to do was the exact opposite—I wanted to run away and hide. I didn't want to be seen. . . .

"At one point my hero, S. J. Perelman, takes me aside backstage and he ushers me into the men's room and sits me on a toilet in a stall and starts giving me a locker room talk. Well, I started laughing hysterically, because here I was sitting on a toilet being given a pep talk by S. J. Perelman, one of my literary heroes. 'What the hell are you laughing at?' he asked in his high-pitched voice. He was always beautifully dressed in Brooks Brothers tweeds, a button-down shirt and foulard tie. 'What are you laughing at? Don't you know $300,000 is riding on this show?' (Today that would be three million.) 'Why don't you take this more seriously?' And I couldn't tell him. I wanted to cry. . . . And I thought, Why isn't the director telling me this? Why is the writer telling me this? Where is the director? . . ."[23]

Al Hirschfeld overheard Sid's harangue in the men's room. "And I sneaked out of there and came up into the sunlight of Philadelphia realizing that we were in deep trouble. That was an incident I shall always remember about Sid and his explosive temperament," he later told an interviewer.[24]

Obviously Perelman, fed up with the failure of other plays he had written, was taking to heart William Saroyan's advice about *The Night before Christmas*. He was taking over the staging himself, sweeping aside theatrical protocol, which demands that the director, not the writer, speak to an actor about his performance.

But Sid was deluded about what worked and what didn't. "In the script there was a joke," Tom Glazer remembers. "The joke consisted of the following. Walter O'Keefe, [as] an advertising executive, wakes up in a futuristic period, and he says to his butler . . . as he is having coffee and breakfast in bed, 'Read me Brooks Atkinson's review of the play last night. *The Times* is over there,' or something like that. So the butler goes over, picks up the *New York Times* and he reads—

and there is a silence for about fifteen seconds, which is a long time on the stage—'Atkinson says,' and he puts down the paper and turns to the audience. 'Atkinson says *Feh!*' Nobody laughed. Nobody knew what the word meant [Yiddish for "It stinks!"].

"Well, you would think they would take out the gag, but Perelman insisted on keeping the damned thing. . . . My guess is that he must have said in New Haven they won't know what the hell it means, wait until they get to New York, they'll know what it means and laugh at the idea of a Wasp like Brooks Atkinson saying it. It stayed in, and night after night nobody laughed."

*Sweet Bye and Bye* opened in New Haven on October 10, 1946, and Sid knew immediately that the show was in trouble. Gene Sheldon's voice was unsuited to his part, and he would have to be replaced. Then, a week's delay in the Philadelphia opening, caused by casting and transportation complications, cost the backers $25,000. According to Vernon Duke, "Dolores Gray was a tower of strength and stopped the proceedings with 'Roundabout' and 'Just like a Man,' transplanted into Bette Davis's *Two's Company* six years later. But even valiant Dolores couldn't carry the whole show on her back, especially a show as incurably sick as ours was. The real nightmare began in Philadelphia, our next stop. Will I ever forget the ten mad hours in Sid Perelman's suite at the Warwick, in the course of which we telephoned every available and unavailable juvenile in New York, Hollywood, and if I remember right, Australia? Sheldon was eventually replaced by Erik Rhodes, a capable character actor, but hardly a musical comedy lead. The entire structure began crumbling with the dress rehearsal at the Forrest, to which the critics had been invited as our opening coincided with the premiere of an important straight play. . . .[25] For the second week of its 'engagement,' our show was moved to the Erlanger [in Philadelphia],[26] probably the most sinister theater in the world, situated in a street chiefly noted for cheap furniture stores. The inside of the Erlanger looked like a furniture store too—I never saw so many empty chairs in my life."[27]

Undoubtedly Sid felt that the musical was too sophisticated for out-of-town audiences and that it would have been a hit if only it had come to New York. But in the period immediately following the war, there were many more theatrical productions than theaters for them to play in. The Shuberts could literally pick and choose what came into New York. They were not enthusiastic about *Sweet Bye and Bye*, and it was unable to find a Broadway home. It closed in Philadelphia and was never revived.[28]

If Perelman had not achieved his dream of becoming a successful playwright, he could at least take solace in the fact that many people considered him the funniest man in America. Every week admirers scanned the pages of the *New Yorker* and the *Saturday Evening Post*, hoping for a new piece by S. J. Perelman. He continued to write regularly for both publications, and two more collections of his work were published in 1946 and 1947 to critical acclaim. The first, *Keep It Crisp*, contained his famous parody of Raymond Chandler's hard-boiled detective novels, "Farewell, My Lovely Appetizer":

> "Well, you certainly look like something the cat dragged in," she said. She had a quick tongue. She also had eyes like dusty lapis lazuli, taffy hair, and a figure that did things to me. I kicked open the bottom drawer of her desk, let two inches of rye trickle down my craw, kissed Birdie square on her lush, red mouth, and set fire to a cigarette.
> "I could go for you, sugar," I said slowly. Her face was veiled, watchful. I stared at her ears, liking the way they were joined to her head. There was something complete about them; you knew they were there for keeps. When you're a private eye, you want things to stay put.

Chandler adored the parody of his work. He and Sid became good friends, had lunch together whenever Sid was in Hollywood and kept up a warm correspondence. In one letter, written in 1951, Chandler quipped, "I am still reading your brutal account of your family's efforts to keep you from being certified as a lunatic, and by God there are times when you don't speak of them at all nicely. Needless to say, I enjoyed seeing you tremendously, although I realize that the gibbons will always come first."[29]

*Keep It Crisp* also contained satires on Tabu (the "Forbidden" perfume), dental surgery and the world of J. P. Marquand. The Marquand spoof began: "Out of these things, and many more, is woven the warp and woof of my childhood memory: the dappled sunlight on the great lawns of Chowderhead, our summer estate at Newport, the bittersweet fragrance of stranded eels at low tide, the alcoholic breath of a clubman wafted on the breeze from Bailey's Beach . . ." When the piece was first printed in the *New Yorker*, E. B. White wrote Perelman's editor, Gus Lobrano, "The title of Sid's piece, 'So Little Time Marches On' is the funniest thing I have read in the magazine for a long time, and the piece was funny, too."[30]

Another piece, "No Dearth of Mirth—Fill Out the Coupon," poked fun at Bennett Cerf, who was not only the editor-in-chief of Random House, but the author of several popular collections of humorous anecdotes and stories. In his piece, Perelman concluded that Cerf— "Barnaby Chirp"—would be the perfect person to run a new organization Perelman had thought of, the Jape-of-the-Month Club:

> ... at specified intervals [subscribers would receive] hand-culled jokes packed in dry ice, suitable for use in domestic arguments, encounters with bill collectors, visits to the dentist—in short, all the trivial, everyday contingencies that recur throughout the year. Simultaneously, it struck me that the only person in America capable of grasping the magnitude of the scheme was Barnaby Chirp. Brilliant young publisher, writer, book reviewer, anthologist, columnist and flaneur, Chirp had fathered many a compendium of hilarious rib-ticklers. His latest, *Laughing Gasp*, had sold six hundred and fifty thousand copies prior to publication; so well had it sold, in fact, that a first edition was never published. His motto, "Git thar fustest with the mustiest jokes," indubitably made him my man, and I rushed to his office to broach the idea. He jumped at it.
>
> "It's the cat's pajamas—a peachamaroot!" he proclaimed, jumping at it. "Here, let me get this stuff out of the way so we can talk." Turning back to his desk, he delivered two radio broadcasts into a lapel microphone, organized a ten-cent book cartel, wrote a thirty-five-thousand-word preface to *Higgledy-Piggledy: An Omnibus of Jocose Jugoslav Stories* and sold the Scandinavian dramatic rights to *Laughing Gasp* to a small Danish producer in the bottom drawer. "Now then," he said, swinging toward me, "we'll fix the annual membership fee of the Jape-of-the-Month Club at twenty-five hundred a year."[31]

Although Cerf was good-natured about the piece—he signed his Christmas telegram to Perelman "Barnaby Chirp"—the relationship between author and publisher was coming to an end. The day before Sid was to leave for Los Angeles for the start of his trip with Al Hirschfeld for *Holiday* magazine, he had lunch with Donald Klopfer. The lunch was pleasant, and Klopfer says that he naturally assumed Random House would be publishing Sid's account of his journey in book form. It was only after Sid left for Los Angeles that Klopfer learned that Sid, without saying a word to anyone, had signed a contract for his travel book with Simon and Schuster.[32]

Some months later, when he was in the Orient, Sid wrote Klopfer a letter, blaming his defection on Random House, which, he felt, had failed to promote and advertise *Keep It Crisp*. But Klopfer stood firm. He replied that recent sales hadn't been good enough to warrant a major advertising campaign and concluded: "In all seriousness, whether you stay with us or go to any other publisher, you have to trust him and you can't be sniping at him at all times. After all, he is in business to sell books; that's the only way he can make money, so that his interests and yours are identical. In all honesty, I hope to God we can get together when you come back, but I only want it if we trust each other and trust each other's judgment."[33]

But Sid never returned to Random House. For the rest of his life, his books were published by Simon and Schuster. He and Donald Klopfer were not on speaking terms for several years, although as time went on, they were civil enough when they met.

Perelman's paranoia—his fear of someone taking advantage of him— did not confine itself to his publishers. In Bucks County, where he and Laura continued to live part of the year, he adopted an attitude toward the local tradesmen and townspeople that was surprisingly snobbish, given his own working-class background and his father's socialistic ideals. Nowhere were his negative feelings about his neighbors and the people who worked for him more blatantly demonstrated than in his book about the trials of country living, *Acres and Pains*, published by Reynal and Hitchcock in 1947. The book contained twenty-one pieces that had been written in 1943 and 1944 and published in the *Saturday Evening Post* and the *Country Book*. It was illustrated by R. Osborn, creator of the cartoon character Dilbert.

Sid's account was packed with unflattering descriptions of weekend guests and greedy, dim-witted locals, who were portrayed as jacking up their prices when they learned he was a Hollywood screenwriter, raiding his liquor cabinet whenever his back was turned and making disparaging remarks about his property.

The locals were not amused when they read Perelman's book. Although there were exceptions, many of them began to dislike Perelman intensely. They thought him egocentric, tight-fisted, hyper-critical and cantankerous—a man who did not mingle with his neighbors and who had a fit if the girl across the road dared to play her Victrola on the lawn for her dance class while he was writing. They puzzled over why his children were shy, silent and withdrawn and why he never mentioned them as they grew older. Many of them liked to hunt, and they knew he violently disapproved of it. As a neighbor said, "He was devastated for weeks every time he saw a wounded deer or animal." They had liked Nathanael West much better, a man who shared their love of hunting and mixed in their society easily. Laura was also far more popular than Sid. The people of Bucks County found her warmhearted and approachable.

Sid particularly despised Frenchtown, New Jersey, a small town on the other side of the Delaware River a few miles away from his farm. He called it Loutsville and wrote of it in a piece entitled "Plus Ça Change": "Of all the hamlets strung along the watery eastern border of Pennsylvania none, I daresay, offers less sustenance to the eye or spirit than Loutsville. From whatever quarter of the compass one approaches it, one is seized by an almost palpable miasma, an ineradicable conviction of doom. The main street, a somber parade of groceries, lunchrooms and package stores, straggles a scant two blocks from a taproom at one end of town to an alehouse at the other, and the inhabitants, as a rule, follow suit."[34]

In Frenchtown, Sid liked to go into a store and ask for a luxury item, knowing full well that the store did not stock it. He would then become furious at the shopkeeper. One store owner fought back and threw him out of the shop, forbidding him ever to return. For a while, whenever he needed a certain item, Sid would have to drive a good distance to get it or else ask a neighbor to buy it for him in the Frenchtown store that had barred him.

Undoubtedly Laura suffered the most from his war against the local tradesmen. The Perelmans' neighbor, artist Mary Faulconer, remembers Laura phoning her one Sunday afternoon and asking her to read the television listings. "For a certain time?" Miss Faulconer inquired. "No, for the whole day," Laura sighed.[35] The newspaper delivery man, it seems, had been omitting the Perelmans from his daily route ever since Sid had had a fight with him.

"But you forgave Sid this type of behavior," Miss Faulconer fondly adds, "because he was so special."

On occasion Perelman could be solicitous and thoughtful of his employees. Lynn Greening, who worked for Perelman one summer when Laura was in California recuperating from an operation, received one of his books with a charming dedication. When his play,

*The Beauty Part,* tried out at the Bucks County Playhouse, Perelman presented her with tickets, and when Lynn was married several years later, he and Laura attended the wedding and gave her a gift. Lynn remembers Perelman as a kindly, shy and very serious person who hesitated when he spoke.[36]

Lynn's mother, Gloria Scoboria, used to check on the Perelmans' farm whenever they returned to their Greenwich Village apartment. She remembers that Sid and Laura hung clothes and old rags on the clothesline to make people think they were still in residence. "He was a very gentlemanly person who spoke the way he wrote," she says.[37]

In *Acres and Pains,* Sid lamented that "A farm is an irregular patch of nettles, bounded by short-term notes, containing a fool and his wife who didn't know enough to stay in the city." In reality he loved the country. Laura's niece, Maxine Winokur, remembers going on long walks with him when she was a young girl. He would identify and discuss every tree on the property. His love of nature was so intense that he communicated it to her, she says. She vowed that when she grew up, she would live in a house in the country, too.

In his piece on Nathanael West, collected in *The Last Laugh,* Sid reminisced about seeing the farm for the first time with Laura and West in 1932: "Their voices shook as they described the stone house on a hillside circumscribed by a tumbling creek, the monumental barn above larger than the cathedral at Chartres. . . . I grudgingly went out with them to see the place, and in a trice also fell for it. The autumn foliage was at its height, and the woods and fields blazed with color. In contrast to the bedlam of New York, the only sound that disturbed the sylvan hush was the distant chatter of crows in the north forty. There was an air of permanence, of solidity, about the house and outbuildings that captivated and reassured."[38]

But possibly it was more than the trees and wild beauty of the Pennsylvania countryside that drew him again and again back to the land. Perhaps he saw the farm as a symbolic restoration of the lost family farm in Connecticut that had once meant prosperity and status to the Perelman family.

In the winter of 1947, Sid left the farm and he did not come back to it for the next nine months. When he returned, he would be a changed person, with a new perspective and fresh creative vision. For he had lived out a fantasy that had enraptured him ever since he was a poor and lonely young man dreaming of the exotic, far-off places he read about in library books. He had gone around the world.

# 13

## "TO COUNT THE CATS
## IN ZANZIBAR"

### *(1947–1949)*

> I do enjoy travel, or I have enjoyed it very much in certain
> parts of the world, notably the Far East. But the thing that has
> impelled me to travel has been the necessity to seek out situ-
> ations, namely dilemmas and imbroglios of all sorts, and I
> think that's an extension of the very nature of written comedy.
> The comic writer describes impossible situations with which
> all of us deal constantly and in order to find more and more
> material, I have discovered that one has to range farther and
> farther away from home.
>
> S. J. PERELMAN
> to Philip French, 1979[1]

In his lifetime Perelman not only went around the world half a dozen
times but also made innumerable trips to England, Africa and the
Far East. He visited every continent, with the exception of South
America, which he tended to regard as "a collection of banana re-
publics." He traveled for a variety of reasons—to get new material
for his humor, to expand his knowledge of the world and, as time
went on, to escape from increasingly painful domestic problems.

Constant travel suited his restless nature. It also enabled him to
stay married to a woman whose unhappiness at times overwhelmed
him, yet for which he found no solution except flight. He could legally
remain a husband and father, a responsible provider, yet become in
a matter of hours a totally free individual, an adventurer answerable
to no one except himself. As much as he craved the solidity and
permanence of a home, he was also afraid of its suffocating monotony.
So whenever he could arrange it, he was on the move, shuttling back
and forth across the globe. "I'm an enemy of stasis in my own case,"

he once admitted to a friend, adding when the friend reminded him that a family was a form of stasis that "I've been imprisoned by my family for far too long to tell you about it. I try to keep as fluid as possible."

His career provided an easy excuse. Unlike the average tourist who must pay his own way, Perelman traveled free and was well compensated for writing his impressions of foreign countries. Slick magazines such as *Holiday* and the *New Yorker*, and later *Travel & Leisure* and the *Sunday Times* [of London], commissioned article after article on the exotic ports he visited, demanding only that they be written in his inimitable comic style. This new direction in his professional life came at precisely the right time, for after nearly two decades of grinding out humor pieces, screenplays and Broadway flops, he needed a change of pace and fresh material to satirize. Although he still had not given up hope of writing a hit play, he was tired and discouraged after the failure of *Sweet Bye and Bye* and in no mood to start work on another full-scale project. Travel writing was also much more lucrative than playwriting. It paid so handsomely, in fact, that he did not have to depend on Hollywood for any extra money.

In 1946, a week before *Sweet Bye and Bye* folded in Philadelphia, Perelman and Al Hirschfeld had lunch with Ted Patrick, the editor of *Holiday*, at the Warwick Hotel. According to Hirschfeld, "Patrick, an old friend of Perelman's, made the happy mistake of asking him what his plans were after the contemplated opening in New York. Perelman lackadaisically responded that he was going swordfishing off the Florida coast . . . But Patrick insisted on compounding his original gambit of probing Perelman's plans for the future. He asked if Perelman would care to write a piece for *Holiday* about his adventures in swordfishing. . . . [Then] Patrick, throwing reason to the wind, boldly made the proposition that perhaps Perelman could change his plans about swordfishing in Florida, that both of us be dispatched to Hollywood to write and draw something about these colorful natives for *Holiday* magazine. Thus it was that after some additional martinis and insane logical conversation, we were commissioned by Mr. Patrick to go around the world."[2]

Sid had known Al Hirschfeld since 1932 when they met in Paris at the Closerie-des-Lilas. Hirschfeld, whose luxuriant black beard amused Perelman immediately, wanted to do a caricature of him, which Perelman only consented to after he learned that it wouldn't cost him anything. "In no time at all—five minutes to be exact—we were laughing and chatting away as though we had known each other five minutes," Sid recalled.[3]

The two men had much in common. Their mothers were Russian immigrants and both had spent their childhoods absorbed in painting, drawing and sculpture. At eighteen Hirschfeld had become art director to David Selznick and worked in the art department at Warner Brothers before going to Paris to study art. But his fame soon rested on his wonderful caricatures of stage personalities, including the actors and actresses in Perelman's only smash hit, *One Touch of Venus*. Over the years he was to draw many caricatures of Perelman himself, including the famous portrait of Sid reclining on a couch, smoking a cigarette, with a devilish look on his face—a sketch used by many of Perelman's friends in their posthumous reminiscences.

Hirschfeld and Perelman were personal friends as well as professional acquaintances. When he was in New York, Sid would often have dinner at the 95th Street townhouse Hirschfeld shared with his wife, German actress Dolly Haas, and their red-haired daughter, Nina, whose name Hirschfeld liked to hide in nearly all of his caricatures.

Of Hirschfeld, Sid once said, "He loves to dress up like Madame Schumann-Heink in a sea-green ballgown trimmed with Alençon lace and triple rope of pearls reposing on his bodice, which he amplifies by stuffing with tissue paper."[4]

Of Perelman, Hirschfeld once told an interviewer, "What he tries to do in his writing I try to do in my drawing . . . he has a sly kind of crackling inward . . . humor . . . It's much more difficult [to do] in words because a line itself is self-regulating but in words you have to really work at it and he does. He's a very meticulous, hard worker and a great craftsman. For instance, when Sid makes an error on a page he doesn't erase it. He does the whole page over again. He used to drive me crazy on the round-the-world thing because it was in '47 just after the war and it was difficult to get these things back to the magazine. We'd have to go through the State Department to send them and sometimes there were special couriers and planes, and we would get to the base and Sid would suddenly realize that he didn't remember whether he said the Celestial Empire or the Empire of China or what. He said I have to make sure . . . and he rips open the envelope and he realizes he had made an error, goes back to the hotel, types the whole thing over again. Couldn't wait for him to get that thing out of his hands, that script."[5]

In January of 1947, Perelman and Hirschfeld started their round-the-world trip in Los Angeles, where Perelman stayed at the Bel Air home of his friends the Hacketts (he would dedicate his account of the journey to them when it was published in book form by Simon and Schuster). Before he and Hirschfeld left for San Francisco, they had lunch at the Town and Country Market with Aldous Huxley, whom Sid had met when Huxley was working on a screenplay at MGM. Huxley later wrote E. McKnight Kauffer about the luncheon, saying that he hoped Perelman and Hirschfeld's trip around the world would be without incident, as many stops on their itinerary were places where the natives shot white men first and then asked if they were Americans.[6]

Undaunted by such reports, the two world travelers sailed from San Francisco on February 11, 1947, on the S.S. *Marine Flier* bound for Singapore, with ports of call at Chinwangtao, Shanghai and Hong Kong. From Hong Kong, Sid went by coastal ferry to Macao, a city widely touted in pulp fiction as the most sinful in the East. He found it "slightly less exciting than a rainy Sunday evening in Rochester."[7]

On this first trip around the world, Sid's lifelong love affair with Far Eastern art began. Over the years he and Laura had bought some valuable Toulouse-Lautrec posters and some Ben Shahn and Horace Pippin paintings. But he was awestruck by the wonderful collection of Buddhas in the National Museum at Bangkok and overwhelmed by the beauty of the Temple of the Emerald Buddha. Departing from his pose of a harried, gullible traveler, he was willing to "gush shamelessly" about the artists of the East.

Arriving in London in September, he and Hirschfeld attended a revue starring Hermione Gingold, whose style, Sid wrote, "may be loosely described as an amalgam of that of Groucho Marx and Tallulah Bankhead."[8] In fact, he and Hirschfeld were so taken with Miss Gingold that they saw the revue three times and later paid the star a visit in her dressing room.

T. S. Eliot was a friend and admirer of Perelman's work, and Sid had hoped to see him. But Eliot was in the country recuperating from an operation and was too ill to have visitors.

Somerset Maugham was another devotee of Perelman's humor. According to Ted Morgan, Maugham's biographer, Ken McCormick, editor-in-chief at Doubleday, had sent Maugham some of Perelman's books, and Maugham had found them very funny:

179

Perelman had just finished a round-the-world trip, ending up in the south of France. One morning he went to the Hotel Negresco barbershop in Nice to get his hair cut. He was waiting for his turn when he noticed something familiar about the man in the barber's chair, and he said to the reflection in the mirror. "Would that by any chance be Mr. Somerset Maugham?" And the reflection replied, "And would that by any chance be Mr. S. J. Perelman?"

Maugham then launched into a very formal speech of welcome. Perelman, he said, had seen the splendors of the East, traveling the silk road, and had finally arrived on the Riviera. The barber interrupted Maugham's oration to say, "Excuse me, Mr. Maugham, shall I snip out the little hairs in your ears?"

"Please, Maurice," Maugham said, continuing his rotund words of welcome.

"What about these little hairs in the nose?" the barber asked.

"Maurice, how many years have you been cutting my hair?" Maugham asked.

"Twenty years, Mr. Maugham."

"Then why do you have to ask? You always interrupt at exactly the wrong moment."

Thereafter Maugham and Perelman established a friendship. To Perelman, Maugham was a marvelous technician, with a kind of diligence he felt was necessary to good writing. Some of his short stories, he thought, were classics, and *Cakes and Ale* was a model of that difficult genre, the comic novel. "If I were forced by some awful fate to be a teacher," Perelman said, "I would make my students read *The Summing Up* and *On a Chinese Screen*, where there is a section on dinner parties at treaty ports that is so brilliant you can pick it up and admire it like a piece of jewelry."[9]

When he returned to the United States, Sid told Heywood Hale Broun about a beautiful many-armed Oriental statue Maugham had in his sumptuous villa, Mauresque, in Nice. Noticing that Perelman was admiring it, Maugham asked, "Do you like it? I find Jews usually do."

"Sid told me he started to get sore," Broun recalls, "but then he thought to himself, 'I like it and I *am* Jewish.' " Later in the visit the two writers discussed Max Beerbohm, whom they both admired and whose work was out of fashion at the time. Sid told Broun that Maugham suddenly turned to him and said in a flat voice, "Do you expect to be remembered? I don't."

Perhaps in homage to Maugham's famous novel, *The Razor's Edge*,

Sid entitled a piece he later wrote for *Diplomat* magazine "The Adventure of the Razor's Edge." In this inspired parody of a Sherlock Holmes mystery, Sid cast himself as both Dr. Watson and a miserly American millionaire named Saul Petty who has lost a razor blade he has used for 1,100 times and wishes Holmes to recover it.

Published in August of 1948, *Westward Ha!, or Around the World in Eighty Clichés* was a bestseller, selling over 60,000 copies, which was twice the total of any previously published Perelman book. Most of the reviews were highly enthusiastic, although some critics, among them Eudora Welty, had some reservations about the new direction Perelman's humor was taking. In the *New York Times Book Review*, she wrote: "Perelman's prose at its pure best, as everybody knows, is highly concentrated stuff. Every line and word count; it is as deadly accurate, as carefully organized and as impressionistic as high comedy or poetry. When this special stuff is given us in its natural form—the set piece—it is wonderful. But when it's made to cover a world journey, it loses its charms with its shape. When writing that's really a high comic performance has to serve for a long sustained account of a trip, taking us over actual hill and dale and following true-life narratives and the known maps, not to mention keeping two strange characters—Perelman and Hirschfeld—alive and in recognizable human guise before us, then the demand on the prose is not a fair one."[10]

His travel writing was not the only new direction Sid's humor was taking. When he and Laura had visited their friends, the Robert Coateses, at their new apartment in Greenwich Village, Mrs. Coates gave him a copy of E. M. Hull's *The Sheik* to read.[11] He was enthralled. Under the general title "Cloudland Revisited," he began reappraising his feelings toward some of the bestselling pulp fiction that had captivated him in the twenties, a technique he would later apply to the silent films he had seen as a youth. Many of these novels had been published by Horace Liveright, who was known for his love of sensational fiction. They included *The Sheik* ("Into Your Tent I'll Creep"), Gertrude Atherton's *Black Oxen* ("Lady, Play Your Endocrines"), Warner Fabian's *Flaming Youth* ("Sodom in the Suburbs"), Elinor Glyn's *Three Weeks* ("Tuberoses and Tigers"), Maurice Dekobra's *The Madonna of the Sleeping Cars* ("Mayfair Mama, Turn Your Damper Down") and Maxwell Bodenheim's *Replenishing Jessica* ("Great Aches from Little Boudoirs Grow.")

When he reread them, Sid found that these novels proved far sillier and less passionate than he remembered, and his accounts of their convoluted plots and inane characters were among the funniest pieces he ever wrote. Of George Barr McCutcheon's *Graustark*, which he reread one rainy weekend in Martha's Vineyard, he wrote: "Our reunion, like most, left something to be desired. I do not think I had changed particularly, perhaps my reflexes were a little less elastic, so I often had to backtrack forty or fifty pages to pick up the thread, and occasionally I fell into a light reverie between chapters, but in the main my mind had lost none of its vacuity and was still as supple as a moist gingersnap. *Graustark*, on the other hand, had altered almost beyond recognition. During the twenty-eight intervening years, it was apparent, some poltergeist had sneaked in and curdled the motivation, converted the hero into an insufferable jackanapes, drawn mustaches on the ladies of the piece, and generally sprinkled sneeze powder over the derring-do."[12]

The "Cloudland Revisited" pieces he had originally written for the *New Yorker* were published by Simon and Schuster in 1949 in a collection entitled *Listen to the Mocking Bird*. Al Hirschfeld did the illustrations, and the dust jacket contained "An Appreciation of S. J. Perelman by George S. Kaufman," which consisted of the following tribute: "I appreciate S. J. Perelman (signed) George S. Kaufman."

Ted Patrick of *Holiday* wanted Perelman to write more funny travel pieces, and on January 21, 1949, Sid set off on another around-the-world adventure. On this trip he was accompanied by Laura, twelve-year-old Adam and ten-year-old Abby, as well as thirteen pieces of baggage, including four trunks, a typewriter, two inflated Schmoos and Abby's cello.

The Perelmans first went to San Francisco by train, then flew to Los Angeles, which to their surprise was blanketed by snow to a depth of nearly an inch in some places. Once the streets were cleared, Sid took the children to MGM, where they met Lassie, who he wrote a friend was "not a dog at all but a cunning simulacrum animated by two dwarf actors." They also watched Jennifer Jones filming a scene from *Madame Bovary*. Their father showed them the Irving G. Thalberg Memorial Building, where he and Laura had slaved in the thirties. It was now known as "The Iron Lung" by the people who worked there. In Hollywood, he saw his old friends Raymond Chandler, Stanley Rose, Groucho Marx, Harry Ruby and Harry Kurnitz. He also went to several parties, which he found exceedingly boring since the main topic of conversation among the guests, most of whom were screenwriters, was how much they had contributed to various pictures. " 'I did seventeen and one-fifth percent of the original story idea of *Wizened*,' they shouted, 'and thirty-two and five-sixteenths percent of the additional dialogue of *He Shot Her Bolt!* Come on outside, you bastard!' " he wrote in *The Swiss Family Perelman*, which was published in November of 1950.[13] The family soon flew back to San Francisco, which Sid liked better than Los Angeles because he felt it was more cosmopolitan and the people had more character. They stayed at the Mark Hopkins Hotel before sailing on the *President Cleveland* for the Far East.

Perelman did not like American liners, finding them far less atmospheric than the French ships he had traveled on in the early thirties. He missed the smell of garlic and spilled French wine, the hot salt water in the bathtubs and the odor of oilcloth in the staterooms. Of more serious consequence was the fact that he had difficulty working aboard ship. The Perelmans had been assigned two cabins, so that Sid, who required absolute silence in order to write, could work without distraction. But at the last minute, the company switched them to a deluxe suite, and it was only after considerable finagling that he was able to borrow an extra two-berth stateroom. There, every day he wrote his pieces for *Holiday*, which were due in New York on the first day of every month.

The family's first overseas stop was Hawaii, which Sid found disturbingly reminiscent of Southern California. From there they sailed to Manila, which even after four years of peace still showed the brutal effects of World War II. In Hong Kong, the family left the *President Cleveland* and boarded a Dutch steamer, the *Tjisdane*, which would take them to Batavia, Semarang, Surabaya, and Macassar.

Before he left San Francisco, Perelman had had drinks with Somerset Maugham, who was celebrating his seventy-fifth birthday at the home of his stockbroker friend, Bertram Alanson. At the party Maugham, who was quite drunk on Dom Perignon, had made Perelman promise that he would visit Banda Neira, one of the Indonesian islands in the Moluccas, which he had used as background in a novel, *The Narrow Corner*.

In Amboina, Sid made good on his promise and sailed alone to

Banda Neira on an auxiliary schooner of the Moluccan Naval Training Service while Laura and the children went on to Macassar.

In Banda Neira, he was haunted by the cadaverous appearance of the natives, many of whom seemed on the verge of starvation. He learned that even though the island abounded in fruits, and the waters teemed with fish, the populace subsisted solely on sago and grated white sweet potato. An outpost of the Dutch in the 17th century and a prosperous center of the spice trade, Banda Neira had suffered a decline. Its baronial mansions, once the homes of wealthy nutmeg planters, had fallen into ruin, with their beautiful tiled roofs collapsing into weed-grown rooms and their furniture slowly rotting to dust

Sid rejoined Laura and the children in Macassar and the family traveled on to Bali and Bangkok. Although he had loved Bangkok on his previous trip with Al Hirschfeld, he found it very unpleasant now. The weather was murderously hot, and both Adam and Abby became ill—Abby with jungle boils she had caught in the Moluccas and Adam with a badly infected leg caused by scratching a mosquito bite. Perelman himself had a severe ear infection and an enlarged spleen, both of which he managed to cure with large doses of sulfa drugs.

As the trip progressed, Sid began to loathe the Dutch. By the time he left the East Indies, he was positive that his mail was being censored and his every move watched by the Dutch authorities and reported to the government. "Faced with the realization that their colonial empire was coming apart at the seams like a wet paper box," he wrote in *The Swiss Family Perelman*, "that after three centuries of befriending the Asiatic brother, their noses were being plucked out of the feedbag and that their homeland within a few years must again shrink to an insignificant pimple on the North Sea, our Dutch cousins were in a truly fearful wax. By some nightmarish process of logic they had succeeded in convincing themselves that the UNO [United Nations] was responsible for their debacle in Indonesia and hence that we, as American nationals, were legitimate targets for their barbs."[14]

In Sorong, an oil company town on the northwestern tip of New Guinea, Sid was appalled when a pompous Dutch bureaucrat refused to let him and his family venture into the fabulous New Guinea jungle, insisting that they tour the oil installation instead. Sid was so furious he appealed to a local diplomat for assistance. In the end they were permitted to explore a bit of the jungle for which the area was famous.

It proved disappointing, as they saw no wildlife or giant butterflies, merely timber and sentries who checked and rechecked their identities. Perelman was further enraged when after emerging from the jungle he was informed by the Dutch bureaucrat that whatever he wrote about Sorong must be submitted to him for approval. He refused to do this and walked off in a huff.

Much as he disliked the Dutch colonials he encountered, Sid bought two things in Bangkok he would cherish all his life. The first was an English sports car, a natty black and red MG Tourer that he had shipped to London at the end of June so he could drive it on a tour of Denmark, Germany and Holland. "It was a handsome little vehicle, its red leather upholstery a rich contrast to the gleaming black body and smart canvas top, the high curving cowl flowing into the rakish cutaway doors, the dash sparkling with more mysterious gauges, meters, and indicators than a Wurlitzer organ," he wrote in *The Swiss Family Perelman.*[15]

The second was a mynah bird, which he bought in a Chinese firecracker shop for the equivalent of seven dollars. Perelman came to dote on the bird, whom he called Tong Cha, boasting to a friend that not only were mynahs the most accomplished of talking birds, but that when he bought him, Tong Cha was already fluent in both Siamese and English. He could say "So what?" (in Siamese, *"so wah di,"* the standard Siamese greeting), "Hello, hello" and his own name, "Tong Cha," a shortened version of *"Koon TongCha,"* meaning "mynah bird." He was also capable of various deafening shrieks and cackles that did not endear him to the hotel staff or guests.

Like Perelman, Tong Cha soon became an experienced traveler. From his many flights, which he was forced to spend in the cargo hold, he picked up the sound of a propellor plane revving up at the end of a runway before taking off. When traveling by train, he was in the habit of giving a piercing shriek as the train emerged from a tunnel. He also liked to wolf-whistle at pretty women, many of whom thought Perelman was responsible.

Sid soon found himself totally neglecting his writing to clean Tong Cha's cage and make sure he received the proper diet, a fantastic mixture of rice, bananas, hard-boiled eggs and tiny chili peppers.

Not everyone adored Tong Cha as much as Sid did. "Tong Cha was a lot like Perelman," says one of the bird's detractors. "He made horrible noises and pecked at you constantly until he drew blood." But Sid wrote a friend that Tong Cha was "perfect." Unlike fickle human beings, he gave love unconditionally. Sid was the only person Tong Cha would let handle him. He would become almost ecstatic when his master fed him or stroked his head.

His friends sometimes felt that Tong Cha was the only thing Sid ever really loved unreservedly. In 1978, a year before his death, when his friend, the artist Mary Faulconer, asked if she could paint him with his beloved bird, who had died some years before, he leaped at the opportunity. Within a day he brought her many photographs of himself and Tong. He also brought a Chinese jacket and trousers he occasionally wore at the farm at Bucks County. "He said he'd meet me and wanted to hand it to me directly," Miss Faulconer recalled, "so I said, 'Well, you can leave it at the desk at the hairdresser's.' But he didn't. He walked in with this shopping bag, with his porkpie hat on, and came right over, and I had my hair in rollers. I said, 'Don't you dare look at me, whatever you do.' And he kind of smiled and he didn't . . . and then he handed me his Chinese clothes."

Sid supplied Mary Faulconer with information about Tong Cha's diet but she balked at painting chopped egg and substituted a few cherries instead. The color of Tong's water cup, he remembered, had been a "cerulean blue." "He was very serious about the whole thing," Miss Faulconer said. "There was no laughing, no joking."

When Mary Faulconer showed Sid the completed portrait, "he took off his glasses, which I had never seen him do, and smiled and said, 'You flatter me.' "[16]

In order to get Tong Cha out of Bangkok, Perelman had to take him to a Siamese veterinary college where, after his temperature was taken, he was given a certificate of health. With Tong Cha in his cage, which was draped in black cloth in the vain hope that he would not emit one of his piercing shrieks, the family flew to India, Iraq and Turkey, where Perelman became exhausted from having to haggle incessantly with Istanbul's immigration and customs officials, for in addition to Tong Cha, he was carrying sixty-seven cartons of cigarettes he had bought cheap in Hong Kong. But these problems seemed to vanish once he saw Istanbul; he and Laura were charmed by the mosques and the Grand Bazaar.

As Sid was three and a half months behind schedule on his pieces for *Holiday*, he wanted to rent a house for at least six weeks and catch up on his work. A Dutch pilot he had met arranged for him to rent a house at St. Jean–Cap Ferrat, a few miles from Nice. But at the last moment the Dutch owners, imagining the Perelmans were millionaires, doubled the rent and insisted they pay their servants' wages, so the family stayed instead at the Hotel Metropole in Beaulieu-sur-Mer.

Adam's leg still had not healed. It appeared to be dangerously infected. Alarmed, the Perelmans called in several doctors who treated the wound to no avail. Then Perelman heard about a Dr. Spinetta, who had lived in Madagascar as a young man and understood the nature of Madagascan ailments. Finally this French physician was able to effect a cure.

Sid interrupted his writing schedule to lunch several times with Maugham at Mauresque in Nice. Rosamond Lehmann, Cecil Day Lewis, Muriel Rukeyser, Ken McCormick and Colonel and Mrs. Spencer Berger of the U.S. Marine Corps Mediterranean task force were among the guests at these gala luncheons. Perelman also brought the children to visit Maugham. Alan Searles, Maugham's secretary, took them on a tour of the house. According to Ted Morgan, when Adam saw all the exotic objects from Maugham's travels, including stuffed birds from Borneo and African masks in the guest bathrooms, he asked, "What do they do in this place? It looks like some kind of damn movie joint."[17]

Much to the amusement of their father, both Adam and Abby speculated behind Maugham's back on whether he was wealthier than a Mr. Sherfizee of Charleston, South Carolina, who had a villa nearby.

After boarding Tong Cha with an old Parisian lady who owned a pet shop on the Left Bank, the Perelmans flew to England, where they picked up the new MG that had just arrived from Bangkok. Zoos fascinated Sid, and as soon as he arrived in London, he headed for the famed one in Regent's Park. There was still rationing in England, and Sid noted that although beef was practically nonexistent in the stores and restaurants, it was obvious that the "big cats" were eating it, as they looked very healthy. In London, he visited his friends Leigh Ashton, Sidney Bernstein and Professor Solly Zuckerman, a well-known zoologist and friend of E. E. Cummings. On this trip he also saw T. S. Eliot, whom he had missed in London two years before. They had lunch at the Garrick Club, where Eliot told Sid about his trip to Sweden that past December to accept the Nobel Prize.

On July 25, the Perelmans left London for Bath. The trip was not a pleasant one, as Sid and Laura both had trouble driving on the left-hand side of the road. Once, when Sid was tired, he inadvertently switched into the right-hand lane, narrowly missing an oncoming car. It gave them all a bad scare, and undoubtedly was a cruel reminder of West's fatal accident.

In Liverpool, Sid left the MG for a checkup. It would be the first of many, for he would own the car for thirty more years and when he died, it would still be in mint condition. As one friend put it, it was "his baby." He was always fussing with it, worrying about it like an anxious mother with a delicate infant. A symbol of his Anglophilia, it was the perfect car for a would-be British squire. It represented success, glamor and refinement, all the elegance and good taste he imagined existed among the aristocracy. It gave him the illusion of having made it in the Gentile world. Yet there was something obsessive too about the care he lavished on it during the long years that lay ahead.

In August, the family flew to Dublin. The city of James Joyce, his boyhood literary hero, lived up to Sid's expectations. It had an 18th-century feeling that captured his imagination. Joyce, he noted with pride, was becoming one of Dublin's major industries. The city was filled with American college professors writing doctoral theses on *Ulysses*, and there were pubs named after the main characters. Ria Mooney, manager of the Abbey Theatre, gave a cocktail party for the Perelmans and afterward took Sid to call on Jack Yeats, William Butler Yeats's brother. They drank sherry in Yeats's studio and talked about Mark Twain, George Ade and the contemporary theater.

When Sid returned to Liverpool from Dublin, he found to his dismay that the garage had outfitted the MG with ugly bathtub-style grips. He quickly discarded them but they left holes in the dashboard. The family moved on to Chester and Oxford, where they visited the university, although Sid seemed more concerned about the damage to his car than about his tour of Brasenose and Magdalen colleges. He was vastly relieved when the dashboard and speedometer were replaced at a nearby MG factory. At their hotel in Oxford, the sink was stopped up, and Laura managed to unclog it by pouring down the remains of some whiskey she had bought in Dublin. Or at least that was the story Perelman told friends. It is possible that she had started drinking again and dumped the alcohol down the sink at his insistence.

After a tour of Copenhagen, Elsinore, Bremen, Amsterdam, and Brussels, the Perelmans returned to Paris to fetch Tong Cha and spent several evenings with Phillippe Soupault at his apartment on the Rue de l'Université. The Surrealist poet and novelist lived up to his reputation for unconventional behavior by spending part of one evening helping Adam throw firecrackers down the stairwell.

On September 29, the Perelmans, with Tong Cha and the MG, sailed on the *De Grasse* from Le Havre to New York. Although Sid had a good time with the Irwin Shaws and the Robert Standishes, who were also on board, he was eager to get home. In fact, he could not return soon enough. There was a woman in New York he badly wanted to see.

# 14
## "BEHIND A FAÇADE"
### (1950–1954)

Sid fell in love with Leila Hadley the night he met her. The year was 1948, and Jack Goodman, his friend and editor at Simon and Schuster, introduced them at a party at "21" to promote *Westward Ha!* Leila, a petite young woman in her early twenties with catlike green eyes, was the kind of woman he had always admired. Not only was she beautiful and intelligent, she possessed a vibrancy and gaiety that refreshed and animated his melancholy nature.

Leila Eliott Burton was born in New York City but had spent part of her childhood in England and Scotland. She was the great-great-great granddaughter of James Boswell, the biographer of Samuel Johnson. A youthful marriage to Arthur T. Hadley II had ended in divorce, but produced a son, Kippy, who lived with her.

Although Leila had an excellent job as a publicist for the cartoonist Al Capp, she was dissatisfied with her life in New York. "I had wanted to leave New York—not the city, which I loved," she wrote, "but the life I lived there, which seemed to claim from me barely more than an acceptance. I wanted to be a stranger in a world where everything I saw, heard, touched and tasted would be fresh and new, because wonder and awareness seemed to have disappeared from my life, leaving an excessive familiarity with an existence of routine."[1]

Leila brought out the romantic, tender side of Perelman's nature—the part few people were permitted to see. With her he felt free to relax his habitual guard and to talk deeply about his work and his matrimonial problems. Their lunches in stylish French restaurants lasted for hours and at one of them he urged her to quit her job and travel:

190

It was too late to cancel my lunch appointment. I went along to the restaurant and waited morosely for the arrival of a man I'll call James. James [Sid] was late and, having experienced an unproductive morning of work, he was also in a cantankerous mood. We picked at the antipasto and idly guillotined a few acquaintances, and by the time we had drunk two glasses of Orvieto and eaten too much manicotti, we had decided that New York was a hateful place inhabited by hateful people. James, who had just returned from the Far East, was contemplating a trip to Africa.

"I've always wanted to go to the Far East," I said mournfully. "It's one of my favorite castles in the air."

"Well, why don't you go then?" James asked. "At the risk of being a bore, may I quote you something from the last chapter of *Walden*." This was a favorite piece of reading of his, and now one of mine, and I believe he knew it almost word for word. " 'If you have built your castles in the air, your work need not be lost; that is where they should be. Now put your foundations under them.' "

"Oh, James," I protested, "you know it's not as simple as that. I don't have any money."

"You make enough," he said.

"I know," I said wearily, "and I spend it."

"Well, if you take my advice," he said, "you'll book your passage now and worry about money later."[2]

Leila took Sid's advice and set off on her travels, taking six-year-old Kippy along. They headed for the Far East and traveled for two years, spending part of their journey aboard the *California*, a small three-masted schooner manned by four young men from California who had sailed across the Pacific and planned to take the boat around the world.

Perelman's witty letters followed Leila's progress from port to port. They were as brilliantly amusing as his pieces for the *New Yorker* and revealed a man who was totally in love.

He wanted to divorce Laura and marry Leila when she returned. But once back in New York Leila seemed apathetic and depressed:

During the next few weeks I found I had less and less to say. The first question my friends asked was, "Well, how was your trip?" But before I got as far as Manila in the telling, I could see their attention wandering, and after a while I just said, "Fine," and let it go at that. Even James, who had urged me on my way, appeared inattentive, willing to hear about the places he himself had been and no more. It was useless to try to tell him about the schooner. It was plain that he wasn't interested. "Now, what are you going to do?" he asked.[3]

One of the reasons for her listless mood may have been that she had fallen in love with one of the crew members of the *California*, a handsome and well-educated young man named Yvor Smitter. A few weeks after her return to Manhattan, she flew to California and married him. The couple settled in California. Several months later they flew briefly to Panama City to celebrate the *California*'s completion of her round-the-world sail. In November of the following year they had a daughter, appropriately named Victoria California.

Perelman was distraught when he heard about Leila's marriage and new life. Later he seems to have resigned himself to her absence, for he started writing to her regularly again. Whenever they were apart—and they were during much of their long, intense relationship—he wrote her faithfully, keeping her posted on all the latest books, plays and gossip, and proclaiming once more his undying affection.

Leila and Yvor moved to Johannesburg, South Africa, where Yvor went back to school to get his Ph.D. in geology and Leila enrolled at the University of the Witwatersrand. They had two more children, Matthew and Caroline. Despite her busy domestic schedule, she continued to write and Sid encouraged her in her efforts. Leila's book about her adventures, *Give Me the World*, was published by Simon and Schuster in 1958. When Leila asked Sid what he thought of it, he replied, "It left a red ridge on my stomach as I lay on my back reading it."[4] Despite this noncommittal reaction, she was to write many other books on travel, among them *Fielding's Guide to Traveling with Children in Europe*.

Meanwhile Sid's own life continued to limp on. In his comic pieces, Laura, the *memsahib*, as he often called her, was portrayed as a woman who squandered his money on expensive clothes from Hattie Carnegie and took a dim view of his lustful feelings for other women. In reality this was an attempt to make light of what had become a bitter impasse in their relationship. By 1951, their marriage was at the breaking point. He and Laura argued frequently in loud, angry voices that could be heard by their neighbors across the road in Erwinna. By October of the following year, they were ready to part. As a first step toward separation, they moved across Washington Square Park to an apartment in an old Victorian building. It was understood between them that Perelman would soon be traveling or living by himself.

Ironically, that summer he and Laura added a bedroom and bath to their farm in Erwinna and installed oil heat to make the house habitable in winter.

They both agreed that they had a talent for making each other miserable; only their long years of living and working together and their duty toward their children had held them together. After twenty-two years of marriage, they felt they had nothing in common and should get a divorce. But then something happened that made divorce out of the question.

Abby was enrolled at the Putney School in Vermont, while Adam, who had had some academic difficulties, was a student at the Rhodes School in New York, where he received special tutoring. On December 12, 1952, when he was fifteen, Adam was arrested for robbing a Greenwich Village woman of thirty dollars at knifepoint in the hallway of her apartment. For this offense, he was sent to the Cedar Knolls School for Wayward Boys in Hawthorne, New York.

Sid refused to discuss Adam's arrest with even his closest friends. Undoubtedly, his attitude was composed of a proud sense of privacy, anger at his son and a deep sense of guilt. He must certainly have been aware that he had been away a good deal and far busier with his own concerns than with the needs of his son. He also knew that most of his friends considered Laura the more concerned parent.

Mrs. Robert Coates remembers Laura interrupting their conversation once in Washington Square Park to strap up Adam's roller skate, oblivious of the fact that its wheels were dirtying the skirt of her elegant dress. It is doubtful that her husband would have been as solicitous. Like so many temperamental men of genius, he found children tiresome nuisances, which was perhaps the reason he preferred animals and birds. He could slap a cover over Tong Cha when he screeched or put his poodles outdoors if they got in the way. Boisterous children and sulky adolescents were difficult to control, and he took revenge on their behavior in his humor—exaggerating their faults to grotesque proportions. In his essays, children are always portrayed as hooligans, little monsters who can be counted on to disrupt one's life. He called them, among other things, "those part-time chimpanzees masquerading as children." His letters to friends also frequently poked fun at his son and daughter. In a letter to I. J. Kapstein, dated December 17, 1944, he wrote: "Otherwise, life creeps along as always; the kids aren't getting any younger and hull down on the horizon. I see the great day when they'll be old enough to get their working papers. . . . They both go to the same school this year and so far have an unblemished record, all zeros."

With Abby, who was shy and introverted, Sid was capable at times of tenderness and concern. He often bragged about her musical abilities and scholastic achievements. When she was a student at the City and Country School in New York, he even took the time and trouble to write a humorous little essay for the school bulletin, "City and Country, Uncle Fagin of Progressive Schools." True to form, he said in it that he hoped Abby would have a flourishing career as an international jewel thief. In his opinion, City and Country was the only school in New York that offered the necessary courses.

Every spring he would take Abby for a walk around the farm to show her the wildflowers. In the late 1950s, he, Mary Faulconer and Abby went to the Philadephia Zoo, which he liked to visit every year. Sid was driving his MG with the top down, when a large piece of sheet metal flew off a passing scrap-iron truck. If Mary Faulconer had not seen an ominous shadow out of the corner of her eye and yelled at Sid to swerve to the right, and if he had not been able to respond immediately, they would all have been decapitated. Abby was so frightened by the near-accident that she got down on the floor in the back of the car. According to Mary Faulconer, the only way Abby and Sid were able to calm down was to drive to Doylestown for chocolate sodas.

But it was with Adam, who as a young man tried to imitate his father's wit and manner of talking, that Sid' deficiencies as a father were painfully apparent. A friend remembers visiting the Perelmans when Adam, who was about twelve and had a weight problem, came into the living room and took a piece of candy from a box on the table. "Get lost!" Sid snarled at his son.

Perelman's testiness with children was not confined to his own. Although he could write charming notes to the children of women he was attracted to, it could be said that his kindly concern was not altogether genuine. Nothing irritated him more than when a friend brought along a child for a weekend visit to Bucks County, or when a child started banging on the piano or interrupting adult conversation at a party. People who continually talked about their children baffled him. He could not understand why they loved their children so much. Hope Hale Davis tells the story of Robert Patterson, a close friend of Perelman's, who remembered one time when he was cradling

Portraits of
Perelman by
Ralph Steiner,
1935.
*Courtesy of
Ralph Steiner.*

Mrs. Weinstein with West's
hunting dogs the year before his
death, 1939.

Reading some "mulch."
*Courtesy of Mrs. Paul McGhee.*

With Ogden Nash (left) and Al Hirschfeld (right) at a rehearsal of
*Sweet Bye and Bye*, 1946. *The Billy Rose Theater Collection, The New York Public Library
at Lincoln Center, Astor, Lenox and Tilden Foundations.*

Leila Hadley.
*Courtesy of Jean Guy of Paris.*

Aboard ship with Adam, Laura and Abby on a trip around the world, 1949.

Laura, Abby and Adam, c. 1949.

With Tong Cha, c. 1950.

Making friends with a cheetah in
East Africa, c. 1954.

On the "All-Girl Safari," 1954.

Perelman with poodle, c. 1955.
*Courtesy of Mrs. Jean Montague.*

Laura and Sid at the Erwinna
farm, c. 1955.

Laura and cat.

Sophie Perelman (right) and her sister-in-law Sophie Mason in Providence, Rhode Island, 1951. *Courtesy of Mr. and Mrs. Vincent Mason.*

Laura and Abby at the Erwinna farm, c. 1960.

A rehearsal for "Malice in Wonderland," an NBC *Omnibus* television show scripted by Sid in 1959. From left to right, front: Perelman, Keenan Wynn, Salem Ludwig, Dan Tobin; rear: Pat Englund, Julie Newmar and James Lee, the director. *Courtesy of Mrs. Tallman Bissell.*

With Benjamin Crocker Clough (left) and I. J. Kapstein (center) after receiving an honorary doctorate of letters from Brown University, 1965. *Courtesy of Mrs. I. J. Kapstein.*

Perelman and his poodles, Misty and Tartuffe, c. 1960.

Sid and Laura at a neighbor's Christmas party, 1967. Laura died three years later.
*Courtesy of Mr. and Mrs. Joseph Meyer.*

S. J. Perelman in 1979, the year of his death.
*Courtesy of Martha Saxton.*

his small daughter and Sid watched him incredulously. "You're in love with that kid, aren't you?" he asked Patterson in a tone of total incomprehension.

His attitude may partially be explained by the bleak, deprived world of his childhood, which he appears to have coped with by withdrawing into fantasy. Because neither of his parents seems to have fulfilled his needs and expectations, it is not surprising that he never learned to be a warm and nurturing parent himself. He may also have viewed children as competitors for attention. Egocentric, insecure about people's attitudes toward him, he may well have thought that it was he—not some child—who was most in need of praise and affection.

In *Hunter of Doves*, Josephine Herbst offers another possible explanation of Perelman's baffling behavior toward Adam:

> And did they still worry about Bartram [Nathanael West], though he was dead? Oh, Bartram was a man who came to stay, and thinking of Nora [Laura] and Baker [Sid], she knew that Bartram was still living with them. He looked at them, too, from their young son's eyes, so like Bartram's that it had been a shock the first time she had seen the boy, so like the uncle, as he came stalking over the lawn and speaking in the same kind of voice with the same shy grace. That dry antagonism of the father toward the son, what was it except a memory of the thorn? For Bartram had been the beloved, would be so long as Nora had life. Baker had been only his surrogate.[5]

In 1950, after returning from his second trip around the world, Sid decided to collaborate with Laura on a dramatic version of George Orwell's *Burmese Days*. Sonia Blair, Orwell's widow, owned the copyright, and after much effort, Leah Salisbury was able to locate her. In September, the Perelmans signed an agreement with Mrs. Orwell, but by April of the following year, Sid had abandoned the idea entirely. His reasons are unknown. Possibly, they were based on his worsening marital situation, which would have made a collaboration with Laura impossible.

In 1951, he sold a series of travel articles to *Redbook*, dealing with his adventures in St. Augustine, Hollywood, Las Vegas, Sun Valley, Acapulco and a dude ranch in Arizona. It was a bitter experience. Although the editors of the magazine promoted the series heavily and even ran a caricature of him on the cover, they found after the first piece was published that their readers were not as responsive to

Perelman's sophisticated humor as readers of the *New Yorker*. In fact, Wade Nichols, the editor assigned to Perelman, had already made 103 changes in his Florida piece in an attempt to simplify his intricate style. Sid was furious when he read the revisions. He also objected to the way Al Hirschfeld was being forced to alter his illustrations to appeal to the readership's taste. Only the thought that the editors might expand the series to a total of twelve pieces stopped him from quitting on the spot.

But reader opinion continued to be so negative that *Redbook* decided to cancel the Mexico installment. The series thus included only five pieces, not the six Perelman had originally contracted for. He had hoped to make a book from the series, *Springtime for Sidney*, but there wasn't enough material for such a project. He wrote Leila Hadley that as far as he was concerned, the only market for a good writer was the *New Yorker*. *Holiday*, he added, had once been a magazine of distinction, but, in his opinion, it had become slick and fatuous. He deplored the attitude of certain magazine editors who insisted that their readers couldn't understand anything but the simplest prose. Such editors reminded him of the stupid, misguided producers he had worked for in Hollywood.

That year, in addition to his travel articles, he completed a series on comedians for *Holiday*, writing profiles of Groucho Marx, Jimmy Durante, George Jessel and Fred Allen, a close personal friend who shared his love of Chinese food. In June of 1951, after speaking at the alumni dinner at Brown University, he went to Hollywood to interview Groucho on the set of RKO where he was filming *A Girl in Every Port*. As Sid wrote Leila Hadley, most of his profiles of the comedians were a tremendous amount of work as they had to be largely invented. In his profile of Groucho he made a lot of jokes about Groucho's stinginess, but in reality Marx was very nice to him—in fact, nicer than he had been when Sid was working on *Horse Feathers* and *Monkey Business*. He even handed out profuse compliments about Sid's work in the *New Yorker*.

During this visit Sid called on Dorothy Parker, who was living in a beach house in Malibu. James Agee, who had just completed the script for John Huston's *The African Queen*, was her houseguest. By nature neat and fastidious, Perelman was disgusted by their style of living. Although he wasn't romantically involved with Parker, Agee was drinking as heavily as she. "Parker says Agee consumed three bottles of Scotch unaided last Friday," he wrote Leila Hadley. "I

196

didn't get Agee's closing quotations on Parker's consumption. They both exist in a fog of crapulous laundry, stale cigarette smoke, and dirty dishes, sans furniture or cleanliness; one suspects they wet their beds." The atmosphere of the house depressed him, perhaps because it reminded him of Laura's battle with alcoholism. His despondency grew even deeper when he learned that many of the screenwriters he had once worked with were being blacklisted.

On February 24, 1950, Perelman, along with Bennett Cerf, Jack Goodman, Roger Butterfield, John Hersey, Arthur Miller, Elmer Rice and many other prominent publishers, writers and play producers, had submitted motion for leave to file brief as *Amici Curiae* in the Supreme Court of the United States in the case of John Howard Lawson and Dalton Trumbo against the United States of America. Lawson and Trumbo were members of the "Hollywood Ten," screenwriters who were blacklisted for being at one time members of the Communist party. In the brief, Perelman and the others stated that "the kind of proceedings before the House Committee on Un-American Activities involved in these two cases effectively restrains, in ways both direct and indirect, the free creation and communication of ideas. . . . The filing of this brief should not be taken to intimate support or sympathy with the political philosophies, whatever they may be, of the two petitioners before the Court. The decision in question threatens the freedom of those of different as well as like mind."[6]

But their efforts were of no avail. In late June, Lawson and Trumbo were sentenced to federal prison at Ashland, Kentucky, for Contempt of Congress. Before leaving for Kentucky, the two screenwriters stopped briefly in New York to attend a fund-raising party given in their honor by Leila Hadley,[7] which was attended by both Sid and Laura.

Although Sid knew many people who were involved in leftist causes—Nathanael West, Dorothy Parker, Lillian Hellman, Ruth McKenney, Lester Cole and Michael Gold—and had contributed articles to the *New Masses* in his youth, his signing of the brief was one of the few times he was actively involved in politics of any sort. Very little of his humor dealt with political theories or the foibles of a particular politician, with the possible exception of "Waiting for Santy," which was more a parody of Clifford Odets' style than it was of communism.

A Democrat, Sid never blindly supported a candidate simply because he was a member of the Democratic party. Although he was an admirer of Adlai Stevenson, whom he considered intelligent, cultivated and possessing the best sense of humor of any American politician, he could not convince himself, as so many of Stevenson's supporters had, that he was another Abraham Lincoln. This natural skepticism influenced his view of American politics. In his opinion, the Democrats were as capable of dirty tricks as the Republicans. He deplored all the hypocrisy, flag-waving, patronage and sly maneuvering that accompanied every election.

Originally, the editors at *Holiday* had wanted Sid to write a profile of comedian Ed Wynn. In 1952, they withdrew the assignment as they didn't want to pay Sid's expenses to Hollywood for only one piece. Sid did not mind. He was eager to resume his "Cloudland Revisited" series for the *New Yorker*, this time on the old silent films he had seen as a young man—Erich von Stroheim's *Foolish Wives*, D. W. Griffith's *Intolerance, 20,000 Leagues, Way Down East, Male and Female* and *Stella Dallas*. Sid had first suggested the idea to Harold Ross several years before and Ross had been highly enthusiastic.

The Museum of Modern Art had an enormous film library, which it shared with its associated branch, the Eastman Foundation in Rochester. Sid's friend, Monroe Wheeler, arranged for him to use the museum's facilities. As each film was being shown, Sid talked into a tape recorder, describing each scene and the subtitle. A secretary then transcribed his tapes, and he used this material as the basis for his pieces on silent movies, which were among the funniest that he ever wrote.

When James Thurber heard from Gus Lobrano that Perelman was writing a new "Cloudland Revisited" series based on the old movies, he sent Sid a letter, offering suggestions: "Don't miss *The Sheik*, which Helen and I saw in England in 1938. It's damn near as funny as *The Vampire* with a skinny man named Adolph Menjou in it. Don't miss Valentino's eyes popping open at the sight of Agnes Ayres, or the wonderful line 'You can tell he's an Englishman by the size of his hands.' Before the audience got to the last word everybody was screaming. . . . You mustn't miss the old Mae Murray pictures and the worst of the W. S. Hart in which he takes off his hat at the sight of a woman while his mouth trembles and his eyes glisten as if he were watching the immaculate conception. And the women were certainly not Virginia Mayo in them pictures, pal . . ."[8] Over the years the two veteran humorists occasionally corresponded, usually to compliment one another on their latest work. When Thurber's *Further Fables for Our Time* was published in 1956,

Sid wrote him an effusive letter, saying how much he enjoyed it. Thurber replied immediately, writing that he would rather get such a letter "from a colleague than from a colleen, college, comic columnist, concubine, Columbus or and so forth."[9]

Privately, Sid regarded Thurber with suspicion. After all, Thurber was his major competitor, a writer to be closely watched. Professionally, their lives were too closely meshed for comfort. Both were identified in the public mind with the *New Yorker*, where they were both edited by Gus Lobrano. They also had the same publisher, Simon and Schuster, and here too their collections were edited by the same editor, Jack Goodman.

Like Perelman, Thurber was an irascible, temperamental man who could be easily set off by something very slight. One of their areas of contention was the quality of the magazine both of them wrote for. Thurber went through phases when he felt that the *New Yorker* was one of the finest publications, although according to his widow, Helen, he, like Perelman, was also capable of damning it.[10] Sid encountered Thurber one evening when Thurber was in one of his reverential moods about the magazine. "I remember one particular occasion at a party in Washington Square," Perelman told Philip French. "Thurber was going on at a great rate about his accomplishments and what not and about the importance of the magazine. And I said something like 'Come, come Jim. After all, it's just another fifteen-cent magazine.' Thurber flew into a passion such as I cannot adequately describe. His eyesight was none too good but he arose and he clawed at my throat. He had to be held away from me and I think that he literally would have destroyed me if he could have. But fortunately Robert Coates and a couple of other powerful men held Thurber and prevented any mayhem. But it was just the fact that I had referred to it somewhat disparagingly that excited his wrath."[11]

Brendan Gill, in *Here at the New Yorker*, recalled Gus Lobrano telling him about "a party at Sid Perelman's in the course of which Thurber had succeeded in making everyone present angry with everyone else, as well as with him. Whitefaced, trembling with vexation, Perelman finally eased Thurber out of the house. The next morning, Thurber was on the phone to Perelman. 'Sid, what a marvelous party! I never had such a good time.'"[12]

By October of 1951, Perelman had become disillusioned with his new publisher, Simon and Schuster. He felt that they had failed to give proper promotion to his latest books, *Listen to the Mocking Bird* and *The Swiss Family Perelman*, both of which had had good reviews but listless sales. Although he had worked for many years without a literary agent, he was then being represented by Mark Hanna, and Hanna advised him to switch to Doubleday, which was delighted to add a humorist of Perelman's stature to its list. A contract was drawn up, but Doubleday let the news leak out before Perelman signed it. When they heard about Perelman's proposed move, Jack Goodman and Albert Leventhal, president of Simon and Schuster, were very upset. As Donald Klopfer had done several years before, they assured Perelman that he was an extremely valued author and asked him to reconsider and stay with the house.

Eventually they were able to convince him to remain. His next collection of pieces, *The Ill-Tempered Clavichord*, was published in 1952 by Simon and Schuster. Dedicated to Gus Lobrano, the book had a jacket illustration by McKnight Kauffer, who was to die two years later after providing his last drawing for a Perelman book.

Sid himself furnished the jacket copy for his own biography: "Behind a façade as inscrutable as a Maltese kitten's dwells one of the protean individuals of our time, termed by many a modern Leonardo. A bibliophile (his collection of drugstore reprints is unrivaled in the hemisphere), a musician of note (he whistles an accompaniment to *Stairway to Paradise* that has rendered even Benny Goodman speechless), and a notable etcher whose admirers crow about his works, S. J. Perelman is a striking reincarnation of a man of the Renaissance. He has wandered much in the earth's far places, where he occupies a niche in the hearts of its peoples besides that of the anopheles mosquito and frambesia. Among his many books are *Filaments* (verse), *The Wind in the Pillows* (nocturnal essays), *Sonya, A Girl of the Limberlost* (medical), and *Bei Mir Bist Du Sean*, a rollicking tale of the Celtic Revival. He is twelve years old."

*The Ill-Tempered Clavichord* was well-received, and many critics were especially impressed with Perelman's latest addition to his "Cloudland Revisited" series, which included reviews of such popular twenties writers as Sax Rohmer and Edgar Rice Burroughs. Observed *Newsweek*: "They combine a deadly parody of book reviewers' prose with arresting sociological observations. As for Tarzan: (Strictly speaking, the saga begins in the African forest with the adoption by a female anthropoid ape of an English baby of lofty lineage.) Only

Perelman's standing as a humorist prevents these essays from being taken seriously."[13]

In April of 1953 the Perelmans gave up their city apartment and moved to Erwinna. Sid retained his office at 513-A Sixth Avenue, coming to New York every week or so.

Ever since he had gone around the world with Al Hirschfeld in 1947, he had dreamed of going to East Africa. Now, six years later, the opportunity presented itself. He heard about an interesting African safari, and when he proposed writing about it to Gus Lobrano and William Shawn (the new editor of the *New Yorker* after Harold Ross's death), both were enthusiastic.

Sporting a bronze-red cavalry mustache of the type worn by well-to-do Englishmen in Nairobi, Sid left for Africa in late December. He stopped briefly in London and Paris, where he saw a number of friends, including T. S. Eliot, C. Day Lewis, Ronald Searle, Alan Moorehead, Norman Lewis, Angus Wilson, Eric Ambler and Philippe Soupault, who was working for UNESCO. One of Sid's close friends was Harvey Orkin, a talent agent and motion picture executive who was a brilliant raconteur. On this particular trip Orkin arranged for Sid to meet one of his clients. Richard Burton was appearing as Hamlet at the Old Vic, and many people thought that his portrayal was the most compelling since John Barrymore's. Perelman liked Burton enormously, finding him unpretentious and sensitive, as well as lively and entertaining.[14]

Although his social calendar was full, Sid—who always dreamed of having an aviary—found time to visit the Regent's Park Zoo, where he spent several hours talking to the head keeper of the birdhouse about white mynahs and other rare exotic birds.

He had acquired another tropical bird, Cyrano, a short-keeled toucan Leila Hadley had sent him from Managua. When he and Laura moved back to Manhattan in 1954, he had to give the toucan to the Philadelphia Zoo, since there was no room for four pets in their Manhattan apartment. Besides Tong Cha and their poodle, Tartuffe, they now had a cat, Kootzie. Later Perelman wrote a humorous account, "Love My Toucan," describing Cyrano's raucous yelling and its effect on the neighbors in Bucks County. The piece was published in the April 7, 1957, issue of *This Week* magazine.[15] Leila Hadley appeared in it as a "Mrs. Hinchingbrooke" who was dropping off the bird at

Idlewild en route to meet her husband in Iraq. Sid described her as "a not unattractive person in a shrunken black dinner dress who exhibited a surprising knowledge of tropical birds for a youngster of 39." According to Perelman, Laura knew about Leila Hadley and accepted the relationship. In the piece he also described Laura's reaction to the news of Leila's gift: " 'How exciting, dear,' said my wife, when I casually introduced the subject. 'But look here—why not send the bird on to Iraq and bring Mrs. Hinchingbrooke home? Isn't that what you've had in mind from the beginning?' "

Perelman arrived in Kenya on January 11, 1954. He had hoped to start his trip months before, but an uprising of the Mau Maus had delayed his departure. After visiting Treetops, a hotel in the bush country,[16] and going on several short safaris, he linked up with the safari that had originally excited his interest. It was the first American "all-girl safari" ever organized in Africa. Led by Beverly Putnam, an employee of Scandinavian Airlines, it had been conceived as a promotional gimmick for the airline. Fourteen women had joined the party. They were scheduled to go to Ruanda-Urundi in Watusi country, and Perelman planned to accompany them there. But when he learned that his itinerary included a later trip to Ruanda-Urundi, he decided to limit himself to an overnight journey with the group across Lake Victoria to Murchison Falls.

Miss Putnam's women were scarcely typical of African safari groups. Many of them cried every time an animal was shot, and they spent a good deal of time squabbling over the three male white hunters who accompanied the expedition. Perelman wrote a humorous account of his brief journey with them, "The Artemisses." It was included in his six-part series about East Africa, "Dr. Perelman, I Presume, or Small-Bore in Africa" for the *New Yorker*.

He toyed with the idea of writing a musical based on this "all-girl safari," and so did the British critic Kenneth Tynan, who thought it would make an entertaining show. When Sid returned from Africa via London, Tynan approached him with the idea of writing an adaptation based on an outline he had written. Sid said he wasn't interested. In April of 1955, when Tynan learned that Sid was working on a musical with Ogden Nash about East Africa to be called *White Rhino*, in which Hermione Gingold would star, he threatened to bring suit if Perelman's book for the show bore any similarity to the outline he had shown him in London. Perelman responded by writing Tynan an uncharacteristically placating letter, saying he had no intention of writing anything based on Tynan's ideas, and the matter was dropped. But Perelman never forgave Tynan, whom he disliked personally. Yet often in the midst of some tirade about Tynan's faults, Perelman would pause and remark grudgingly that he *was* an excellent writer.

A play based on *Burmese Days* and a musical about the all-girl safari were only two of the ideas Perelman had for new projects in the mid-fifties—and subsequently dropped. In 1954, he also proposed to Heywood Hale Broun that they collaborate on a dramatic adaptation of Eric Linklater's *Mr. Byculla*. At that point Broun had written only newspaper stories, and he was puzzled why the author of *One Touch of Venus* would want to collaborate with him. But Sid told him that as a literary writer he had trouble with theatrical dialogue and that since Broun was an actor, he would know how lines ought to be spoken.

Sid also told Broun that his plays had been flops because they didn't have the right star or director. He felt that *Mr. Byculla* would be a perfect vehicle for Robert Morley, and he told Broun that if Morley didn't like their play, they would rewrite it until he did.

"About this point Sid had been talking vaguely about our arrangement," Broun says, "and I said, I guess it ought to be written down, and suddenly I get this curt letter from Sid's agent saying that I would get 20%. I thought, 20%—Sid had always talked about us being colleagues and working together, and I called Sid, and he said, 'Oh well, you know I don't really concern myself with this. I just tell Mark Hanna to do whatever.' So I signed on for the 20% because I didn't have anything else better to do. But we didn't get the rights anyway. Somebody else got them. . . . But it was a view to me of the stonier side of Sid, and other people told me later, 'He's fine until it comes to money.' "[17]

In late January of 1954, shortly after Perelman left for Africa, Adam escaped from the Cedar Knolls School at Hawthorne. He hitched a ride to White Plains and then took a train to New York. Several days later he was arrested in Greenwich Village and charged with assaulting and robbing two women at knifepoint. At the Charles Street station house, he readily admitted holding up the two women. Police discovered a seven-inch bowie knife he was carrying, which he said he had bought for seven dollars the day before. When Laura, who was subletting an apartment at 25 Fifth Avenue, was told of Adam's arrest, she was very distraught and told reporters: "I always kept in touch with the school. I didn't know until yesterday that he had escaped. I thank God none of the women was injured by him. I don't know why my boy did it. I have a daughter, Abby, fifteen, and my concern now is for her. The publicity may hurt her."[18]

Sid's friends were divided in their opinions about Adam's motives. Some felt that he was emotionally troubled from an early age, others that Sid, when he was in a manic state, was cruel and belittling to his son, literally driving a normal young boy into abnormal behavior.

Adam reportedly told a friend later that he had attacked the women to "embarrass" his father. Deeply affected by his parents' conflicts and incessant quarrels, he was perhaps punishing his father for his numerous infidelities, which he believed had caused his mother much heartache. According to many friends, the family was split down the middle in their loyalties: Adam was very close to his mother, while Abby felt a greater rapport with her father.

Adam pleaded guilty to the assaults on the two women and was given an indeterminate term up to five years at the Elmira Reception Center in Elmira, New York. To the Perelmans' relief, the court took a sympathetic view of his case, regarding him as a confused adolescent rather than a hardened criminal. At Elmira, he received a complete psychiatric examination and then was sent to a place that was a combination farm, school and clinic. He was not sentenced to any period of confinement.

When Heywood Hale Broun told Perelman how sorry he was about the boy's difficulties, Sid curtly informed him that he didn't wish to discuss the matter. Robert Gottlieb, Sid's editor at Simon and Schuster following the death of Jack Goodman, met with a similar response. "I remember just after Adam was arrested, I called Sid, which was very difficult for me to do, simply to say, I read about this, if there's any way we can help, if there are money problems, just let me know. He couldn't talk about it. It didn't exist."[19]

Although Sid may have had his differences with Adam in the past, he experienced much more anguish than he was willing to admit over his son's present difficulties. To those few people with whom he ever talked intimately, he confided that both he and Laura had broken down and cried when they had seen Adam in the Tombs. Although formerly leery of psychiatry, Sid began seeing an analyst. It is reported that he consulted psychiatrists intermittently for the rest of his life, but whether these sessions helped his troubled relationship with his family in any dramatic sense is debatable. His moods, which fluctuated from depression to elation, appear to have been controlled only by medication.

Soon after his return from Africa, Sid went into a deep depression. He was unable to write for six months. Leila Hadley's marriage, his own marital situation, from which he seemed unable to extricate himself, and Adam's problems—all had taken their toll. Even writing a letter to a friend loomed as a gigantic task.

In the early fall of 1954 he and Laura went to Martha's Vineyard for a few weeks, as they did every year. Severe hurricanes battered the island, but curiously the unremitting rain and turbulent winds seemed to enliven Sid's mood and restore his capacity for work. Once again he was able to write the kind of pieces people thought so hilarious but that in reality took grim effort and hours of toil.

# 15

## AROUND THE WORLD
## IN 80 DAYS

### (1955–1956)

> Squat, muscular, intensely dynamic, he was the very pattern
> of the modern major moviemaker—voluble, cunning, full of
> huckster shrewdness, slippery as a silverfish, and yet undeni-
> ably magnetic. In short, a con man, a *tummler* with a bursting
> Napoleonic complex.
>
> S. J. PERELMAN,
> "Around the Bend in Eighty Days"[1]

Perhaps it was more than a lucky coincidence that Sid, emerging
from one of his darkest depressions, should have received a phone
call in July of 1955 from producer Mike Todd. To a man who had
feared that his literary career was over, a contact with the flamboyant
Broadway showman was like a tonic. A nonstop talker, possessed of
a volcanic energy that allowed him to do many things at once, Mike
Todd was definitely larger than life. He was so full of wild contradictions and extravagant plans that Sid, who was always fascinated
by excessive behavior, felt rejuvenated on the spot.

Todd wanted Sid to come to Hollywood and brush up the dialogue
of his first movie, *Around the World in 80 Days*, based on the Jules
Verne novel. Sid did not hesitate to accept the offer. He had written
nothing during his depression and needed money badly.

When he arrived in Hollywood, Sid was at first amused by Todd's
high-powered behavior. It reminded him of the exaggerated self-
importance of some of the producers and stars he had known in
old-time Hollywood. Like the Groucho known to the public, the forty-
eight-year-old Todd, chomping perennially on a cigar, was an over-
blown, outrageous personality. Sid, an inhibited person who longed

206

not to be, could not help but enjoy the spectacle of Todd holding phone conversations simultaneously with three different people, or flying all over the globe in search of exotic locales or buying fantastically expensive jewelry for his new girlfriend, Elizabeth Taylor, whom he liked to introduce to people as "Miss Lizzie Schwarzkopf."

"They were not an incongruous couple," Sid told Brenda Maddox, one of Elizabeth Taylor's biographers, many years later, "because they were both so showbiz. They engaged a lot in a kind of arguing banter that was very hard on their hearers, but there is no doubt he was very fond of her."[2]

Some of Todd's antics, Sid observed, were as crazy as any he had created for the Marx Brothers. Once, when a nautical sequence for *Around the World in 80 Days* was being filmed off Balboa, Todd refused to let one of the thirty-three assistant directors in his employ throw garbage into the ocean to attract seagulls. Gulls, he insisted, were entitled to first-class treatment, like everyone else who worked in his movies. He instructed one assistant director to throw sardines instead.[3]

Born Avrom Hirsch Goldbogen in Minneapolis in 1907, Todd was the son of an impoverished Polish rabbi. As a young man, he flitted from one profession to another. He was shill to a pitchman selling fake gold watches, a soundproofer of sound stages, a gagwriter for Olsen and Johnson. He made and lost two fortunes in the construction business before winding up as a highly successful Broadway producer with four hits running simultaneously on Broadway. Gambling losses then plunged him into bankruptcy. But Todd had no intention of giving up his scale of living, which included a penthouse in New York, an estate in Westchester, suites of lavish offices and smoking fifteen Dunhill cigars a day, all individually "selected and wrapped for Mr. Michael Todd." "I owed a million and a half," he said. "What was I supposed to do—cut down on my cigars?"[4]

In 1950, after paying back most of his debts, Todd formed the Thomas-Todd Company with Lowell Thomas, the commentator, to develop a wide-screen process called Cinerama. Todd and his son, Michael Junior, shot most of the sequences for *This is Cinerama*, a film made in this technique. It included a famous roller-coaster ride, but according to Todd's biographer, Art Cohn, "he was dissatisfied with the necessity of having to use three cameras, three projection machines and three separate strips of film that made imperfectly meshed images—and intimate scenes—impossible."[5] He sold out his interests in Cinerama, and with the technical assistance of Dr. Brian

O'Brian of the University of Rochester he developed a process that gave the effect of Cinerama with a single camera and film. Called Todd-AO, the process was first used in Samuel Goldwyn's 1955 *Oklahoma!*, starring Gordon MacRae, Gloria Grahame and Shirley Jones, with dances choreographed by Agnes de Mille.

*Around the World in 80 Days* was the second feature film made in this process. It starred David Niven as the supercilious Victorian traveler Phileas Fogg; Cantinflas, the acclaimed Mexican comedian, as Passepartout, his valet; and a twenty-two-year-old unknown, Shirley MacLaine, as Aouda, an Indian princess Fogg rescues from the suttee, and whom Todd picked for her "whimsical, pixieish, quality." The well-known English actor Robert Newton was cast as Inspector Fix, a private eye who thinks Phileas Fogg is an escaped bank robber.

Richard Sale, a British writer, had written an early screen version of the famous Verne novel. But Todd hadn't liked it, so he asked the film's director, John Farrow, to write a new script. Farrow, with the help of James Poe, a screenwriter, took the dialogue from Verne's book and transformed it into a screenplay. It was Perelman's job to polish up this script.

In July, Sid went to Hollywood for three weeks. He found the movie colony as isolated and provincial as ever. As he later told Joe Hyams, he felt out of place as a humorist in an industry devoted to problem pictures and war epics. Even getting a haircut in Beverly Hills proved a frustrating experience. "I went into the barber shop where a tall, cool young lady at an escritoire greeted me," he said. "I asked for a haircut. She countered by asking what studio I was with. I told her I wasn't with a studio. Still smiling brightly, she asked if my secretary called for an appointment.

"I told her I had no secretary but did have need for a haircut. She unrolled an elaborate chart with every hour of the day broken up into fifteen-minute sections and said she might find the time for me next week.

"Obviously I was the first square to come in off the street without studio, secretary, recommendation, appointment or visa. The young lady so discomfited me I stumbled backwards into a tie rack and ended up getting the haircut two months later in Singapore—without an appointment."[6]

In early August, Sid returned to New York to work on the script in the blistering heat. In the meantime, Todd, who had flown to Chinchón, Spain, to look at a location for a bullfighting sequence, decided that Sid should also be on hand for the filming. Todd returned to New York and then flew back to Spain again with Sid, his lawyers and some aides accompanying him. During the flight he played gin rummy with his cronies and tinkered with the dialogue Sid had written, or as Art Cohn put it, "rewrote in one hundred percent Todd-AO."[7]

It is reported that Todd once said of Perelman: "He writes great dialogue, but it's strictly *New Yorker*. The circulation of the *New Yorker* is three hundred and fifty thousand. I want this picture to be seen by over a hundred million."[8]

In London, the party missed its connecting flight to Spain and Todd took everyone to the Dorchester Hotel, where the hotel staff displaced some visiting Arabian royalty from their sumptuous suite so Todd could make several international phone calls in comfort. To fly his group to Madrid, he chartered an eight-passenger plane, plying Sid and the others with roast chickens and box lunches which, as the flight was bumpy, were an ordeal to contemplate. In Madrid, Todd fought constantly with Farrow, a veteran of many Hollywood films. Fed up, Farrow quit the picture. Todd immediately hired a new director—Englishman Michael Anderson, who had never directed a Hollywood picture before.

Todd then hired the entire population of Chinchón to play the audience in the bullfight sequence. But the townspeople did not fill up the arena, so he imported hundreds of extras from nearby Madrid. The bullfight sequence was one of the highlights of the film. The Spanish matador Luis Miguel Dominguín killed three bulls, but Sid had little stomach for the sequence. He told a friend that his sympathies were all with the bulls. Unlike Ernest Hemingway, he saw no beauty in the sport and loathed seeing animals tortured and killed.

After the shooting ended, Todd squeezed Sid and several others back into his plane, and they all flew to Biarritz so he could play baccarat for a few hours. Then the party flew to London. Although Todd insisted that his chief screenwriter stay again at the Dorchester, Sid refused and checked into his favorite hotel in London, Brown's, which he liked to call "Brown's Hotel for Distressed Gentlewomen."

By September, Sid's initial infatuation with Todd's flamboyant style had turned into unmitigated loathing. He had always despised the showman Billy Rose for his vulgarity, but Todd, he felt, was even worse, a cheap huckster given to childish temper tantrums, a megalomaniac who insisted that Sid be on call twenty-four hours a day.

Once, Todd telephoned Sid's friend A. J. Liebling, whom he didn't know, in the middle of the night when he hadn't seen Perelman for a few hours. During the London sequence, he ordered Sid to get a hatpin from the wardrobe department for Hermione Gingold, and the only thought that sustained Sid as he fetched one was that one day he would write about Todd with all the sarcasm he could muster.[9] In late September, he wrote an exasperated letter to T. S. Eliot in which he described Todd as "a combination of Quasimodo and P. T. Barnum," adding that his trip to Europe in connection with the picture was the worst he had ever made.[10]

In November, Sid was back in Hollywood, doing some additional dialogue for Marlene Dietrich, Red Skelton, Frank Sinatra, Noel Coward and George Raft—stars Todd had somehow convinced to play bit parts in the picture in return for an expensive car or a valuable painting. The only reason Sid consented to do the additional dialogue was that Todd had finally agreed to pay his price, which Mark Hanna had raised. But Todd's money was running low by then, and Sid by the skin of his teeth was able to extract his final week's salary from him before it ran out altogether.

"Week after week, it took cajolery, pleas, and threats of legal action to collect one's salary," Sid wrote in "Around the Bend in Eighty Days," collected in *Vinegar Puss*. "All the while, of course, our impresario lived like the Medici, running up awesome bills that he waved away airily on presentation. Whether they were ever settled, even after he hit the mother lode, was doubtful. His *chutzpah*, however, was indisputable, for as became more and more obvious daily, his million-dollar epic was a classic shoestring operation. . . . To this day, I venture to say, nobody knows where or how Todd promoted the wherewithal to make his chef d'oeuvre, or who got what share of the golden hoard. All I know is that my pittance was extracted only by deep surgery."[11] Sid told friends that he and Todd used to meet regularly in a parking lot where he gave Todd new pages of the film script in exchange for a check.

Nevertheless, by late fall Sid's financial worries were temporarily over. He had received $29,000 for his work on *Around the World in 80 Days*, as well as over three thousand dollars for his share of royalties from a Producers Showcase live NBC television presentation of *One Touch of Venus* that aired on August 27, 1955, directed by Fred Coe.

Unfortunately, his domestic problems still plagued him. In April of 1955 he and Laura had moved again, this time to an apartment at

134 West 11th Street between Sixth and Seventh Avenues. The new apartment was a floor-through with a terrace in a remodeled brownstone. They redecorated it in the mustard and lime green colors they were so fond of. Their frequent moves during this period seem to reflect their restlessness and discontent, as well as a longing for escape from their problems. But the new apartment and the new paint job did not ease the friction between them. Laura was growing increasingly bitter and depressed about her life, and her state of mind was exacerbated by Adam's recent difficulties. She and Sid fought constantly. Physically, she began to show the strain. Always a heavy smoker, she began to chain-smoke, lighting one cigarette after another. Her movie-siren good looks had faded, and it was a matronly, careworn woman who looked at the world with a sad, resigned smile. She and Perelman, who called each other "Babe" and in later years, "Mr. and Mrs. P.," were seldom photographed together alone. Always an adored poodle, cat or bird was in the picture. As a friend said, "She looked as if she had been through the wars."

Laura's prediction in her diary that she could easily become an alcoholic had proved a sadly accurate one. "When the children were very small, she was just drinking heavily, but as they began to grow and get into their teens, she became an alcoholic," a friend says. "In those first years of their marriage, she and Sid were a dear couple to their friends, but then as life went on and things got complicated, it was grisly."

Yet Laura by sheer force of will was making every effort to come to terms with the reality of her beloved brother's death and her loneliness and disappointment. Some years before, aware that she, like her good friend Dorothy Parker, had a severe drinking problem, she joined Alcoholics Anonymous. For the most part she was successful in staying sober, although there were occasional lapses, especially during periods of extreme stress. She never quite got used to the idea of being an abstainer. She liked to tell her friends that she hoped when they invited her to dinner they would serve a dessert with a splash of brandy in it so that she could have a taste of liquor.

Her tipsiness, when she was off the wagon, was usually not obvious. A slow-moving dignified woman, she merely moved more languorously than usual. A friend remembers driving with her from New York to the Bucks County farm. The trip seemed endless, and the friend wondered why it was taking so long until she looked down at the gear box and saw that Laura had been driving the entire time in second gear. "But she had such dignity and presence that I didn't dare mention it to her," says the friend.

Laura sometimes asked Shirley Meyer, her next-door neighbor in Erwinna, to go to lunch with her. "I knew what that meant," Mrs. Meyer says. "I planned to be away all day long, although all we did was drive from here to Doylestown. She'd always be taking her laundry, and we'd go to lunch and then we'd drive all the way to Flemington and come back, and it would take all day long because she would drive at 25 miles per hour. . . . I think she just wanted to get rid of the day."[12]

Mrs. Meyer found Laura a warm and compassionate person, as did Robert Gottlieb. "She had that spiritually rattled look of a once beautiful, large woman who had gone through very difficult times," he says. "She always reminded me of a great wounded bird. But I found her a very sympathetic, touching and moving person and I was very fond of her."[13]

Perelman was loath to admit Laura's drinking problem to anyone. He seems to have tried ignoring it, as he ignored many other painful things in his life. The only place where he acknowledged his wife's dependence on alcohol was in his humor, where it appeared more as a fashionable—and lovable—bad habit than the torment it must have been for everyone in the family. In *The Swiss Family Perelman*, Sid admits to resorting to some underhanded tactics to make Laura see the folly of going to Siam:

> "Well, you've made your bed," I said cruelly. "I wash my hands. Bye-bye Martinis." The blow told! I saw her blanch and lunged home. "There's not a drop of French vermouth between San Francisco and Saint Tropez." For an instant, as she strove with the animal in her, my fate hung in the balance. Then, squaring her shoulders, her magnificent eyes blazing defiance, she flung the shaker into the grate, smashing it to smithereens.
>
> "Anything you can do, I can do better," she said in a voice that rang like metal. "Fetch up the seven-league boots. Thailand, here I come."[14]

Laura and Sid's spirits brightened considerably when they learned that Adam, whom they visited monthly in Elmira, would be released at the end of February 1956. They arranged for him to work for a friend of theirs who owned a large printing plant near Harrisburg, Pennsylvania. Sid wrote a friend that Adam "looked well," seemed to be "coping with his environment," and was "very cheered up" by the news of his impending release and new job. A few months later Sid was pleased by reports that Adam was adjusting to his new life and being very cooperative. During the following year, 1957, he remained optimistic about Adam's "becoming a responsible young man" when his son began working at a scientific instrument company near Wanamaker's and attending night school. Adam was then living at home, and Sid wrote that he found him more emotionally mature, as well as sobered by the events of the past few years.

Abby had graduated from Putney School in June of 1955. That summer she worked for a second year as an apprentice at the Bucks County Playhouse. Pat Englund, an actress who later played April Monkhood in Perelman's 1962 play, *The Beauty Part*, met Abby at that time. She recalls: "She broke my heart. You could see that she was a very sensitive, intelligent young girl. She was very fragile, very febrile, very young, and I always wondered what kind of woman she became because she was interesting. She was not like the other young girls. You could see that this was a person who had come to her late teens with a lot of baggage. She was quite beautiful in a way—not in a conventional way—but I thought she was beautiful."[15]

As a child, Abby had wanted to be a writer. For a time her favorite writer was Conan Doyle, whom her father also vastly admired. Like her mother, she loved miniatures, and a classmate recalls being very touched when Abby gave her a tiny object as a gift.

In September, Abby entered Pembroke. But she did not respond to college life any better than her mother and dropped out after two months. Professors there recall her as being depressed and immature. "A drifty kind of person who is hard to make contact with," is how one friend of Perelman's describes her. She spent the remainder of the year at home, working part-time at a Doubleday bookstore and taking classes at New York University so that she would be prepared to take college boards in May and enter another college the following September. It is reported that both her parents were upset by her decision to leave Pembroke. Sid told a friend he was worried that she had too much time on her hands. There was nothing for her to do but read, practice her cello and go to the movies endlessly. His own doleful nature and Laura's personal problems only increased the tension at home. But in the fall of 1956 Abby was accepted at St. John's College in Annapolis, where the curriculum was based on the one hundred great books and the intellectual atmosphere was more in tune with her personality. She appears to have been happy there.

*   *   *

After the Perelmans attended Abby's graduation from the Putney School, they visited J. D. Salinger and his new wife, Claire, at their mountaintop retreat in Windsor, fifty miles away. Sid was pleased to find Jerry, as he called him, looking so well and thought matrimony obviously agreed with him, although he wondered how his wife would be able to tolerate his solitary life.

Sid had enormous regard for Salinger, both as an exceptionally talented writer and as a person. He dedicated one of his collections, *Baby, It's Cold Inside*, to him. Respecting Salinger's fierce desire for privacy, he refused to divulge any information about his personal life, even to close friends such as *Holiday* editor Caskie Stinnett, who some years later questioned him about their relationship. "When Perelman visited in Maine, he sometimes stopped in Vermont to visit Salinger en route back to New York," Stinnett says. "One day on the sundeck, when Perelman and I were having a drink and talking aimlessly, he said he was going to see Salinger after he left me, and I inquired pointedly about Salinger and his reclusive life. It was then that Perelman said—quite apologetically because he was a very polite man— that he would prefer I not ask him to talk about Salinger since he felt that Salinger would not like it. I told Perelman that I could understand his feeling, and the conversation drifted on to some other subjects."[16]

In the fall of 1955, a new collection of Perelman's pieces, *Perelman's Home Companion*, was published. It consisted mainly of pieces from earlier books that were no longer in print. Although Sid again blamed the lackluster sales on Simon and Schuster's failure to advertise the book properly, he seemed contented with his publishers at the moment and did not talk about a move to any other house.

*Around the World in 80 Days* opened at the Rivoli Theatre in New York on October 17, 1956, to an invited audience who received playbills because Todd insisted that his movie was a "show" and not a film. Todd persuaded Sid to attend the opening, and at the party afterward he basked in the congratulations of Moss Hart, Max Gordon and Richard Rodgers, among others.

The premiere was almost cancelled, however, for Todd was again involved in controversy, this time with his screenwriters. Although both John Farrow and James Poe had worked on the script, Todd insisted that only Perelman receive screen credit. Enraged, Poe took up the matter with the Writers Guild of America, who supported his contention that his name appear as well as John Farrow's. Ed North, president of the Screen Writers branch of the Guild, said that the credit committee made its decision after reading "a screenplay written by Poe in collaboration with John Farrow, a mimeographed script typed from a movieola version of the film with dialogue contributions by Perelman, plus statements by Poe and Farrow."[17] Todd, however, refused to honor the Guild's ruling and was placed on its unfair list. Undoutedly he felt that Perelman's name had more "show business" value than Poe's, who although he was one of Hollywood's most skilled screenwriters, was far less known to the general public.

Poe then informed Todd that he would try to restrain the opening of the film unless he was granted screen credit. Earlier, in a complaint filed against Poe in Santa Monica Superior Court, Todd had asked for damages of $250,000 and the return of $2,166 he said he had overpaid Poe.[18]

Poe, whose later credits included *Cat on a Hot Tin Roof* and *Lilies of the Field*, won out against Todd. But when the film premiered at the Rivoli, the screen credit appeared as "Screenplay by S. J. Perelman based on the Jules Verne novel." Later, it was changed to "Screenplay by James Poe, John Farrow, and S. J. Perelman from the classic by Jules Verne."

Sid remained aloof from the controversy. As he wrote Leila Hadley, taking sole writing credit for the picture when he hadn't seen it might be dangerous.

Despite the behind-the-scenes feuds and power struggles, *Around the World in 80 Days* was a smash hit, adored by audiences who sometimes paid as much as $100 a ticket on the black market to see it. The critics loved it too and attributed much of its charm to its literate screenplay. "For this free-wheeling treatment of the Jules Verne classic, S. J. Perelman has written a screenplay full of comic joy and immense relish," wrote John Beaufort in the *Christian Science Monitor*.

The film won all sorts of awards, including the Best English Language Film of 1956 by the New York Film Critics. Perelman was acclaimed the best screenwriter of the year for his adaptation. (It was the first time the New York critics in their twenty-two years of voting awards had included screenwriting as a category.) The film also won five Academy Awards, including ones for best picture, color cinematography, musical score, film editing and screen adaptation (shared by Farrow, Poe and Perelman).[19]

Sid did not attend the Academy Award ceremonies, which were held jointly at the Pantages Theatre in Hollywood and the Century Theatre in New York on March 27, 1957. According to his friend James Lee, he felt awkward about appearing after the bitter battle over the screen credits.[20] The actress he so admired, Hermione Gingold, delivered his acceptance speech for him. It was the hit of the evening.

"I am delighted to accept this objet d'art for Mr. Perelman, who regrets that he cannot be here for a variety of reasons—all of them spicy," Miss Gingold announced in her naughtiest voice. "He asks me to say, however, that he is dumbfounded, absolutely flummoxed. He never expected any recognition or acclaim for writing *Around the World in 80 Days* and, in fact, did so on the express understanding that it would never be shown.

"Now that the fat is in the fire, though, he will endeavor to live up to it or, rather, to live it up. He's a very happy boy, and I'm a very happy girl. Bless you."[21]

On October 17, 1957, Mike Todd invited 18,000 people to a gala party at Madison Square Garden to celebrate the first anniversary of the film's run on Broadway. Countless millions watched on television. There were bands and elephants and champagne and a gigantic cake almost the size of an apartment building. Despite all this, the party was a monumental failure. Gate crashers consumed most of the food and champagne and when Elizabeth Taylor, now Mrs. Mike Todd, tried to cut the cake, some of the layers collapsed and fell at her feet.

Again, Sid was not present. By then, he was furious with Todd, who had ignored him since the premiere. Some time before the opening he had proposed to Todd that Cervantes' *Don Quixote* would be a natural sequel to *Around the World in 80 Days*, but he backed out of writing the screen adaptation when Todd agreed to meet his price. "Listen, I was exposed to that megalomaniac for fifteen months while making the movie. Isn't that enough?" He told a *New York Herald Tribune* reporter who asked him why he wasn't attending the Madison Square Garden celebration, "Oh, I see him around now and then. He travels so much you can't miss him. He has an infinite capacity for taking planes. But if you really want to know what I think of Mike Todd, I think he's the cutest kid at 729 Seventh Avenue, where there are a lot of cute kids."[22]

As his parting shot at Todd and Hollywood in general, Sid took the "objet d'art" that Hermione Gingold had accepted for him and used it as a doorstop in his office.

# 16

## "A WRITER OF LITTLE LEAVES"

### (1957–1960)

Although he made fun of it, Sid's Oscar for the screenplay of *Around the World in 80 Days* was a tremendous boost to his career. Suddenly he was very much in demand as a writer, and both Mark Hanna and Irving Lazar, his new agent for movie work, were besieged with offers. Sid told his agents to turn down most of these offers, including the opportunity to write the screenplay for *Auntie Mame* and a new Cinerama film. After years of scrounging, he could pick and choose his screen assignments.

In early January of 1957, Sid spent a high-pressured two weeks writing a script for an *Omnibus* show on the history of burlesque, "The Big Wheel," starring Bert Lahr. It was televised on January 27, and Sid himself appeared briefly in one scene, depicting the peak era of "bald-headed row." The show was a success, but a week earlier Sid had enjoyed what he considered a far greater triumph: His new collection, *The Road to Miltown or, Under the Spreading Atrophy* was published to great critical acclaim. Dorothy Parker wrote a first-page review in the *New York Times Book Review* and in her glowing assessment of her friend's work, she observed: "Mr. Perelman stands alone in this day of humorists. Mr. Perelman—there he is. Robert Benchley, who was probably nearest to Perelman, and Ring Lardner, who was nearest to nobody, are gone, and so Mr. Perelman stands by himself. Lonely he may be—but there he is."[1]

Sid was in Hollywood on publication day. He wrote Leila Hadley that he took a special perverse delight in being congratulated and "fawned on by some yahoos I had detested for years."

Dorothy Parker's review worked its magic. Other newspapers,

following the *Times*'s lead, published equally ecstatic reviews. *The Road to Miltown* became a bestseller, earning back some of the heavy advances Jack Goodman had given Perelman during the past few years.

It was the last book Sid and Jack worked on together. In August of 1957, Goodman, who had been in ill health for a year, died of a cerebral hemmorhage at the age of forty-eight. Robert Gottlieb succeeded him as Sid's editor. Jack Goodman's death deeply grieved Sid, for like Gus Lobrano, who had died the year before, he was among the few people in publishing Sid liked and deeply respected.

As for his relationship with the *New Yorker*, Sid easily made the transition to William Maxwell, a fiction editor under Katharine White, who edited his pieces for a few months, and then to William Shawn, who became editor of the *New Yorker* following Harold Ross's death from lung cancer in 1951. Shawn would continue to edit Perelman's work until Sid's death in 1979.

After Gus Lobrano's death, Katharine White wrote Perelman a note, reassuring him about his future at the magazine. Sid replied that he deeply appreciated the gesture. Privately, he disliked Mrs. White, writing that "following Gus Lobrano's death, [she] has consolidated her editorial power to such an extent that she sits astride the magazine and is slowly throttling the life out of it. Its whole character has changed, none of the vivacity, the gaiety it used to have is apparent any more."

He was not the only *New Yorker* writer to take umbrage at the magazine's editorial policies. Some years before, Edmund Wilson had written a letter to Mrs. White, who was then his editor, complaining about the extensive editing at the magazine:

> The editors are so afraid of anything that is unusual, that is not expected, that they put a premium on insipidity and banality. I find, in the case of my own articles, that if I ever coin a phrase or strike off a picturesque metaphor, somebody always objects. Every first-rate writer invents and renews the language; and many of the best writers have highly idiosyncratic styles; but almost no idiosyncratic writer ever gets into *The New Yorker*. Who can imagine Henry James or Bernard Shaw—or Dos Passos or Faulkner—in *The New Yorker?* The object here is as far as possible to iron all the writing out so that there will be nothing vivid or startling or original or personal in it. Sid Perelman is almost the sole exception, and I have never understood how he got by.[2]

The light amount of editing that Lobrano had performed on Sid's earlier pieces contributed to his smooth and amicable relationship with the magazine. But Lobrano's death, coupled with Sid's new fame as a screenwriter, made him question whether he should continue writing for it. Suddenly he began to object to what he called "their august editorial decisions, their fussy little changes and pipsqueak variations on my copy." He felt that he had "fallen, virtually, into a state of servitude" and was strongly tempted to quit. Finally he worked out an arrangement that permitted him much more freedom to work for other publications while still retaining "the first reading" agreement he had had for years as well as the right to receive bonuses and cost-of-living increases. By the late 1970s, he would be paid from $3,000 to $3,500 for an article, plus expenses.

Writing for television began to occupy most of his time. In June of 1957, he finished a television script for the opening broadcast of *The Seven Lively Arts*, a new series on CBS dealing with drama, dance and music. The series was produced by John Houseman, whom Sid had met many years before in Greenwich Village. Sid himself was scheduled to appear on the show he had written, "The Changing Ways of Love," to discuss the shifting styles of romance from the 1920s to the 1950s.

From the start, there were differences between writer and producer about the approach to the material. Sid wanted to do a saucy parody and was taken aback when Houseman's assistants presented him with masses of statistics about sex and love. For his part, Houseman felt that although Sid "could not have been more cooperative and industrious . . . his style was better suited to the printed page than to broadcasting, where his tone seemed consistently forced and over-blown."[3]

In the light of what was to come, these artistic differences would soon seem negligible. John Crosby, the television critic of the *New York Herald Tribune*, was the host of the series. Crosby was extremely nearsighted, and John Houseman thought that his image as master of ceremonies might be improved if he wore contact lenses instead of his usual tortoiseshell glasses. "He agreed," Houseman recalled in his memoirs, *Final Dress*, "and the most expensive optician in the city was put to work on two pairs of contact lenses with the assurance that they would be ready long before the start of rehearsals."[4]

But Crosby's contact lenses were uncomfortable. In fact, they irritated him so much that he told Houseman he couldn't wear them on the show. Houseman urged him to go back to wearing his glasses, but Crosby replied that wasn't necessary. He was going to memorize his lines, so that he would not have to rely on cue cards for his delivery. "I was against it," Houseman says, "but John was adamant and there was no way to sway him."

Houseman's fears were realized when "The Changing Ways of Love" was broadcast live on Sunday, November 3, 1957. In the middle of his opening speech about love, John Crosby froze. He could not remember his lines. And since he was wearing neither his glasses nor his contact lenses, he could not read the cue cards that an assistant was desperately waving in front of him. To Houseman and others in the control room, his pause—eighteen and a half seconds in all—seemed an eternity. "Finally, like members of Sleeping Beauty's court, we sprang back to life. Orders flashed over the intercom . . . Sid Perelman, pacing nervously behind a flat, was seized and hustled before a camera which caught him in a state of bewildered alarm as Crosby's voice, partially restored, reading from a boob card that the assistant was holding directly under his nose, introduced him as 'S. J. Perelman, Academy Award winner for the screenplay of *Around the World in 80 Days* and himself a survivor of the reckless twenties.' Whereupon Perelman, his glasses flashing and his voice shrill with forced gaiety, went into his act and heroically launched the first of his jokes into a void of bewilderment and despair."[5]

Fellow television critics had a field day over Crosby's stage fright, making all sorts of cracks about the producers forgetting to give him tranquilizers. They were divided about Perelman as a television personality. Jack Gould in the *New York Times* noted that "the humorist resembled a road company Groucho Marx trapped in the Smithsonian Institution."

According to John Houseman, it was announced on the air that "The show had been written by S. J. Perelman, who had won an Academy Award for the screenplay of the film, *Around the World in 80 Days*. Before we had gone off the air, the phone rang. It was the father-in-law of James Poe who was the writer who had originally written the script, and Mike Todd had then given it to Perelman. There had been a terrible, rather bad-tempered arbitration about it, and the Screen Writers Guild gave credit to Poe and second credit to Perelman, and we'd announced that he had written it. So his father-in-law, who was an eminent lawyer, said that this was a disgrace and he was going to sue CBS for libel and demand a retraction. And so we said well, we're sorry, you're right, the credits were that way so next week we'll amend this. So next week we go on the air, and at the end of the show, Crosby says, 'Just a correction . . . last week we said that *Around the World in 80 Days* was written by S. J. Perelman, whereas in fact it was written by . . . Joe Smith.' Everyone was staggered. Our phone rang again. It was the father-in-law in a rage. And then the third week we had to go on once again and say, well, we want to get a final correction. It was written by James Poe and Sid Perelman.''[6]

Sid remained good-humored about the contretemps. Although he was nervous about being thrown into the limelight suddenly, he had still managed to control his stage fright and improvise suitable lines.

In fact, Jack O'Brian in the *New York Journal-American* wrote, "Perelman could turn into quite a TV attraction, certainly an offbeat fellow visually, a cheerful low comedy intellectual in a Brooks button-down, probably the first litterateur of his amiable broad stripe able to project intelligent nonsense since the late Bob Benchley brightened up whatever art he enlivened. . . . Perelman's analyses of matters amatory had the fine old Benchley touch, the fresh, gay, gentle nudge, as in his study of women's dresses before and after World War I. Noting some eighteen yards of material went into milady's prewar frock and only three antebellum yards necessary, a prelude to the end of feminine mystery, Perelman concluded: 'Women became six times more available.' ''[7]

Evidently encouraged by such remarks, Sid appeared that year as a panelist with John Mason Brown and Neva Patterson on Dr. Bergen Evans's *The Last Word* on CBS-TV, a series about the proper use of the English language.

Sid's next television project was a musical adaptation of *Aladdin*, set in China, which was produced by Richard C. Lewine as part of the *DuPont Show of the Month* on CBS. The cast included Sal Mineo, Tab Hunter, Anna Maria Alberghetti, Cyril Ritchard, Dennis King, Basil Rathbone and Una Merkel. The score was by Cole Porter, and in September of 1957 Sid went to Hollywood to confer with him about the show.

But despite all the talent associated with it, *Aladdin* was a flop, both as a television musical when it was aired on February 21, 1958, and a year later when it was presented at the Coliseum Theatre in London for a brief run. The critics panned Mineo's performance as

Aladdin, as well as Sid's script, which they found "unclever." They even criticized Cole Porter's songs. According to Porter's biographer, Charles Schwartz, the gravely ill songwriter "never wrote anything else after *Aladdin*. It is indeed ironic that someone who had contributed so many musical hits to the world should end his songwriting career on such a dismal note."[8]

On January 18, 1959, Sid's adaptations of some of his stories about life in Hollywood, "Malice in Wonderland—Three Hollywood Cameos," were televised on *Omnibus*,[9] a prestigious cultural series which after a long run on CBS and a short stint on ABC was then occasionally seen on NBC. The plot revolved around a naive psychiatrist, Dr. Randy Kalbfus, played by Keenan Wynn, who goes to Hollywood as a technical adviser on a psychological thriller and lets Hollywood go to his head. Sobbing "I'm sorry, Sigmund," he is seduced by Audrey Merridew (Julie Newmar), a statuesque blonde Southern cracker who'll do anything to further her acting career. Sporting a beret, Dr. Kalbfus soon divorces his wife. He becomes obsessed with the idea that Sophia Loren wants to marry him. His only hope for sanity is to return to New York and be analyzed himself.

The cast also included Andrew Duggan as a hammy Western star, Pat Englund, Pert Kelton as Julie Newmar's embittered mother, Norma Crane as Kalbfus's discarded wife and Dan Tobin as another psychiatist who goes to Hollywood.

Of the several television scripts Sid had written in the past few years, "Malice in Wonderland" was the most successful. Jack Gould in the *New York Times* wrote that Perelman's "finished wit was quite the most funny program of this or several seasons past. . . . Mr. Perelman's cracks alone could have sustained the show. They have lost neither their scintillating hilarity nor devastating applicability. The Actors Studio, the *Reader's Digest*, motherhood, Freud, the East, the South, and the glamorous vacuum of Hollywood all received their due share.

"But Robert Saudek, the *Omnibus* producer, and James Lee and Michael Dreyfus, the directors, saw to it that the Perelman spirit arrived on the screen with a minimum of loss. There were many fine inventive touches that implemented the author's intent and heightened the satirical impact . . . Someone should find a network of which Mr. Perelman could be president."[10]

In 1963, Sid wrote a humorous account of his experiences as a television writer—"Be a Television Writer! Earn No Money!"—for

the November issue of *TV Guide*. Of his work on *Aladdin*, he offered
the following remarks: "As for *Aladdin*, that belongs to the ages. Statistics compiled by trained investigators working under Vichyssoise
estimate that this production put more viewers to sleep than all the
tranquilizers sold in the same year. From across the country, television repairmen reported countless instances of picture tubes clogged
with a flocculent white substance resembling kapok, which, on analysis, proved to be *Aladdin*. Subsequently CBS received three tons of
mail about the program, half of it containing veiled threats against
Mineo, the other half containing unveiled ones."[11]

On April 2, 1958, Adam, twenty-one, was arrested at his apartment
at 606 East 9th Street. He was charged with the assault, robbery and
attempted rape of two women in separate attacks. One of the women
was Lucy Goldthwaite, a forty-year-old editor at *McCall's*, and the
other Cora Weiss, a thirty-three-year-old graduate student at Hunter
College and a social worker at Beekman Downtown Hospital. In both
attacks, the women fought back, and Adam fled. In the Goldthwaite
assault, Adam took the woman's purse, which contained thirty-five
dollars. He later insisted that he threw it into an ashcan without
taking out the money. When he was arrested, Adam told the police
that he had no reason for the attacks, except that he "had a com-
pulsion to do it."[12]
Originally no bail was allowed on two of the charges at Adam's
arraignment in felony court. But his lawyer, Harris B. Steinberg, was
able to persuade General Sessions Judge George M. Carney to release
him on $5,000 bail. In court Steinberg said his client had been under
a doctor's care because of "a great deal of mental turmoil and anxiety."[13] On May 29, Adam was discharged on his own recognizance,[14]
and it is unclear whether he was convicted.

In college, Sid had dabbled in the occult with Nathanael West. His
fascination with it deepened around the time Adam got into trouble.
He began to consult the tarot cards and use the Ouija board, a device
invented in the twenties for recording messages from the dead. One
night Sid's friend Bill Cole brought him back to his apartment for
drinks. At that time Cole's roommate was Maurice Dolbier, book critic
of the *New York Herald Tribune*. Dolbier was a devotee of the Ouija
board, and Cole, after introducing the two men, asked Dolbier to bring
out the board. "Perelman and I, with our eyes closed and fingers

lightly resting on the pointer, moved and we got the usual preliminary nonsensical mishmash, which Bill gamely spelled out," Dolbier recalled some years later. "Then, with eyes opened, we asked if we could get in touch with certain deceased authors. We asked for Robert Benchley and asked how he liked it up there. Swiftly he responded: 'What do you mean . . . UP here?' We asked Ring Lardner what he thought of that year's World Series. The reply was pure Lardner: 'What Serious? Are you series?' We asked F. Scott Fitzgerald about the newly published memoir by Sheilah Graham of their love affair. 'Ah, Sheilah,' the pointer moved quickly. 'My better-late-than-never girl . . .'

"*Life* magazine, doing an article on Perelman, heard of our occult meanderings and thought it a good photo opportunity. While we sat waiting for the cameras to be set up, Perelman suggested that we fill the time with trying to get a message from Ernest Hemingway. The message came: 'You busy boys are all wrong. You should be in Valhalla with me.' Perelman nodded. 'That's Hemingway all right. Who but he would think he was in Valhalla?' "[15]

Philip Hamburger, Perelman's close friend and a staff member of the *New Yorker* since 1939, recalled spending a fall evening in Erwinna with Sid. "It was a crisp fall evening, the sort of evening when Sid might decide to tell a particularly hair-raising ghost story. But this evening he called for a Ouija board.

"I gave a short laugh, thinking it was some kind of joke. Sid cut me off with a severe look. 'I take the Ouija very seriously,' he said 'A few months ago I visited friends in the Adirondacks, and we got out the board and tried to reach Robert Benchley. But they didn't take the board seriously. Thanks to the noise and laughter, I never reached Benchley, and I had some questions to put to him, especially about humor. Tonight I want to reach Harold Ross. I want to ask Ross the same questions.'

"Sid asked me to place my hands on the board. Nobody made a sound. We sat a long time, but nothing happened. I felt somewhat embarrassed—and he seemed enormously disappointed."[16]

How seriously Sid believed in the occult is debatable. Like the aging, blind Thurber, who turned to ESP and religious miracles for comfort, did part of him yearn to embrace something that would ease the strain of his personal problems? Or was his curiosity merely an intellectual one, piqued by reading about the obsessions of two men he greatly admired—Alfred Russel Wallace, the 19th-century naturalist, and Sir Arthur Conan Doyle, creator of Sherlock Holmes, both of whom believed wholeheartedly in spiritualism?

Some clue to Sid's true feelings may be found in "Is There a Writer in the House?" In this piece collected in *The Last Laugh*, he made light of his occult adventures, claiming they had something to do with the consumption of too many vodka martinis. Leila Hadley believes that the occult, for Sid, was an entertainment, a jest. "He was interested in it the way he was interested in a million other things," she says.

A few days before *Adam's* release, on May 21, 1958, Sid was formally inducted into the National Institute of Arts and Letters, the highest ranking honor society of the arts in the United States. Robert Penn Warren proposed the nomination, and Conrad Aiken and Lillian Hellman seconded it. In his remarks Warren said: "S. J. Perelman has accomplished three things. First, he has created a character—the character of Perelman as we know him, a combination of brash confidence and befuddlement that strikes a sad, shadowy echo in our breasts. Second, he has developed a style which is elegant in a parody of elegance. Third, he is funny. He is very funny. Isn't that enough?"

An active member of the Academy, Sid donated a corrected manuscript, "Short Easterly Squall, with Low Visibility and Rising Gorge," in 1958. He also served on the Committee on Grants for Literature from 1960 to 1962, as well as on the Departmental Committee for Literature from 1977 to 1980. An admirer of Joseph Heller's *Catch-22*, Sid tried to sponsor the novel at a Grants comittee meeting, but was the only member to vote for it. He was delighted when Heller's novel received excellent reviews in the *New York Times* and *New York Herald Tribune* and hoped that his colleagues would reconsider it.

When Heller did receive an Award in Literature from the Institute in 1963, Perelman was asked as the only really enthusiastic sponsor of his work to write his citation: "To Joseph Heller, novelist, born in New York City, for rambunctiousness of humor and gutsiness of style which do not undercut but accent a sense of pathos in the human story."

*The Most of S. J. Perelman*, the most comprehensive collection of Perelman's comic essays, was published in the fall of 1958. Chronologically arranged, it contained ninety-six pieces he had written during the past thirty years, eight of them never included in a collection before, in addition to two complete books, *Acres and Pains* and *Westward Ha!* Dorothy Parker wrote the introduction, which was based on her *Times* book review of *The Road to Miltown*. In his concluding note, Perelman described his own unique talent: "If I were to apply for a library card in Paris, I would subscribe myself as *feuilletoniste*, that is to say, a writer of little leaves. I may be in error, but the word seems to me to carry a hint of endearment rather than patronage . . .

"In whatever case I should like to affirm my loyalty to it as a medium. The handful of chumps who still practice it are as lonely as the survivors of Fort Zinderneuf; a few more assaults by television and picture journalism and we might as well post their bodies on the ramparts, pray for togetherness, and kneel for the final annihilation. Until then, so long and don't take any wooden rhetoric."[17]

Perhaps in a gesture of reconciliation and appreciation for her creative help and fortitude during all the years of their marriage, Sid dedicated this collection to his wife. Evidently the tribute did not help, for the following year Laura said that she intended to divorce him. He managed to talk her out of it, and by that summer their marriage had improved sufficiently for her to visit him in Rome, where he had been staying since April at the Grand Hotel, writing a screenplay for Titanus Films that would star Harry Belafonte. It was never produced. He wrote James Lee, who had codirected "Malice in Wonderland" and was subletting his New York office, that he liked Rome even though the women were too fat and had dreadful taste in clothes and that he was sick to death of eating pasta. He conceded that Rome, like London, was a wonderful city to walk in, and he delighted in browsing through the antique shops and bookstores along the Via Babuino.

But he also wrote Jim that he felt lonely. There was no one for him to talk to, and so he was very happy when Laura came to Rome, followed by Abby in June. The three of them went to Positano for several weeks. While Laura and Abby went sightseeing at Pompeii, Paestum and Herculaneum, he stayed at the hotel and continued to work on the picture, dictating to his secretary.

On August 22, while the Perelmans were in Rome, thieves broke into their Bucks County farm, taking, among other items, many of Sid's valuable Oriental and African sculptures. Sid later vented his anger against the robbers in a piece, "Open Letter to a Cold-Slough Mob," in which he warned the thieves that "fourteen of the sculptures you took possess properties of a most curious and terrifying nature, as you will observe when your limbs begin to wither and your hair falls out in patches."[18]

In September, several weeks after Laura and Abby sailed for New York on the *United States*, Sid finished the first draft of his screenplay. Then he flew to London, where he planned to do some preliminary work on some satiric pieces about English life for the *New Yorker*.

# 17

## THE BEAUTY PART

### (1961–1963)

In the summer of 1961, Laura learned that she had breast cancer. A mastectomy was performed at Beth Israel Hospital, and it was hoped that the disease was arrested. Although members of AA visited Laura at the hospital, their support did not help her through the shock of the operation. Unfortunately, too, a doctor who was unaware of her drinking problem gave her a bottle of brandy as a gift, and depressed and fearful, she began drinking again.

Laura spent most of the summer recuperating in Los Angeles. Sid remained alone at the Erwinna farm. He obviously had difficulty facing her illness. When she came home from the hospital to their New York apartment, he left for Bucks County immediately, leaving her, weak and still wearing a catheter, in the care of a friend. In letters to friends and acquaintances during that period, he made no mention of her operation or convalescence, but said she was vacationing in California for several weeks and was contemplating a trip alone to India that year.

That he was deeply depressed, however, was evident. A photograph taken of him in 1962 by Irving Penn reveals a man submerged in gloom and despair, a man who had spent the previous winter unable to write.

According to Laura's friend Elizabeth McGhee, cancer was Laura's biggest fear. "She always called it 'the Big Casino,'" Mrs. McGhee says. "Her mother had died of it, as well as many other members of the Weinstein family. There was a great anxiety after her mother's death, and although her mother was a difficult woman, there was still a great bond between them."[1]

228

It had been an especially troubled year for the family. The previous summer, Abby, who had graduated from St. John's, announced her engagement to the Reverend Winfry Smith, an Episcopalian minister who was her tutor at college and considerably older than herself. According to many sources, Sid violently objected to the marriage, even though he had been raised as an atheist. "The idea of a Jewish girl marrying an Episcopalian minister killed Sid," a friend says. Reportedly his angry reaction distressed Abby deeply and plunged Laura into gloom.

But Abby defied her father, and she and her fiancé were married at the Church of the Ascension in Greenwich Village. The wedding reception was held at the Perelmans' Greenwich Village apartment. "Few people paid any attention to the couple," reports a friend. "They were leaving for their honeymoon, and nobody was saying good-bye, so a friend and I flung open a downstairs window and threw Uncle Ben's rice at them. Then we heard this terrible racket as the rice was being sucked back into the air conditioner."

That summer Sid was occupied with writing a new play. Called *An Evening with S. J. Perelman,* it was the first play he had written since the disastrous *Sweet Bye and Bye* as well as the first play he attempted without a collaborator. He began thinking about it in 1959 after the success of "Malice in Wonderland." "We started kicking around an idea for a play of similar satiric approach for Broadway," he told an interviewer. "The 'we' included several friends, including James Lee, who directed the TV program."[2]

*The Beauty Part,* as it was later called, was based on the same format as "Malice in Wonderland." It was a series of related sketches based on some *New Yorker* pieces that were connected by what Sid called "a certain element of story."

This time the target of Perelman's satire was the American obsession with acquiring culture. "It seems incumbent on everyone to express themselves in words and paint," he told Paul Gardner of the *New York Times.* "Self-improvement is fine. It's all right for people to leap around in homemade jerseys, but that isn't self-expression."[3]

The absurdity of artistic pretensions without substance had struck Perelman years before when he was riding in the elevator at the Hotel Sutton and between floors the operator had gravely informed him, "I'm having trouble with my second act."

The title Sid chose for his new play had to do with the tradeoff between bad and good. "People say, 'My uncle got a job in a cafeteria,' " Sid explained. " 'He has to work all night, but the beauty part is he can bring home stale Danish pastry.' "

Mike Ellis, who lived in Bucks County with his wife and family, was running the Bucks County Playhouse at that time. "One day in 1960 Sid was at the house and Harvey Orkin was there, and it was a regular Sunday in Bucks County with a lot of people around," he recalls, "and Harvey took me aside and he said, 'Listen, how would you like to give Sid $5,000 to write a play?' ($5,000 was a lot of money in those days.) And I said, 'why not?' And that's what he did. And some time later Sid came up with a play and I read the first version, and I was sick. It was no play, and I was really concerned about what would become of this and how it could be possibly shaped into a play. The first version had forty-eight different characters which were later cut down to whatever the final number was, twenty-eight or something of the sort, and no discernible story line whatsoever. It was an absolute nightmare and it was to be directed by Jimmy Lee, who was a playwright and director."4

*The Beauty Part* was tried out at the Bucks County Playhouse in New Hope, Pennsylvania, in the summer of 1961. It starred veteran comedian Bert Lahr, who played six roles in a virtuoso performance that ranged from Milo Leotard Allardyce DuPlessis Weatherwax, the lecherous husband of an heiress to a garbage disposal fortune, to Hyacinth Beddoes Laffoon, a steely-eyed female publisher of such lurid magazines as *Spicy Mortician* who was saucily based on the legendary *Look* editor Fleur Cowles; Harry Hubris, a wily Hollywood magnate who also masquerades as a Cambodian houseboy trying to steal a novel; Nelson Smedley, a senile "snackateria" mogul who is convinced that there are Communists in his chocolate sodas; and Judge Herman J. Rinderbrust, a television justice who cares mostly about how he looks on camera. Lahr, who tossed off these impersonations like a quick-change artist, was easily the main attraction of the show, although other members of the cast included Larry Hagman, Jack Gilford, Neva Patterson and Patricia Englund.

The summer stock audiences adored the play, and Mike Ellis, the producer, wanted to bring it to Broadway. But Sid decided that although he needed the money a Broadway hit might bring, the show needed redirecting as well as rewriting, and it would be wiser to revamp it before proceeding further.

"The changes mostly evolved from Jimmy Lee and Harvey Orkin,"

230

Mike Ellis says. "They were both very old friends of his, and I would say . . . that they were really the ones who were responsible for making some order out of the chaos that originally existed."

*The Rising Gorge*, Perelman's sixteenth collection, was published that autumn. Sid was especially pleased by the jacket illustration. An irate image of a man, it was by one of his favorite artists, Ben Shahn.

*The Rising Gorge* contained Sid's *New Yorker* account of his trip to the East Coast of Africa as well as two of the pieces he had written about Florida and Hollywood for *Redbook*. It also included "The Importance of Healing Ernest," which had originally appeared in *What's New* magazine. This was a humorous account of the "medical therapy" Sid said he had administered to Hemingway while the latter was recuperating at a Nairobi hotel after his plane crashed in Uganda in January of 1954.

Hemingway committed suicide shortly before *The Rising Gorge* was published. Recalled Frank Metz, art director of Simon and Schuster: "We were in the country and we had a very young baby, and Sid called up very early on a Sunday morning. I mean it was about six-thirty or quarter to seven, and he said, 'Did you hear the news? Ernest Hemingway committed suicide. How do you think it will affect my book? What state is it in, is it on press?' And I said, 'I don't really know, you have to call the people in the production department and find out whether it's too late. What's the problem?' 'Well, it's the story about Hemingway. I'm afraid that people will take it the wrong way because now he's dead.' It was a part of his soul, I guess, that this kind of thing tortured him, whether he had inadvertently injured someone. In the end I don't think the story was ever changed. And he never mentioned it again. It was one of those odd telephone calls out of the blue."[5]

In a different vein was "Eine Kleine Mothmusik," which dealt with Sid's clothes obsession and his relationship to "Mr. Stanley Merlin, owner of the Busy Bee Cleaners on MacDougal Street." Sid is concerned about whether Merlin has properly cleaned and put into cold storage an expensive garbardine suit of solari cloth. The correspondence between the vacationing author and the fictional Merlin, defending his reputation as a dry cleaner, becomes a hilarious duel, made all the funnier by a series of imaginary contretemps and malapropisms.

The character of Merlin was based on Sid's actual dry cleaner in Greenwich Village. In reality this gentleman was an excellent dry cleaner. A friend had recommended him but later she recalled, "The next thing I knew, a story about Sid's terrible dry cleaner appeared in the *New Yorker*. Then the dry cleaner wouldn't speak to me."

Burling Lowrey, reviewing the new collection of comic essays in the *Saturday Review of Literature*, wrote: "S. J. Perelman is the most durable, and, over the long haul, possibly the most brilliant of that familiar group of humorists whose wit fructified in the Twenties and Thirties and who found a spiritual home in the pages of the *New Yorker*. . . . Perelman is at his best when creating sharp capsule sketches of human gargoyles, such as 'a saccharine Southern Gentlewoman with marcelled blue hair, false choppers and the profile of an iguana. . . .' "

In the fall of 1961 Sid acted as a script consultant to comedy television show writer David Schwartz, who was preparing a pilot of *Acres and Pains* for CBS. Walter Matthau and Anne Jackson were to portray Laura and Sid. But the series seems never to have been made.

For the next twenty-one months Sid rewrote *The Beauty Part*. Before he was completely satisfied with the script, he would write it and rewrite it at least ten more times.

Rewritten and redirected, the play opened at the Music Box Theatre on December 26, 1962. The new director was an Englishman, Noel Willman, who had directed the highly successful *A Man for All Seasons* the year before. Bert Lahr played the six leading roles he had played at the Bucks County Playhouse. The new cast included Charlotte Rae, Alice Ghostley and Joseph Leon, as well as Larry Hagman, Patricia Englund, David Doyle, Bill La Massena and Arnold Soboloff, all of whom had been in the original production.

Larry Hagman played the role of Lance Weatherwax, a witless young man who decides to become an artist after his father's shocking disclosure that the "genesis of our scratch is the garbage disposal business." To his dismay, Lance discovers in the course of his odyssey that the arts are as much of a business as anything else in America and that artists are motivated not by a pure love of their craft but by money. At the play's conclusion, Lance, considerably wiser from his experience, accepts Milo Weatherwax's materialistic values, as his father pelts the audience with greenbacks from a baby bassinet held tenderly in his arms.

232

In structure as well as theme, *The Beauty Part* had much in common with Nathanael West's comic novel, *A Cool Million*. In both the central character is a naive young man in pursuit of an ideal. For West's Lemuel Pitkin, it was the American dream of a good and prosperous life, for Lance Weatherwax, personal fulfillment in the arts. But their dreams prove monstrous illusions, perverted by human greed, avarice and materialism. All the characters the young men meet along the way are monsters, reflecting the worst in human nature and the bitterness and disillusionment of their creators.

Of the two satires, West's was the more savage and uncompromising. At the end of *A Cool Million*, Lemuel Pitkin is annihilated, while Lance Weatherwax at the conclusion of *The Beauty Part* realizes the folly of his idealism and becomes as grasping and self-seeking as the rest of the complacent middle class.

Although Sid maintained that *The Beauty Part* was merely an "amusing" play about untalented people with artistic pretensions, critic Marilyn Stasio maintained that "the comedy is also a devastating satire on American values, with especial acidic scorn for society's debasement of art and culture into bogus fabrications of their pure selves. In Perelman's vision of culture-consuming America, the acclaimed artist is he who prostitutes his principles to become a pseudo-artist. Success descends not on the creator of pure art, but on the dilettante practitioner of pseudo-arts, like interior decorators and designers, and on the cultural scavengers like agents, editors, and producers who batten off the talents of true creators."[6]

*The Beauty Part* revealed a great deal about Sid's own conflicts as an artist. Like Lance Weatherwax, he had been a romantic, vulnerable young man with starry-eyed notions about art. But experience soon taught him that like all the corrupt and jaded artists Weatherwax meets during the course of the play, he would have to become a commodity if he were going to support himself as a writer. Like Goddard Quagmeyer, the idealistic artist who goes Hollywood, he too had to "sell out," going to Hollywood and wasting his talent on a succession of mediocre films.

Superficially, Sid seemed to have come to terms with being a commercial writer. When an interviewer asked him why he wrote, he replied cheerfully: "I loathe writing. On the other hand, I'm a great believer in money."[7] This was a self-deception, however, for few commercial writers wrote as meticulously and exquisitely as he did. Sid cared deeply about the craft of writing, often spending an entire day on one sentence. He judged other writers severely, damning them if their style or intelligence failed to measure up to his incredibly high standards. He especially scorned writers who were commercially successful, and in some cases it wasn't merely their slipshod writing and the banality of their ideas that aroused his resentment. For despite the disdain he displayed in *The Beauty Part* toward artists who prostitute their talents in a country culturally unsophisticated, Sid himself longed for a big commercial success in show business. He was envious of people who made a fortune out of their writing. It was one of the major disappointments in his life that he was never a playwright of mass appeal like George S. Kaufman or Neil Simon.

"As far as I'm concerned, Sid's major ambition was to make as much money as possible however it had to be done," Mike Ellis says. "His main thrust always was how much money he could make. The main value of writing a play is that if it's a hit, the income goes on indefinitely while you are doing other things that also bring you income, and of course, that isn't true of motion pictures and short stories."

*The Beauty Part* should have made him the successful Broadway playwright he had always dreamed of being. Audiences and critics loved the show. *Newsweek* called it "lovely lunacy,"[8] while Howard Taubman in a *New York Times* review that was never printed observed that "It has taken all these years to make an awesome discovery—that S. J. Perelman and Bert Lahr were made for one another."[9]

Despite the favorable notices, *The Beauty Part* closed after only 84 performances. Why should a play that everybody adored, that the critics raved over, with a star of Lahr's magnitude, fail to be a smash hit? Perelman was famous, and his script the most hilarious he had ever written for the stage.

On December 8, 1962, two and a half weeks before the play was to open, the printer's union went on strike against New York's nine newspapers. It lasted for 114 days. The effect of this strike on the Broadway theater—and especially on *The Beauty Part*—was devastating. Without reviews to guide them, advertisements and ticket information, the theater-going public stayed away in droves.

Although Perelman, Mike Ellis and Harvey Orkin were convinced it was the newspaper strike that closed *The Beauty Part*, Marilyn Stasio believes that other factors were also to blame. In her book, *Broadway's Beautiful Losers*, which includes a trenchant analysis of the play and why it failed, she observed: "Because it opened during the debilitating New York newspaper strike of 1962–1963, *The Beauty Part* illustrates first of all the truly crucial importance of the daily press to the health of the theatre industry. Secondly, because it was critically caught between two interim bookings, the show also illustrates the complexities of producing and managing a Broadway show—a single judgmental error on the part of a producer, and even a popular show can lose its momentum and suddenly fold. Finally, because the comedy is a satire and one whose pungent wit is aimed directly at the class of people who comprise the bulk of the general Broadway audience, *The Beauty Part* is eloquent proof of the extraordinary difficulties faced by non-formula shows trying to succeed within Broadway's conventionally structured producing system."[10]

Mike Ellis tried a number of gimmicks to make the public aware of the show's critical acclaim. He printed the unpublished reviews on fliers, which were then distributed in cigar stores and in laundry and film packages. Skywriting also advertised the show, and contests were instigated—but nothing offset the lack of newspaper reviews. The play, which had already lost $70,000 on the road, continued to lose money on Broadway every week. A month after it opened, Ellis asked Perelman, Lahr and Willman to take royalty cuts.

Joseph Leon, who played Goddard Quagmeyer, remembers Sid as looking very worried during rehearsals. "His face was constantly red and his blue eyes watery, like a bloodhound's."[11] Gisella Orkin also remembers him as being very strained. "He wanted Harvey to go to all the rehearsals," she recalls, "and he was very upset when Harvey did not go to the theater on Christmas Eve."[12]

Undoubtedly Sid felt that his entire future in the theater rested on the play's success. He took a keen interest in every aspect of the production, writing detailed memos to Ellis and Willman, in which he made clear his disapproval of some of the actors and their interpretations of certain scenes, saying he would like to replace them if possible. As in *Sweet Bye and Bye*, he also breached theatrical protocol by haranguing certain actors about the way they performed their parts.

But *The Beauty Part* posed special problems for actors. "It is very difficult to find people who can speak the words that Sid wrote," Mike Ellis says. "Sid wrote words that were meant to go into the brain through the eye, and to get a group of people whose style can encompass the writing is very difficult to achieve."[13]

Patricia Englund, who played April Monkhood in both the Bucks

235

County and Broadway productions, is an actress with the kind of informed intelligence necessary to bring a Perelman character to life. "It's a different kind of acting," she observes. "You have to come in from above, to let the words carry you. You mustn't be dimensional, you mustn't be real, you can't act too much, because he didn't write real people, he wrote cartoons, and yet they were quite recognizable as types. When he gave you those thumbnail sketches of people, you knew all about them—you knew what kind of dreadful human beings they were."[14]

But the actors' failure to interpret their parts properly wasn't the only problem bothering Perelman. He was dissatisfied with Ellis's handling of the show and felt he wasn't doing enough to make it a hit even under the circumstances. "I had two major problems with Sid," Ellis says. "One is I had a very difficult decision to make in Philadelphia as to whether to take the show into New York at all. We got no concessions from Actors' Equity because the situation was unprecedented. There was no way of knowing how long the strike would last, so I either had to open and take my chances that the strike would end or I had to not open and continue to pay the actors until the strike ended, but the bottom line was that if I wanted to take the show into New York, I now had to borrow $40,000. Well, $40,000 was an awful lot of money in those days, and it took me many, many years to get out of debt from that. . . . After the show closed, one of the things I tried to do to get out from debt was to make settlements with the creative people to whom money was owed, and Sid was the most difficult to settle with. . . . For a long time he would only speak to my wife because of our arguments about the financial settlements."[15]

When the play continued to lose money on Broadway, Sid refused to sit down with Ellis and talk about possible solutions. His old paranoia reasserted itself. Ellis had now become another enemy in a long line of enemies, a person who was only interested in making money at his expense.

Frustrated, Ellis wrote Sid a long letter, imploring him to see the necessity of taking a cut in royalties.[16] Sid at last relented. He was to receive 10 percent of the gross each week up to $25,000 and 10 percent of any gross over $35,000 but waived his royalties on grosses between $25,000 and $35,000 for ten weeks.

Bert Lahr and Noel Willman agreed to take similar cuts. Superficially, Sid appears to have gotten along better with Lahr than he had with Groucho many years before. With Lahr, there were none of the battles about Perelman's literary references that had marred his association with the star of *Horse Feathers*. Sid called Lahr "the last of the great clowns," and said of him, "He was able to take what I wrote and interpret it perfectly."[17]

In his biography of his father, *Notes on a Cowardly Lion*, John Lahr writes that "Perelman and Lahr seemed an unlikely team. I remember them sitting in a coffee shop across from the Shubert Theatre in New Haven when the play began its pre-Broadway tryouts in 1962. They confronted each other in avid discussion. Perelman, with brush mustache and wire-rimmed glasses, fitted the image of a dry litterateur, or a well-preened buyer for Sotheby's. Small and quiet, he spoke carefully, with a hint of hardness in his voice. Perelman accepted Lahr's suggestions and his worry with stoic kindness. Perelman's mind, like his choice of clothes, was careful and stylized. Whatever his emotions, his image to the world was one of aloof propriety. Their rapport was immediate. In private, the civilized veneer of that relationship was sometimes questioned. 'He's rough. He's rough. He wanted every line to stay just the way he wrote it. Finally, Noel Willman, the director, told him before we came into New York that some of them had to be changed.' "[18]

Despite their private reservations about one another, Sid and Lahr worked together beautifully and in the process managed to tone down the other's theatrical shortcomings. "However, Lahr had difficulty with some of Perelman's convoluted literary cadences. Perelman's combination of hifalutin' English and Yiddish jargon could keep Lahr's exuberance from taking control. . . . Perelman struggled to adapt his most baroque rhythms to Lahr's vocal range. The tension was healthy but frustrating. Perelman's language took on an economy and dramatic impact it sometimes lacked on the printed page."[19]

A few years after *The Beauty Part* closed, Sid wrote a rather mean-spirited piece about Lahr, "Dear Sir or Madam," collected in *Baby, It's Cold Inside*, in which he accused Lahr (Smiley Grimes, as he called him) of being temperamental about his costume for Hyacinth Beddoes Laffoon and "wrenching my lines out of recognition." Undoubtedly, he was angry at Lahr for refusing to do *The Beauty Part* in London. According to John Lahr, "Perelman wrote him frequently urging him to consent to a London production, where Perelman reigned as the King of American humorists, and where Lahr had never tested his talent. Lahr refused. 'They just couldn't pay my price.' In 1966, when he was finally promised a salary that would have made him the highest-paid performer ever on the English stage (five hundred pounds a week), he agreed to perform it, only to have the opportunity fizzle. As a consequence, a fine show bowed to the demands of commercial theatre."[20]

In mid-February of 1963, as *The Beauty Part* was about to close on Broadway, Sid was in Nairobi, preparing to depart for the Seychelles, a group of British islands in the Indian Ocean that were noted for their beauty and that he had always longed to visit.

"The reviews were raves, and we thought the show was a smash," Harvey Orkin told Marilyn Stasio. "All the talk between us and the producers was about what we should do with the show in its third year, and who should be cast in the road company when the show went on tour, and whether to take the profits in spread. Sid was really flying high, and he took a trip to Africa. When we closed the show two months later, I finally had to cable Sid in Africa. He wrote a *New Yorker* piece about that cable, and in it I think he referred to his agent as 'Toby Swindler [sic].' "[21]

When Sid received Orkin's cable about the show's imminent demise, he was thrown into a state of indecision. Should he cancel his trip to the Seychelles or return to New York for the play's closing? To help him make a decision, he visited two astrologers in Nairobi. Although convinced that it was a waste of time "to hire Indian fakirs to dream up disasters for me when I was perfectly capable of doing it myself," he returned to New York. "I knew now where my duty lay—not on an island paradise eating lotus but patrolling Times Square, where I could keep an eye on chiselers named Toby Swingler who betrayed a man the moment he turned his back."[22] He later told Heywood Hale Broun that it was a decision he always regretted.

After the play closed, Sid had no desire to write at all. His inertia was broken briefly in June, when he spent five weeks in London as chief writer for Elizabeth Taylor's television debut on CBS in a travelogue entitled "Elizabeth Taylor's London." It was aired on October 6, 1963. Sid hated writing it, and his task was not made easy by the presence of four producers and Miss Taylor's remaining incommunicado the entire time.

In an article later published in *TV Guide*, Sid denounced television writing. About his work for Elizabeth Taylor he wrote: "Within a month, the bulk of the work was finished, and the producers and I foregathered to 'polish' the script, a ritual in which anything that might be construed as amusing is painstakingly removed . . . In due course the script was hacked and altered beyond recognition, and it was time for the vultures from the advertising agency to descend. Scores of experts flapped in to pontificate on what was wrong with the script, all clad in Italian silk suits and tab collars. Their suggestions were, of course, embodied *in toto*, and the finished product, sparkling and flavorful as a plate of cold gruel, was ready for the oven."[23]

In London, Harvey Orkin arranged for him to meet with Peter Sellers, another one of Orkin's clients. Sid hoped to persuade Sellers to play all of Bert Lahr's parts in a movie version of *The Beauty Part*, which he hoped would eventually be made. Three years later, in 1966, Walter Shenson, a producer, tried to interest United Artists in making a film from Perelman's comedy, and Sid himself wrote an outline of a screen treatment. But United Artists—and later two other distributors—turned down Shenson's offer, and the film was never made.

# 18

## "A LIVING NATIONAL TREASURE"

### (1964–1970)

The failure of *The Beauty Part* was one of the biggest disappointments of Sid's career. But far more devastating was the news that Laura had cancer. Although he might have been unwilling to admit it, Laura had played a major part in his literary career. She had boosted his morale, collaborated with him on two plays and some of his screen writing and always been on the lookout for situations that he might turn into comic pieces. But now, she withdrew into herself and her fears about her illness, and he was left entirely on his own. A very important source of creative support and encouragement was gone from his life from that time on.

Although he would live another sixteen years, he would write no more plays or screenplays, or attempt the comic novel people were always pressing him to write. For the rest of his life he would not risk himself artistically but would repeat the kind of pieces that had served him so brilliantly in his youth, trying to refit them into the mold of the new American culture, with which he found himself more and more out of sync. For the world itself had become his biggest competitor. It had changed, becoming in its violence and bizarreness a grotesque parody of itself, something that, as a member of an older generation, he could not deal with.

Anger, which had always been lying beneath the surface of Sid's glittering prose, now began to dominate his pieces. Increasingly, they became more personal vendettas rather than rib-tickling romps. Wordiness and an excessive attention to obscure references and foreign words began to muddy his meticulous style. His comic persona was no longer the wistful, bespectacled boy from Providence but an

240

angry, cantankerous man, condemning almost everyone and every-thing. He began to lose the comic writer's most precious gift—a sense of humor.

Travel was always Sid's passion, his escape, his anodyne. In the last twenty years of his life, he would be constantly on the move. As he grew older, the trips became sillier and more desperately outlandish.

In 1964, the Perelmans returned to Europe, taking their poodle Misty with them. (Sid adored the dog and often took her to restau-rants; as he was being interviewed, she would sit on a chair and dine on rare roast beef.) In France, they bought a Peugeot sedan and toured the château country before heading for Paris, where Sid took great delight in an exhibition of Siamese art from the National Museum in Bangkok.

To avoid the English quarantine on animals, the Perelmans put Misty in a Paris kennel and flew to London for a two-week visit, staying at their favorite hotel, Brown's.[1] In London, Sid delivered a speech at the British Society of Authors eightieth anniversary dinner, but as he was speaking, the microphone went dead, and few people heard him, with the exception of T. S. Eliot, who was sitting next to him and who applauded loudly at the end.

Groucho Marx was in town for a television appearance, and he and Sid had a pleasant dinner together at the American Embassy before being interviewed by Kenneth Tynan at the Connaught Hotel. Sid had by then patched up his quarrel with Tynan over the all-girl safari musical.

One evening he and Laura had dinner with the Eliots. The poet's appearance alarmed Sid. He thought that Eliot looked in poor health, and he was right. Eliot had only a year to live. The Perelmans flew back to Paris and, after retrieving Misty from the kennel, drove to Vevey, Switzerland, where Sid finished an article for the *Saturday Evening Post*. In Switzerland they dined with Oona and Charlie Chap-lin. Although Sid was generally unimpressed by comedians, he ad-mired Chaplin and thought he was "a great man." As a child, Sid was so enamored of him that he had even done an imitation of Chap-lin. "A cane, a mustache, baggy trousers . . ." he recalled.[2]

In July, after a brief visit to Venice, the Perelmans drove to Yu-goslavia, Hungary and Rumania in search of Dracula's castle. Sid found the Balkan countries drab and depressing and wrote Jim Lee and his wife, Neva Patterson, that visiting them reaffirmed his belief in capitalism. Later he wrote several articles about his adventures in the Balkans for the *New Yorker* and *Venture* and subsequently incorporated the material into "Misty Behind the Curtain," collected in *Chicken Inspector #23*. As for Misty, she appears to have enjoyed the trip better than her master and mistress. "She bore it with infinite patience," Sid told reporter Mary Blume. "They all wanted to know whether we wove anything with her wool."[3]

Both Sid and Laura contracted influenza on their return to the United States. Sid recovered quickly, but Laura, who did not have her husband's strong constitution, was still ill by October. They remained at the Bucks County farm while their apartment in the city was painted (they were still living at 134 West 11th Street) and planned to return permanently to the city in mid-October. On October 16, 1964, word came that Sid's mother, Sophie, age eighty-one, had died in Los Angeles at the Cedars of Lebanon Hospital of a myocardial infarction, the result of arteriosclerotic heart disease.[4] For thirty years Sophie had lived alone in Los Angeles in a modest house that Sid had bought for her, until old age and poor health had forced her to move into a retirement home.

I. J. Kapstein and his wife visited her there in the late 1950s. She complained bitterly to them that Sid never came to see her, that all he did "was write the checks." Then, her green eyes blazing, she demanded the truth from Kapstein, "Tell me, Kap, do you think Sid is all *that* funny?"[5]

Vincent Mason, Sid's cousin, also sensed that an estrangement between mother and son followed Joseph Perelman's death. After Sid was married and living on Washington Square, Sophie took Vincent to see his apartment. Sid was not at home, and as she and Vincent walked through the silent rooms, with their Oriental sculpture and valuable paintings, she made Vincent promise not to touch anything.[6]

The letters Sid wrote to friends shortly after his mother's death do not say a word about her demise. Yet this should not be construed to mean that he was unaffected by it. In fact, he seems to have been so appalled by illness or death in his family that his instant reaction was to repress its existence. Paradoxically, however, he could be consoling and kind to friends who had suffered a bereavement.

In June of 1965, Sid, who was always bitter about not graduating from Brown University because of his failure to pass trigonometry, received an honorary doctorate of letters from his alma mater. No doubt he felt a tremendous sense of vindication and triumph when he received the following citation:

> Great humor enlightens and criticizes even as it amuses. Yours will endure as literature and as wit, but also as an analysis of our customs and beliefs, our follies and faiths. Read with joy, remembered with pleasure, and contemplated with better understanding, your works are a treasury of yesterday, today, and tomorrow.

The next morning Sid flew to Washington to a reception for Presidential scholars. John Cheever, John O'Hara and John Updike also attended this reception, and Updike read selections from his works. Perelman was an admirer of Cheever, but did not care for John Updike, whose work he found too sexually explicit for his tastes.

Sid's feelings about O'Hara were mixed. He liked some of O'Hara's work, but found O'Hara quick to take offense. Once, many years before, in Hollywood, Laura, who was pregnant, went to a doctor for a routine examination. Sid went with her. When they left the doctor's office, they saw a Rolls-Royce parked at the curb. They knew it was John O'Hara's car because it had his initials carved into the steering wheel. As a joke, Sid wrote on a piece of paper "Dear John, it's no worse than a bad cold" and slipped the note under the windshield wiper. He never heard from O'Hara, and many months later returned to New York. One day, while he was at the *New Yorker* office, his friend Joseph Mitchell told him that O'Hara was furious at him. Perplexed, Sid asked him why. Mitchell replied that O'Hara was outraged when he had learned Sid was spreading rumors that he had gonorrhea. Sid then remembered what he had written and said, "I don't know why that should upset him." "Well, because he does have gonorrhea," Mitchell said.

Over the years Perelman had closely guarded Nathanael West's memory and literary reputation. Under the terms of West's will, Laura received 25 percent of any proceeds from the sale or royalties of her brother's literary works. Her sister, Hinda Rhodes, also received 25 percent, and Patrick Bransten, West's adopted son by his marriage to Eileen McKenney, received the remaining 50 percent. Perelman scrupulously advised his wife in matters pertaining to the West estate. In West's lifetime, *Miss Lonelyhearts* had been made into a movie twice by 20th Century–Fox, and in 1963, Laura sold the movie rights to *The Day of the Locust* to Joseph Strick—Allen Hodgdon for $30,000, after it had been optioned for some time. Joseph Strick wanted Edward Albee to write the screenplay, and when Albee refused, Strick tried to recruit Perelman. But Sid turned down the offer, possibly because the deal was on a speculative basis with no money up front.

Sid hated almost everything written about West. The only critiques he approved were Malcolm Cowley's introduction to the Avon edition of *Miss Lonelyhearts* and Robert M. Coates' preface to the New Directions reprint of the novel. He particularly objected to Richard B. Gehman's 1950 introduction to *The Day of the Locust,* which he felt was opportunistic and an invasion of his brother-in-law's privacy. A number of people were interested in writing critical studies and biographies of West, but Sid refused to cooperate. He wrote I. J. Kapstein that half of his mail came from young people interested in doing Ph.D. theses on West, and if he answered all their questions, he would have no time for his own writing. He also told Kapstein that he had started writing his own memoirs, for which he had signed a contract with Simon and Schuster in 1960. Entitled *Smiling, the Boy Fell Dead,* it would contain certain reminiscences of West, and hence he had no desire to share his memories.

For years after his death, West still continued to be an influence on the Perelman household. He made his presence known in Laura's air of mourning and in Adam, who as a little boy so resembled his uncle that John Sanford, West's close friend, thought that Adam was "Pep shrunk to two feet high."[7] One might go so far as to say that there were two men fighting for dominance in the Perelman family— Sid Perelman and the by now idealized memory of his brother-in-law. As much as he loved West, Sid must have found it burdensome at times to compete with a dead man for literary fame and his family's affections. Undoubtedly he was aware of the fact that several of West's friends were of the firm opinion that the reason he never departed from a successful comic formula to risk writing a serious novel was that he feared comparison with West. Characteristically, Perelman never brought up the question of West when asked why he had never attempted a full-scale novel. "To me the muralist is no more valid than the miniature painter. In this very large country where size is all and where Thomas Wolfe outranks Robert Benchley, I am content to stitch away at my embroidery hoop."[8] No wonder that late in life he began referring to West in his correspondence and essays as "Nathanael West," "West," or "N. W.," never by the more familiar or intimate "Nat" or "Pep."

In October of 1965, Dr. Jay Martin, who taught a popular course in American studies at Yale University, asked Sid to speak to his students about Nathanael West. Sid agreed, and after he had delivered his lecture, he spent some time with Martin. Finding him knowledgeable as well as sympathetic to West's work, Sid granted Martin's request to write West's biography. He wrote I. J. Kapstein that he found Martin not only "likeable and smart, [but] devoid of the idiotic ingenuousness-plus-vaulting ambition that [had] distinguished previous so-called scholars."[9] Reportedly, many years before, Sid had let a student see West's papers, only to discover that the student later disappeared with one of West's valuable original manuscripts, which he subsequently deposited in a university library. This bitter experience may have soured him on all other scholars interested in the facts of West's life.

According to Jay Martin, although his biography of West was authorized, Sid did not restrict him in any way. "He felt Farrar, Straus & Giroux should be the publisher, as the house had published *The Complete Works of Nathanael West*," Martin says. "He arranged a contract for me, then withdrew from the negotiations. He was thoroughly cooperative throughout and did not object to my interviewing people he personally disliked."

Martin spent several days interviewing Laura about West. "She was very moved and touched and sensitive still at that point on the subject of talking about her brother. This was the first time she had ever talked to a stranger about him."[10] It was his impression that she still had not reconciled herself to his death.

The Perelmans usually spent part of the winter in Key West, Florida. On a Tuesday afternoon, December 28, 1965, six days after the twenty-fifth anniversary of West's death and less than a month after Sid wrote Jay Martin telling him how pleased he was that he was undertaking West's biography, an accident occurred that was strangely similar to the one that had killed West and Eileen. Sid was driving his Peugeot southward at about 45 miles an hour on Route 301 five miles below Orangeburg, South Carolina, when an oncoming car, driven by twenty-year-old William S. Thomas of Cope, South Carolina, swerved directly in front of him, colliding with the front end of the Peugeot and totally demolishing it.

Both Sid and Laura were injured in the accident. They were taken by ambulance to Orangeburg Regional Hospital. Sid had lacerations on both knees and a chipped left elbow. He was treated in the emergency room and released. Laura was more seriously hurt. She sustained a broken fibula alongside her left knee and a severe blow to the coccyx as well as contusions of the left temple. After being treated in the emergency room, she was discharged but immediately readmitted on the advice of a physician. She remained in the hospital until New Year's Eve.

Since their car was a total loss, Laura and Sid continued on to Miami aboard the Seaboard Railroad. For almost a month, she continued to experience severe pain and difficulty in walking, and was under sedation. She remained under the care of Captain James Benavides of the U.S. Hospital in Key West.

Their poodle Misty was unhurt, as had been Julie, West's pointer, untouched in the accident that had claimed two lives.

On December 31, 1965, William S. Thomas was found guilty of criminal negligence in failing to yield the right of way to Perelman, but the charge was later dismissed.[11]

Sid's letters to Ogden Nash and I. J. Kapstein describe the details of the accident, his fury over the stupidity of the other driver, and the magnitude of Laura's injuries, but they do not mention the psychological trauma it must have caused them to be reminded of the tragedy twenty-five years before that had altered the course of their lives. Judging from E. B. White's recollection of Perelman's reaction to the accident, Sid defended himself against emotion and shock by retreating into a realm he loved and felt safe in—the abstract world of language. In a 1968 letter to William K. Zinsser, White wrote: "He [Perelman] and Laura showed up here in Sarasota a couple of winters ago. They had been in an automobile accident—a bad one, the car a complete wreck. Laura came out of it with some bruises, Sid with a new word. The car, he learned, had been 'totalled.' I could see that the addition of this word to his already enormous store meant a lot to him. His ears are as busy as an ant's feelers. No word ever gets by him."[12]

In late September of 1966, a seventeenth collection of Perelman's work, *Chicken Inspector #23*, was published. Dedicated to William

Shawn, it was the first new collection of his work in five years. Much to Sid's delight, Ogden Nash, who disliked prose as a medium, consented to review the book for *Life* magazine. "Perelman, like Pope, is not for high school dropouts," Nash observed."It is not essential that to savor him fully, you be reasonably well up on modern art, the Rover Boys, Proust, the promotion material of the Morticians' Association, the Georgics of Vergil, the lore of the safari and the exotic customs of the mysterious East. But it helps. His eyes, peering through the sort of steel-rimmed spectacles we associate with kindly old horse-and-buggy doctors, rove continually over the foibles and fatuity of his era, and when they spot a particularly virulent boil or carbuncle, his lancet is ready and ruthless.

"Unlike the ordinary husband who grows to resemble his wife, Perelman has grown to resemble his writings. His figure is lean, sharp and precise; his jaw seems more angular as his hair thins, and his irascibility increases, and his trim moustache would not be out of place under a pith helmet on a plantation in Kenya. His wardrobe is as cosmopolitan as his wit.

"Perelman's style is so uniquely his own that his readers in the *New Yorker*, which long ago established the peekaboo custom of printing the contributor's name at the tail of the article rather than the head, need only glance at the first paragraph to identify its author. He exposes the fool in his folly not through reduction, but through magnification, to the absurd, so that the subject stands larger than life and twice as ludicrous, foot in mouth and egg on his chin, hoist by his own asininity. . . . Here is a happy chance to laugh at some of the perfect asses in this imperfect world. Perelman swats good, like a fool-killer should."[13]

Sid was enormously pleased by the review and wrote Nash to thank him. He was very fond of the kindly, good-natured poet, corresponding with him frequently and often enclosing funny clippings, jokes from the newspapers or whimsical names he had come across in the phone book. A great admirer of Nash's work, Sid was especially pleased by the 1968 holiday issue of the *New Yorker*, which included pieces by Nash, Frank Sullivan and himself. Nash's wit and erudition never failed to impress him, and as he once wrote Nash, it bothered him that as time went on his humor wasn't sufficiently appreciated.

Undoubtedly Nash's wonderful review blunted the sting of Victor S. Navasky's blast at the new collection in *Book Week*, attacking Perelman for directing his wit against such frippery as Dove Soap, commercials, his English tailor and ladies who are afraid of mice rather than at Ngo Dinh Diem and Stokely Carmichael.[14] But Perelman shrugged off the attack and told book columnist Martha MacGregor that such criticism had dogged him since he had written for the *New Masses*. "Why wasn't I in there tickling people and making them see the tragedy of the proletariat? It isn't enough to make people laugh, there must be a message," he lamented.[15]

Perelman's unwillingness to tackle serious subjects disturbed other critics. Inevitably, they compared his writing to West's. Laurence B. Chase, writing in the *Brown Alumni Monthly*, noted: "Unfortunately, Perelman's early ability to stir up controversy has not continued in his subsequent writing. Perhaps the sadness about humorists in the outside world is that they're never taken seriously. Were anyone to treat Perelman's writing seriously he would find that there's a lot of similarity between it and West's writing, both thematically and stylistically.... The obvious difference is that nobody ever gets hurt in Perelman's vignettes; people suffer under West's pen. Perelman, in short, sugar-coats the pill to the extent that his writing gives all the immediate delight of, and as little lasting nourishment as, cotton candy. Taken in the same small amounts that you take cotton candy, all of his writings are a delight, pure and simple."[16]

Perhaps Sid's reluctance to tackle controversial themes again had to do with his fear of being compared with West. He knew that the critics would compare any attempt at serious literature with the work of his brother-in-law, who was well on his way to becoming a cult figure. Perhaps he felt that in such a contest, West would be the victor and it was safer for him to stick to familiar ground.

On one occasion he told Ralph Tyler that he considered writing a comic novel as difficult a form as the autobiography he had been working on for years without success. "There are very few successful comic novels," he said. "*Lucky Jim* was one and Max Beerbohm's *Zuleika Dobson* for part of its length is a really marvelous book and then it sort of falls apart. Evelyn Waugh did several; I don't know whether you could describe them as comic necessarily, although there is a good deal of humor.

"About the ninth page of ordinary double-spaced type, you have to be very careful. It's almost an instinctive feeling I have, and consequently to sustain a comic novel for, let's say, two hundred pages, demands a very good comic idea to begin with and a great deal of invention."[17]

One might add that the unique nature of Perelman's talent prevented him from writing savagely comic novels like West's. His genius
lay in caricature, in his marvelous command of language, not in the
depiction of character, emotion or social satire.

On September 30, 1966, the Perelmans gave up their New York
apartment. A second burglary in August, plus the increasing pollution
in the city, inspired them to move permanently to Erwinna. Sid also
moved out of the office at 13th Street and Sixth Avenue where he had
worked for fifteen years. Their plan was to use the Bucks County farm
as their headquarters and to travel as much as possible. Although
Sid missed being within walking distance of a first-rate corned beef
sandwich, he nevertheless seemed to find working in the country more
productive and satisfying than writing in Manhattan.

In the spring of the following year, the Perelmans traveled through
England and France for six weeks. A month or so after their return,
Sid entered the exclusive New York Doctors Hospital for a prostate
operation. Released after two weeks, he went to Erwinna to conva-
lesce for a month. He was sixty-three years old and, aside from the
prostate condition, in excellent health. Lean, muscular and aristo-
cratic looking in his English tweeds, he bore little resemblance to the
way he had described himself in a recent piece as "a portly house-
holder whose nose resembled an exploded boysenberry."[18]

Alexander King had changed the way books were promoted when
he appeared on the Jack Paar television show in the late 1950s. His
book was published in the midst of a newspaper strike, and there
were no reviews. King, who was convinced he was dying of a kidney
ailment and therefore not accountable for his actions, violently con-
demned the Catholic Church on the air. Paar and the audience were
staggered, and at the end of King's diatribe, Paar held up a copy of
his book, and telling the audience it was very funny, advised them
to buy it. Within a month the book was selling 10,000 copies a week.

Sid was friendly with King and his wife, Margie. In fact, he had
been responsible for bringing King's book, *Mine Enemy Grows Older*,
to the attention of Simon and Schuster. But Sid deplored the trend
King had started and wrote a satirical piece for *TV Guide*, "Now Silent
Flows the Con," about his own television appearances promoting
*Chicken Inspector #23*. He hated talk shows and most talk show hosts,
with the exception of Dick Cavett[19] and Martha Deane, both of whom
had cultivated tastes and actually read the books of the writers they

interviewed. Sid also felt that publishers, by putting authors on television, had found another way to wriggle out of advertising books
themselves. In his opinion, writing had become a form of hucksterism,
and books were being merchandised as if they were soap powder. He
wrote his friend, sculptor Karl Fortess, that from now on he would
make as few television appearances as possible.[20]

That December Sid planned to visit Europe and East Africa to work
on some pieces that *Holiday* had commissioned. But the editors at
*Holiday* postponed Sid's trip until the following September, and Sid
feared it would be cancelled altogether as Lyndon Johnson was
threatening to curb American tourism. Sid then proposed that he rent
Earl Mountbatten's castle in Galway, Ireland, for a week and write
a piece about it for the magazine.[21] But renting the castle proved
prohibitively expensive, and *Holiday* wanted Sid to pay some of the
expenses himself, which he was reluctant to do.

Eventually he and the editors were able to work out the financial
details. On April 26, 1968, he left for London, arriving at Classiebawn
Castle near Sligo on May 4th. The 600-acre property faced the Atlantic, and one day there were three hailstorms within an hour. Sid's
only companions were the staff of three servants. Sid wrote Neva
Patterson a charming letter about his experiences and instructed her
to think of him from now on as "Sidney Heathcliff."

When he returned, he learned, to his disappointment, that his East
African trip had been cancelled. *Holiday* was in deep financial trouble,
and many members of the staff were being fired. To save money, the
editors not only refused to pay his expenses on a piece, but wanted
to cut his fee for an assignment, which was $2,000 to $2,500 plus all
expenses, by over 30 percent. This he refused to countenance. *Holiday*
was no longer to be a travel magazine but one concerned with people's
leisure activities, and Sid hated its new format, which he felt resembled *Esquire* merged with *Playboy*.

The editors of the new *Holiday* offered Sid two assignments—one
on the French Sûreté, the other a profile of Charlie Chaplin—but both
pieces involved a tremendous amount of work, which he was loath
to undertake at a reduced price. He eventually agreed to do the Sûreté
piece, however, traveling to Boston to do research.

The editorial changes at *Holiday*, in addition to the generally gloomy
prospects for magazine publishing, which was being adversely affected by television, deeply depressed Sid. Ever since the early 1960s

he had feared for the future of his kind of humor. In 1962 he had told *Life* reporter Jane Howard: "Humorous writing—humor meant to be read—is shrinking and passing out of existence. As a class this sort of writer is doomed. A young man or woman so impelled today usually ends up as one of a six-man gag team."[22]

He continued to work intermittently on his autobiography, but reliving the past proved difficult. When he spoke about the project at all, it was jokingly. "I've just reached the part where I graduate from nursery school with blazing honors," he told Israel Shenker of the *New York Times*.[23]

On September 26, Sid and Laura sailed on the S.S. *France* for a five-week vacation in England, France and Switzerland. Although most of Perelman's trips were paid for by the magazine for which he was going on assignment, he financed this particular trip himself. He felt that both he and Laura needed a change of pace before facing the long Erwinna winter. In Switzerland, he and Laura particularly enjoyed visiting the zoos at Zurich and Basel. Long fascinated by apes, they spent time observing the gorillas and their antics.[24]

From Switzerland they flew to London, a city Sid always enjoyed, for the English regarded him as America's foremost humorist. Laudatory articles about his work appeared frequently in *Punch*, and he was invited everywhere. On this particular trip, he talked with the editors of the *Sunday Times* [of London] about doing some pieces for them. He wrote a friend that although the money was trifling compared to the fees he commanded in the United States, he felt more than compensated by the wonderful reception of his work in England and by the people's kindness toward him.

On November 12, he and Laura flew back to the United States via Philadelphia. It was a cold and miserable homecoming. A violent storm had struck the East, and on their return to Erwinna, they found the power shut off at the farm and subzero temperatures. Chilled and exhausted, they contracted the flu, which laid them low for several weeks. Again, the flu depleted Laura especially, and it was a long time before she recovered.

Sid's old ambivalence about the city versus the country resurfaced. To escape the difficult winter months in Erwinna, he and Laura sublet an apartment for January and Februay at 136 East 76th Street.

In early May of 1969, Sid traveled to Providence to speak at a party for I. J. Kapstein, who was retiring from Brown University, where he had had a distinguished career as an English professor. With humor and tenderness, Sid recalled his and "Kappy's" years together in Greenwich Village:

> Kapstein, using his newfound literacy, worked for the publishing firm of Alfred A. Knopf and I [was] a free-lance comic artist for magazines that invariably went bankrupt the moment they bought my drawings. Ah, those were the halcyon days in the Greenwich Village of 1927. What if we often went to bed hungry, if there was no money to ransom our laundry or pay the rent? Were we down-hearted? The answer is yes— we were miserable.[25]

In 1968, Sid had written the preface, "Browser's Delight," that accompanied a highly successful facsimile edition of the 1897 Sears Roebuck catalogue, published by Chelsea House. He had enjoyed the experience, and the following year agreed to write the preface for a Chelsea House reprint of a book originally published in 1886 and entitled *Professional Criminals of America* by Inspector Thomas Byrnes of the New York Police Department. Sid had long been fascinated by criminals and rapscallions, and his preface, "Don't Blame Inspector Byrnes," was one of his most charming pieces.[26]

In September of 1969, the Perelmans returned to London. They stayed at Brown's Hotel until the middle of October, at which time they rented a flat in Hay's Mews (off Berkeley Square) for three months, using it as a base for writing and travel.

Sometime before, Abby's marriage to the Reverend Winfry Smith had ended in divorce. During their stay in London, Sid and Laura were joined by Abby. Like her parents, she had a passion for zoos and the family often visited menageries in England and Switzerland.

One of Sid's purposes in going to London was to find an English agent. Michael Korda, whom he liked no better than Bennett Cerf, was now his editor at Simon and Schuster;[27] he recommended Deborah Rogers, whom Sid liked and asked to represent him.

He was also in the market for a new English publisher. Many of his previous works had been published in England by Max Reinhardt, Ltd., which subsequently merged with John Lane to form Bodley Head, and by William Heinemann, Ltd., but Sid had eventually become dissatisfied with both houses. He had a one-book arrangement with Hodder and Stoughton to publish *Chicken Inspector #23*, but since he had not been pleased by their handling of it, had decided that fall to move to Weidenfeld and Nicolson, where his editor was Tony Godwin. But Sid soon had the same complaints about Weidenfeld that he had about all his American publishers and previous British ones, namely slow payment of advances, poor jacket design—and, of course, his major complaint: failure to advertise.

Some of his editors felt that he abandoned them as soon as their usefulness to him was over, even though they had the illusion during their association that he had valued them personally. "Sid was very professional to work with and very pleasant," says Robert Gottlieb. "We spent a good deal of time together—dinners in New York, or weekends at his place in Bucks County. It was all very polite, courteous—I think he prided himself on his elegance of manner—but he could not deal with anything disturbing. He was one of those people who had to walk away from anything that was trouble or even personal. I can furnish a very minor example of this from my own relationship with him. When in 1968 I left Simon and Schuster, where I had been editor-in-chief, I had worked with many writers. I discussed them all with my colleagues at S and S, trying to decide which ones might want to come with me to Knopf and which ones should stay put. And I remember saying that there was absolutely no reason for Sid Perelman to leave, because I didn't perform any real function for him editorially—I just shepherded his books through. We'd had a very pleasant relationship for a dozen years, but he was at Simon and Schuster before I was, and I was simply his custodian. I couldn't imagine that he would want to leave, much as I might have liked him to.

"I wrote a personal letter to Sid, explaining why I was leaving and what his choices were and my feelings about them. Of the perhaps eighty authors I worked with, Sid was the only person I never heard from—ever. I ceased to exist when I ceased to serve him. I wasn't angry or hurt—it was expectable behavior. In fact, the worst of it is that I *wasn't* surprised. I'm afraid that's the kind of man he was: He needed people who were there for him in one way or another; their own dramas were of no real interest to him because he was so totally involved in his own."[28]

Sid's own drama intensified again that winter in London. After forty-two years of married life, he asked Laura for a divorce. According to a friend, "she was very unhappy with this information, but nevertheless acceded to it." Instead of visiting Paris for Christmas, as they had planned, both Sid and Laura contracted the flu and were forced to cancel their trip. On January 9, 1970, they flew back to Philadelphia.

Laura never recovered from the flu. On February 2, 1970, she entered a hospital in Flemington, New Jersey, for extensive tests. The prognosis was serious. A divorce was now out of the question. Sid realized he could never abandon her. She returned home for two brief stays and then was readmitted to the Hunterdon Medical Center. There she sank into a coma and died on April 10, 1970. She was fifty-eight years old.

Her fears about a recurrence of "the Big Casino" had become a dreaded reality. Her death was caused by a breast cancer that had metastasized to the chest, causing an obstruction of the superior vena cava, which drains blood from the brain. The immediate cause of death was listed as cerebral edema.[29]

In her will (dated January 15, 1958, with a first codicil attached November 3, 1966), Laura left her entire estate to her husband. In the event that Perelman failed to survive her, she bequeathed her estate to Adam and Abby. Abby was to receive her money without stipulation, but Adam's share of the estate was to be placed in trust, with the Perelmans' lawyer and friend of many years, James H. Mathias, acting as trustee.[30]

Lynn Greening, who had worked as a gardener for Perelman in 1961 while Laura was in California recuperating from a cancer operation, later became a nurse. At the time of Laura's illness, she was a nurse's aide at the Hunterdon Medical Center.

"Mrs. Perelman came in one time, and she had a bad spell and shortness of breath, and she must have been very frightened," Lynn remembers. "She came in and got in her room, and her husband was outside, and she said, 'Don't let Mr. P in here,' so I guess she thought she was going to pass away, and she didn't want him to have to witness it, and I thought that was a wonderful thing, to think so much of him. A lot of people would have wanted their husbands there so they could get their support."[31]

Sid's behavior during Laura's last illness and death struck many of their friends and neighbors as bizarre. One neighbor went to the hospital to visit Laura, only to find a NO VISITORS sign on the door. Later, she learned that it was Sid—not Laura's doctor—who had not wanted her to have visitors.

"Sid didn't inform people close to Laura that she had died, giving them no opportunity to mourn," a friend says. "There was no funeral service for her. Nothing." Many people who had known the Perelmans for years were also surprised to find that after his wife's death, Sid had no interest whatsoever in maintaining a friendship with them. He simply cut them out of his life.

After Laura died, Sid stayed alone on the farm where they had lived for thirty-seven years until Abby came to stay with him for a period of time. After she left, he visited his friends, the Peter Cusicks, at their apartment on Central Park West, returning to Erwinna to look after the farm and the animals, which now included a horse, Mister X, and his poodles Misty and Tartuffe. It was not until summer that he was able to write.

Not even Eudora Welty's glowing front-page review of his new collection, *Baby, It's Cold Inside*, in the August 30th issue of the *New York Times Book Review* could alleviate his gloom. "What I predict now could really be put in the form of a nomination: that S. J. Perelman be declared a living national treasure. This would be a good time for it. He has a new book today, and we need the treasure," Miss Welty wrote.

". . . The value of the word has declined. Parody is among the early casualties of this disaster, for it comes to be no longer recognizable apart from its subject. Parody makes its point by its precision and strictness in use of the word, probing to explore the distinction between the true and the false, the real and the synthetic. It's a demanding and exacting art, and there are few with the gift of penetration, and the temerity, let alone the wit and the style, to practice it. Right now, it's in danger of becoming a lost cause. The only writer I know who can save it is the author of this book. He stands alone. We already owe him a great deal for years of utter delight but we owe him even more now.

"Not for nothing is the book called *Baby, It's Cold Inside*. Back of some of these pieces, and not very far, lies deep sadness, lies outrage. What an achievement Mr. S. J. Perelman makes today, that out of our sadness and outrage we are brought, in these little leaves, to laugh at ourselves once more."[32]

Sid soon realized that he would never be able to live alone on the farm with all its memories and associations. He decided to put it up for sale and move to England, perhaps permanently, although as he wrote Karl Fortess, he hated making definitive statements that he

255

later reneged on. The four months he had spent with Laura in London that past autumn convinced him that he would like to live in England for a longer period. An added incentive was that his friend, British writer Chaim Raphael, had recently gotten him elected to the Reform Club, where Phileas Fogg had started his trip around the world. This set Sid thinking about duplicating Fogg's fabulous itinerary in a piece for the *New Yorker*.

On October 13, 1970, Sid sold the farm for $108,000. It comprised a little over 87 acres (he and Laura had bought approximately seven additional acres of land in 1961 from Lilly Hochman, a neighbor). The purchaser was William C. Musham, a Philadelphia businessman.

Approximately two weeks before, on September 25, a crowd of five hundred bidders gathered on the lawn of the farm, listening to auctioneer Ken Brown from Brown Brothers of Buckingham knock down the house furnishings, memorabilia and collector's items that Sid and Laura had accumulated during the many years of their marriage. As the afternoon wore on, the buyers carried to their cars toleware coffee pots, 19th-century prints, cherry night tables, lamps, even a rusty stereoscope and a boat made of cloves, which Ken Brown had offered for sale with the comment, "If you grow tired of it, you can throw it into a stew." Mister X, the brown horse that Abby used to ride whenever she visited her parents, was sold for $80 to an Ottsville woman, while Perelman's four-door black 1965 Rover, which he had bought to replace the demolished Peugeot, brought the highest price of any of the items sold—$1,300.

The crowd kept hoping for a glimpse of Perelman, but he did not attend the auction. Nor did Adam or Abby. When Abby learned of the auction, she and her new boyfriend, Joe Aronson, came to Erwinna, and they worked furiously for several days, packing up items she wanted to keep in storage in Aronson's parents' home in upstate New York. Many of Sid's friends and neighbors also stayed away from the sale. They were appalled by Sid's decision to sell everything he owned, including personal items such as Laura's clothing and favorite knickknacks. They felt that this wholesale destruction of the home that the couple had shared for so many years revealed a lack of feeling. Many thought that he was cash-crazy and callous with regard to the feelings of his children. "It was like eating the flesh of the dead," one woman said.

But there were a few possessions that Sid refused to part with: a

256

thousand books, which he put into storage; the oak swivel chair he sat on while writing; a horn-handled pen knife that had belonged to Nathanael West; and his vintage four-door MG, which he was thinking seriously about shipping to England.[33] As he wrote Karl Fortess, "Somehow, the thought of driving it to Abingdon on Thames, where it came from, and asking the Morris Garage people to tune it up so I can use it for another 21 years appeals to me. What do you think?"[34]

The impulsive sale of his farm and possessions, a decision he was later to regret, was indicative of Sid's state of mind following Laura's death. "He was enormously depressed when Laura died," says a woman who knew him well. "He did that terrible thing in that terrible burst of grief and just sold everything, got rid of everything, and left for England. . . . He could erupt in anger all the time, but I have never known Sid so totally irritable and grief-stricken all at the same time.

"He didn't want to say he was totally wrong, but he said he wished he hadn't. Sid also had that compulsive rightness. He had to be right and correct and precise and that's why he was obsessed with words."

Many people remember Sid as being keyed-up and manic during this period. One source recalls Sid, who was by nature a shy, quiet man, chattering nonstop and telling her gleefully that with the sale of the farm and most of his possessions, he was richer than he had been in his entire life. Suddenly, too, he became extremely dependent on her and her husband. "Before Laura's death, he had been rude and ignored us," she says.

Sometime during this period Sid watched a television talk show in which a movie star announced that he had taken out a telephone contract for a large sum of money with Bell Telephone Company when he was making a foreign film. The film was never made, but Bell Telephone refused to refund his money. He was so angry that he announced his private number on television and invited the millions of people watching to call anyone they wanted. Sid jumped at the opportunity. He began calling everyone he knew in far places.

On the weekend before he was to leave for London, Sid was a guest at the home of Betty Blue Moodie, a friend who lived in Bucks County. Mrs. Moodie recalls that Sid called her at the last minute from New York and said he wanted to come to Bucks County to take one last look at his MG, which he had decided not to ship to England but to put in storage in a garage in Erwinna. As Mrs. Moodie was entertaining other guests that weekend, there was only an uncomfortable, unheated guest room available, but Sid was so desperate he came anyway. During the entire weekend he was very agitated and never stopped talking.[35]

Mrs. Moodie also recalls that Sid spent his last weekend in the United States calling friends all over the world. He was elated, high-spirited, full of anecdotes and jokes. To people who knew him well, his behavior seemed out of control, suggesting that he was on the verge of a nervous collapse.

In September, when Sid was packing his books for storage, Mc-Candlish Phillips, a reporter for the *New York Times*, telephoned him for an interview. Sid told him, "The fact that I think it's volcano time in this country is not responsible for the move, though I'm just as appalled as everyone about the conditions. I've had all the rural splendor that I can use, and each time I get to New York, it seems more pestilential than before. . . . Plants can live on carbon dioxide, but I can't. I think T. S. Eliot used the phrase 'twice-breathed air.' I'd hesitate to say how many times the air in New York has been re-breathed."

Sid also told Phillips that he had spent some time in London the previous winter and found there what seemed "a far more rational society than our own. The obvious good manners and consideration of people there toward each other may be only selfish, but it's good enough for me," he said.

"Today the news in this country is so filled with insanity and violence that the newspapers from which I derive many of my ideas have scant room for the sort of thing that turns me on—the bizarre, the unusual, the eccentric. In Britain, they still have the taste for eccentricity."[36]

*Volcano . . . pestilential . . . carbon dioxide . . . insanity . . . violence.* These were the words of a man suffocated by conflicting emotions that seemed impossible to untangle, a man who desperately needed to get away from himself.

On October 21, 1970, amid much press coverage and hullabaloo, America's foremost humorist left the United States for England and a new, presumably happier, life.

# PART THREE

1970–1979

# 19

## "ALONE IN THIS DAY OF HUMORISTS"

### *(1970–1972)*

Perelman's move to London in 1970 created a storm of controversy. The press was filled with articles and editorials questioning the wisdom of his decision. Although unaware of his intense inner turmoil, many journalists seemed to sense that he was motivated more by personal reasons than by a profound dissatisfaction with his native land. Philip Wagner in the *Philadelphia Evening Bulletin* predicted that Perelman "will learn expatriates can't escape themselves . . . they can't help looking back over their shoulders and wondering what they have actually gained,"[1] an opinion echoed in the *Christian Science Monitor* by Melvin Maddocks, who observed, "An expatriate travels, not to find a new home, but a new self."[2]

As might be expected, many prominent New Yorkers were infuriated by Perelman's blast at their city, taking it as a personal affront. "A contemptible act," Brendan Gill, drama critic of the *New Yorker*, was quoted as saying in the *Los Angeles Times*. "The man should be put into chains."[3]

Others, including Jimmy Breslin, resident essayist for *New York* magazine, a new weekly in rivalry with the *New Yorker*, used the occasion to tear down Perelman's literary reputation.

"Perelman? He's looking for a world that's gone. People don't laugh at him anymore. What did he ever write that you remember? Did he write 'Walter Mitty?' Thurber did. It's all gone for Perelman. The round table at the Algonquin, the match game at Bleeck's—that's all in the past. He won't find anything different in London. It's all the young now. He's coming over there even after the Beatles are gone. Even they are over the hill now. That's how young it is over there."[4]

Privately many of Sid's friends felt that he had made a huge mistake by being so vocal about his decision to emigrate. Writing to a friend, E. B. White commented: "It seems to me that if a man decides to shake off the dust of America and go somewhere else, he would be smart to sneak away with the least possible noise. Then, if he later changes his mind and wants to return to his native land, he can do it without incurring the gibes and jeers of the populace."[5]

Sid seemed surprised by the public's reaction. Perhaps he had begun to realize that the move to London, the sale of his farm, and the auctioning off of his possessions had been precipitous. Distraught by Laura's death, he had acted on impulse and made quick decisions he might ultimately regret.

In "A Farewell to Bucks," published in the *New York Times*, he wrote with a special note of poignancy about the deer and other wildlife on his former country estate:

> They used to come over the brow of the hill every evening at 6:40 during the Huntley-Brinkley broadcast in a slow-moving tapestry: First a doe, sniffing the air for possible danger to the two fawns following her, then a half-grown step-brother and finally the antlered sire, all nibbling intently as they made their way toward the salt block down the western slope of our farm. Once in a while, when the volume of our TV set crackled with the bark of guns in Vietnam or the snarl of jet, the deer would lift their heads and listen, but most of the time they were too busy feeding to notice.
>
> How many thousands of years they and their ancestors had followed that particular track was problematical. Certainly long before the big stone barn had been raised on the ridge and equipped with hex signs to ward off spells or the cattle, these original inhabitants of the land—and the pheasants, groundhogs, squirrels, moles and all the other rightful owners of the place—had been quietly going about their business of balancing the ecology. . . .
>
> The other morning in Philadelphia I recalled those many evenings when my wife and I used to skim off the horrors of the day's news and the deer moved silently through the dusk. A little group of us—the seller, the buyer, our respective real estate agents and lawyers—were gathered at a title company's office to conclude the formalities of the change of ownership, and as our pens scratched away at the countless documents, I began thinking about the permanent residents—the quadrupeds, the winged ones, the blind burrowing irrigators of the soil, and the myriad scaly, antennaed insects and reptiles whose claim to these fields and hills so far predated ours. Did they suspect, in their unimaginable dreams,

that five faceless folk had met in a glassed-in partition to accomplish this world-shaking agreement? The longer I thought about it the less likely it seemed and the more unreal the whole exercise became.[6]

His mood of disillusionment with America had evidently softened, for in an interview with Robert Taylor of the *Boston Globe* just before he sailed, he said that he did not plan to live in England permanently. "I'm not settling in England as an expatriate," he said. He blamed the *Times* reporter for creating a false impression of his plans. "He must have been wearing a leaky headset. He got me standing in the rubble at an uncomfortable moment. Anyway, I intend to come back here frequently and continue this shabby little trade of mine."[7]

On October 21, 1970, Perelman sailed on the S.S. *France* for Southampton, where he aroused great excitement among the passengers, who mistook him for Groucho Marx.[8] In London, he stayed briefly at the Reform Club, a great brownstone building on Pall Mall, and then moved in December to a flat he sublet from a South African woman painter. There, at 15 Onslow Gardens, he lived in untypical disarray with unanswered mail and packs of his favorite chocolates scattered about on chairs and his necktie hung on a rubber plant by the window.[9]

But he did not stay at home very long. For a bizarre idea had occurred to him, a desire to prove that like the fictitious Phileas Fogg, he could go around the world in eighty days. He would follow Fogg's itinerary exactly, leaving from the Reform Club, where Fogg had begun his journey, and using the modes of travel available in Victorian times—railroad, steamer, carriage, yacht, trading vessel, sledge and elephant. "Anyone can jet around the world in a 747," he said. "The point of the exercise is to do it Phileas Fogg fashion." As far as possible, he planned to follow Fogg's itinerary—traveling from London to Suez to Bombay to Calcutta to Hong Kong to Yokohama to San Francisco to New York to London. Exactly eighty days later, he would return to the Reform Club to celebrate his triumph, saying nonchalantly, as Fogg had done, "Here I am, gentlemen."

Fogg's companion on his trip around the world had been Passepartout, his French manservant. But Perelman's image of himself as a Lothario demanded that he have a female companion. He chose his secretary, Dianne Baker, a tall, pretty American girl, the daughter of a West Texas minister.

At eight o'clock on the evening of March 5, 1971,[10] Sid and Mrs.

263

Baker, accompanied by photographers, stepped out of the Reform Club into historic Pall Mall. A hansom cab drove them to Charing Cross Station, where they boarded the night train for Paris. In France the next day they lunched with David K. E. Bruce, former head of the U.S. delegation at the Paris Vietnam peace talks and his wife, Evangeline, at the Hotel Crillon. Also present was Ronald Searle, who would illustrate the book Sid planned to bring out in 1972 in celebration of the hundredth anniversary of Fogg's famous trip. Journalist Mary Blume, Lady Christian Hesketh (one of Sid's dearest friends, who had flown to Paris especially for the occasion) and Janet Flanner of the *New Yorker* completed the luncheon guests. Miss Flanner presented Sid with some Lanvin handkerchiefs as a farewell present.

On the following day Sid and Mrs. Baker traveled by train to Rome, where they dined with Robert Edwards and his wife, Luisa. Edwards had just produced *Death in Venice*. Sid had also worked for him in 1959 on an Italian film that was never finished. After traveling to Naples, they sailed for Istanbul.

So far the trip seemed to be progressing smoothly, even luxuriously, and Sid was optimistic. In eastern Turkey, however, less than fifty miles from the Iranian border, they were stopped by a violent snowstorm and forced back to Erzurum. Desperate to keep to his schedule, Sid broke his own rules about using modern transportation and flew back to Ankara so he could make air connections to Kuwait. "During the flight Sid wove an elaborate fabrication regarding the overland trek through Iran. 'We drove straight through so fast I didn't have time to stop off anywhere. We'll have to get some books on Iran so I can describe the countryside.' I was sworn to secrecy," Dianne Baker later wrote in an article about the trip for *Harper's Bazaar*.[11]

From Kuwait, they boarded a steamer for Bombay. Sid dreaded this part of the trip. He had never liked India or the Indians, and he especially abhorred Indian bureaucrats, who delighted in making things difficult for tourists, forcing them to spend hours filling out official forms. Disembarking in Bombay, he found his worst fears realized. He and Mrs. Baker were subjected to an interminable delay, possibly complicated by the fact that a passenger on the ship, a Hindu woman, had committed suicide that morning by leaping overboard.

"I'm forced to report that I found the subcontinent of India just as hysterical, scatterbrained, shrill and bureaucracy-ridden as it ever was ... I have been forced to conclude that deep down, no matter how placid the surface, there's a screw loose in the Indian mentality," he declared.[12]

When Phileas Fogg had been unable to travel all the way to Calcutta by train, he bought an elephant and reached his destination on schedule. Originally, Sid had planned to duplicate this feat, until he learned that riding fifty miles on an elephant would make him seasick. He decided to travel only ten miles on the animal. Much to his surprise, finding an elephant to ride on in India proved an almost insurmountable problem. It seemed that the only elephants in the entire country available for hire belonged to the Maharajah of Jaipur. This meant that Sid and Mrs. Baker had to fly to New Delhi, drive 200 miles to Jaipur, and then after they had ridden the elephant ten miles, drive back to New Delhi. According to Mrs. Baker's account, when they arrived at the Maharajah's Amber Palace, Sid, decked out in white safari jacket, custom-made white silk trousers, blue T-shirt and silk sashcoat, scrambled up into the silver howdah of a brilliantly caparisoned elephant named Rosebud, which the guide claimed was "the same elephant Jacqueline Kennedy rode during her visit to India."

" 'Highly improbable,' Sid said," Mrs. Baker reports. " 'We've landed in the Disneyland of India.' Nonetheless, he leapt into the howdah with all the enthusiasm of a delinquent Weight Watcher on a binge in a Viennese bakery. Rosebud took off at a fast lumber. A hundred yards later, I heard an agonizing shriek. Rosebud made an abrupt about-face and returned at a gallop to the launching pad. Ashen-faced, Sid descended. 'I'm getting seasick. You ride this infernal beast if you've got the guts.' He tottered over to the Chevy and collapsed in air-conditioned comfort."[13]

The next seven days increased Sid's irritability and gloom. From New Delhi, he and Mrs. Baker flew to Madras, which he found depressing. After Madras they crossed the Bay of Bengal on an Indian freighter. The cargo consisted of thousands of bushels of onions that reeked unbearably in the blazing heat. The ship was filthy and swarming with rats and giant cockroaches. The food was abysmal. According to Mrs. Baker, "we ate lamb curry for breakfast, chicken curry for lunch, fish curry for dinner, and stewed onions at every meal. I dissolved in sweat, sunbathing on the poop deck while S.J.P. read or suffered in stony silence."[14]

Unable to tolerate such conditions any longer, they disembarked at Penang and flew to Singapore, where Sid retreated to his hotel room for three days. When he emerged, he took Mrs. Baker to Chinatown, where they visited the bird shops on Rochor Road. "I propose to convert you to my enthusiasm for the Chinese. They're such clean, intelligent people," she quoted him as saying.[15]

In Hong Kong, a few days later, he fired Mrs. Baker. "Ever since Bombay, Sid had been prone to moody silences followed by temper tantrums. I attributed his irascible humor to fatigue and disappointment in failing to follow Fogg's trail faithfully. I was dead wrong. He was plotting a scheme to trade me in for a mynah bird. It happened in Hong Kong. Without warning the ax fell. I'd hardly unpacked my bags when Sid gave me an air ticket back to London with a curt, 'It'll cost me $2,500 to get you back via the itinerary. The air fare is $611. You're no longer of value to me.' There was no other explanation or reason given for this abrupt dismissal."[16]

Under the name Diane Ellis, Dianne Baker published her version of the trip, "Halfway Around the World in 40 Days with S. J. Perelman," in the May 1972 issue of *Harper's Bazaar*. Her comments about her traveling companion did not make a flattering portrait. Sid was described as a testy, easily depressed man who refused to shake the dirty hands of Moslem children because he feared contracting a disease, a man who spent most of his time engaged in a non-Phileas Fogg pursuit, namely sulking in his hotel room.

In his own account of the trip, "Around the Bend in Eighty Days," serialized in the *New Yorker* and later collected in the anthology *Vinegar Puss*, Sid blamed everything on Mrs. Baker's boyfriend. "The discus thrower at Cal Tech with whom she had confessed an earlier infatuation at the time I hired her had re-entered her life. Currently living in London, he had been wooing her assiduously throughout our journey—indeed, had proposed by cable in Singapore, importuning her to curtail the trip and join him at the altar."[17]

This was his fictional alibi. In reality, their personalities had clashed violently. If Mrs. Baker found Perelman moody and cantankerous, he found her bossy and dominating. He blamed the blow-up in Singapore on the overbearing way she had told him to wrap up some books he was sending back to London.

Again perhaps Sid's irascibility could be blamed on the fact that he badly missed Laura—whether subconsciously or otherwise. For years, he had traveled with her to all corners of the globe. She kept him company in lonely, uncomfortable circumstances and shared his new experiences with a zest to match his own. Not only had she helped him with his work, she also had been the subject of innumerable caricatures in the travel pieces he wrote about their adventures together. But Laura was dead, and he needed a woman to perform her function in his fiction. Like the youthful Laura, Mrs. Baker was tall and dark, but there all resemblance ended. Mrs. Baker had no tolerance for his quick changes of mood, nor did she know how to rouse him from his depressions as Laura time and again had been able to do somehow.

For the remainder of his life, Sid would keep on looking for an ideal female companion to replace his wife in his travels, but all his efforts would result in disaster. The fantasy could never measure up to the truth.

Like many men, Sid was repelled by women his own age. Their wrinkles and stooped figures were to him marks of waning sexuality, and he had no wish to be identified with them. At age sixty-seven he still felt young and vigorous, capable of attracting women in their twenties and thirties. His itinerary from Hong Kong to San Francisco had called for him to sail on the *President Wilson*, but he decided to fly when he encountered a number of elderly female tourists at his hotel in Hong Kong. "Phileas Fogg never had to contend with these blue-haired American ladies with a Southern accent," he told a reporter. "My mind boggles at the thought of having to spend nineteen days with an entire shipload of these creatures."[18]

In Hong Kong, just before he fired Dianne Baker, he bought a mynah bird. He called it Tong Cha II, after Tong Cha, the beloved mynah bird he had bought in 1949 in Bangkok and kept until its death.

With Tong Cha II, he flew to Tokyo and then to Los Angeles, where he visited Neva Patterson and James Lee, arriving at the door with a box of brown rice he asked Neva to cook for the bird. Back in New York, he stayed at the Hotel Algonquin for a week, visiting friends, doctors and dentists before sailing on the *Queen Elizabeth II* for England. It was a dismal crossing. "Somehow, all the blue-haired ladies from Santa Barbara, all the elderly pirates with liver spots I had eluded on the *President Wilson* had mysteriously hurtled across the world to enliven the passage. They held cocktail parties morning, noon and night, danced the tango in paper hats, and generated such jollification that the crossing became one endless gala . . . And when the mighty vessel drew into her berth at Southampton, terminating the longest five-day voyage in memory, I felt that I had paid my debt to Phileas Fogg."[19]

Although Sid accomplished his goal and went around the world (though in 76 days, to be exact), the trip itself was a humiliating fiasco. Pretending to be a fictitious Victorian gentleman in the 20th century had proved an impossible—indeed ridiculous—fantasy. For Sidney Joseph Perelman, Phileas Fogg was yet another role in a long series of personas—man about town, intrepid world traveler, dashing Lothario, elegant dandy—that he tried to don in a search for self-identity, an adolescent dream of grandeur inevitably doomed to failure.

On a professional level as well, the trip had been a disaster. To meet his schedule, Sid had had to break his much publicized ground rules and fly instead of following in Fogg's footsteps. He was also forced to bypass certain countries and cities that had been accessible to travelers in Fogg's day. As he said in an interview in the *Los Angeles Times*, "It was infinitely more difficult to do the trip now than it was one hundred years ago."[20]

In no respect had this frenzied safari measured up to his two previous trips around the world—the first with Al Hirschfeld in 1947, the second with his family in 1949. Years had elapsed since he had undertaken those adventures with their sense of heady excitement and high hopes. He was sixty-seven years old now, and Laura was dead, and even though he would have been loath to admit it, going around the world for a third time was a melancholy attempt to retrace not Phileas Fogg's footsteps but possibly his own. Buying another mynah bird in Hong Kong was another indication of his terrible yearning for a past forever gone. Yet he knew inwardly that even if he revisited the old places and duplicated the actions of his younger self, the past could never be recaptured. Even Tong Cha II was nothing like his predecessor. He only said "Hello" and hated to be petted.

Like the blue-haired Southern ladies who were desperate for gaiety and glamor in their declining years, Sid would have to come to terms with being old and alone.

# 20

## "ADIEU TO ONSLOW SQUARE"

### *(1972–1975)*

When Sid returned from Hong Kong with Tong Cha II, he found that his South African landlady had returned to London unexpectedly, and a new flat had been found for him—at 14 Onslow Square.

It was a beautiful apartment, more luxurious than his first. It boasted a concert grand piano, a marble fireplace, matching white couches and a sunny, well-equipped kitchen. Once his favorite art works and thirty-one cases of books were moved in, it seemed like a haven where he could settle down for life. He hung Tong Cha II's cage next to a kitchen window where the bird could watch the neighborhood cats.

Life in England was reasonably pleasant for a while. People invited Sid to parties, he was interviewed in all the newspapers and lionized by the intelligentsia. In 1970 he had met Princess Margaret at a gathering at the Kenneth Tynans'. They had chatted, and he had given her his specially made cigarette lighter when her own had failed to work.

The British intellectuals considered him America's foremost humorist. They adored his dazzling wordplays and delicious parodies of great English writers. He had lunch at some of the most exclusive clubs, and was entertained for the weekend at fashionable house parties given by the nobility. Living alone as he was now, he occasionally became rattled about his social engagements and would arrive much later than the prescribed hour or else not appear at all.

Laura had arranged such social matters for him in the past. Perhaps he missed her more than he knew. Some of his friends felt that his equilibrium had been shattered by her death, for his behavior seemed to alternate between manic activity and listless melancholy.

269

To Constance Sayre of Simon and Schuster, who moved to England when he did, Sid gave the impression of a man determined not to live in the past. "He needed people around him, needed attention," she says. "After Laura died, he didn't know where he wanted to be, wanted to do . . . He did not dwell on the past at all. He was more concerned with creating his new life, inventing it almost, inventing the Perelman of the 1970s. What will he do now? What will he be now? It seemed a life very much for the present rather than the past. Of course he was always looking for new material, and so he wasn't interested in presumably dwelling on what was old material that had been worked and revised."[1]

At 14 Onslow Square Sid sat down in his freshly painted study and tried to write a series about the trip he had taken. The work was slow-going, for as he wrote to a friend, his other trips around the world had been filled with comic incidents, whereas the Phileas Fogg episode had been mainly tedious. He found that he had to invent most of it.[2]

Between bouts at the typewriter he roamed the city or dropped in on friends—Mel Calman, a writer and cartoonist, and his wife, Karen; Shirley Conran, author of *Lace;* Chaim Raphael, Norman Lewis, Vera Russell, Ernie Anderson; the writer Max Wilk and his wife, Barbara; and Lady Christian Hesketh, who often entertained him at her estate in Northamptonshire.

One of Sid's very close friends in London was Eric Lister, an extroverted and energetic Englishman from Manchester who owned an art gallery specializing in the work of naive and primitive painters. In the 1970s he accompanied Sid on many trips throughout England, Europe and Tunisia. In his reminiscences, *Don't Mention the Marx Brothers*, published in 1985 in England, Lister describes meeting Sid for the first time at his gallery in 1967:

I observed a small ultra-dapper elderly gentleman sporting a brown Locke's pork-pie hat, English "raised-seam" cheviot-tweed sports jacket, Brooks Brothers Oxford button-down shirt, silk-knitted tie, steam-pressed grey flannel trousers and hand-made well-patinated brogues. With some trepidation, I took the plunge. "Mr. Perelman, I presume."

The face that turned towards me was a caricaturist's delight. Round and florid with jowls like antique waxed rosewood carefully shaved for half-a-century in close collaboration with Mr. Gillette. The straight, grey, thick, bristly moustache carefully matched an eyebrow (either one). Appearing beneath those bushy caterpillars were the once-seen-never-forgotten Perelman eyes. Large, dark and inscrutable, the right one looking directly at me, the other staring disconcertingly over my left shoulder into infinity. The entire ocular effect was magnified by an ancient pair of minute oval silver spectacles. As memorable a trademark as the Perelman eyes was the Perelman voice. Soft, croaky, hesitant, slightly breathless and topped with an East Coast nasal twang, as American as the cherry on a chocolate malted ice cream soda.[3]

Lister seems to have been a far more amusing and steadfast companion than the women Sid always hoped would enliven his travels. Like Laura, he understood his quirks and knew how to jolly him out of his black moods. An accomplished clarinetist, he shared Sid's love of jazz; on their travels he took care of many of the arrangements. He was also an expert on vintage cars. Lister introduced Sid to Blyume's, a Jewish restaurant in Soho, where Sid feasted on *kneidlach* soup and corned beef sandwiches, and he and Lister verbally sparred with one another, their conversation larded with Yiddish phrases. In his memoir, Lister emphasizes Sid's "lightheartedness," portraying him as a loveable curmudgeon. And perhaps with Lister he was more buoyant and relaxed than he was with other people, for during his life Sid seems to have been the most contented when he was in the company of an outgoing and amiable Jewish male—a Nathanael West, I. J. Kapstein, Al Hirschfeld, Harvey Orkin or Eric Lister—who shared his intellectual interests and wild sense of the ridiculous.

As time went on, there were fewer invitations to the manor houses and chic flats, perhaps because Sid seldom reciprocated with invitations of his own. "He was a marvelous guest and he was an absolutely non-host," says a friend who spent a lot of time with him in London. "Once he brought along two extra guests when he was invited to a total stranger's home. He didn't tell his host the other people were coming. He just showed up with them. . . . I think his penuriousness must have had something to do with his eventually leaving London because several people told me that they would have him to dinner, for the weekend, to the country, but there was never any reciprocity, and I think he got dropped, and then that's when he got lonely."

He had lunch and dinner with Groucho Marx. Groucho seemed frail, but his mood wasn't as black as it had been in California, where Sid had seen him last. Still, Sid was shocked by Groucho's deterioration. It was hard to believe that "this creaky old man" had once been the "bouncy" and audacious star of *Monkey Business*. Later, when Groucho was very ill and near death, Sid went to a birthday party given for him by Erin Fleming, Groucho's constant companion in his last years. As Sid's friend Louise Kerz describes the scene: "The birthday party was in Groucho's bedroom. Groucho was in bed, drugged up, and everyone stood around. Erin Fleming called everyone in. Sid and Groucho had a conversation."[4]

Neva Patterson was there, and she describes the party in more detail: "Erin Fleming said to Groucho, 'You've got to get to bed'— she was very good with him. 'You've had too much Christmas' or something like that, and he went to bed, and she put on his pajamas and he came in wearing them, and he had scuffies—Dr. Dentons with simulated pompons on them—and he said 'I've gotta sing a couple of songs,' and he sang 'Hello, I Must Be Going,' 'On the Banks of the Indiana,' and 'I Love a Piano.' "[5]

Sid and Groucho's relationship may have softened at the very end of Groucho's life, but Sid still harbored certain grudges against him. He told Louise Kerz that he had never gotten over the reading of the script of *Monkey Business* and Groucho's utter silence after the reading ended. As though the hurt had happened yesterday, he would grow visibly angry. "Imagine that—not saying a word!" He described Groucho to her as "one of the most detestable people [he had] ever met."

England was beginning to lose some of its charm for Sid. On closer inspection it proved depressingly modern and drab. Gone were the days of Edwardian splendor. South Kensington, where he lived, was peopled not with dashing, mysterious figures like Sherlock Holmes, but "by stiff-backed Anglo-Indian women living in genteel penury, stalking out three or four times a day to buy one egg or a lemon."[6]

As time went on, he began to condemn the British almost as fiercely as he had damned New Yorkers. The English were repressed, smug, provincial and condescending, he said. Furthermore they talked so rapidly that he couldn't understand a word they were saying. But the worst thing about them was their sense of humor. It was entirely different from his own.

He had sublet his flat on Onslow Square for a year, but well before the lease was up, he could not wait to vacate the premises. In an unpublished piece, "Adieu to Onslow Square," he wrote about the beautiful white couches, the marble fireplace, his hundreds of books and favorite works of art from the Orient. "Well, Lord knows how I got it all sorted out, but finally the packing cases, the cartons of excelsior, shredded newspaper and wisps of plastic were toted off, and the place was ready to be lived in. I slipped into my brand new smoking jacket, the red velvet kind with the braided shawl collar, went into the reception room and sat down on one of the white couches, sidewise to the marble fireplace. After awhile I noticed how remarkably quiet it was. You couldn't hear a voice or a sound. You certainly couldn't hear the mynah bird way out in Gloucestershire shrieking at the friends I'd given him to. After awhile I decided it would have made more sense for the mynah to have given *me* to the friends in Gloucestershire because I sure didn't belong in this flat, seated on this white couch between the marble fireplace and the concert grand. So I took off the smoking jacket, put on my hat and went down to Walton Street to the estate agents where I had a heart-to-heart talk with Miss Olive Crouchbody."[7]

In his memoir, Eric Lister reports that before Sid left England, he sold his enormous library to a South Kensington dealer, retaining only a few dozen books for himself. He gave Lister his jazz records and some personal belongings, including a Mickey Mouse picture frame that Eileen McKenney, who had worked for the Disney Studios, had given him many years before.[8] Sid was obviously in a depression, and Lister tried to talk him out of his decision. After the books were sold, Lister called up Sid's friend, Max Wilk, who fortunately was able to buy some volumes back from the dealer.[9]

In May of 1972, after six months in London, Sid sailed to New York on the S.S. *France*. He insisted that it was only for a visit, but once in New York he immediately sublet a furnished apartment on 220 East 73rd Street. "English life, while very pleasant, is rather bland," he told Israel Shenker in a widely quoted interview in the *New York Times*. "I expected kindness and gentility and I found it, but there is such a thing as too much couth.

"Their rye bread has no caraway seeds, and their name for corned beef is salt beef—and it doesn't compare with what you can get on the Upper West Side or on the Lower East Side. . . .

"When I'm away, I miss the tension, the give and take. I feel it's a great mistake for any writer to cut himself off from his roots. One's work suffers by trying to transplant it to another milieu.

"My style is mélange—a mixture of all the sludge I read as a child, all the clichés, liberal doses of Yiddish, criminal slang, and some of what I was taught in a Providence, Rhode Island, school by impatient teachers. When I tried to think of an idiomatic expression in London, I had to reach for it. I felt out of touch with the idiom. . . .

"What I would like to do hereafter is to spend my winters in New York and three or four months of each summer in England. That still leaves the spring and autumn unaccounted for, and maybe then I can let my beard grow and become the castaway God intended me to be."[10]

In New York he socialized with old friends, who included the Hirschfelds, the Philip Hamburgers, Ruth Goetz and the Hacketts, who gave him a birthday party every year and whom Sid regarded as "saintly" people.

But in late September he was on the move again, traveling to London, France, Italy and the Far East on assignment for *Travel & Leisure*, a magazine backed by the American Express Company and edited by the former staff of the now defunct *Holiday*. He had been commissioned to write several pieces for a series to be entitled "Nostasia in Asia": on the Hunzas, a people in the remote Himalayas who supposedly lived to be a hundred and twenty as the result of eating apricot pits;[11] on Hong Kong; on the Ainus in northern Japan; and on Banda Neira, the remote island in East Indonesia that Somerset Maugham insisted he visit in 1949 and that he wrote about in *The Swiss Family Perelman*.

Caskie Stinnett was the new editor of *Travel & Leisure*. "As a writer, Sid was difficult to deal with," he recalls. "I think the reason for that was that the *New Yorker* so pampers its writers by giving them everything they want, including a tremendous amount of money and lots of time and so much space to write in, that when they go to another publication such as *Holiday* and *Travel & Leisure*, almost everything they don't get they feel is an affront to them as a writer."

According to Mr. Stinnett, little things upset Sid. He hated to produce receipts after he had gone on a trip, and was cantankerous about money. He was also stubborn about being edited, even if it was a question of merely cleaning up an awkward sentence. But Mr. Stinnett understood his tough attitude. "Undoubtedly he felt that editing might deflate the humor," he says.[12]

In Rome, Sid spent some time with Abby, who was living there with her second husband, Joe Aronson, whom she married in Edgartown, Massachusetts, on September 29, 1970. An excellent artist, Aronson had spent four years in Florence prior to their marriage. In 1972 he won the Prix de Rome, and he and Abby had gone to Italy for two years. A short, dark man, Aronson had been in Abby's class at the City and Country School. Sid liked him and was upset when the marriage broke up several years later. He told one of his women friends that he did not think his daughter was "suited to matrimony."

After spending some time with them, Sid flew on to Indonesia. It had always been one of his favorite places, and he spent a memorable two and a half weeks there, cruising on a sailing ship through the Banda and Aratura Seas lying between New Guinea and Australia. He visited remote island groups such as the Kai, the Aru and the Tanimbar, which still remained as they had been in the 1850s, when Alfred Russel Wallace had visited them.

After stopping off at Bali, which he found disappointingly commercialized, he flew to Sydney and then to Alice Springs in the Australian outback. Although he found Australia dull, his trip to the outback was not without incident.

On his flight to Alice Springs, the plane, with thirty-eight passengers aboard, was hijacked. It was the first incident of its type in Australia. "I didn't realize it was real until I saw the gun aimed directly at my bosom, which at the time was full of Indonesian rice," he told a reporter. "When the plane stopped at Alice Springs, the hostess advised us that anyone who was ill or subject to heart attacks would be allowed to leave. To my surprise, everyone but seven or eight immediately got up and left. I couldn't imagine why the others stayed. As we left, the hijacker asked each passenger to show his ticket, examined it, and then said, 'Get out.' My immediate reaction was to ask myself how a poltroon would behave in these circumstances. That's exactly how I behaved. I got off the plane."[13]

At the time of the hijacking, Perelman was carrying nine large Ming plates he had purchased in Indonesia. Somehow he managed to leap off the plane without damaging a single one. "I never wrote about it," he told Sukey Pett of the Associated Press, "because except for that one remark by the stewardess it wasn't really funny. The hijacker was killed by the police but not before he wounded a detective."[14]

The erratic pattern of Sid's life continued. He seemed unable to stay long in one place. In the next seven years he would zigzag back and forth across the world like a distracted butterfly, using almost any excuse to remain constantly on the move.

Yet his ceaseless trips seemed to bring him no happiness, no answer to what he was really searching for. "He didn't know what he wanted," a friend says. He was critical of almost everything, and his letters to friends became increasingly jaded.

In February of 1973, after returning from Australia, he tried communal living in a house in Sarasota Springs, Florida, which he rented with Lillian Hellman, Frances and Albert Hackett and a couple of young poets. It was not a successful experiment.

For one thing, he loathed Sarasota Springs. It was too full of old people to suit his taste. Nor did he like the rented house, which was so crowded with furniture and knickknacks it resembled an auction gallery. Nor did he enjoy the cooking, which was done at first by a Mennonite lady and an Armenian student who spent the day baking chocolate cakes, and then by Lillian Hellman, who was good at fish and spaghetti, but made a pot roast that tasted like a "shag rug." The temperature of Florida was disappointingly cold, the social life dull and Sid complained that Lillian Hellman spent too much time on the phone, conversing with Renata Adler, Mike Nichols and her secretary in New York. The monotony of his life in Florida was enlivened only by a visit from Harvey Orkin, his agent, who brought two pounds of corned beef from Sid's favorite New York delicatessen as a house present.

The Hacketts he found congenial, but the personality of Lillian Hellman grated on his nerves in this day-to-day contact. He found her arrogant and bossy, and he was scarcely sympathetic to her much-publicized feuds. After her contretemps with Diana Trilling, he wrote Caskie Stinnett that "maybe the girls should book with the Pond Lecture Bureau as a wrassling act for Chatauquas and country fairs. Or the best seven out of nine falls at the next Authors' League social. I'm sure Halston could run up something real nifty in the way of red and blue rosettes for their trunks. Then the winner could be matched against your fave Bella Abzug."

He felt that Hellman took herself and her own life much too seriously. She "mythologized" everything, particularly her famous love affair with Dashiell Hammett. After reading *Scoundrel Time*, he wrote a friend that "Lil has begun to confuse herself with George Sand. I see all the preliminary symptoms of *folie de grandeur;* she regards herself as a historical character, and as someone who has known her

276

since 1928 or thereabouts, I am becoming alarmed lest those men in the white jackets armed with butterfly nets suddenly appear and entice her into their wagon."

A lifelong admirer of beautiful women, Sid often made derogatory though witty remarks about Lillian's looks. His attitude was cruel, considering how sensitive he was about his own appearance—which, however, he also was quick to make wisecracks about. As he was leaving the Reform Club on his third trip around the world, he told Lewis Chester of the *Sunday Times* that "even built-up shoes could not conceal that [he was] 'almost a dwarf...' "[15] and on another occasion he told Alan Coren, the editor of *Punch*, "I never get over the shock of being Rex Harrison inside and then catching sight of myself in one of these damn mirrors."[16]

Leila Hadley feels that in many cases Sid's wild criticisms of other people were externalized criticisms of himself. "For example, he always denigrated people who were short, like Billy Rose," she says.

Miss Hellman retaliated by telling other people how stingy he was. When Diane Johnson, Hammett's biographer, took Sid to lunch to discuss his reminiscences of the detective writer, she hooted with laughter when she learned that Miss Johnson had paid for it.[17] According to Heywood Hale Broun, both Hellman and Perelman were by nature acerbic and grouchy people, and it was amazing they got along with one another as well as they did.

Broun remembers one day when he and Sid ran into Lillian on the street. Lillian greeted Sid warmly and said, "Why don't we open up one of those little triangular shops under the steps of an office building where we can sell candy?" Sid replied wryly to the suggestion, "Good idea. Fine line for old Jews."[18]


By late March Sid was ready to return to New York. There he rented two rooms on the 15th floor of the Gramercy Park Hotel on Lexington Avenue and decided to make it his official headquarters.

Many years before he had said in an interview, "My ambition is to live out of a paper suitcase in the Dixie Hotel and take off at will."[19] Like the Sutton, the old Dixie Hotel, in the West Forties, boasted a colorful clientele—actors and circus performers, including midgets, were frequent guests. Sid sometimes stayed there, and according to Heywood Hale Broun, some of his happiest writing was done at the Dixie, for as soon as he had finished a piece and delivered it to the

*New Yorker*, he would go directly to Port Authority and take a bus back to Erwinna.

The Dixie had long since been torn down, and the Gramercy Park Hotel was more elegant, but in choosing to live as a hotel guest, he was living out the old fantasy—of a man without ties, a transient, a wanderer with a minimum of possessions, a man free as a wild bird.

His rooms were small and plainly furnished. The hotel furniture was enlivened only by a few personal possessions—his Royal Quiet portable typewriter, and the attractive oak swivel armchair on which he sat to do his writing, plus a 17th-century head of Kuan Yin that Leila Hadley had given him, and several paintings and photographs by artist friends. In his bathroom he put up a photograph of Jetta Goudal, one of the beautiful silent screen stars he had worshiped in his youth. "When Jetta falls off the wall, I will die," he told a friend. She outlived him by five years, dying at the age of eighty-six, on January 16, 1985.

The hotel was near several of his favorite restaurants, and not far away from a delicatessen he liked—so he dined out frequently. He loved to eat well and never worried about his weight, which, thanks to heavy smoking and a highly nervous temperament, never varied throughout his life. According to a friend, he "had a sweet tooth and loved chocolate fudge sundaes and rich desserts topped with whipped cream." He had lived all over the world but was not a gourmet, preferring the simple Jewish food of his childhood or Chinese food. Eric Lister writes that he loathed vegetables and health foods.

After Laura's death, Sid continued to have relationships with many women. Some of his involvements were with women he had been seeing off and on for years; others were with women he met after Laura's death. Among the latter were Diane Daniels, an attractive blonde from Westport, Connecticut, who was a friend of the Max Wilkses; and Irene Kemmer, a friend of Laura's to whom he dedicated *Vinegar Puss*. A widow, Mrs. Kemmer visited Sid when he was living in London and shared his interest in travel and the occult.

These two relationships, as well as the others in his life, were kept in separate compartments. Just as it had been when Laura was alive, Sid protected the names and reputations of his ladyfriends, and none of them knew about the existence of the others. Many of the letters he wrote to them were highly erotic in a most amusing way.

One such letter, written from Australia to a longtime friend and mistress, includes a spicy account of a chance sexual encounter with a woman Sid supposedly met while traveling in Indonesia. He describes a tall, dark, voluptuous lady he notices at the Jakarta Airport—a woman so beautiful and alluring he can't take his eyes off her. As they board the plane, he realizes that both he and she are carrying identical flight bags, which have been mixed up by the baggage attendant so that Sid has hers and she has his. Rummaging through her bag, he finds cosmetics and a leather-bound diary. Judging by the diary's torrid entries (which of course he "quotes" in Krafft-Ebing style), he realizes that the lady is ravenous for a man.

Slipping the diary back into the flight bag, he strolls casually to the rear of the plane. "Naturally my heart (and particularly another vital organ) swelled at the opportunity this mix-up offered." The lady sat beside an unoccupied place. Sliding into the seat beside her, Sid handed her her bag and confessed he had read her diary:

> I was of course watching her reaction out of the corner of my eye, and baby, it was a peach.
>
> "That was a rather nasty thing to do," she said, endeavoring not to raise her voice. ". . . And what emotion did it arouse if any?"
>
> "A rather complex one," I said. "In part a desire to help, to assist—to *succor* you, so to speak. To ride to the assistance of a damsel in distress as any true gentleman would."
>
> "M-m-m," she said reflectively, pondering my words. Then she leaned closer to me, and as she did so, I was offered an unobstructed view down the front of her cleavage. They were really magnificent breasts—like ripe mangoes, and the coral-tinted nipples (longing, I felt, to be succored and titillated) sent a galvanic charge to my cock. "You say in part," she went on. "Was that the only emotion?"
>
> "Not at all," I said. "Permit me to show you." I reached over and took her hand which she made no effort to withdraw, and placed it on my fly where there was a quite noticeable elevation. "How *fascinating*," she said, averting her head, and speaking rather dreamily as if she had no connection with what was transpiring. "But tell me—how can I be sure that that isn't just a pocket flashlight?"

Thus impishly he goes on, obviously bent on tickling the prurience of his real girlfriend or perhaps merely making her laugh.

A letter written to Paul Theroux in 1976 reveals the delight Sid still took in attracting pretty young women even at the advanced age of seventy-two:

Dear Paul,

Between the constant repetition of "White Christmas" and "Jingle Bells" on station WPAT and the increasing frenzy of Saks' and Gimbel's newspaper ads as these fucking holidays draw near, I have been in a zombie-like state for weeks, totally incapable of rational thought or action. I must have arrived at near-paralysis yesterday afternoon when I was in the 4th-floor lingerie section ("Intimate Apparel") in Saks 5th Avenue. I had just purchased two such intimate garments for gifties to a couple of ladies of my acquaintance, a tall blonde and a somewhat shorter brunette. For the former I had chosen a black lace chemise in the style known as a teddy back in the Twenties (familiar to you as the scanty garment worn by Rita Hayworth in the war-time pinup). For the shorter brunette, a similar peach-colored job. Both of these real silk, parenthetically, and as I signed the charge slip, I knew that when the bill comes in after January 1st, I would kick myself for my prodigality. Anyway, while the hard-featured saleslady was wrapping them up with appropriate mash-notes to each bimbo, I went upstairs to the men's dept. to buy myself a cheap tie-tack. When I returned for the feminine frillies, I found (a) that the saleslady had forgotten to identify which box was which, and (b) that she had switched the notes. In other words, the blonde Amazon would find herself with the brunette's undershirt and some steamy sentiment addressed to the latter, and vice versa. I broke out into a perspiration—it's tropically hot in those department stores anyway—and insisted on the saleslady clawing open the boxes, which meant destroying all the fake holly berries, silver cord and mish-mash they were entwined in. This of course put her in a foul temper, and meanwhile a waiting queue of customers became incensed. The upshot was a group shot of seven or eight people leering and cackling obscenely as I stood there holding the two chemises and the notes appropriate to the recipients. Given the savoir-faire of Cary Grant I might have risen above it but the only savoir-faire I possess is Oliver Hardy's, and little enough of that....[20]

Sid occasionally discussed marriage with a few of the women he dated. However, he never became engaged nor did he ever live with a woman.

Why did he not remarry once he was free? Perhaps because it would have spoiled the romantic fantasies he preferred to revel in. Or perhaps he regarded marriage as an entrapment. It was associated with the dead weight of Laura's unhappiness and the long, burdensome responsibility he must have felt for her welfare. Once he became a widower, he was eager to remain free to improvise a new life and taste new experiences, and to do so he had to keep moving, not tie himself down to a serious commitment. To the end of his days he was a man who avoided powerful emotions, either other people's or his own.

"He was tight. He was tight on a lot of levels," says a beautiful actress who was the recipient of many of Sid's torrid—and playful— love letters, but who was never his mistress. "And by tight, I don't mean cheap. I mean contained, and I'm sure that was difficult in terms of his children and in terms of loving. It was probably easier for him to be freer with strangers, freer in his letters than it was on a one-to-one, intimate level."

Several of his women friends were struck by the powerful hold Laura still exerted over him after her death. "He admired her greatly," says Diane Daniels, who dated Sid from 1974 until the beginning of 1979 when she became engaged to another man. "He felt that she had keen insight about people. After she died, he told me that he had dreams about her."[21]

Another woman, a college professor who enjoyed a relationship with Sid that spanned several decades, said, "After Laura died, he became sentimental about her. When I visited Sid at his hotel in London, there were pictures of her in his room. I had never seen any before."

Many of the women who were involved with Perelman still speak tenderly about him years after his death. To an impartial observer he may have been small and insignificant-looking, an unlikely man to have been such a Lothario, but in the courtly, romantic way he treated women and in the brilliance and variety of his literary achievements, he possessed a charisma that attracted them far more than mere good looks.

What kind of woman was Perelman attracted to? In general, most were like himself—sophisticated, amusing, intelligent and civilized, yet oddly evasive, somewhat cryptic, private people who tended to protect themselves. Today many of them live in fear that their names will be connected with him romantically. Many portray themselves as "just good friends." "My relationship with Mr. Perelman is not a matter for the public record," writes Irene Kemmer. Although Mrs. Kemmer declined to be interviewed, she offered the following anecdote in a letter:

On September 23, 1979, I was seated on a plane moving from Peking to Nanking. The man beside me was the shy, reserved, yet very bright English journalist who served as guide to our party of 10 in order to perfect his study of the countless dialects in the Chinese language.

As a rule, Simon spoke very little, and we travelers went so far as to find him properly inscrutable. Knowing this, I was surprised and very delighted to find him trying to "make conversation." His opening query was a wish for my impressions of Peking.

Then he asked if I knew anyone who had already made the Chinese trek. I said I did—that it was a New York friend who had attempted, the previous year, to drive a vintage car from Paris to Peking. Simon showed great excitement, and said, "Oh, you mean S. J. Perelman. Isn't it too bad that he died."

I was frozen. Then my heart began the kind of flip-flops I didn't think it could sustain. My head hammered out a reminder that I hadn't seen a scrap of news printed in a language I could read in many weeks, and that perhaps Simon had heard something in his frequent telephone calls made to the West during our travels. If it was true, I didn't want to know. I changed the subject, and we soon landed.

The journey continued, and on October 12, I flew into JFK. A man from San Francisco (a stranger, too) asked to share my cab into town. The first stop was his—the Gramercy Park Hotel, and the home of SJP. The coincidence was staggering.

I got to my address, tore out the keys, tore up the 5 flights of stairs, and dialed the number of SJP's apartment. The familiar voice gave a delighted laugh and said, "Welcome home from old Cathay." The chat was mercifully brief. I was on my knees with relief and fatigue. After computing the number of days it would take for a 16-hour jet lag to recede, we made a date for October 19. I went to bed and slept like a rock. I was never to hear SJP's voice again. On the 17th, he died.[22]

Perelman also continued to see Leila Hadley, who by a curious twist of fate had since married the man who had bought Sid's farm in Erwinna.

"I met William Musham [her third husband, a business executive] at Derald Ruttenberg's sixtieth birthday party on February 16, 1976," she states, "and I was fascinated that he owned Sid Perelman's place in Bucks County. I married him on May 29, 1976. I had been up to that place several times before when Laura was alive, and I knew that Sid always kept his MG there, that car that was like another child. And then when William and I were married, Sid came up and visited quite a lot of times, and that's why I planted all those trees and put in 10,000 daffodils."[23]

Leila Hadley and William Musham, who were divorced in 1979, turned the farm, which they renamed Northern Cross Farm, into a showplace. They put in a pool and tennis court, and there were peacocks on the property. According to Leila, Sid approved of these changes and was grateful that they cared as much as he did about the land.

After Laura's death, Sid had a sheet brass plaque made and one day he nailed it on one of the pin-oak trees on the property. It read: "In memory of Laura Perelman and Nathanael West. S. J. Perelman."

Another woman he was deeply fond of was Prudence Crowther, whom he met eight months before he died.

Prudence, who was working at the *New York Review of Books*, sent Sid a humorous piece she had written, which was later published in the *New Yorker*. They began to correspond, and Sid expressed a desire to meet her. They soon became friends.[24] Many of his friends felt that Prudence brightened his life considerably. They noticed that he seemed less reserved and distant around the tall, dark young woman. Neva Patterson, who spent the evening with them on the weekend before Sid died, says, "He really was terribly fond of her. She is a charming, brilliant girl and obviously they were mad about one another. I think it meant the world to him to have a beautiful young woman adoring him. We had a happy evening. The only difference I noticed in him was that his hearing was beginning to deteriorate a bit, but otherwise he was his old wonderful self."[25]

Other friends saw him in a very different light in his last years. They felt he was lonely and unfulfilled despite his air of self-sufficiency. George Brounoff, who had known Sid since the twenties, says, "I had a feeling about him that after Laura died, he seemed not to have much interest in anything. If you read his pieces in those years, they went downhill, too, I think. But you had to really be an expert in his kind of humor to see the difference between a winner and a mediocre piece."[26] And writer Martha Saxton sensed "anger behind his remoteness."

He would tell her stories that clearly he had told many times before. They were well-crafted, with a punch line and lots of characters. Obviously he was thinking of using them in his pieces or had used them in social situations before. "He wasn't particularly spontaneous. He didn't like to reveal himself," she recalls.[27]

"There was a palpable loneliness about him that moved me," re-called Richard Merkin, who met Sid in the last few years of his life.[28]

The decline of his career undoubtedly was one of the major reasons for his unhappiness. Says Constance Sayre: "Sid never sold that many copies and he never was a big best seller, and I think that always irked him. . . . He had been published over the years probably with less enthusiasm, and then when *Chicken Inspector #23* appeared with the front-page review in the *New York Times Book Review* by Eudora Welty, it made everyone at Simon and Schuster sit up and pay attention and say we mustn't forget about this author, he's been with us all these years, and then the book didn't sell that well, and I think he was always upset about that and it got to be harder and harder to sell his books, although certainly everyone was greeted with this great outpouring of enthusiastic reviews, but the numbers weren't there. . . . It made Sid very cranky to be considered this 'national treasure' and not sell."[29]

In the fall of 1974, the past circled back in the form of a revival of *The Beauty Part* at the American Place Theatre in New York. Recalls Susan Sullivan, who played April Monkhood in the new production and who met Perelman at this time: "He had his own rhythm, and it was a sort of slow rhythm, and it had nothing to do with age. He didn't seem old to me. He seemed very young, although he moved slowly, and he had an enormous twinkle to his eye and to his spirit, and he had a real eye for the women. But he was rather quiet when you were with him. His personality, at least in my experience with him, seemed to evolve through his letters and through his writing. He was much more aggressive and it was as if his inner being could manifest itself. But on a one-to-one level he was much quieter and more secretly mischievous."[30]

Sid was excited by the prospect of the revival. Soured by the play's earlier failure, he hoped it might be a smash under more favorable circumstances. "I was so disheartened by this kick in the belly," he said, "I retired from writing for the theater. If the play succeeds this time, who knows? It might revive my faith."[31]

The American Place Theatre was a subscription theater, and *The Beauty Part* had a limited run from October 23 to November 23. It was not a hit, although it had some favorable reviews, especially in the *New Yorker*. But Clive Barnes of the *New York Times* wrote a scathing criticism not only of the play but of the actor chosen to play the late Bert Lahr's roles: comedian Joseph Bova. As a result Broadway did not beckon, and Sid's faith in theater writing was never revived.

Another blow followed. His new collection of essays, *Vinegar Puss*, published in March of 1975, was negatively reviewed by Anatole Broyard of the *New York Times*. "There is a sour note in some of the pieces that was not there before," wrote Broyard. "You can sense the author forcing his material too, falling into the hostility and aggression that seem to be occupational diseases of the comic. . . . Mr. Perelman used to be the world's most inspired manic: Now he is often simply manic. He builds up a set piece about a Hong Kong tailor only to produce a mandarin suit that doesn't fit. He buys an antique snuff box somewhere in the Orient only to discover back in London that it does not contain snuff. He is invariably a victim of confidence men, scattered in wait for him all over the globe.

"Most disappointing of all, Mr. Perelman is guilty of bad taste. In a piece called 'The Machismo Mystique,' he descends to one of the world's oldest and worst jokes—the one about the midget with an inverse sexual endowment. There is also quite a bit of leering, in several other pieces, over bust measurements—another 'joke' that is older than the author himself and far less deserving of immortality.

"When the world was younger, Mr. Perelman's free associations were freer. They bubbled like champagne, but now you can hear the machine grinding them out. . . . While Mr. Perelman used to sound disenchanted, he now sounds disillusioned, and proud of it."[32]

Anatole Broyard was not the first person to point out the declining quality of Perelman's work. Several magazine editors in the United States and England were also of the opinion that Sid's writing was funny only on rare occasions now. In 1970 they had begun turning down material he submitted. Even his time-honored standby, the *New Yorker*, had started holding some of his pieces "in inventory"—a diplomatic way of putting off publication. Sid was furious that some of these "inventoried" pieces had delayed their inclusion in *Vinegar Puss*.

He blamed the changing times for his difficulties as a comic writer. "Reality has overtaken the comic writer," he told Marilyn Stasio of *Cue* magazine. "That's the plight of the satirist today. This was confirmed for me when I saw the movie *M*A*S*H*. For the first time I was struck with something that was actually beyond satire. Not war itself, but the horror of people being blown to bits and then patched together again. It is called black humor, but I have always questioned it. It is black, but it is not humor.

"I write about social mores, about our vulnerabilities. But these days it is difficult to find subjects to satirize. I'm frozen in my period, as are my contemporaries of the thirties and forties, writers like Thurber, E. B. White, Frank Sullivan. We're slightly appalled by the change in manners, the tremendous revolution in morals. Society seems to have reached a point of tastelessness and meaninglessness that is beyond anything you can kid."[33]

Robert Gottlieb felt merely that Sid had written himself out. "His best material was his earlier material. For me, most of what he wrote in the last fifteen years or so was not very good. He still had the manner but he no longer had the charge. His anger and irritation began to dominate his sense of comedy."[34]

Heywood Hale Broun felt that Sid could not help becoming dated. "We are moving into the age of Woody Allen and Donald Barthelme, and out of the age of Sid Perelman," he said. And Dorothy Parker mourned for the madness and zaniness of the past: "There just aren't any humorists today. I don't know why. I don't suppose there is much demand for humor, although there ought to be. S. J. Perelman is about the only one working at it, and he's rewriting himself. Humor now is too carefully planned. There is nothing of the madness Mr. Benchley and some of the others had in my time, no leaping of minds."[35]

The golden age of American humor was dying with its last practitioner.

# 21

# "ONE LAST CHUCK
# OF THE DICE"

## *(1975–1979)*

The handful of my Hollywood contemporaries still alive . . . were enjoying a pleasurable second childhood. They busied themselves coloring comic books, played with stage money doled out by their business managers, and occasionally as an extra treat, were permitted to drool on television.

S. J. PERELMAN, *Eastward Ha!*

In March of 1975 Sid set off on his sixth global tour—visiting England, Scotland, France, Russia, Greece, Israel, Iran, Bangkok, Penang, Malaysia, Malacca, Singapore, Borneo, Java, Australia, Tahiti and finally, "the most primitive civilization of all, the Hollywood colony I had known in the thirties."

He was gone seven and a half months and then returned to Europe the following May to research more locales. The pieces he wrote were serialized in *Travel & Leisure* and then collected in *Eastward Ha!*, which was illustrated by Al Hirschfeld, who did not accompany him.[1]

As Anatole Broyard had written in his review of *Vinegar Puss*, "Mr. Perelman is a more irascible traveler even than Tobias Smollett whose 'Travels in France and Italy' is a little classic of vituperation. All the beautiful cities in the world have been bastardized by skyscrapers. Food all over the world is inedible. Cupidity knows no nationality. There is no more native craft or culture, even in the remotest islands of the Far East."[2]

Perelman especially hated Israel and Russia. Of Israel, he wrote, "What magic, what ingenuity and manpower it has taken to recreate Grossinger's, the Miami Fontainebleau, and the Concord Hotel on a barren strand in the Near East!"[3] As for the Soviet Union—"Yalta

287

contains sanitariums that ignite more hypochondria in the onlooker than the Magic Mountain. . . . That Chekhov managed to glean any literary nuggets from Yalta is merely added proof of his stature."[4]

Nor did he much care for Santa Barbara, where he lectured for a month at the University of California. The town was too full of old people waiting to die, he complained. And the students got on his nerves, always asking him silly questions about whether Harpo could really speak and how they could break into television writing.

In the early spring of 1977 Sid parted with four of his most valuable modern paintings, selling them at the Sotheby Parke Bernet Galleries in New York. The total sale came to $51,250, and the net to Perelman $30,000.[5] "It seems time to simplify, like Thoreau," he said.[6] But actually he may have needed the money—to support his restless life-style and help his children when necessary. He had also felt that the insurance on the paintings, which had lain in storage since 1970, was becoming prohibitive.

With money and a new collection of essays behind him, Sid might have been expected to rest from his travels and settle down in New York for awhile. But in May of 1977, he took off again for London in search of a small house in the country. He was fed up with New York taxes and pollution, he said. For a brief time he was interested in a small town in Shropshire called Ludlow, midway between Shrews-bury and Hereford. He had written to Karl Fortess that "I rather fancy myself as an *alte kocker* with a knobbed stick, attended by standard grey poodle, thrusting kids out of my path and exchanging greetings with Miss Marple, who delivers my mail on a bicycle."[7]

But Sid's vision of a country home abroad remained a fantasy. He never purchased property in either Ludlow or Cork, Ireland, which also appealed to him. He stayed on at the Gramercy Park Hotel, moving to an upstairs suite when he returned from England in July of 1977.

He had gone to England partly to settle problems with his pub-lishers. Furious over what he felt was Weidenfeld's failure to promote both *Baby, It's Cold Inside* and *Vinegar Puss*, he now had a new English publisher, Eyre Methuen, which was to publish *Eastward Ha!* in the United Kingdom as well as reissue *The Most of S. J. Perelman*, which was long out of print. He also had a new British agent, Pat Kavanagh of A. D. Peters, who handled many other prominent authors, including Arthur Koestler.

On April 10, 1978, Sid received a special achievement medal at the 29th Annual National Book Awards ceremony held in Carnegie Hall. This was the first time the Association of American Publishers had ever awarded such a medal. It read: "Special Achievement Award to S. J. Perelman for a sustained and exceptional contribution to American writing." Accepting the award from TV critic Gene Shalit, Sid said that he would treasure it second only to the one he had received from the Ottoman Empire—"The Turkish Order of Chastity, Second Class."

In 1978, Sid presented the New York Film Critics' Award to Woody Allen and Marshall Brickman for their screenplay of *Annie Hall*. In his speech, Sid reminisced about working with Ogden Nash in 1936 at MGM on a screenplay of *How to Win Friends and Influence People*, "an expensive vehicle for Fanny Brice, Claude Rains and Esther Williams that fortunately never made it out of the garage. If it had, it would have been known as the Edsel of the entertainment business. . . . From time immemorial, Hollywood producers have been obsessed by the problem of how to make pictures without using writers. They tried every imaginable device, such as employing the half-dozen apes reputed to have tapped out all the plays of Shakespeare. In final desperation, they sometimes wrote the screenplays themselves—but these grossed even less than the chimpanzee version. . . .

". . . The world already knows what intense pleasure Woody Allen has given us, and never more so than with his latest film. The third time I saw it, I realized what an inexpressible debt of enjoyment I owe him. I'm grateful for this occasion to proclaim it.

"I have to add of course that, in the end, Woody had to use a writer. And he could not have chosen a better one, a more agreeable and a smarter one, than Marshall Brickman."[8]

A few weeks later Sid and a female companion were seated at Elaine's, a New York restaurant frequented by literary celebrities, when Sid saw Woody Allen and Marshall Brickman across the room. Sid's companion suggested he send Allen his card. Agreeing, he wrote, "My dear Mr. Allen, won't you please join us for a Dr. Brown's Cel-Ray Tonic?" The waiter reluctantly delivered it, sighing that everyone in the place was sending his card to Woody Allen. Minutes went by and then Allen, looking astounded, appeared at Sid's table, saying, "I don't believe it. I thought it was a joke." It was the first time the two masters of surrealist humor had ever met.[9]

\*     \*     \*

In March of 1978, at the casual suggestion of Martha Saxton and her husband, photographer Enrico Ferorelli, Sid began planning an extraordinarily difficult recreation of the famous 1907 Peking-to-Paris road race, in which Prince Borghese and four or five other motorists had participated. It was still considered one of the most grueling races of all time.

The original race had started in Peking in February and ended months later on the cobbled streets of Paris. The route had taken the competing motorists through the Gobi Desert, Mongolia, Siberia, Russia, Poland and Germany. Many of the cars had to be taken apart in certain places and carried by coolies piece by piece across the great Yangtze gorges.

Sid planned to drive the natty black and red MG he had bought in Bangkok in 1949 from Paris to China, reversing the original route. He was seventy-four years old, and the car thirty years old, but both man and automobile were in reasonable health, trim and dapper and elegant. The car had only 19,300 miles on it and had been cared for by a superb mechanic in Erwinna. If he were successful, Sid told his friends, he would be the first foreign civilian ever to drive into China. "I tend to be numbered increasingly among the geriatrics," he said. "Perhaps this is why I'm striving to drive from Paris to Peking—one last chuck of the dice."

It would also be a chance to make a splash in the world press. As though he had finally despaired of making any more big money at writing, he seemed more and more frantic to attract attention by unique adventures, by feats of derring-do. Perhaps he thought it would help the sales of his books. Or perhaps he did it merely out of some vast nostalgia for the daring heroes he had read about as a boy. Whatever his motives, he had set himself an ordeal that made the Phileas Fogg venture pale by comparison.

Still he was game. When Harold Evans, who had commissioned the trip for the *Sunday Times* [of London], tried to talk him out of the Paris-to-Peking route, suggesting that Sid should retrace the Grand Tour popular with young English aristocrats in the 18th and 19th centuries, Sid replied that such a trip lacked excitement.

Since the MG was old and possibly subject to breakdowns, both men felt that Sid should not drive the car alone. Sid suggested that there be a back-up car to carry replacement parts for the MG, supplies and gas. But this time Evans disagreed, saying a back-up car would

290

detract from the romance of the adventure. In the end he and Sid compromised. A small trailer was attached to the MG and loaded with supplies, including 100,000 Band-Aids and 30 boxes of Lomotil, which Sid insisted on taking in case of emergencies.

As traveling companions Sid would have his friend Eric Lister and Sid Beer, who was in charge of the Huntingdonshire MG Museum, which had agreed to furnish the necessary spare parts.

Being Sid, he insisted on taking along a woman—Delta Willis, a tall, pretty blonde from Pine Bluff, Arkansas, who had been recommended by Martha Saxton. Perelman had always been partial to tall women, and Delta, the vice-president of a film company called Survival Anglia Ltd., loomed over six feet.

Miss Willis knew that part of her job was to be caricatured, and she was right. As soon as he hired her, Perelman told journalist Mary Blume, "In case I am pursued by brigands, I intend to throw portions of this lady to impede them as I hurtle on."[9] His threat was never made good, for Delta Willis also wanted to write a book about the trip and she was dismissed before the adventure began.

Sid and his two male companions started the journey from the Arc de Triomphe on the Champs-Elysées on September 2, 1978. Sid was driving, but it was mainly for publicity purposes, for at age seventy-four, he no longer trusted himself behind the wheel. During the trip Eric Lister and Sid Beer shared nearly all the driving. For the next twenty-seven days, they drove through Central Europe, the Balkans, Turkey, Iran, Afghanistan, Pakistan and India. The car performed well, but Perelman's relationship with his traveling companions did not progress as smoothly.

Once they left Germany, the food and accommodations were miserable. All three men had to sleep in one room, which greatly annoyed Perelman, who felt that such arrangements were like being in the Boy Scouts. Once they reached Bombay, there was no decent land route, so they had to fly with the car to Hong Kong. Along the way it had been stripped of all its MG insignia by souvenir hunters. For the next six weeks Sid cooled his heels trying to get permission to enter China, while Lister and Beer returned to London.

"It must be obvious to observers of human nature that a couple of curmudgeons like Sid and I [sic] placed in a cocktail shaker with a normally reserved English gentleman as the third ingredient would create a bitter potion when shaken for too long," Lister later wrote.

"... The tragedy that this trip created was the irreparable rift it caused between Sid and myself. The last time I saw him was in our suite at the Peninsula Hotel in Hong Kong."[10]

Finally Sid was granted a visa to enter China and was able to fly to Peking with Nancy Nash, a Hong Kong journalist and photographer. Two days after his arrival in Peking, however, he became ill with acute bronchitis and had to be hospitalized for five days in Peking's Capital Hospital. While he was there, the staff referred to him as "the famous foreign pen-driver."

The Chinese at last agreed to have the MG shipped to Peking. Sid, who was still feeling unwell and very disconsolate, decided to forego Peking altogether and have the MG shipped back to England by boat. He would fly back to Hong Kong and then return to London.

What he did not know was that there was a lorry strike in England, and the car could not be unloaded when it got to Southampton. Instead it was shipped to Hamburg, Germany. To complicate matters, when at last the MG reached the United States, it was sent to Baltimore, not Philadelphia as he had specified. Perelman blamed all these mishaps on Sidney Beer, who he felt had deliberately messed up the arrangements in retaliation for their disagreements on the road.

The last lap of this ill-fated journey cost Sid five hundred dollars more—when he had to have the car trucked from Baltimore to Pennsylvania, where his expert mechanic would get it back into running order.

For three and a half months after his return to America, Sid tried to write about his trip. But the dazzling wordplay, the clever bon mots for which he was so famous, would not come. He had gone around the world six times in his life, but this was the most unpleasant journey of all, a physical and mental fiasco from beginning to end. In the past he had somehow managed to find humor in hardship and tangled arrangements, but this time he found nothing funny in any aspect of his trek to the Far East. It was grotesque, obscene. "The car behaved like a dream, and my two companions like a nightmare," he told a friend.

Although he proposed to give Harold Evans eight pieces he had written for the *New Yorker* as a substitute for the humorous series he had promised the *Sunday Times*, it was the first time in his long career as a writer that he had failed to deliver a major piece.[11] On September 4, 1979, he wrote Paul Theroux that "after a lot of bleeding cuticle, I decided to abandon it. I guess there are certain subjects—or maybe one's subjective reactions to them—that in spite of the most manful attempts, are totally unproductive."

That summer he gave up smoking. Some of his friends thought he had aged and seemed in fragile health. Others, like the Philip Hamburgers, with whom Sid and Ruth Goetz had dinner two nights before he died, found him unaffected by the rigors of his frustrating journey and in cheerful spirits. His relationship with Prudence Crowther seemed to be giving him new life—yet several of his English friends were deeply concerned about him. The last time he had seen them in England, he confided that he had suffered a number of "little heart attacks." Still he accepted dinner invitations, dressed nattily, ate well—and admiring the *New Yorker* profile Kenneth Tynan had written about Louise Brooks, the silent movie star, he planned to drive up to Rochester, New York, and see her in the fall—or whenever his MG was ready for travel.

On October 17, 1979, playwright Edward Chodorov, who was an old friend of Sid's, was planning to meet him for dinner. He phoned Sid that morning to confirm their dinner date. After ringing Sid's room at the hotel several times and receiving no answer, he asked the hotel manager to see if Sid was all right.

After Sid's death, a rumor circulated among many of his friends that he had died in *flagrante delicto*. "He would have loved the rumor," a ladyfriend says. But it was not true. He died alone, dressed in pajamas and a robe. The time of death was estimated at eleven-thirty A.M.

His death at age seventy-five had been caused by a massive heart attack, brought on by arteriosclerosis.[12] It was the same disease that had killed his mother. Like him, Sophie had died in autumn, on October 16, just one day before the date of his death.

As a dabbler in the occult, Sid might have noticed that October 17th was a peculiarly significant date in his life. It was the day *Around the World in 80 Days* had opened many years before to such fanfare. October 17th was also the birthday of a man who even though he had been dead for thirty-nine years still cast a mysterious shadow across his life—Nathanael West.

All over the world English-speaking readers mourned him. After years of reading his semiautobiographical pieces, many felt they knew him personally. He had made them laugh when they didn't feel like laughing. People quoted their favorite Perelman lines and remembered the names of his outlandish characters.

Sid's obituaries tried to assess his enormous influence not only on the Marx Brothers, but also on American humor and writing in general.

The *New Yorker*'s surprisingly brief obituary (in "The Talk of the Town" under *Notes and Comments*) emphasized that "the English language was his element; he dwelled in it, was nourished by it, loved it—revelled in it."[13] The *New York Times*'s front-page obituary was more extensive and detailed. It quoted William Shawn as saying, "He was one of the world's funniest writers. He was also one of the few remaining writers in America who devoted themselves wholly to humor. Over the years, people often put pressure on him to write something they considered serious—a novel, say—but he was never diverted from doing what he apparently was born to do, which was to write short humor pieces. . . . He was widely appreciated as a humorist, but people were so enormously entertained by him that they sometimes overlooked his great originality and his literary brilliance. He was a master of the English language, and no one has put the language to more stunning comic use than he did."[14]

The opinion was that he was a great parodist, at his best when parodying a novel, classic or otherwise, a silent film, advertisement or passing trend. *Time* called him "a major stylist in a minor form whose value cannot be over-estimated."[15] Many of the tributes also pointed out that his humor was a major influence on everyone working in modern comedy, from Spike Milligan and Peter Sellers to Marshall Brickman and Woody Allen.

The British were more analytical in their appraisal of the man and his work. In the *New Statesman*, Russell Davies pointed out that "In his own country, Perelman was latterly in danger of being cast as little more than a talented eyewitness, wittily recalling the supposed greats of Broadway, Hollywood and the *New Yorker*. And this was no doubt one of the reasons why we in Britain saw so much of him during the Seventies. . . . The more you look at Perelman's collected works . . . the more you realize that there's a complete social commentary on the United States embedded in it: more securely embedded, indeed, than ever it was in works of conscious compilation like Mencken's *Americana* . . . Perelman never pretended to be the common man. The central thread of his style was smoothly learned, frankly literary; so it enabled him to reach up and clobber pomposity effortlessly, but also to reach down and use for his civilized purposes the countless wild barbarisms of the madly mixed American language. His career, in effect, was one long refusal to let go of the incompatible life below for the sake of the seductive enlightenment above. He remained a gently pained observer—for, as one of his titles states, 'It Takes Two to Tango, but Only One to Squirm.' "[16]

Ironically, no obituary of Perelman appeared in the *Times of London*, the paper for which he did so much work in the last years of his life. He died during the time when the management of the paper was involved in a union dispute and had temporarily suspended its publication.

Perelman left an estate of approximately $400,000 before taxes, as well as an English estate of $11,562. In his will, dated December 3, 1975, he directed that after his debts were paid, the remainder of his estate be divided equally between Adam and Abby.[17]

In a statement to the court assessing the value of Perelman's literary estate, agent Peter Matson said that Perelman's income came principally from the sale of short pieces and not from the royalties from his twenty anthologies. His income for the past ten years had been derived almost solely from the sale of articles to the *New Yorker* and *Travel & Leisure*.

After his death, Sid's remaining art works were appraised and sold. They included a Toulouse-Lautrec poster entitled "Divan Japonais," the Ming head of Kuan Yin that Leila Hadley had given him, as well as art works by friends, including a lithograph by Jack Levine and a collage by Saul Steinberg. On November 25, 1980, his papers, which included over two hundred manuscripts in his personally monogrammed suitcase pasted with labels of his favorite airlines and hotels, were put up for auction at the Sotheby Parke Bernet Galleries. They were acquired for $15,500 by the New York Public Library's Berg Collection of English and American Literature.

Sid's MG was sold by the Vintage Car Store of Nyack, New York, to Thomas W. Barrett III of Scottsdale, Arizona, for $10,000.

Sid and Adam had reconciled in the early 1970s. Adam often had dinner with his father in Greenwich Village or visited him at his suite at the Gramercy Park Hotel. As a Christmas gift in 1977, Sid gave each of his children a check for $3,000.

After he was released from Elmira, Adam, according to a knowledgeable source, enrolled—and then dropped out of—an evening high school for adults at New York University. Except for the incident in 1958, when he was twenty-one, he never displayed any criminal behavior again. Says a woman friend of Adam's who wishes not to be identified: "He made it a point to stay away from his mother and father's home as much as possible. He had a series of odd jobs and then became interested in the restaurant business. For thirteen years, he was a bartender and manager of Googie's, a bar on Sullivan Street in Greenwich Village. He no longer works there, but frequents the place.

"As a young man, Adam had a great deal of difficulty coping with what he perceived to be Sid's inability to take things seriously," Adam's friend continues. "He also hated what he calls his father's 'immigrant's paranoia' about people and money. But oddly enough, the older and more bitter and fragile Sid became, the more Adam grew to understand him, even love him in a special way.

"If you were to meet Adam today, you would find that he's a tall, heavyset bachelor of about fifty who loves to eat and drink well. Aside from inheriting ginger-colored hair the same shade as Sid's mustache, he bears little resemblance to his father. He looks very much like his mother and has her languorous manner. Although Adam is sometimes brusque with strangers, he can be very talkative and charming once he is put at his ease. His great ambition is to have the novels he's written published. He identifies with the West side of the family and is convinced that Laura had more writing talent than either Perelman or West, but that Sid withheld his emotional support, preventing her from growing as a person and a writer."

Divorced from Joe Aronson, Abby was living at the time of her father's death with Ken Weinstein, a gunsmith, in West Hurley, New York, near Woodstock. It is reported that the auction in which Sid sold many of the family possessions had deeply wounded her. When she came to stay with him in Erwinna after Laura's death, neighbors were struck by her withdrawn manner. Other people, who met her later in connection with the settling of Sid's estate, have described her as "an interesting and enigmatic" person, echoing Pat Englund's impressions of her as a young woman.

Although Abby, like her brother, had her disagreements with Sid, after his death she would fiercely protect his memory, refusing to grant interviews about him and her mother. It is possible that she

296

was protecting what she felt was his sense of privacy, as Sid zealously guarded Nathanael West's after his death, but her refusal to discuss her father's life or career may also stem from her reluctance to relive a very painful past. "It was a traumatic childhood, and Abby doesn't want any reminder of it," a friend says. "Quite frankly, considering their parents' tempestuous relationship, it is to their credit that Adam and Abby were able to survive and make individual lives for themselves."

At present Abby lives a quiet, reclusive country life. Friends of Perelman's who are in touch with her report that she is a well-informed and keen observer of nature, deriving much enjoyment and solace from it, as did her mother and father. Much of her time is devoted to studying bird and wild animal behavior and to gardening. "She has a passion to see things *grow*," a friend says. After Sid's death, both she and Adam authorized a book of his letters, to be edited by Prudence Crowther. It will be published by Viking in the near future.

In July of 1981, Simon and Schuster published *The Last Laugh*, a posthumous collection of Sid's final seventeen pieces. They were mostly reprinted from the *New Yorker* and also included portions of Sid's autobiography, which he contracted to write in 1960 but which he never finished and which was considered unpublishable by his executors. Reviewing the anthology for the *Saturday Review*, Marshall Brickman wrote: "Despite his generous acknowledgments to Ade, Leacock, Sullivan and others, he cut a path that was unique, original, and inevitably a trap for those who admire his work enough to try and emulate or analyze it. His genius defies criticism. He was the maestro, nonpareil, incomparable, beyond interpretation. As he himself once said, 'Before they made Perelman, they broke the mold.' "[18]

But Hope Hale Davis, who had known Perelman since the twenties, found it difficult to read the posthumous collection "as purely a comic *omnium gatherum*." In *The New Leader*, she observed:

> Unlike West, who with *Miss Lonelyhearts* was able to express the ultimate in compassion, Perelman had let surrealism limit his view of life. I think some of his wildest outside loops spring from the hysteria of a prisoner gone berserk. He had locked himself into his style—or rather, his hodge-podge of others' styles—almost inadvertently, as he suggests in the segment of *The Hindsight Saga* describing his struggles before making contact with the Marx Brothers.

He had to think twice in those days, I remember, before buying a cup of coffee. And he had no taste for being poor, having grown up on a Rhode Island farm where his father was making an unlikely, un-Jewish try at scraping a living from the soil. To add to his discontent his college friend Pep, in a vain quest for acceptance on Fraternity Row, had set standards in English tweeds and leather from which Sid, despite his mockery, would never free himself. When at last he sighted the glint of Hollywood gold he had not only his family responsibilities but the demands of the roller-coaster life of a screenwriter to hold him in his groove.

At a time of general worry and fear, Perelman provided relief and ever-renewable joy to millions, in more countries than were raced through in his film *Around the World in 80 Days*. His memoir offers hints of the price he paid, albeit disguised as comedy. He tries to make Groucho's real-life outrages as funny as his imagined *Monkey Business*. Perelman calls Elizabeth Taylor a "renowned vedette," which in English means, according to the ever-needed dictionary, "a small naval launch used for scouting." It is partly his obvious effort to be humorous about such matters as greed, malice and treachery that gives *The Hindsight Saga* its effect of gloom.[19]

Sid was cremated on October 19, 1979, two days after his death. As had been the case with Laura, there was no funeral or formal memorial service of any kind. Several close friends gathered at the Hirschfelds' a few days later. Marc Connelly spoke movingly about Sid, and at Al Hirschfeld's request, Mary Faulconer brought the portrait of Sid and Tong Cha she had painted the year before, and they passed it around. His ashes were buried under a tree in West Hurley, New York, not far from Abby's home.

Several months later, on January 28, 1980, a "Salute to S. J. Perelman," directed by Janet Sternburg, opened the Writers in Performance Series at the Manhattan Theatre Club on East 73rd Street. Friends and colleagues, including Al Hirschfeld, Morley Safer, Prudence Crowther, Marc Connelly, William Zinsser, Neva Patterson and Ruth Goetz, gathered to read from Perelman's works and to reminisce about the man who had meant so much to them. Adam and Abby were also present. Afterward there was a display of family pictures that Adam furnished, accompanied by a phonograph recording of Sid reading from one of his pieces.

But it was Heywood Hale Broun's heartfelt tribute that made Sid and his humor come vividly alive again, much more than the photographs of the past ever could:

"When I think of Sid I remember the time he told me about meeting Sax Rohmer. At one point in their talk Rohmer spoke of pacing the terrace of Shepheard's Hotel in Cairo talking to someone he called Oppy.

"After a moment of incomprehension Sid realized that the nickname referred to E. Phillips Oppenheim.

"As he told me this, Sid, though dressed as usual like an Edwardian baronet, suddenly looked and sounded like a Providence schoolboy— 'My God, what wouldn't any of us give to be a fly on the wall at that meeting—Rohmer and Oppenheim talking over plots in Egypt!'

"It seems to me that Sid was a Providence schoolboy a good deal of the time, and I loved him for it, and the zest he had for that world into which all we weedy, hard-reading schoolchildren have disappeared for hours at a time, that world where soldiers of fortune stride into smoke-filled dens in Singapore, where indolent noblemen smile with deceptive gentleness as their rapiers hiss out of the scabbard, that world where a London clubman reveals the whereabouts of a giant ruby and gets a couple of comrades out of the smoking room to scale the Himalayas and find it, that world where glorious improbable things happen, things which made bearable the boring years of high school and the boring years that come after high school.

"Sid grew up to make wonderful fun of the real world, and to have a love-laugh relationship with the world of fantasy, and he ran through the English language as zestfully as the lovers in the bad movies he cherished ran through sunlit mountain meadows.

"Sometimes, as in the case with all who ask of life more than it can give, he had stretches of depression. He never thought much of his ability to inspire affection, and in those dark periods, probably never realized how many people schemed together to try to ease his pain.

"All of us will miss him, will visit with him in his books, and will send our hopes vaulting over the stone walls of reality in the wish to believe that as spies, adventurers, cavalry colonels and beautiful women murmur together on a terrace behind him, he is pacing between Sax and Oppy, finding out what they talked about so long ago."[20]

In America and England, people kept on writing humor. Although some of it was funny and quite talented, none of it was like Sid's. For his genius was unique, and when he died, a special type of humor—highly literate and inventive, yet cranky and thoroughly irreverent—passed from the contemporary scene. But then perhaps no other modern writer was willing to match his commitment to words. "He lived to turn his experiences into brilliant language," says Martha Saxton.

Whether this was a rare gift or a feverish obsession is unimportant in the last analysis. For he made us forget for a brief time our own pain and sorrows—and enter a wild, wonderful realm of fantasy that was sublime.

# WORKS BY S. J. PERELMAN*

### FICTION AND COLLECTED ESSAYS

*Dawn Ginsbergh's Revenge*, Horace Liveright, Inc., 1929.
*Parlor, Bedlam and Bath* (with Quentin Reynolds), Horace Liveright, Inc., 1930.
*Strictly from Hunger*, Random House, 1937.
*Look Who's Talking!*, Random House, 1940.
*The Dream Department*, Random House, 1943.
*Crazy Like a Fox*, Random House, 1944.
*Keep It Crisp*, Random House, 1946.
*The Best of S. J. Perelman*, Random House, 1947.
*Acres and Pains*, Reynal and Hitchcock, 1947.
*Westward Ha!*, Simon and Schuster, 1948.
*Listen to the Mocking Bird*, Simon and Schuster, 1949.
*The Swiss Family Perelman*, Simon and Schuster, 1950.
*The Ill-Tempered Clavichord*, Simon and Schuster, 1952.
*Perelman's Home Companion*, Simon and Schuster, 1955.
*The Road to Miltown*, Simon and Schuster, 1957.
*The Most of S. J. Perelman*, Simon and Schuster, 1958.
*The Rising Gorge*, Simon and Schuster, 1961.
*Chicken Inspector #23*, Simon and Schuster, 1966.
*Baby, It's Cold Inside*, Simon and Schuster, 1970.

*For a list of comic essays that have not been collected in the above anthologies, consult *An Index to Literature in the New Yorker* and the *Reader's Guide to Periodical Literature*, keeping in mind that when Perelman's pieces for the *New Yorker* and other magazines appeared in book form, their titles were often changed. In compiling this list of Perelman's works, I am indebted to the earlier researches of Geoff Brown in the May 1975 Monthly Film Bulletin.

*Vinegar Puss*, Simon and Schuster, 1975.
*Eastward Ha!*, Simon and Schuster, 1977.
*The Last Laugh*, Simon and Schuster, 1981.

## REVUES AND PLAYS

*The Third Little Show*, 1931
*Walk a Little Faster*, 1932
*All Good Americans* (with Laura Perelman), 1933
*Even Stephen* (with Nathanael West), 1934 (not produced)
*The Night before Christmas* (with Laura Perelman), 1941
*One Touch of Venus* (with Ogden Nash), 1943
*Sweet Bye and Bye* (with Al Hirschfeld), 1946
*The Beauty Part*, 1962

## FILMS WITH SCREENPLAY CREDITS

*Monkey Business*, Paramount Pictures, 1931.
*Horse Feathers*, Paramount Pictures, 1932.
*Hold 'Em Jail*, RKO, 1932.
*Sitting Pretty*, Paramount Pictures, 1933.
*Florida Special*, Paramount Pictures, 1936.
*Ambush*, Paramount Pictures, 1939.
*Boy Trouble*, Paramount Pictures, 1939.
*The Golden Fleecing*, MGM, 1940.
*Around the World in 80 Days*, United Artists, 1956.
    Uncredited contributions:
        *The Big Broadcast of 1936*, Paramount Pictures, 1935.
        *Sweethearts*, MGM, 1938.

## TELEVISION SCRIPTS

"The Big Wheel" (*Omnibus*), ABC-TV, 1957.
"The Changing Ways of Love" (*The Seven Lively Arts*), CBS-TV, 1957.
"Aladdin," CBS-TV, 1958.
"Malice in Wonderland" (*Omnibus*), NBC-TV, 1959.
"Elizabeth Taylor's London," CBS-TV, 1963.

# NOTES ON SOURCES

Unless otherwise specified, the letters cited are in the possession of the recipients.

### INTRODUCTION

1. Quoted in William Zinsser's "That Perelman of Great Price is 65," *New York Times Magazine*, January 26, 1969, p. 25.

### 1. JOSEPH AND SOPHIE

1. Jane Howard, "The Cranky Humorist," *Life*, February 9, 1962.
2. Author's interview with Allen Saalburg.
3. "So Little Time Marches On," in *The Most of S. J. Perelman*, Simon and Schuster, New York, 1958, p. 235.
4. This account of Joseph and Sophie's background depends mainly on interviews by the author with Vincent Mason and George and Archie Bashlow, S. J. Perelman's cousins. I am indebted to Mrs. Estelle Mason for her additional research into the family's genealogy and property holdings in the United States in the late 19th century.
5. *Providence Sunday Journal*, January 6, 1963.
6. Alexander and Lillian Feinsilver, "From the American Scene: Colchester's Yankee Jews," *Commentary*, July 1955, pp. 64–66.
7. Report of the Immigration Commission, Vol. 22, Immigrants in Industries, "Recent Immigrants in Agriculture," Washington, D.C., 1911, p. 15.
8. Colchester Land Records 24: 371, 373.
9. Ibid., 36: 409.

10. Ibid., 36: 520.
11. Ibid., 39: 209.
12. Ibid., 39: 212, 213.
13. Ibid., 39: 277.
14. Ibid., 36: 671.
15. Myra McPherson, "Puns and Names with S. J.," *Providence Sunday Journal*, October 25, 1970. Alan Brien, "The Man in the Ironic Mask," *Quest*, November 1978, p. 4.
16. S. J. Perelman, State of New York Certificate and Record of Birth, #3160, February 1, 1904.
17. I. J. Kapstein, "Sid (1904–1979)," *Brown Alumni Monthly*, December 1979, pp. 31–35.
18. Ibid.
19. S. J. Perelman, "Around the Bend in Eighty Days," in *Vinegar Puss*, Simon and Schuster, New York, 1975, p. 52.
20. S. J. Perelman, "How I Learned to Wink and Leer," *New York Times Magazine*, April 23, 1978, p. 16.
21. Author's interview with Celia Ernspos Adler.
22. Author's interview with I. J. Kapstein.
23. *Holiday*, December 1952.
24. Zinsser, *New York Times Magazine*, 1969.
25. S. J. Perelman, Introduction, *The Best of S. J. Perelman*, Random House, New York, 1947.

## 2. "AH, THE COLLEGE BOYS, THE COLLEGE BOYS"

1. Upton Sinclair, *The Goose-Step: A Study of American Education*, privately published, 1923.
2. Laurence B. Chase, *The Plastic Agents*, Independent Studies Thesis (unpublished), Brown University, 1962, p. 44.
3. Ibid., p. 45.
4. Ibid., p. 46.
5. Letter from Eleanor F. Horowitz to the author.
6. Author's interview with William A. Dyer, Jr.
7. Quentin Reynolds, *By Quentin Reynolds*, McGraw-Hill, New York, 1963, p. 51.
8. John Sanford, "Nathanael West," *The Screen Writer*, 1946, pp. 10–13.
9. James F. Light, *Nathanael West: An Interpretative Study*, Northwestern University Press, Chicago, 1961, pp. 5–6.
10. Jay Martin, *Nathanael West: The Art of His Life*, Farrar, Straus & Giroux, New York, 1970, p. 68.
11. Author's interview with John Sanford.

12. Martin, p. 56.
13. Author's interview with Vincent Mason.
14. *Brown Daily Herald*, December 8, 1923, p. 3.
15. *Casements*, May 19, 1924, pp. 14–15.
16. Letter from Professor Fredson Bowers to the author.
17. *Brown Jug*, 1924, p. 14.
18. Author's interview with Edward Goldberger.
19. *Brown Jug*, June 1924, p. 15.
20. Quoted in *The Plastic Age*, a novel by Percy Marks, with an afterword by R. V. Cassill, "Lost American Fiction," Edited by Matthew J. Bruccoli, Southern Illinois University Press, Carbondale, Illinois, 1980, p. 333.
21. Alan Brien, *Quest*, November 1978.
22. *Brown Daily Herald*, November 22, 1924, p. 2.
23. Ibid., November 25, 1924, p. 3.
24. *Brown Jug*, January 1925, p. 19.
25. *Brown Daily Herald*, January 6, 1925, p. 2.
26. *Jug* editors were often called into the Dean's office. William A. Dyer, Jr., who preceded Perelman as *Jug* editor, recalls that many jokes and cut-lines under the cartoons in the magazine had a suggestive double meaning. When Dean Randall would call in the editor to demand an explanation, his response would be to plead total ignorance.
27. *Brown Daily Herald*, March 18, 1925, p. 4.
28. *Brown Jug*, October 1924, p. 17.
29. *Brun-Mael*, 1926, p. 49.
30. Laurence B. Chase, "When Perelman Went to Brown," *Brown Alumni Monthly* (date unknown).
31. *Liber Brunensis*, 1924, p. 142.
32. *Brown Jug*, June 1925, p. 15.
33. *Liber Brunensis*, 1925, p. 102.

### 3. "A Sumptuous Living"

1. William Zinsser, "That Perelman of Great Price is 65," *New York Times Magazine*, January 26, 1969, p. 72.
2. Ibid.
3. Author's interview with Parke Cummings.
4. Corey Ford, *The Time of Laughter*, Little, Brown and Company, Boston, 1967, p. 111.
5. Author's interview with Richard Merkin.
6. *Judge*, August 15, 1925, p. 30.
7. Ibid., September 12, 1925, p. 5.
8. Ibid., September 26, 1925, p. 9.

9. Author's interview with John Richmond.

10. "Weekend with Jimmy Durante," *Holiday* (date unknown).

11. Author's interview with Philip Lukin.

12. Joseph Perelman, Certificate of Death, City of Providence, October 2, 1926, Register #2968.

13. Hope Hale Davis, "The Sad Side of Perelman," *The New Leader*, July 27, 1981, pp. 16–17.

14. Author's interview with Hope Hale Davis.

15. Jay Martin, *Nathanael West: The Art of His Life*, Farrar, Straus & Giroux, New York, 1970, p. 111.

16. Ibid.

17. Author's interview with George Brounoff.

18. *The Sepiad*, February 1929, p. 7.

19. Author's interview with Mrs. Samuel Kaufman.

20. The City of New York Certificate of Marriage Registration of Sidney Joseph Perelman to Lorraine Weinstein, June 20, 1929, C42249.

21. Bennett Cerf, *At Random: The Reminiscences of Bennett Cerf*, Random House, New York, 1977, p. 41.

22. Ibid. p. 79.

23. S. J. Perelman, *Dawn Ginsbergh's Revenge*, Horace Liveright, Inc., New York, 1929, p. 12.

24. S. J. Perelman, "Tomorrow—Fairly Cloudy," in *The Best of S. J. Perelman*, Random House, New York, 1947, p. 185.

25. *Dawn Ginsbergh's Revenge*, p. 23.

26. Ibid., p. 95.

27. Ibid., p. 102.

28. Ibid., pp. 194–95.

29. Ibid., pp. 222–23.

30. Author's interview with Victor D. Schmalzer.

31. S. J. Perelman, *The Last Laugh*, Simon and Schuster, New York, 1981, p. 148.

32. Ibid.

33. In March of 1937, Perelman signed an agreement letting Liveright Publishing Corporation retain exclusive rights for the publication of *Dawn Ginsbergh's Revenge* and *Parlor, Bedlam and Bath* in exchange for releasing him from his contractual obligation to write another book for the house. W. W. Norton, Inc., which has since acquired the Liveright imprint, now owns the rights to these two books. According to Victor Schmalzer, treasurer of W. W. Norton, the firm approached Perelman several times about a reprint of *Dawn Ginsbergh's Revenge* (now a collector's item). But he never replied to their inquiries, possibly because he felt he had nothing financially to gain from a reissue.

### 4. "I Told You I'd Wax Roth Some Day"

1. William Zinsser, "That Perelman of Great Price is 65," *The New York Times Magazine*, January 26, 1969, p. 72.
2. Letter to the author from H. N. Swanson.
3. "The Dick Cavett Show," First Interview, November 29, 1977.
4. Quentin Reynolds, *By Quentin Reynolds*, McGraw-Hill, New York, 1963, p. 66.
5. Ibid., p. 67.
6. *New York Times*, November 30, 1930, p. 9.
7. *Saturday Review of Literature*, July 12, 1930.
8. S. J. Perelman and Quentin Reynolds, *Parlor, Bedlam and Bath*, Horace Liveright, Inc., New York, 1930, pp. 239–40.
9. Author's interview with James Lee.
10. Jay Martin, *Nathanael West: The Art of His Life*, Farrar, Straus & Giroux, New York, 1970, p. 116.
11. Author's interview with John Sanford.
12. Perelman was always hazy about the date of his first meeting with Groucho. In some accounts, he said it was 1930, in others that he attended a performance "one October evening in the fall of 1931." But *Animal Crackers* closed on Broadway on April 6, 1929, after a run of 191 performances. Obviously Perelman met Groucho earlier than he thought, which indicates the rapidity with which Groucho rushed him off to Hollywood.
13. Although Perelman also later maintained that *Monkey Business* was originally conceived of as a radio show, there is no evidence that such a show ever existed except in his own account. At the time, there was no mention in the trade papers of serious negotiations by any network or with the Marx Brothers. Furthermore, when the Marx Brothers signed a movie contract to film *Monkey Business*, they were still on a publicity tour for the film of *Animal Crackers*. In a letter to I. J. Kapstein, dated October 31, 1930, Perelman talks about writing a skit for the Marx Brothers to play in movie theaters through the Midwest. Undoubtedly this, not a radio show, was the actual origin of *Monkey Business*.
14. S. J. Perelman, *The Last Laugh*, Simon and Schuster, New York, 1981, p. 147.

### 5. Enter Groucho Marx

1. "On the Road to Miltown," National Education Television film, 1966.
2. *Women's Wear Daily*, May 3, 1972, p. 50.
3. Groucho Marx, *The Groucho Letters*, Simon and Schuster, New York, 1967, p. 191.

4. Ibid.
5. Leo Rosten, *Look*, March 28, 1950.
6. *Variety*, June 10, 1964, p. 20.
7. *The Observer*, June 14, 1964, p. 21.
8. Not quite. Sid and Groucho were photographed together, sitting atop a car, in 1930 during the filming of *Monkey Business*.
9. Charlotte Chandler, *Hello, I Must Be Going: Groucho and His Friends*, Doubleday and Co., New York, 1978, p. 272.
10. West View by Burt Prelutsky, *Los Angeles Times*, 1971.
11. Robert Altman, Jon Carroll and Michael Goodwin, "Portrait of the Artist as an Old Man" (source unknown).
12. Author's interview with Alistair Cooke. According to Cooke, Groucho's wisecrack about Ruby looking like "a dishonest Abraham Lincoln" was Ruby's own line about himself. "He was, in life," Mr. Cooke says, "a much funnier man than Groucho."
13. Howard Kissel, "S. J. Perelman: Fifty Years of Laughter Later," *Women's Wear Daily*, October 23, 1974, p. 138.
14. S. J. Perelman, *The Last Laugh*, Simon and Schuster, New York, 1981, p. 151.
15. Ibid., pp. 151–52.
16. Edmund Wilson, *The Thirties: From Notebooks and Diaries of the Period*, edited with an introduction by Leon Edel, Farrar, Straus and Giroux, New York, 1980, p. 344.
17. S. J. Perelman, *The Last Laugh*, p. 132.
18. Letter to the author from Teet Carle.
19. Mel Calman, "Perelman in Cloudsville," *Sight and Sound*, Autumn 1978, p. 248.
20. Quoted in Joe Adamson, *Groucho, Harpo, Chico and Sometimes Zeppo: A History of the Marx Brothers and a Satire on the Rest of the World*, Simon and Schuster, New York, 1973, p. 135.
21. Perelman got even with Groucho several weeks later at a dinner party he and Laura gave for the Marx Brothers and their wives at the Garden of Allah. When Sid went to get their coats, he found Gherky, his dog, curled up inside Groucho's wife's mink coat and staring at the remains of her feathered cloche bonnet, which he had just devoured.
22. Mary Blume, "Perelman Recalls His Marxian Past," *Los Angeles Times*, June 9, 1967, p. 20.
23. Adamson, p. 136.
24. Ibid., pp. 138–39.
25. Paul D. Zimmerman and Burt Goldblatt, *The Marx Brothers at the Movies*, G. P. Putnam's Sons, New York, 1968.
26. *New York Times*, October 18, 1931.

27. S. J. Perelman to Betty White Johnston, October 17, 1931.
28. *Life*, October 30, 1931.
29. *The Canadian Forum*, February 1933, p. 175.
30. Adamson, p. 170.
31. According to *Variety*, this was in line with the cost-conscious policy of Warner Brothers and other studios during the early thirties. Rather than sign contracts with writers, they preferred a week-to-week arrangement.
32. Wilson, p. 336.

6. LAURA

1. Jay Martin, *Nathanael West: The Art of His Life*, Farrar, Straus & Giroux, New York, 1970, p. 159.
2. *Philadelphia Record*, July 6, 1941, p. 5.
3. Edmund Wilson, *The Thirties*, p. 191.
4. When Josephine Herbst and John Herrmann had met West earlier that fall at the Sutton Hotel, they persuaded him to visit them in Erwinna for several days. His visit was a success. The three novelists got along famously, and during West's stay, they urged him to take an extended vacation from his job at the Sutton and come to Bucks County for six weeks; there, without distractions, he might be able to finish *Miss Lonelyhearts*. On October 12, 1932, West moved into Warford House in Frenchtown, New Jersey, and started commuting three times a day to Erwinna across the bridge that connected New Jersey and Pennsylvania. He was invited to eat all his meals at the Herrmann farmhouse.
5. Wilson, p. 314.
6. Ibid., pp. 329–30.
7. Josephine Herbst, *Hunter of Doves, Botteghe Oscure*, 1954, pp. 316–17.
8. Ibid., p. 327.
9. Ibid., p. 328–29.
10. Ibid., p. 323.
11. Ibid., pp. 338–39.

7. "A DREARY INDUSTRIAL TOWN"

1. William Cole and George Plimpton, "S. J. Perelman," *Writers at Work: The Paris Review Interviews*, Second Series, The Viking Press, New York, 1963, p. 252.
2. Author's interview with Allen Saalburg.
3. In his profile of Dorothy Parker in *The Last Laugh*, Perelman claimed that he had met her in 1932 at a party given by Poultney Kerr, the "bibulous producer of *Sherry Flip*." These were his fictitious names for

Courtney Burr, sometimes also referred to as "Poultney Groin," and *Walk a Little Faster*.

4. Howard Barnes, *New York Herald Tribune*, June 2, 1931.
5. Vernon Duke, *Passport to Paris*, Little, Brown and Co., Boston, 1955, p. 272.
6. Ibid., p. 275.
7. *New Yorker*, December 17, 1932, pp. 26–27.
8. *New York Times*, December 8, 1932.
9. *New York Sun*, December 8, 1932.
10. S. J. Perelman, "Scenario," in *The Best of S. J. Perelman*, Random House, New York, 1947, p 57.
11. *New York Post*, July 30, 1934, p. 8.
12. Tom Dardis, *Some Time in the Sun*, Charles Scribner's Sons, New York, 1976, pp. 156–57. For a full discussion of Nathanael West's film career, see Jay Martin's *Nathanael West: The Art of His Life* and Tom Dardis's *Some Time in the Sun*.
13. Ibid., p. 167.
14. S. J. Perelman, "Nathanael West: A Portrait," *Contempo*, July 25, 1933.
15. Author's interview with Joseph Schrank.

## 8. "STRICTLY FROM HUNGER"

1. S. J. Perelman, *The Last Laugh*, p. 182. MGM contract files reveal that the Perelmans also signed contracts for three films during this period: *Maytime*, starring Jeannette MacDonald and Nelson Eddy; *Loyalty;* and a new version of *Her Cardboard Lover*, starring Norma Shearer and Robert Taylor. These films were eventually produced, but the extent of the Perelmans' contribution is unclear. In any event, they did not receive screen credit, nor did they receive it for Paramount's *The Big Broadcast of 1936*, another film they reportedly worked on.
      In 1936 Perelman also worked at MGM with Ogden Nash on a screenplay of *How to Win Friends and Influence People*. It was never produced.
2. *Variety*, June 3, 1936.
3. Lester Cole, *Hollywood Red: The Autobiography of Lester Cole*, Ramparts Press, Palo Alto, California, 1981, pp. 141–42. Some years later Perelman wrote a piece about working on the film, "Three Loves Had I in Assorted Flavors," collected in *Baby, It's Cold Inside*, Simon and Schuster, New York, 1970.
4. Ibid., pp. 191–92.
5. S. J. Perelman to Bennett Cerf, September 15, 1936, Random House Collection, Columbia University Libraries, Rare Book and Manuscript Division.

6. Vincente Minnelli with Hector Arce, *I Remember It Well*, Doubleday and Co., Garden City, New York, 1974, p. 106.
7. S. J. Perelman, "Vincente Minnelli," *The Best of S. J. Perelman*, Random House, New York, 1947, p. 230.
8. Minnelli, p. 92.
9. S. J. Perelman to I. J. Kapstein, March 1, 1937.
10. Letter to the author from Israel Shenker.
11. Philip Hamburger, "Unforgettable S. J. Perelman," *Reader's Digest*, March, 1980, p. 102.
12. Author's interview with Louise Kerz.
13. William Cole and George Plimpton, "S. J. Perelman," *Writers at Work: The Paris Review Interviews*, Second Series, The Viking Press, New York, 1963, pp. 248–49.
14. Letter to the author from Professor Constance B. Hieatt. The skit for Clairol was used at the Clairol Pavilion at the New York World's Fair, 1964–65.
15. Interview with Stephen Banker, *Tapes for Readers*, Washington, D.C., 1979.
16. Ibid.
17. Quoted in the *New York Times*, October 18, 1979.
18. *Tapes for Readers*, 1979.
19. Phil Thomas, interview with S. J. Perelman, Associated Press (undated).
20. Author's interview with Heywood Hale Broun.
21. S. J. Perelman, "Waiting for Santy," *The Best of S. J. Perelman*, p. 15.
22. *New York Mirror*, August 13, 1937.
23. *New Republic*, September 1, 1937, p. 108.
24. S. J. Perelman to I. J. Kapstein, March 1, 1937.
25. Bennett Cerf to S. J. Perelman, August 19, 1937, Random House Collection, Columbia University Libraries.
26. S. J. Perelman to Donald Klopfer, July 5, 1938, ibid.
27. S. J. Perelman, *The Last Laugh*, 1981, p. 173.
28. Ibid., p. 186.
29. "On the Road to Miltown," National Education Television Film, 1966.
30. Quoted in John Keats's *You Might as Well Live: The Life and Times of Dorothy Parker*, Simon and Schuster, New York, 1970, pp. 215–16.
31. "On the Road to Miltown," NET film, 1966.
32. *The Letters of F. Scott Fitzgerald*, edited by Andrew Turnbull, Charles Scribner's Sons, New York, 1963, p. 584.
33. *The Notebooks of F. Scott Fitzgerald*, edited by Matthew J. Bruccoli, Harcourt, Brace and Jovanovich, New York, 1978, pp. 316–17.
34. Lillian Hellman, *An Unfinished Woman*, Little, Brown and Company, Boston, 1969, p. 63.

35. Dashiell Hammett to Lillian Hellman, May 3, 1931, quoted in *Dashiell Hammett: A Life* by Diane Johnson, Random House, New York, 1983, p. 101.
36. Steven Marcus's taped interview with Albert Hackett, quoted in Diane Johnson's *Dashiell Hammett*, p. 123.
37. Diane Johnson, *Vanity Fair*, May 1985, p. 118.
38. *Time*, August 12, 1940, p. 66.
39. *The Sun*, February 9, 1939.
40. *Variety*, January 26, 1939, p. 3.
41. *Variety*, April 12, 1939.
42. Bennett Cerf to S. J. Perelman, February 26, 1940, Random House Collection, Columbia University Libraries.
43. S. J. Perelman to Bennett Cerf, March 30, 1940, ibid.
44. Donald Klopfer to S. J. Perelman, March 7, 1940, ibid.
45. S. J. Perelman to Belle Becker, May 12, 1940, ibid.
46. Alexander Woollcott to Bennett Cerf, May 25, 1940, ibid.
47. S. J. Perelman to Bennett Cerf, July 14, 1940, ibid.
48. Bennett Cerf to S. J. Perelman, July 16, 1940, ibid.
49. *New York Times*, November 7, 1940.
50. Perelman and Augustus Goetz once collaborated on a humorous piece for the *New Yorker*. Entitled "Home is Where You Hang Yourself," it was about the tribulations of dealing with real estate agents and buying a place in the country.
51. *Time*, August 12, 1940, pp. 66–67.
52. George S. Kaufman to S. J. Perelman, December 9, 1940, unpublished memo.

## 9. TRAGEDY

1. Jay Martin, *Nathanael West: The Art of His Life*, Farrar, Strauss & Giroux, New York, 1970, p. 268.
2. Ibid., p. 269.
3. Tom Dardis, *Some Time in the Sun*, Charles Scribner's Sons, New York, 1976, p. 163.
4. Ibid., p. 169.
5. Ibid., p. 170.
6. Martin, p. 323.
7. Lester Cole, *Hollywood Red*, p. 157.
8. Martin, pp. 373–75.
9. Ibid., p. 375.
10. Josephine Herbst, *Hunter of Doves*, p. 329.
11. Ibid., p. 329.

12. Lester Cole, *Hollywood Red*, p. 157.
13. Martin, p. 376.


10. AFTERMATH

 1. Jay Martin, *Nathanael West: The Art of His Life*, Farrar, Straus & Giroux, New York, 1970, p. 10.
 2. Ibid., p. 398.
 3. Sheilah Graham, *The Real F. Scott Fitzgerald: Thirty-Five Years Later*, Grosset and Dunlap, New York, 1976, pp. 205–206.
 4. Martin, p. 11.
 5. S. J. Perelman to John Sanford, January 11, 1941.
 6. S. J. Perelman to John Sanford, August 2, 1942.
 7. Saxe Commins to S. J. Perelman, January 17, 1941, Random House Collection, Columbia University Libraries.
 8. Leah Salisbury to S. J. Perelman, January 9, 1941, Leah Salisbury Collection, Columbia University Libraries.
 9. *The New Yorker*, April 19, 1941, p. 29.
10. It was during this period, when Perelman was researching criminal argot for *The Night before Christmas*, that he met D. W. Maurer, an English professor at Louisville University. An expert on underworld slang, Maurer was the author of *The Big Con*, a definitive work on the confidence game. Perelman liked to say that Maurer was a remarkably well-adjusted man— it wasn't every English professor who could rush out of a romantic poetry lecture and meet "a pay-off man just out of the stir."
11. Many people thought that *The Night before Christmas* was a flop because of its title. It was subsequently retitled *Little Bank Around the Corner* when revived by an amateur group in Toledo, Ohio, in 1952 and *Larceny Below* when reprinted by Samuel French, Ltd., in 1950.
12. *Sunday Herald Tribune*, April 27, 1941.
13. Leonard Maltin, program notes for a course on American Film Comedy, Museum of Modern Art, Department of Film, May 13, 1976–January 4, 1977.
14. S. J. Perelman, Comedy Material, Larry Adler, May 13, 1942, Leah Salisbury Manuscript Collection, Columbia University Libraries.
15. Larry Adler to Leah Salisbury, August 14, 1942, ibid.
16. S. J. Perelman to Leah Salisbury, August 16, 1942, ibid.
17. Scott Meredith, *George S. Kaufman and His Friends*, Doubleday and Company, Garden City, New York, 1970, p. 554.
18. S. J. Perelman, *The Dream Department*, Random House, New York, 1943, pp. 39–40.
19. Diana Trilling, *The Nation*, February 27, 1943, pp. 320–21.

20. *Time*, February 1, 1943, pp. 84–85.
21. Ibid.

## 11. ONE TOUCH OF VENUS

1. Cheryl Crawford, *One Naked Individual: My Fifty Years in the Theatre*, Bobbs-Merrill Co., Indianapolis, 1977, p. 118.
2. Ibid., p. 122. In November of 1942 the *New York Times* announced that Perelman and the Revuers—nightclub performers who included Adolph Green, Betty Comden and Judy Holliday—were collaborating on a revue, to be produced by Cheryl Crawford. Although Perelman wrote six sketches for the show, it was never produced.
3. Ibid., p. 124.
4. Mary Martin, *My Heart Belongs to Daddy*, William Morrow and Co., New York, 1976, p. 108.
5. Author's interview with Agnes de Mille.
6. Mary Martin, p. 110.
7. *New York Times*, March 23, 1944.
8. Agnes de Mille, *And Promenade Home*, Little, Brown and Company, Boston, 1958, p. 90.
9. Crawford, pp. 128–29.
10. Author's interview with Elia Kazan.
11. Crawford, p. 130.
12. De Mille, pp. 100–101.
13. Crawford, p.132.
14. Ibid., p. 134.
15. *New York Herald Tribune*, October 8, 1943, p. 12.
16. *Newsweek*, October 18, 1943, p. 86.
17. *PM*, October 8, 1943, p. 22.
18. *Daily News*, October 17, 1943, p. 68.
19. John O'Hara to Joseph Bryan III, October 20, 1943, *Selected Letters of John O'Hara*, edited by Matthew J. Bruccoli, Random House, New York, 1978, p. 182. Perelman got even with O'Hara a couple of years later. When "Frou-Frou, or the Future of Vertigo" was reprinted in a Modern Library edition, he instructed Donald Klopfer to change the sentence "What between amnesia (inability to find my own rubbers) and total recall, you might think I'd have have the sense enough to sit still and mind my own business." The words "total recall" were changed to "O'Hara's Disease (ability to remember all the cunning things I did last night)."
20. The annual Donaldson Awards, in which people involved in the theater voted on outstanding achievement on Broadway that year, were first

presented during the 1943–1944 season. *One Touch of Venus* was voted second best musical of the season. Perelman and Nash received second place for the Best Book of the season for a musical and Ogden Nash won second place for Best Lyrics.
21. *Baltimore Sun*, April 23, 1944.

## 12. PERSONA

1. *Life*, February 9, 1962, p. 85.
2. Author's interview with Caskie Stinnett.
3. Author's interview with Philip Hamburger.
4. Author's interview with Paul Theroux.
5. Author's interview with Leila Hadley.
6. Author's interview with William Zinsser.
7. Author's interview with Mrs. Robert Coates.
8. Author's interview with Robert Gottlieb.
9. Author's interview with Frank Metz.
10. Author's interview with Mike Ellis.
11. Author's interview with Louise Kerz.
12. Author's interview with Allen Saalburg.
13. Author's interview with Betty White Johnston.
14. Author's interview with Heywood Hale Broun.
15. Ibid.
16. William A. Raidy, Newhouse News Service, December 14, 1974.
17. Author's interview with Allen Saalburg.
18. Sukey Pett, Associated Press, March 19, 1978.
19. Published in 1947, the Modern Library edition was titled *The Best of S. J. Perelman*. In addition to the pieces published in *Crazy Like a Fox*, it contained an introduction by "Sidney Namlerep" and four additional essays.
20. *New York Times Book Review*, July 2, 1944.
21. H. N. Swanson to Leah Salisbury, May 31, 1946, Leah Salisbury Manuscript Collection, Columbia University Libraries.
22. *New York Times*, October 29, 1948.
23. Author's interview with Tom Glazer.
24. "Perelman's Revenge, or The Gift of Providence, Rhode Island," edited and presented by Philip French, BBC Radio 3, broadcast January 12, 1979.
25. George Kelly's comedy, *The Fatal Weakness*, starring Ina Claire.
26. The Erlanger seems to have been an unlucky theater for Perelman's friends, too. *Park Avenue*, a musical by George S. Kaufman and Nunnally Johnson, played there just before *Sweet Bye and Bye*. It too was a flop.
27. Vernon Duke, *Passport to Paris*, pp. 436–37.

28. In 1951 Perelman and Hirschfeld revamped the "Executives Anonymous" sketch from *Sweet Bye and Bye* for Leonard Sillman and *New Faces*. But Sillman never used the sketch.
29. Raymond Chandler to S. J. Perelman, September 4, 1951, *Selected Letters of Raymond Chandler*, edited by Frank MacShane, Columbia University Press, New York, 1981, pp. 286–87.
30. *Letters of E. B. White*, edited by Dorothy Lobrano Guth, Harper & Row, New York, 1976, p. 259.
31. S. J. Perelman, *The Best of S. J. Perelman*, pp. 215–16.
32. Author's interview with Donald Klopfer.
33. S. J. Perelman to Donald Klopfer, February 2, 1947; Donald Klopfer to S. J. Perelman, March 3, 1947, Random House Manuscript Collection, Columbia University Libraries.
34. S. J. Perelman, "Plus Ça Change," in *Baby, It's Cold Inside*, Simon and Schuster, New York, 1970, p. 238.
35. Author's interview with Mary Faulconer.
36. Author's interview with Lynn Greening.
37. Author's interview with Gloria Scoboria.
38. S. J. Perelman, *The Last Laugh*, pp. 166–67.

## 13. "To Count the Cats in Zanzibar"

1. Philip French, "Perelman's Revenge," BBC Radio 3, broadcast January 12, 1979.
2. Al Hirschfeld, *The American Theatre as Seen by Hirschfeld*, George Braziller, New York, 1961.
3. S. J. Perelman, *Westward Ha!*, in *The Most of S. J. Perelman*, Simon and Schuster, New York, 1958, p. 311.
4. Quoted in Alan Brien's "The Man in the Ironic Mask," *Quest*, November 1978, p. 94.
5. French, BBC Radio 3.
6. *The Letters of Aldous Huxley*, edited by Grover Smith, Harper & Row, 1969, p. 564.
7. S. J. Perelman, *Westward Ha!*, p. 343.
8. Ibid., p. 388.
9. Ted Morgan, *Maugham: A Biography*, Simon and Schuster, New York, 1980, p. 512.
10. *New York Times Book Review*, August 8, 1948.
11. Author's interview with Mrs. Robert Coates.
12. S. J. Perelman, "How Ruritarian Can You Get," in *Listen to the Mocking Bird*, Simon and Schuster, New York, 1949, pp. 88–89.
13. S. J. Perelman, excerpts from *The Swiss Family Perelman*, in *The Most of S. J. Perelman*, p. 33.

14. Ibid., p. 74.
15. Ibid., p. 173.
16. Author's interview with Mary Faulconer.
17. Ted Morgan, *Maugham*, p. 308.


### 14. "BEHIND A FAÇADE"

1. Leila Hadley, *Give Me the World*, Simon and Schuster, New York, 1958, p. 2.
2. Ibid., p. 4.
3. Ibid., p. 339.
4. Author's interview with Leila Hadley.
5. Josephine Herbst, *Hunter of Doves*, p. 332.
6. In the Supreme Court of the United States, October Term, 1949, Motion for Leave to File and Brief *Amici Curiae* Submitted on Behalf of Publishers, Writers and Play Producers, pp. 4–5.
7. Bruce Cook, *Dalton Trumbo*, Charles Scribner's Sons, New York, 1977, p. 209.
8. James Thurber to S. J. Perelman, July 7, 1952, Ohio State University Libraries.
9. James Thurber to S. J. Perelman, July 5, 1956, ibid.
10. Author's interview with Mrs. James Thurber.
11. Philip French, "Perelman's Revenge," BBC Radio 3, broadcast January 12, 1979.
12. Brendan Gill, *Here at the New Yorker*, Random House, New York, 1975, p. 294.
13. *Newsweek*, October 27, 1952, p. 119.
14. S. J. Perelman to Neva Patterson, December 28, 1953.
15. Retitled "Love Sends a Little Gift of Noses," the piece was collected in *The Rising Gorge*, Simon and Schuster, New York, 1961.
16. Some years later Perelman learned that he had been among the last visitors to Treetops. The day after he left, the Mau Mau set fire to the tree and destroyed the hotel.
17. Author's interview with Heywood Hale Broun.
18. *New York Journal-American*, January 1954; *New York Times*, March 17, 1954.
19. Author's interview with Robert Gottlieb.


### 15. *AROUND THE WORLD IN 80 DAYS*

1. S. J. Perelman, "Around the Bend in Eighty Days," in *Vinegar Puss*, Simon and Schuster, New York, 1975, p. 34.

2. Brenda Maddox, *Who's Afraid of Elizabeth Taylor?*, M. Evans and Company, New York, 1977, p. 127.
3. "When This World was Wider," *Life*, October 22, 1956.
4. *Michael Todd's Around the World in 80 Days Almanac*, edited by Art Cohn, Random House, New York, 1956, p. 9.
5. Ibid., p. 10.
6. Joe Hyams, "This is Hollywood," *New York Herald Tribune*, November 14, 1955.
7. Art Cohn, *The Nine Lives of Michael Todd*, Random House, New York, 1958, p. 376.
8. Ibid.
9. Perelman later did. Both "Around the Bend in Eighty Days," collected in *Vinegar Puss*, and "Three Little Photoplays and How They Grew," collected in *The Last Laugh*, contain funny—and merciless—descriptions of Todd's personality.
10. S. J. Perelman to T. S. Eliot, September 29, 1955.
11. S. J. Perelman, *Vinegar Puss*, p. 35.
12. Author's interview with Shirley Meyer.
13. Author's interview with Robert Gottlieb.
14. S. J. Perelman, *The Swiss Family Perelman*, in *The Most of S. J. Perelman*, 1950, pp. 8–9.
15. Author's interview with Pat Englund.
16. Author's interview with Caskie Stinnett.
17. *New York Times*, September 30, 1956.
18. *New York Times*, October 11, 1956.
19. *Around the World in 80 Days* became one of the most successful films of all time. As of 1982, it was the fourth highest dollar earner in United States film history, achieving domestic film rentals of $23,120,000. Seventeen months after its premiere, Mike Todd died after his private plane, "The Lucky Liz," crashed in a thunderstorm over New Mexico. The film was re-released in movie theaters in 1968 by Mike Todd, Jr., and distributed by United Artists. In 1981, ownership reverted to Elizabeth Taylor, Todd's wife when he died, and she subsequently sold the worldwide distribution rights to Warner Brothers. By 1984, the year the all-star extravaganza was re-released for a second time in movie theaters, many of the people associated with it—Todd, John Farrow, James Poe, David Niven, Robert Newton, Perelman and a number of the star cameos—were dead.
20. Author's interview with James Lee.
21. *New York Times*, March 28, 1957.
22. Quoted in the *Providence Evening Bulletin*, October 22, 1957.

## 16. "A WRITER OF LITTLE LEAVES"

1. *New York Times Book Review*, January 20, 1957, p. 1.
2. Edmund Wilson to Katharine White, November 12, 1947, in *Letters on Literature and Politics, 1912–1972*, edited by Elena Wilson, Farrar, Straus and Giroux, New York, 1977, p. 411.
3. John Houseman, *Final Dress*, Simon and Schuster, New York, 1983, p. 98.
4. Ibid.
5. Ibid., p. 105.
6. Author's interview with John Houseman.
7. *New York Journal-American*, November 5, 1957.
8. Charles Schwartz, *Cole Porter: A Biography*, The Dial Press, New York, 1977, p. 259.
9. "Malice in Wonderland" was based on three Perelman essays: "And Thou Beside Me, Yacketing in the Wilderness," "Rent Me and I'll Come to You" and "Physician, Steel Thyself."
10. *New York Times*, January 19, 1959.
11. *TV Guide*, November 1963, pp. 6–7.
12. *New York World Telegram*, April 2, 1958; *New York Mirror*, April 2, 1958.
13. *New York Times*, April 3, 1958.
14. Certificate of Disposition No. 320708, Docket No. 6267, 1958, Criminal Court of the State of New York.
15. Maurice Dolbier, "Medium is the Message," *Providence Journal*, November 21, 1982.
16. Philip Hamburger, "Unforgettable S. J. Perelman," *Reader's Digest*, March 1980, p. 103.
17. S. J. Perelman, *The Most of S. J. Perelman*, Simon and Schuster, New York, 1958, pp. 431–32.
18. S. J. Perelman, "Open Letter to a Cold-Slough Mob," *The Rising Gorge*, Simon and Schuster, New York, 1961, p. 203.

## 17. *THE BEAUTY PART*

1. Author's interview with Mrs. Paul McGhee.
2. William Glover, *The Courier-Journal*, August 20, 1961.
3. Paul Gardner, *The New York Times*, October 9, 1962.
4. Author's interview with Mike Ellis.
5. Author's interview with Frank Metz.
6. Marilyn Stasio, *Broadway's Beautiful Losers: The Strange History of Five Neglected Plays*, Delacorte Press, New York, 1972, p. 160.
7. *Life*, February 9, 1962.
8. *Newsweek*, January 7, 1963, pp. 58–59.

9. *New York Times*, December 26, 1962 (unpublished review).
10. Stasio, pp. 158–59.
11. Author's interview with Joseph Leon.
12. Author's interview with Gisella Orkin.
13. Author's interview with Mike Ellis.
14. Author's interview with Patricia Englund.
15. Author's interview with Mike Ellis.
16. Mike Ellis to S. J. Perelman, January 25, 1963, University of Pittsburgh Libraries, Special Collections Department.
17. John Lahr, *Notes on a Cowardly Lion: The Biography of Bert Lahr*, Alfred A. Knopf, New York, 1969, p. 305.
18. Ibid., pp. 306–307.
19. Ibid., p. 309.
20. Ibid., p. 311.
21. Stasio, p. 162.
22. S. J. Perelman, "Caution—Beware of Excess Prophets," *Chicken Inspector #23*, Simon and Schuster, New York, 1967, p. 58. In reality, Sid was very fond of Harvey Orkin, whom many people considered one of the most amusing men who ever lived. A motion-picture executive, talent agent, novelist, and Emmy-award-winning television writer, Harvey Orkin became famous in England as a wit and ad-libber when he starred in a BBC television program entitled "Not So Much A Program, More a Way of Life." The show took so many potshots at the Royal Family that it was cancelled, but viewers demanded that it—and Mr. Orkin—be put back on the air.

Sid and Harvey Orkin met when Orkin was working as an agent at the William Morris Agency. Although Gisella Orkin, Harvey Orkin's widow, says that when her husband and Sid got together, "they would complain about money, the world situation, and get gloomier and gloomier," Priscilla Morgan, Sid's neighbor in Bucks County, feels that Harvey Orkin brought out the playful side of Sid's personality. She recalls the time she went out to her house for the weekend and as soon as she stepped in the door, had the odd feeling that something was wrong. She couldn't figure out what it was—nothing seemed touched—and it was only later that she realized that all the furniture in the house had been moved a couple of inches from its original place. Sid and Harvey later confessed to being the culprits.

In the last months of his life—he died in 1975 at the age of fifty-seven—Harvey Orkin published a novel, *Scuffler*. Sid described his friend's work in these terms: "A magnificent study in American guile. I haven't laughed out loud with such sheer enjoyment in a month of Sundays. This is the kind of gusto missing from American humor since Ring Lardner laid down his lance."

23. S. J. Perelman, "Be a Television Writer—Earn No Money!," *TV Guide*, March 7–13, 1964.

18. "A LIVING NATIONAL TREASURE"

1. Letter from Shirley Hazzard to the author. Miss Hazzard writes that she and her husband, Francis Steegmuller, recall running into Perelman some years later "in his London period, in the lounge of Brown's Hotel— where we were staying and where he had stayed. He asked how we liked the hotel; my husband said we had a long and good association with it, but that he thought it fair to say that, considering the price, it was remarkable that the floorboards creaked. Perelman replied, 'I find the morning croissants creak too.' This was an inspired onomatopoeic characterization of Brown's breakfast croissants."
2. *Newsweek*, January 7, 1963, p. 59.
3. *Los Angeles Times*, June 9, 1967.
4. Sophie Perelman, Certificate of Death #20710, October 16, 1964, Los Angeles County, California.
5. Author's interview with I. J. Kapstein.
6. Author's interview with Vincent Mason.
7. Author's interview with John Sanford.
8. William Cole and George Plimpton, "S. J. Perelman," *Writers at Work: The Paris Review Interviews*, Second Series, The Viking Press, New York, 1963.
9. S. J. Perelman to I. J. Kapstein, January 27, 1966.
10. Author's interview with Dr. Jay Martin.
11. S. J. Perelman to I. J. Kapstein, January 27, 1966.
12. *The Letters of E. B. White*, edited by Dorothy Lobrano Guth, Harper & Row, New York, 1976, pp. 573–74.
13. *Life*, September 23, 1966.
14. Victor S. Navasky, *Book Week*, October 16, 1966.
15. Martha MacGregor, "The Week in Books," *New York Post* (date unknown).
16. Laurence B. Chase, "S. J. Perelman/Nathanael West—Two for the hee haw or tender is the blight," *Brown Alumni Monthly*, February 1971.
17. *Bookviews*, March 1978.
18. Christopher Lehmann-Haupt, *New York Times Book Review*, September 11, 1966.
19. Perelman was interviewed by Dick Cavett twice—on November 29, 1977, and April 3, 1978. The staff found him "sweet and vulnerable," and "not caustic at all." He was nervous and ill at ease, however, and before the second show, Dick Cavett reportedly had to spend an hour in the green room, warming him up.
20. S. J. Perelman to Karl Fortess, March 5, 1967.
21. Perelman's piece about renting Earl Mountbatten's castle in Ireland was

entitled "A Shamrock in My Head." It was collected in *Baby, It's Cold Inside.*

22. *Life*, February 9, 1962.

23. "A Bucks County Chicken Inspector Ventures into the City," *New York Times*, September 27, 1968.

24. "Mad About the Girl," in *Vinegar Puss*, describes Perelman's passion for Achilla, a lowland gorilla from the Cameroons, and her baby, Quarta, one of the first infant gorillas ever reared in captivity, whom he and Laura went to Basel especially to see in the fall of 1968.

25. I. J. Kapstein, "Sid (1904–1979)," *Brown Alumni Monthly*, December 1979, p. 34.

26. In 1977, Perelman also wrote a preface for John Train's *Remarkable Names of Real People, or How to Name Your Baby*, published by Clarkson N. Potter.

27. Perelman's feelings about Michael Korda and modern-day publishing were summed up in "Under the Shrinking Royalty the Village Smithy Stands," collected in *The Last Laugh*, 1981.

28. Author's interview with Robert Gottlieb.

29. Laura Perelman, Certificate of Death #19916, April 10, 1970, New Jersey State Department of Health.

30. Laura Perelman, Last Will and Testament, January 15, 1958, Register's Office, Doylestown, Pennsylvania.

31. Author's interview with Lynn Greening.

32. *New York Times Book Review*, August 30, 1970.

33. *Philadelphia Evening Bulletin*, September 26, 1970; *Newark Evening News*, September 26, 1970.

34. S. J. Perelman to Karl Fortess, August 18, 1970.

35. Author's interview with Betty Blue Moodie.

36. *New York Times*, September 18, 1970.

## 19. "ALONE IN THIS DAY OF HUMORISTS"

1. *Philadelphia Evening Bulletin*, September 26, 1970.

2. *Christian Science Monitor*, December 2, 1970.

3. Richard Dougherty, "Perelman's Drop-Out Caper Irks New Yorkers," *Los Angeles Times*, January 17, 1971.

4. Ibid.

5. E. B. White to Stanton Waterman, December 30, 1970, *Letters of E. B. White*, edited by Dorothy Lobrano Guth, Harper & Row, New York, 1976.

6. *New York Times*, December 3, 1970, p. 47.

7. *Boston Sunday Globe*, November 22, 1970.

8. Letter from Edward R. Brace to the author.

9. *Christian Science Monitor*, February 22, 1971.

10. Although newspaper accounts claim that Sid left the Reform Club at 9:00 P.M., he wrote a friend that he left at 8:00 P.M., the exact time of Phileas Fogg's departure.
11. Diane Ellis, "Halfway Around the World in 40 Days with S. J. Perelman," *Harper's Bazaar*, May 1972, p. 80.
12. *Los Angeles Times*, April 4, 1971, p. 15.
13. Ellis, p. 82.
14. Ibid.
15. Ibid.
16. Ibid.
17. S. J. Perelman, "Around the Bend in Eighty Days," in *Vinegar Puss*, Simon and Schuster, 1974, pp. 72–73.
18. *Los Angeles Times*, April 24, 1971.
19. S. J. Perelman, "Around the Bend in Eighty Days," in *Vinegar Puss*, Simon and Schuster, New York, 1975, p. 74.
20. *Los Angeles Times*, April 24, 1971.

### 20. "Adieu to Onslow Square"

1. Author's interview with Constance Sayre.
2. Although a separate book about the around-the-world trip was never published, Perelman's account was serialized in the *New Yorker* and the *Sunday Times* [of London], as well as collected in *Vinegar Puss*, published in 1975.
3. Eric Lister, *Don't Mention the Marx Brothers: Escapades with S. J. Perelman*, The Book Guild, Sussex, England, 1985, p. 2.
4. Author's interview with Louise Kerz.
5. Author's interview with Neva Patterson.
6. "Watch Out World: Here Comes S. J. Perelman," *People*, 1972.
7. S. J. Perelman Manuscript Collection, Berg Collection of English and American Literature, The New York Public Library.
8. Lister, p. 54.
9. Lister, p. 48.
10. *New York Times*, September 20, 1972.
11. Perelman never visited the Hunzas. Because of his well-known opposition to the policies of Indira Ghandi, he decided that it would be unsafe for him to visit India. Instead, he went to the Seychelles Islands in 1973, which he had always longed to see but which failed to live up to his expectations. The final article in the series was about his impressions of Burma. This was a substitute for his proposed article about his trip to Australia, which, with the exception of the hijacking, had proved boring and uneventful.
12. Author's interview with Caskie Stinnett.

13. *Time*, November 27, 1972.
14. Associated Press, March 19, 1978. Perelman's claim that he never wrote anything about the hijacking was untrue. He did write a piece, "A Fling with Ming," which to the author's knowledge was never published.
15. *Sunday Times*, March 7, 1971.
16. *Punch*, October 24, 1979.
17. Diane Johnson, *Vanity Fair*, May 1985, p. 18.
18. Author's interview with Heywood Hale Broun.
19. Robert S. Kane, "Playbill," February 25, 1963. Sometimes Perelman was quoted as saying "my ambition is to live out of a paper suitcase at the Mills Hotel and take off at will." The Mills Hotel was in Greenwich Village. It is possible that Sid stayed there, too.
20. S. J. Perelman, *The Last Laugh*, 1981, pp. 12–13.
21. Author's interview with Diane Daniels Megargel.
22. Letter from Irene Kemmer to the author.
23. Author's interview with Leila Hadley.
24. Author's interview with Prudence Crowther.
25. Author's interview with Neva Patterson.
26. Author's interview with George Brounoff.
27. Author's interview with Martha Saxton.
28. Author's interview with Richard Merkin.
29. Author's interview with Constance Sayre.
30. Author's interview with Susan Sullivan.
31. William A. Raidy, *Chicago Daily News*, November 2–3, 1974.
32. *New York Times*, March 21, 1975.
33. Marilyn Stasio, "The Perelman Part," *Cue*, November 11, 1974.
34. Author's interview with Robert Gottlieb.
35. Quoted in John Keats's *You Might as Well Live: The Life and Times of Dorothy Parker*, Simon and Schuster, New York, 1970, p. 288.

### 21. "One Last Chuck of the Dice"

1. *Eastward Ha!*, for which Perelman received a $15,000 advance, was published by Simon and Schuster on October 19, 1977. The book sold approximately 20,000 copies.
2. *New York Times*, March 21, 1975.
3. S. J. Perelman, "Unshorn Locks and Bogus Bagels," *Eastward Ha!*, 1977, p. 70.
4. S. J. Perelman, "The Millennium and What They Can Do With It," *Eastward Ha!*, p. 51.
5. S. J. Perelman to Karl Fortess, May 2, 1977. Ben Shahn's *Four-Piece Orchestra* and *Governor Rolph-Mooney Billing* brought $20,000 and $9,000

respectively, Stuart Davis's *Yellow Cafe* $5,250, and the Horace Pippin still life went for $17,000.

6. *New York Times*, April 20, 1977.

7. S. J. Perelman to Karl Fortess, April 11, 1977.

8. Quoted in *Film Comment*, March–April, 1978.

9. Author's interview with Delta Willis.

10. Mary Blume, *International Herald Tribune*, July 8–9, 1978.

11. Eric Lister, *Don't Mention the Marx Brothers: Escapades with S. J. Perelman*, The Book Guild, Sussex, England, 1985, p. 106.

12. On December 23, 1979, two months after Perelman's death, the *Sunday Times* [of London] published "Perelman's Last Piece," Sid's only account of the Paris-to-Peking trip. The piece was mostly an excoriation of Delta Willis ("Goody Tuchoux") and what he considered her attempt to beat him into print.

13. S. J. Perelman, Certificate of Death 156-79-116726, October 17, 1979, City of New York, Bureau of Vital Records, Department of Health.

14. *The New Yorker*, October 29, 1979, p. 29.

15. *The New York Times*, October 18, 1979, p. 1.

16. *Time*, October 29, 1979.

17. Russell Davies, *The New Statesman*, October 26, 1979.

18. S. J. Perelman, Last Will and Testament, December 3, 1975, Manhattan Surrogate Court, Case #4818/1979.

19. *Saturday Review*, July 1981. This famous self-deprecation appeared in the jacket copy of *The Road to Miltown:* "S. J. Perelman is S. J. Perelman, which is an extravagant compliment in itself. In the words of one who knew him well, or as well as he wanted to know him, just before they made S. J. Perelman, they broke the mold."

20. Hope Hale Davis, "The Sad Side of Perelman," *The New Leader*, July 27, 1981, pp. 16–17.

21. Tribute by Heywood Hale Broun, "Salute to S. J. Perelman," Writers in Performance Series, Manhattan Theatre Club, New York, January 28, 1980.

# SELECTED BIBLIOGRAPHY

ADAMSON, JOE. *Groucho, Harpo, Chico and Sometimes Zeppo: A History of the Marx Brothers and a Satire on the Rest of the World.* New York: Simon and Schuster, 1973.

ARCE, HECTOR. *Groucho: The Authorized Biography.* New York: G. P. Putnam's Sons, 1979.

BERNSTEIN, BURTON. *Thurber: A Biography.* New York: Dodd, Mead and Company, 1975.

BRIEN, ALAN. "The Man in the Ironic Mask." *Quest*, November 1978.

BROUN, HEYWOOD HALE. *Whose Little Boy Are You? A Memoir of the Broun Family.* New York: St. Martin's/Marek, 1983.

BROWN, GEOFF. "Checklist 103–S. J. Perelman." *Monthly Film Bulletin*, May 1975.

BRUCCOLI, MATTHEW J. *Some Sort of Epic Grandeur: The Life of F. Scott Fitzgerald.* New York: Harcourt Brace Jovanovich, 1981.

———. ed. *The Notebooks of F. Scott Fitzgerald.* New York: Harcourt Brace Jovanovich, 1978.

———. *Selected Letters of John O'Hara.* New York: Random House, 1978.

BRYAN, JOSEPH, III. *Merry Gentlemen (and One Lady).* New York: Atheneum, 1985.

CALMAN, MEL. "Perelman in Cloudsville." *Sight and Sound*, Autumn 1978.

CHANDLER, CHARLOTTE. *Hello, I Must Be Going: Groucho and His Friends.* Garden City: Doubleday and Company, 1978.

CHASE, LAURENCE B. *The Plastic Agents.* Independent Studies Thesis (unpublished), Brown University, 1962.

———. "S. J. Perelman–Nathanael West: Two for the hee haw or tender is the blight." *Brown Alumni Monthly*, February 1971.

COHN, ART. *The Nine Lives of Michael Todd.* New York: Random House, 1958.

————, ed. *Michael Todd's Around the World in 80 Days Almanac*. New York: Random House, 1956.

COLE, LESTER. *Hollywood Red: The Autobiography of Lester Cole*. Palo Alto: Ramparts Press, 1981.

COOKE, ALISTAIR. "The American in England: Emerson to S. J. Perelman." The Rede Lecture, 1975, Syndics of the Cambridge University Press, Cambridge, England.

CRAWFORD, CHERYL. *One Naked Individual: My Fifty Years in the Theatre*. Indianapolis/New York: Bobbs-Merrill Company, 1977.

DARDIS, TOM. *Some Time in the Sun*. New York: Charles Scribner's Sons, 1976.

DAVIS, HOPE HALE. "The Sad Side of Perelman." *The New Leader*, July 27, 1981.

DE MILLE, AGNES. *And Promenade Home*. Boston: Little, Brown and Company, 1958.

————. *Dance to the Piper*. Boston: Little, Brown and Company, 1952.

DUKE, VERNON. *Passport to Paris*. Boston: Little, Brown and Company, 1955.

FORD, COREY. *The Time of Laughter*. Boston: Little, Brown and Company, 1967.

GILL, BRENDAN. *Here at the New Yorker*. New York: Random House, 1975.

GRAHAM, SHEILAH. *The Garden of Allah*. New York: Crown Publishers, 1970.

————. *The Real F. Scott Fitzgerald: Thirty-Five Years Later*. New York: Grosset and Dunlap, 1976.

GRANT, JANE. *Ross, the New Yorker and Me*. New York: Reynal and Company, 1968.

GUTH, DOROTHY LOBRANO, ed. *The Letters of E. B. White*. New York: Harper & Row, 1976.

HADLEY, LEILA. *Give Me the World*. New York: Simon and Schuster, 1958.

HAMBURGER, PHILIP. "Unforgettable S. J. Perelman." *Reader's Digest*, March 1980.

HELLMAN, LILLIAN. *An Unfinished Woman*. Boston: Little, Brown and Company, 1969.

HERBST, JOSEPHINE. *Hunter of Doves. Botteghe Oscure*, Spring 1954.

HIRSCHFELD, AL. *The American Theatre as Seen by Hirschfeld*. New York: Braziller, 1961.

————. *Show Business is No Business*. New York: Simon and Schuster, 1951.

HOUSEMAN, JOHN. *Final Dress*. New York: Simon and Schuster, 1983.

HOWARD, JANE. "The Cranky Humorist." *Life*, February 9, 1962.

JOHNSON, DIANE. *Dashiell Hammett: A Life*. New York: Random House, 1983.

KAHN, E. J., Jr. *About the New Yorker and Me: A Sentimental Journey*. New York: G. P. Putnam's Sons, 1979.

KAPSTEIN, I. J. "Sid (1904–1979)." *Brown Alumni Monthly*, December 1979.

KAZIN, ALFRED. "S. J. Perelman: No starch in the dhoti, s'il vous plaît." In

*The Open Forum: Essays for Our Time.* New York: Harcourt, Brace and World, 1961.

KEATS, JOHN. *You Might as Well Live: The Life and Times of Dorothy Parker.* New York: Simon and Schuster, 1970.

KRAMER, DALE. *Ross and the New Yorker.* Garden City: Doubleday and Company, 1951.

LAHR, JOHN. *Notes on a Cowardly Lion: The Biography of Bert Lahr.* New York: Alfred A. Knopf, 1969.

LISTER, ERIC. *Don't Mention the Marx Brothers: Escapades with S. J. Perelman.* Sussex, England: The Book Guild, 1985.

MACSHANE, FRANK. *The Life of Raymond Chandler.* New York: E. P. Dutton and Company, 1976.

——, ed. *Selected Letters of Raymond Chandler.* New York: Columbia University Press, 1981.

MARSCHALL, RICHARD, ed. *That Old Gang O' Mine: The Early and Essential S. J. Perelman.* New York: William Morrow and Company, 1984.

MARTIN, JAY. *Nathanael West: The Art of His Life.* New York: Farrar, Straus & Giroux, 1970.

MARTIN, MARY. *My Heart Belongs to Daddy.* New York: William Morrow & Company, 1976.

MARX, GROUCHO. *The Groucho Letters.* New York: Simon and Schuster, 1967.

MARX, SAMUEL. *Mayer and Thalberg: The Make-Believe Saints.* New York: Random House, 1975.

MEREDITH, SCOTT. *George S. Kaufman and His Friends.* Garden City: Doubleday and Company, 1970.

MINNELLI, VINCENTE, with Hector Arce. *I Remember It Well.* Garden City: Doubleday and Company, 1974.

MORGAN, TED. *Maugham: A Biography.* New York: Simon and Schuster, 1980.

NIVEN, DAVID. *The Moon's a Balloon.* New York: G. P. Putnam's Sons, 1972.

REID, RANDALL. *The Fiction of Nathanael West: No Redeemer, No Promised Land.* Chicago/London: University of Chicago Press, 1967.

REYNOLDS, QUENTIN. *By Quentin Reynolds.* New York: McGraw-Hill, 1963.

SANFORD, JOHN. "Nathanael West." *The Screen Writer,* 1946.

SHENKER, ISRAEL. *Coat of Many Colors: Pages from Jewish Life.* Garden City: Doubleday and Company, 1985.

——. *Words and Their Masters.* Garden City: Doubleday and Company, 1974.

"S. J. PERELMAN." In *Writers at Work: The Paris Review Interviews,* Second Series. Edited by Wiliam Cole and George Plimpton; introduction by Van Wyck Brooks. New York: Viking Press, 1963.

SMITH, GROVER, ed. *The Letters of Aldous Huxley.* New York: Harper & Row, 1969.

STASIO, MARILYN. *Broadway's Beautiful Losers: The Strange History of Five Neglected Plays.* New York: Delacorte Press, 1972.

TAYLOR, ROBERT. "S. J. Perelman Takes a Powder." *Boston Sunday Globe*, November 22, 1970.

THURBER, HELEN, and EDWARD WEEKS, eds. *Selected Letters of James Thurber*. Boston: Little, Brown and Company, 1981.

TURNBULL, ANDREW, ed. *The Letters of F. Scott Fitzgerald*. New York: Charles Scribner's Sons, 1963.

TYLER, RALPH. "S. J. Perelman." *Bookviews*, March 1978.

WEST, NATHANAEL. *The Complete Works of Nathanael West*. New York: Farrar, Straus & Cudahy, 1957.

WILK, MAX. *And Did You Once See Sidney Plain?: A Random Memoir of S. J. Perelman*. With drawings by Al Hirschfeld. New York: W. W. Norton, 1986.

WILSON, EDMUND. *Letters on Literature and Politics (1912–1972)*. Edited by Elena Wilson. New York: Farrar, Straus & Giroux, 1977.

———. *The Thirties: From Notebooks and Diaries of the Period*. Edited with an introduction by Leon Edel. New York: Farrar, Straus & Giroux, 1980.

ZIMMERMAN, PAUL D., and BURT GOLDBLATT. *The Marx Brothers at the Movies*. New York: G. P. Putnam's Sons, 1968.

ZINSSER, WILLIAM. "That Perelman of Great Price is 65." *The New York Times Magazine*, January 26, 1969.

# INDEX

Abbott and Costello, 141
Academy Awards, 215–16
*Accent on Youth* (play), 107
*Acres and Pains* (Perelman), 173, 175, 226, 232
Adams, Samuel Hopkins, 57
Ade, George, 63, 64
Adler, Larry, 143–44
Adler, Renata, 276
Agee, James, 196–97
Aiken, Conrad, 225
*Aladdin* (musical), 221–23
Albee, Edward, 244
Algonquin Roundtable, 117
*All Good Americans* (play), 101, 106, 107
Allen, Fred, 25, 196
Allen, Gracie, 74
Allen, Woody, 289, 294
Altman, Robert, 74
Ambler, Eric, 201
*Ambush* (film), 120–21
*American Boy, The* (magazine), 22
*American Mercury*, 31
American Theatre Wing, 166
Anderson, Sherwood, 57
*Animal Crackers* (film), 69, 71, 76, 83
*Annie Hall* (film), 289
Anthony, Norman, 45, 47, 63
Arnold, Edward, 141
Aronson, Boris, 97, 98, 168
Aronson, Joe, 256, 274–75, 296
*Around the World in 80 Days* (film), 111, 206–10, 214–17, 220–21, 293, 298
Ashton, Leigh, 187
Astor, Mary, 115
Atherton, Gertrude, 57
Atkinson, Brooks, 99
"Author, Author!" (radio show), 121, 123, 159
Ayers, Lew, 125

*Baby, It's Cold Inside* (Perelman), 214, 237, 255, 288
Bacon, Lloyd, 142
Baker, Diane, 263–67
Baker, Kenny, 149
*Ballyhoo* (magazine), 63
Banning, Margaret Culkin, 63
Barnes, Howard, 154
Barrymore, Ethel, 101, 140
Barton, Ralph, 48
Bashlow, George, 23
*Bat, The* (film), 122
Bay, Howard, 152
*Beauty Parlor* (West), 102
*Beauty Part, The* (play), 175, 213, 229–30, 232–40, 284
Beer, Sidney, 291, 292
Beerbohm, Max, 180, 248
Beery, Wallace, 79, 141
Behrman, S. N., 109
Bel Geddes, Norman, 97
Belafonte, Harry, 226
Bemelmans, Ludwig, 146
Benchley, Robert, 73, 99, 114, 116, 117, 217, 221, 286
Benson, Sally, 155
Berlin, Irving, 101
Bernstein, Aline, 147
Bernstein, Sidney, 187
*Black Oxen* (Atherton), 57
Blair, Sonia, 195
Blume, Mary, 242, 264, 291
Boland, Mary, 121
Booth, Shirley, 140
Borgenicht, Miriam, 114
*Born to Be Wild* (film), 129
*Botteghe Oscure* (journal), 93
Boulton, Whitney, 130
Bova, Joseph, 285
Bow, Clara, 79

Bowers, Fredson, 38
*Boy Trouble* (film), 121
Bransten, Patrick, 132, 243
Bransten, Richard, 132
Breslin, Jimmy, 261
Brice, Fanny, 74, 92, 99
Brickman, Marshall, 289, 294, 297
*Broadway's Beautiful Losers* (Stasio), 234
Bromfield, Louise, 166
*Brooklyn Daily Eagle*, 49, 56
Brooks, Louise, 165, 293
Broun, Heywood Hale, 113, 159–60, 162, 166, 180, 203, 204, 238, 277, 286, 298–99
Brounoff, George, 54, 283
*Broun's Nutmeg*, 123, 159
Brown, John Mason, 140, 221
*Brown Alumni Monthly*, 249
*Brown Daily Herald*, 30, 35, 38, 41, 42, 44
*Brown Jug*, 30, 35, 36, 38–42, 45, 47, 48
Broyard, Anatole, 285, 287
Bruce, David K. E., 264
*Burmese Days* (Orwell), 195
Burns, George, 74
Burr, Courtney, 91, 92, 97–99, 101, 116, 140
Burroughs, Edgar Rice, 200
Burton, Richard, 201
Butterfield, Roger, 197

Cady, Jerry, 129
Caldwell, Erskine, 68
Calloway, Cab, 109
Calman, Mel, 270
Campbell, Alan, 106, 116, 117, 122–23, 142
Cantinflas, 208
Capp, Al, 190
Carle, Teet, 79–80
Carroll, Jon, 74
Carson, Jack, 142
*Casements* (magazine), 36–38
*Catch-22* (Heller), 225
Cavett, Dick, 64, 249
CBS, 219, 221–23, 232, 238
Cerf, Bennett, 57, 109, 114, 115, 123–26, 130, 166, 172, 197, 252
Chalmers, Gordon Keith, 38
Chandler, Charlotte, 74
Chandler, Raymond, 171, 183
Chaplin, Charlie, 241, 250
Chapman, John, 155
Chase, Laurence B., 29, 248
Cheever, John, 243
"Chester, Susan," 49, 56, 67
*Chicken Inspector #23* (Perelman), 242, 246, 249, 252, 284
*Children's Hour, The* (Hellman), 68
Chodorov, Edward, 116, 293
Chodorov, Jerome, 140

Christians, Mady, 140
Clark, Bobby, 97
*Clipper* magazine, 138
Clough, Benjamin Crocker, 25, 30, 31
Coates, Robert, 68, 181, 199, 244
Coates, Mrs. Robert, 158, 181, 193
Coe, Fred, 210
Cohn, Art, 207, 209
Cole, Bill, 223–24
Cole, Lester, 53, 107–8, 130–33, 197
*College Humor*, 62–63, 65, 76, 85, 113, 142
Columbia Pictures, 102, 129, 142
Commins, Saxe, 114, 130, 166
Conan Doyle, Arthur, 213, 225
Conklin, Chester, 79
Conklin, Peggy, 140
*Connecticut Yankee in King Arthur's Court, A* (film), 167
Connelly, Marc, 117, 298
Conran, Shirley, 270
*Contact* (magazine), 88, 99, 113
Cooke, Alistair, 75
*Cool Million, A* (West), 102, 128, 139, 233
Cooney, Joseph, 46
Corbett, Lenora, 149
*Corn Is Green, The* (play), 140
*Country Book*, 173
Cowan, Lester, 155, 168
Coward, Noel, 98, 168
Cowles, Fleur, 230
Cowley, Malcolm, 244
Crane, Norma, 222
Crawford, Broderick, 142
Crawford, Cheryl, 147, 149, 151–53, 167
*Crazy Like a Fox* (Perelman), 166
Crew, Regina, 115
Crosby, Bing, 167
Crosby, John, 219–21
Crowther, Prudence, 283, 293, 297, 298
Cummings, E. E., 57, 67, 187
Cummings, Parke, 46

Daniels, Diane, 278, 281
Dardis, Tom, 102
Davies, Russell, 294
Davis, Hope Hale, 51–52, 194, 297
Davis, Owen, 140
*Dawn Ginsbergh's Revenge* (Perelman), 56–61, 65, 69 79, 114
Day, Marjorie, 24
*Day of the Locust, The* (West), 99, 102, 118, 130, 131, 139, 244
Deane, Martha, 249
de Mille, Agnes, 149–52, 154, 208
De Sylva, Buddy, 107, 108
Deutsch, Helene, 142
Dietrich, Marlene, 147–49
Dix, Richard, 79
Dolbier, Maurice, 223–24

*Don't Mention the Marx Brothers* (Lister), 270
Dorgan, Tad, 23
Doyle, David, 232
Drama Critics' Circle Award, 141
*Dream Department, The* (Perelman), 145–46
*Dream Life of Balso Snell, The* (West), 52, 53, 56
Dreiser, Theodore, 57
Dreyfus, Michael, 222
*Duck Soup* (film), 71, 76
Duggan, Andrew, 222
Duke, Vernon, 97–99, 170
*DuPont Show of the Month, The* (TV show), 221
Durante, Jimmy, 49–50, 196
Dyer, William A., Jr., 36, 37

Eastman, Ruth, 47
*Eastward, Ha!* (Perelman), 163, 287, 288
Eddy, Nelson, 115
Edwards, Robert, 264
Eliot, T. S., 117, 179, 187, 201, 210, 240, 258
Ellis, Mike, 159, 230, 234–36
Englund, Patricia, 213, 222, 230, 232, 235–36, 296
Erskine, John, 159
Evans, Bergen, 221
Evans, Harold, 83, 290, 292
*Even Stephen* (Perelman and West), 104
Eyre, Methuen, 288

Fabian, Warner, 57
Fadiman, Clifton, 69
Farrell, James T., 68
Farrow, John, 208, 214–15
Faulconer, Mary, 174, 186, 194, 298
Faulkner, William, 57
Faunce, William H. P., 40, 44
Feinsilver, Alexander and Lillian, 19
Ferber, Edna, 153, 166
Ferorelli, Enrico, 290
Fields, Joseph, 140
Fields, W. C., 79, 141
*Final Dress* (Houseman), 219
Fitzgerald, F. Scott, 63, 116–18, 133, 137
Fitzgerald, Zelda, 63, 137
*Five Came Back* (film), 129, 130
*Flaming Youth* (Fabian), 57
Flanner, Janet, 264
Fleming, Erin, 272
*Florida Special* (film), 107
*Follow Your Heart* (film), 129
Ford, Corey, 47, 63
*Foreign-Born* (Herrmann), 88
Fortress, Karl, 250, 255, 257, 288
Freedley, Vinton, 149
*Freeman, The* (journal), 45

French, Philip, 176, 199
Freud, Sigmund, 57
Fuller, R. B., 47
Furness, Betty, 101
*Further Fables for Our Times* (Thurber), 198

Gardner, Ava, 168
Gardner, Paul, 229
Gehman, Richard B., 244
Ghostley, Alice, 232
Gibbs, Wolcott, 140–41, 155
Gilford, Jack, 230
Gill, Brendan, 199, 261
Gimbel, Mrs. Adam, 101
Gingold, Hermione, 179, 202, 210, 216
*Girl in Every Port, A* (film), 73, 196
*Give Me the World* (Hadley), 192
Glazier, Tom, 169
Gleason, Jackie, 142
Godwin, Tony, 253
Goetz, Augustus, 125, 133
Goetz, E. Ray, 98–99
Goetz, Ruth, 125, 274, 293, 298
Gold, Michael, 88, 92, 153, 197
Goldberger, Edward, 37, 39
*Golden Fleecing, The* (film), 125
Goldsmith, Theodore A., 151
Goldwyn, Samuel, 208
*Good Hunting* (play), 129
Goodman, Benny, 114, 115
Goodman, Jack, 190, 197, 198, 200, 204, 218
Goodrich, Frances, 106, 108
Goodwin, Michael, 74
*Goose-Step, The* (Sinclair), 28
Gordon, Max, 214
Gottlieb, Robert, 158, 204, 212, 218, 253, 286
Goudal, Jetta, 165, 278
Gould, Jack, 220, 222
Grable, Betty, 100
Graham, Sheilah, 118, 137
Grahame, Gloria, 208
Gray, Dolores, 168, 170
Greening, Lynn, 174–75, 254
*Greenwich Village* (film), 106, 107
Gross, Milton, 47
*Groucho and Me* (Marx), 73
*Grouchophile, The* (Marx), 75
*Guardian*, 75

Haas, Dolly, 178
Hackett, Albert, 106, 108, 119, 140, 179, 274, 276
Hackett, Frances, 274, 276
Hadley, Leila, 158, 190–92, 196, 197, 201, 205, 215, 217, 225, 277, 282–83, 295
Hagman, Larry, 230, 232
Hall, Mordaunt, 83

Halliday, Richard, 149
Hamburger, Philip, 111, 158, 224, 274, 293
Hammett, Dashiell, 68, 86, 108, 119–20, 276, 277
Hanna, Mark, 200, 203, 210, 217
Harburg, E. Y., 97, 98
Harper's Bazaar, 126, 150, 264, 266
Hart, Moss, 101, 140, 145, 214
Haxton, Florence, 51
Held, John, Jr., 48, 63
Heller, George, 167
Heller, Joseph, 225
Hellman, Lillian, 68, 88, 108, 117, 119–20, 140, 197, 225, 276–77
Hemingway, Ernest, 57, 231
Herbst, Josephine, 88, 93–96, 103, 120, 132–33, 195
Here at the New Yorker (Gill), 199
Herold, Donald, 47, 63
Herrmann, John, 88
Hersey, John, 197
Hesketh, Lady Christian, 264, 270
Hieatt, Constance B., 112
Hirschfield, Al, 166, 169, 172, 177–79, 181, 182, 184, 196, 201, 268, 271, 274, 287, 298
Hodgdon, Allen, 244
Hoey, Evelyn, 91, 98
Hold 'Em Jail (film), 100
Holiday, 25, 73, 157, 172, 177, 182, 183, 186, 196, 198, 214, 250, 274
"Hollywood Ten," 197
Hope, Bob, 155
Horne, Lena, 109
Horse Feathers (film), 71, 76, 82, 84–86, 100, 196, 237
Houseman, John, 219–20
How to Win Friends and Influence People (Carnegie), 148, 289
Howard, Jane, 157, 251
Hunter of Doves (Herbst), 93–96, 132, 195
Huxley, Aldous, 179
Hyams, Joe, 208

I Stole a Million (film), 130
Ill-Tempered Clavicord, The (Perelman), 200
Ingersoll, Robert, 22, 25
Ingster, Boris, 132

Jackson, Anne, 232
Jaffe, Sam, 142
Jessell, George, 196
Johnson, Diane, 119, 277
Johnston, Betty White, 159
Johnstone, Will, 69, 78–81, 83
Jones, Shirley, 208
Joy, Colonel Jason, 107–8

Joyce, James, 188
Judge (humor magazine), 45–48, 52, 56, 62, 63, 113

Kalmar, Bert, 83, 84
Kalmar and Ruby Songbook, 109
Kapstein, I. J., 22, 24, 25, 35–37, 40, 49–51, 56, 110, 115, 161, 193, 242, 244–46, 251–52, 271
Karson, Nat, 168
Kavanaugh, Pat, 288
Kauffer, E. McKnight, 145, 179, 200
Kaufman, George S., 69, 74, 76, 82, 115, 117, 127, 141, 145, 153, 182, 234
Kaufman, Mrs. Samuel, 55
Kaye, Danny, 155, 167
Kazan, Elia, 149, 151–52
Keating, Fred, 101
Keep It Crisp (Perelman), 171, 173
Kelly, Fred, 168
Kelly, Gene, 140, 168
Kelton, Pert, 222
Kemmer, Irene, 278, 281–82
Kerz, Louise, 111, 159, 272
King, Alexander, 249
Kissel, Howard, 76
Klopfer, Donald, 115, 123, 172–73, 200
Knopf, Alfred A., 57, 158
Kober, Arthur, 68, 104
Korda, Michael, 252
Krasna, Norman, 68
Krasnow, Harry, 30
Kronenberger, Louis, 155
Kurnitz, Harry, 168, 183
Kurtz, Frank, 166

La Massena, Bill, 232
Lady in the Dark (play), 140, 147
Lahr, Bert, 217, 230, 232, 234–37, 285
Lahr, John, 237
Lambert, Eleanor, 109, 110
Land is Bright, The (play), 153
Larceny, Inc. (film), 142
Lardner, Ring, 64, 73, 217
Lasky, Jesse, 78
Last Laugh, The (Perelman), 175, 225, 297
Last Word, The (TV show), 221
Laurence, Paula, 153
Laver, James, 107
Lawrence, Gertrude, 140, 149
Lawson, John Howard, 197
Lazar, Irving, 217
Leacock, Stephen, 47, 64
Lee, Billy, 121
Lee, James, 67, 216, 222, 226, 230, 241, 267
Lehmann, Rosamond, 187
Leon, Joseph, 232, 235
Leventhal, Albert, 200

Lewis, Al, 140
Lewis, Cecil Day, 187, 201
Lewis, Norman, 117, 201, 270
Liebling, A. J., 210
*Life* (humor magazine), 45, 63, 83
*Life* magazine, 17, 150, 224, 247, 251
Light, James F., 33
Lightner, Winnie, 83
Lillie, Beatrice, 97–99
Linden, Rachel, 79
Linklater, Eric, 203
Linz, Elizabeth Jane, 44, 51
*Listen to the Mocking Bird* (Perelman), 182, 200
Lister, Eric, 270–71, 273, 278, 291–92
Liveright, Horace, 56–57, 60, 65, 68, 79, 102, 114, 181
Lobrano, Gus, 110, 111, 172, 198–201, 218, 219
Lockridge, Richard, 99
*Look Who's Talking* (Perelman), 123–26
Loos, Anita, 106
Lorentz, Pare, 47
*Los Angeles Times*, 74, 261, 268
Lowrey, Burling, 232
Lukas, Paul, 140
Lukin, Philip, 50

McAlmon, Robert, 88
McCormick, Ken, 179, 187
McCullough, Paul, 97
MacDonald, Jeanette, 115, 116
McGhee, Elizabeth, 228
McGowan, Jack, 101
MacGregor, Martha, 248
McGuinness, James K., 109
MacGunigle, R., 99
McKee, Donald, 47
McKelway, St. Clair, 132
McKenney, Eileen, 121, 131–33, 137, 138, 243, 245, 273
McKenney, Ruth, 121, 131–32, 140, 197
MacLaine, Shirley, 208
McLeod, Norman, 81
MacRae, Gordon, 208
Maddox, Brenda, 207
Mainbocher, 150, 154
Mankiewicz, Herman, 78–81, 83, 116, 142
Manville, Tommy, 101
Marcus, Steven, 119
Margaret, Princess, 269
Marion, George, Jr., 79
Marks, Percy, 28, 31, 39–40, 43, 51, 104
Marquand, J. P., 171
*Martha* (Marks), 43
Martin, Jay, 34, 53, 132, 245
Martin, Mary, 149–52, 154, 168
Marx, Chico, 69–71, 80, 84
Marx, Groucho, 61, 63, 65, 69–77, 80–

85, 106, 144, 183, 196, 237, 240, 271–72, 298
Marx, Harpo, 26, 70, 71, 80, 81, 84, 163, 288
Marx, Zeppo, 80
Marx Brothers, 26, 64, 69–73, 75, 76, 78–85, 141, 159, 207, 294, 297
Mason, Vincent, 242
Mathias, James H. 254
Mathieu, Beatrice, 67, 110
Matson, Peter, 295
Matthau, Walter, 232
Maugham, W. Somerset, 117, 179–80, 183, 187
Max Reinhardt, Ltd., 252
Maxwell, William, 218
Mayer, Louis B., 108, 109
Mencken, H. L., 31, 42
Merkin, Richard, 48, 284
Metz, Frank, 158–59, 231
Meyer, Shirley, 212
MGM, 102, 106, 115, 119, 125, 148, 179, 182, 289
Miller, Arthur, 197
Milligan, Spike, 294
Milne, A. A., 59
*Mine Enemy Grows Older* (King), 249
Minnelli, Vincent, 109–10
Mineo, Sal, 221, 223
*Miss Lonelyhearts* (West), 56, 68, 69, 88, 91, 102, 103, 130, 243–44, 297
*Mr. Byculla* (Linklater), 203
*Mr. and Mrs. North* (play), 140
Mitchell, Joseph, 243
Mizner, Wilson, 78
*Monkey Business* (film), 71, 78–83, 100, 196, 271, 298
Monterey, Carlotta, 48
Moodie, Betty Blue, 257–58
Mooney, Ria, 188
Moorehead, Alan, 201
Morgan, Ted, 179, 187
Morley, Robert, 203
*Most of S. J. Perelman, The* (Perelman), 225, 288
Mostel, Zero, 117
Murray, Mae, 81
Musham, William C., 256, 282–83
*My Sister Eileen* (McKenney), 121, 131–32, 40

Nash, Nancy, 292
Nash, Ogden, 147, 148, 151–55, 167, 168, 202, 246, 247, 289
Nathan, George Jean, 31, 42
National Institute of Arts and Letters, 225
National Labor Relations Board, 108
*Native Son* (play), 141
Navasky, Victor S., 247–48
*New Masses*, 123, 197, 248

New York Film Critics' Award, 289
*New Yorker*, 48, 67, 71, 74, 76, 99, 110–11, 113, 123, 131, 132, 138–40, 143, 145, 148, 155, 158, 161, 166, 171, 177, 182, 191, 196, 198, 199, 201, 202, 209, 218, 224, 227, 229, 231, 232, 238, 241, 243, 247, 256, 261, 264, 266, 274, 278, 283–85, 292, 293–95, 297
Newmar, Julie, 222
Newton, Robert, 208
Nichols, Mike, 276
*Night Before Christmas, The* (Perelman), 127, 137, 139–42, 169
Niven, David, 111, 208
Nock, Albert J., 45
Nolan, Lloyd, 125
North, Ed, 215
Norton-Taylor, Duncan, 37
*Notes on a Cowardly Lion* (Lahr), 237
*Nymph Errant* (musical), 107

Oakie, Jack, 101, 107
O'Connor, Donald, 121
Odets, Clifford, 113–14, 197
O'Hara, John, 140, 155, 243
O'Keefe, Walter, 168, 169
*Oklahoma!* (musical), 150, 208
Oliver, Edna May, 100
*Omnibus* (TV show), 217, 222
*One Touch of Venus* (musical), 147–55, 168, 178, 203, 210
O'Neill, Eugene, 48, 57
Oppenheim, E. Phillips, 299
Orkin, Gisella, 235
Orkin, Harvey, 201, 230, 234, 235, 238, 239, 271, 276
Orr, Forrest, 140
Orwell, George, 195
Osato, Sono, 150, 152, 154
Osborn, R., 173

*Pal Joey* (play), 140, 141, 155
Paramount Pictures, 65, 78–80, 83, 102, 107, 120, 141, 167
*Paris Interlude* (film), 101
Parker, Dorothy, 59, 106, 116–18, 122–23, 142–43, 196–97, 211, 217, 226, 286
*Parlor, Bedlam and Bath* (Perelman and Reynolds), 63, 65–67
Parr, Jack, 249
Patrick, Ted, 177, 182
Patterson, Neva, 221, 230, 241, 250, 267, 272, 283, 298
Patterson, Robert, 194–95
Penn, Irving, 228
Perelman, Abby, 59, 110, 121, 162, 182, 184, 187, 193–94, 204, 213–14, 226, 229, 252, 254–56, 274–75, 295–98
Perelman, Adam, 59, 110, 113, 118, 121, 122, 162, 182, 184, 187, 189, 193–95,

203–5, 212–13, 223, 225, 244, 254, 256, 295–96, 298
Perelman, Joseph, 17–18, 20–23, 25–26, 34, 45, 50, 242
Perelman, Laura West (née Lorraine Weinstein), 37, 51, 53–57, 59, 62, 67–69, 78, 86–97, 101, 102, 106–8, 110, 112, 114–17, 119–23, 125, 130–33, 137–38, 140, 142, 155, 159–64, 166, 168, 173–75, 179, 181, 182, 184, 186–88, 191–93, 195, 197, 201–5, 210–14, 226, 228, 229, 240–46, 251, 253–57, 266–67, 269–71, 278, 280–83, 296, 298
Perelman, Sophie, 17–18, 20–22, 24–26, 242, 293
*Perelman's Home Companion* (Perelman), 214
Perrin, Nat, 76, 81
Pett, Sukey, 275
*Philadelphia Evening Bulletin*, 261
Phillips, McCandlish, 258
Pickford, Mary, 155, 168
*Plastic Age, The* (Marks), 28, 31, 40, 43
Poe, James, 208, 214–15, 220–21
Porter, Cole, 149, 221–22
Prelutsky, Burt, 74
*President's Mystery, The* (film), 129
*Punch*, 251, 277
Pusey, J. Carver, 81
Putnam, Beverly, 202

Queen, Ellery, 121
Quinn, Anthony, 142

Rae, Charlotte, 232
Raft, George, 210
Randall, Otis, 42
Random House, 109, 113–15, 124, 130, 139, 140, 145, 172, 173
Raphael, Chaim, 117, 256, 270
Raphaelson, Samson, 107–8
Rasch, Albertina, 97
Rathbone, Basil, 221
Ratoff, Gregory, 101, 142
Ray, Robert, 120
*Razor's Edge, The* (Maugham), 180
Rea, Gardner, 47
*Redbook*, 195–96, 231
Republic Studios, 129
*Return to the Soil* (West), 102
Reynolds, Quentin, 31, 37, 43, 51, 63–65, 68, 159
Rhodes, Erik, 170
Rhodes, Hinda Weinstein, 54, 55, 243
Rice, Elmer, 197
Richmond, John M., 49–51, 161
*Rising Gorge, The* (Perelman), 231
Ritchard, Cyril, 221
RKO, 73, 80, 100, 102, 129, 132, 196

*Road to Miltown, The* (Perelman), 217–18, 226
Robinson, Gladys, 141–42
Robinson, Edward G., 141–42
Rodgers, Richard, 214
Rogers, Deborah, 252
Rogers, Ginger, 101
Rogers, Will, 113
Rohmer, Sax, 200, 299
Roosevelt, James, 122
Root, Wells, 101
Rose, Billy, 143, 209, 277
Rose, Stanley, 183
Ross, Harold W., 47, 110, 198, 201, 218
Ruby, Harry, 75, 76, 83, 84, 109, 183
Ruggles, Charles, 121
Rukeyser, Muriel, 187
Ryskind, Morrie, 69, 74

Saalberg, Allen, 17, 97, 159, 165
Safer, Morley, 298
Sale, Richard, 208
Salinger, J. D., 214
Salisbury, Leah, 140–44, 155, 195
Sanford, John, 32, 34, 68, 102, 138, 139, 244
Saroyan, William, 141, 169
*Saturday Evening Post*, 144, 171, 173, 241
*Saturday Review of Literature*, 65, 232, 297
Saudek, Robert, 222
Saunders, Walter "Fats," 50, 91
Saxton, Martha, 283, 290, 291, 300
Sayre, Constance, 284
Sayers, Jo Ann, 140
Schrank, Joseph, 104–5, 129
Schwartz, Charles, 222
Schwartz, David, 232
Scoboria, Gloria, 175
*Scoundrel Time* (Hellman), 276
Screen Playwrights, 108, 109
Screen Writers Guild, 107–9, 118, 215, 220
Searle, Ronald, 201, 264
Segal, Vivienne, 140
Sellers, Peter, 239, 294
Selwyn, Edgar, 125
Selznick, David, 178
*Serena Blandish* (play), 109
Seuss, Dr., 63
*Seven Lively Arts, The* (TV show), 219
Shahn, Ben, 179, 231
Shalit, Gene, 289
Shaw, Irwin, 189
Shawn, William, 111, 201, 218, 246–47, 294
Sheehan, Winfield, 107, 108
Sheekman, Arthur, 76, 81, 82
Sheldon, Gene, 168, 170
Shenker, Israel, 111, 251

Shenson, Walter, 239
Shepard, Alice, 89, 91
*Show* magazine, 73
Shubert, Lee, 152
Simon and Schuster, 69, 158, 173, 178, 182, 190, 192, 199–200, 204, 214, 231, 244, 249, 253, 284, 297
Sinclair, Upton, 28–29, 31
*Sitting Pretty* (film), 101
Smith, Winfry, 229, 252
Smitter, Yvor, 192
Soboloff, Arnold, 232
Soupault, Phillippe, 188–89, 201
Spewack, Bella, 147, 148
Spewack, Sam, 147, 148
*Spirit of Culver, The* (film), 130
Standish, Robert, 189
Stasio, Marilyn, 233–36, 238, 285
Steinberg, Saul, 295
Sternberg, Janet, 298
Stevenson, Adlai, 197–98
Stewart, Donald Ogden, 63, 116
Stewart, James, 101
Stinnett, Caskie, 157–58, 214, 274, 276
Strick, Joseph, 244
*Strictly From Hunger* (Perelman), 113–15, 123, 124
Stromberg, Hunt, 115, 116
Sullivan, Frank, 247, 286
Sullivan, Susan, 284
*Sunday Times* (London), 177, 251, 277, 290, 292
Swanson, H. N., 63, 64, 142, 155, 167–68
Swarthout, Gladys, 121
*Sweet Bye and Bye* (musical), 167–70, 177, 229, 235
*Sweethearts* (film), 115–16
Swerling, Jo, 142
*Swiss Family Perelman, The* (Perelman), 183–85, 200, 212, 274

Tashlin, Frank, 168
Taubman, Howard, 234
Taylor, Deems, 159
Taylor, Elizabeth, 207, 216, 238, 298
Taylor, Robert (actor), 101
Taylor, Robert (writer), 263
Thalberg, Irving, 91, 106–9, 115
Theroux, Paul, 158, 279, 292
*Thin Man, The* (Mammett), 68, 86
*Third Little Show* (revue), 97
*This is Cinerama* (film), 207
*This Week* magazine, 201
Thomas, Lowell, 207
Thoreau, Henry David, 22
Thurber, Helen, 198, 199
Thurber, James, 73, 146, 198–99, 224, 286
*Ticket to Paradise* (film), 129
*Time* magazine, 121, 126, 146, 294
Titanus Film, 226

Tobin, Dan, 222
Todd, Mike, 206–10, 214–16, 220
Todd, Thelma, 81, 101
Traube, Shepard, 167
*Travel & Leisure*, 177, 274, 287, 295
Trilling, Diana, 145, 276
Truex, Ernest, 120
Trumbo, Dalton, 129, 197
Tunney, Gene, 159
*TV Guide*, 223, 238, 249
20th Century–Fox, 102, 107, 142, 243
Tynan, Kenneth, 73–74, 202–3, 241, 269, 293
Tyler, Ralph, 248

United Artists, 122, 239
Universal, 102, 130, 168
*Up in Central Park* (film), 167
Updike, John, 243

Van Doren, Carl, 121
Van Gelder, Philip H., 38
Van Gelder, Robert, 114
*Vanity Fair*, 48, 63
*Variety*, 73, 107, 121, 125
*Venture*, 242
Verne, Jules, 208, 215
Viking, 297
*Vinegar Puss* (Perelman), 153, 210, 266, 278, 285, 287, 288
Violinski, Solly, 81
*Vogue*, 150
Vorkapich, Slavko, 80

Wagner, Charles A., 114
Wagner, Philip, 261
*Waiting for Lefty* (Odets), 113
*Walk a Little Faster* (revue), 89
Walker, Robert, 168
Wallace, Alfred Russell, 224–25, 275
Wallis, Hal, 142
Walt Disney Studios, 132, 273
Warner, Jack, 108
Warner Brothers, 83, 142, 178
Warren, Robert Penn, 225
*Watch on the Rhine* (play), 140, 141
Waters, Ethel, 109
Watson, Lucile, 140

Watts, Richard, Jr., 101
Waugh, Evelyn, 248
Weidenfeld and Nicholson, 253, 288
Weill, Kurt, 147, 150, 152, 154, 168
Weinstein, Ken, 296
Weinstein, Lorraine, *see* Perelman, Laura West
Weinstein, Nathan, *see* West, Nathanael
Welty, Eudora, 166, 181, 255, 284
Wescott, Glenway, 166
West, Nathanael (Nathan Weinstein), 19, 32–34, 37, 40, 43, 44, 49, 50, 52–56, 59, 67–69, 77, 84, 86–89, 91–94, 99, 102–6, 108, 110, 118–22, 128–33, 137–40, 145, 161, 163, 174, 175, 188, 197, 223, 233, 243–45, 248–49, 257, 271, 283, 293, 296, 297
Weston, Ruth, 140
*Westward Ha!* (Perelman), 72, 181, 190, 226
*What's New* (magazine), 231
Wheeler, Bert, 100
Wheeler, Monroe, 198
White, E. B., 73, 171–72, 246, 262, 286
White, Katharine, 218
Wilde, Oscar, 113
Wilk, Max, 270, 272, 278
Williams, Emlyn, 140
Williams, Hope, 101
Williams, William Carlos, 88, 103
Willis, Delta, 291
Willman, Noel, 232, 235–37
Wilson, Angus, 201
Wilson, Edmund, 67, 68, 78, 84, 90–91, 218
Winchell, Walter, 63
Winokur, Maxine, 175
Winsor, Kathleen, 166
Woolley, Monty, 97
Woolsey, Robert, 100
Wyman, Jane, 142
Wynn, Ed, 198
Wynn, Keenan, 222

Yeats, Jack, 188

Zinsser, William, 46, 63, 158, 246, 298
Zorina, Vera, 149
Zuckerman, Solly, 187
*Zuleika Dobson* (Beerbohm), 248